The Ordeal of
American POWs
in Burma, 1942–1945

Building the
Death
Railway

The Ordeal of American POWs in Burma, 1942–1945

Building the Death Railway

Edited by
Robert S. La Forte &
Ronald E. Marcello

A Scholarly Resources Inc. Imprint
Wilmington, Delaware

The paper used in this publication meets the minimum requirements of the American National Standard for permanence of paper for printed library materials, Z39.48, 1984.

Scholarly Resources Inc.
104 Greenhill Avenue
Wilmington, DE 19805-1897

Library of Congress Cataloging-in-Publication Data

Building the death railway : the ordeal of American POWs in Burma,
    1942–1945 / edited by Robert S. La Forte and Ronald E. Marcello.
        p.   cm.
    Includes bibliographical references.
    ISBN 0-8420-2428-X
    1. World War, 1939–1945—Prisoners and prisons, Japanese.
2. World War, 1939–1945—Concentration camps—Burma. 3. World
War, 1939–1945—Conscript labor. 4. Burma-Siam Railroad—History.
5. Prisoners of war—Burma—History—20th century. 6. Prisoners of
war—United States—History—20th century. I. La Forte, Robert S.
(Robert Sherman), 1933–   . II. Marcello, Ronald E.
D805.B9B85   1993
940.54'7252'09591—dc20   92-27641
                                                                       CIP

To the Men of the Lost Battalion Association
(Second Battalion, 131st Field Artillery Regiment, Thirty-sixth Division
[Texas National Guard] and the USS *Houston*),
Drs. Philip Bloemsma and Henri Hekking,
and those who never came back

Contents

Introduction

Men form bonds for a multitude of reasons, but few bonds last as long as those that link the soldiers, sailors, and marines of the USS *Houston* and the Second Battalion, 131st Field Artillery Regiment, Thirty-sixth Division, Texas National Guard. Brought together in early 1942 in a Japanese prison camp in Java, their experiences later in the jungles of Burma and Thailand built relationships that still endure, creating "a bond closer than blood." Each year the survivors gather as members of the Lost Battalion Association to remember events that happened one-half century ago—in another place, at a different time. Then they were young, part of an armed force subdued by a brutal military machine bent on conquering Asia to erect a "new order" and bring "the world under one roof." For, in spite of Japan's anti-imperialistic slogan "Asia for Asians," its leaders planned to dominate the area through the establishment of its Greater East Asia Co-Prosperity Sphere.

These Americans met as units in May 1942 at Bicycle Camp, a Japanese prison in the center of Batavia, now Djakarta, the capital of Java. The camp was so named because it had been home to the Tenth Battalion Bicycle Force of the Netherlands East Indies Army. Many of these men would suffer conditions worse than the veterans of Bataan, but their small number has kept them from becoming as well known as the survivors of that infamous Death March. They were a handful: 668 soldiers, sailors, and marines,* out of approximately 25,000 American prisoners of war in the

---

*Most personnel figures used in the following pages are from the Lost Battalion Association's roster, and although the roster's accuracy cannot be established, it does seem to provide the most accurate accounting possible. The figure 668 does not include 1) Battery E, Second Battalion, 2) officers from the *Houston*, and 3) technicians drawn from both units, all of whom were sent from Java to Japan, nor 4) a few men who stayed in the Netherlands East Indies after January 1943, and 5) twenty-three artillerymen detached to the Nineteenth Bomb Group, sometimes referred to as the Nineteenth Bombardment Group. It does include seventeen men of the Twenty-sixth Brigade. The reasons for these distinctions are discussed in the text.

Pacific. What they experienced was living terror, as they worked to build the "railroad of death," the Burma-Thailand railway that paralleled the Kwae Noi (Kwai) River in northwestern Thailand and southeastern Burma.

In the popular mind the men who worked on the Death Railway were British. The 1957 Oscar-winning movie *The Bridge on the River Kwai* made this inevitable. Pierre Boulle's book, *Bridge over the River Kwai*, on which the movie was based, was good enough historical fiction that screenwriters, with their ability to mimic reality, created a script that most would accept as truth. In addition to the film, popular studies that touch on the building of the railway deal primarily with Australian, British, and Dutch prisoners. These three nationalities constituted a large part of the prisoners of war used in the construction, although Asians, who were the largest number of workmen, are mentioned in passing, if at all.

Little has been presented about the 668 Americans who worked on the Burma-Thailand railway in 1942 and 1943. The survivors of the cruiser *Houston*, which the Japanese sank in the Sunda Strait between Java and Sumatra, and the members of the Second Battalion today call themselves "The Lost Battalion." Technically, the guardsmen of the Second were the Lost Battalion, believing after their capture in Java by the Japanese that they were forgotten, "lost" to America's military officialdom.

The members of the Lost Battalion, however, will not forget. As the association's official history states: "Each year since 1945, the survivors of . . . hell, with their families, meet . . . in August, to keep their bond of brotherhood inviolate, and to remember and to pay honor to the 173 Brothers in Arms who died in the prison camps."*

Their story begins about a decade before Pearl Harbor, on September 7, 1929, at a shipyard in Newport News, Virginia, when the Navy launched the USS *Houston* (CA30). After the shakedown cruise, she sailed to the Orient to serve briefly as the flagship of the Asiatic Fleet. Back in American waters by the fall of 1933, she became President Franklin D. Roosevelt's favorite vessel. Called the Little White House because of the president's four extended vacations on board between 1934 and 1939, the *Houston* was a beautiful ship. About six hundred feet long, slicing through the warm waters of the Pacific at a top speed of thirty-two knots, she resembled a naval greyhound. Her nine 8-inch guns could throw a projectile eighteen

---

*Although verification of numbers of deaths is difficult, it appears that 133 members died in conjunction with the building of the railroad, including deaths in Burma, Thailand, and Indochina. Recent estimates of total deaths suggest that 166, not 173, actually died in captivity. One member, not included in the 133, died of cancer in Singapore in May 1945.

miles, while 5-inch and 1.1-inch (pom-pom) antiaircraft batteries and .50-caliber machine guns were lethal challenges to attacking aircraft.

As trouble developed with Japan the *Houston* returned to the Far East and again assumed the role of flagship, this time for fleet commander Admiral Thomas C. Hart, a forty-two-year veteran. In mid-1941, Captain Albert Rooks, who would command the ship for the remainder of her time afloat, took over. Although Rooks was a superb seaman, as he would demonstrate in a few months, his vessel would be no match for Japan's naval forces, which included more and newer ships and enjoyed air supremacy. Still, Rooks and his crew would win glory and perform admirably under impossible circumstances.

When the war warning came from Washington in late November 1941, the *Houston* was undergoing extensive repairs at Cavite Naval Base in Manila Bay. Without waiting for radar or new searchlights to be installed, Captain Rooks sailed into Iloilo on the island of Panay, where he and the crew readied the ship for war. The order of battle envisioned by War Plan Orange, which had been revised in 1938 and as such incorporated into Rainbow 3, the newest war plan, was no longer feasible, if it ever had been.* The Navy's high command considered the Philippines expendable, ordering the fleet to defend the Malay barrier and Australia.

The *Houston* spent December 1941 and January 1942 on convoy duty in the waters and ports of the East Indies and northern Australia. On February 4 she was part of a force dispatched to attack a Japanese convoy in Makassar Strait. Before reaching the area, she came under air attack and took a bomb that permanently disabled the aft 8-inch gun turret, blew a twelve-foot hole in the main deck, and badly damaged the crew's head and the radio room. Worse still, the attack killed forty-eight seamen and wounded twenty. The *Houston* put in to Tjilatjap, Java, where the wounded were first attended to by Corydon McAlmont Wassell, the naval lieutenant commander who gained fame when Gary Cooper portrayed him in the 1944 motion picture *The Story of Dr. Wassell.*

After burial of those killed during the attack, and following hasty and incomplete repairs, the ship put to sea on February 8 and performed convoy duty out of Darwin, Australia. On February 16 a group of ships that she was escorting came under attack by forty-five Japanese bombers and flying

---

*Some general information in this chapter comes from John H. Bradley, Jack W. Dice, and Thomas E. Griess, *The Second World War: Asia and the Pacific*, The West Point Military History Series (Wayne, NJ: Avery Publishing Group, 1989); and Ronald H. Spector, *Eagle against the Sun: The American War with Japan* (New York: Free Press, 1985).

Area of Japan's Thrust into Asia, 1941–42

boats. Captain Rooks masterfully maneuvered the *Houston* in defense of the transports and cargo vessels, and none was lost. Nevertheless, the convoy returned to Darwin after the attack and two days later, on February 18, suffered another massive air raid. The *Houston* avoided harm, having been ordered to leave port and to join a fleet being assembled at Java, but this time the Japanese destroyed many of the vessels she had saved earlier.

Because Japanese radio reported erroneously on several occasions that their forces had sunk the *Houston*, her crew and naval personnel dubbed her "The Galloping Ghost of the Java Coast." The *Houston* was back at Surabaja, Java, on February 24 and the next evening sailed again as part of a flotilla sent to confront a Japanese task force bound for Java. On Friday evening, February 27, she was part of the biggest naval battle since Jutland in World War I, the Battle of the Java Sea.

In the engagement, American, British, Dutch, and Australian (ABDA) naval forces, under the command of Admiral Kerel W. F. M. Doorman of the Dutch Navy, suffered a devastating defeat, losing more than one half of the Allies' ships. ABDA forces did not sink a single Japanese vessel nor damage any troop transports, but the *Houston*, fighting without her aft turret, temporarily disabled a Japanese heavy cruiser.

Breaking contact at dark, Doorman's remaining ships sailed to Tanjong Priok, port of Batavia, where Vice Admiral Conrad E. L. Helfrich of the Dutch Navy, commander of ABDAFLOAT, ordered them to return to Tjilatjap. Another force was assembling there to continue resistance to the Japanese. The next night, Saturday, February 28, the Australian cruiser HMAS *Perth* and the *Houston* unexpectedly confronted a vastly superior enemy armada in the Sunda Strait, between the islands of Java and Sumatra. Without plan, in a chaotic melee called the Battle of Sunda Strait, Japanese war ships sank both vessels. By 12:45 A.M., March 1, the *Houston* had taken multiple hits from shells and torpedoes. By the time her officers gave the order to abandon ship for the second time, most of the crew and Captain Rooks were dead. Out of the crew of 1,070 men, the Japanese captured only 372. The rest died in the battle.*

Japanese ships picked up some of the survivors, but most made it ashore to be taken prisoner by the Imperial Army or turned over to the Japanese by Javanese natives, who disliked the Dutch, specifically, and Occidentals, in general. Within three days most of the Americans had been captured. They initially received acceptable treatment, but Japanese support troops soon put them to work helping to unload transports at Banten Bay.

---

*Alan Payne, "The Battle of Sunda Strait," *Naval History* 6 (Spring 1992): 30–34.

They appeared to have reached the limit of endurance, having been on alert for more than one week and involved in two naval battles in the previous two days.

Nevertheless, they were then forced to carry the supplies that they had unloaded inland to Serang, where the Japanese imprisoned the POWs in the Banton Park theater or, in the case of a few seamen, in the nearby Rangkasbitung jail. After one week the Japanese moved forty sailors from the overcrowded theater to the Serang city jail. Almost from the beginning of captivity their treatment was horrendous. In addition to the viciousness of the guards, the Japanese, who were unprepared for several hundred prisoners, added to the POWs' discomfort by housing them in cramped, squalid quarters and by failing to provide adequate amounts of food and water.

On April 5 the Japanese separated most of the ship's officers from the crew, interrogated them savagely, and then sent them on to Japan. Ten days later, on April 15, they transferred the remaining officers and most of the rank and file to Bicycle Camp, which one member of the Lost Battalion later called the "Hilton Hotel" of Japanese POW compounds. When the majority arrived in Batavia, a few seamen from the *Houston* were already there. Because their living conditions improved considerably, they began to speculate about their future. Some of the seamen expected an American army to march into the camp and free them. When American soldiers marched into Bicycle Camp in May 1942, the ship's crew was understandably disillusioned. Rather than liberate the *Houston* survivors, the Second Battalion, 131st Field Artillery Regiment, Thirty-sixth Division of the Texas National Guard joined them as POWs.

The story of the Second Battalion had begun more than a year earlier, in November 1940, when President Roosevelt had mobilized them because of the unsettled nature of world affairs. Despite the threat of American involvement in wars raging on two continents, most of the guardsmen expected that active service would not last beyond a year. The battalion's units initially mustered at their local armories or in nearby bivouac areas. From mid-December through early January, they moved to Camp Bowie near Brownwood, Texas, about 125 miles southwest of Fort Worth. The Second Battalion consisted of three firing batteries, a service battery, a headquarters battery, and a medical detachment. Battery D was from Wichita Falls, Battery E from Abilene, and Battery F from Jacksboro. Headquarters Battery came from Decatur (of "Eighter from Decatur" fame) and Wichita Falls, Service Battery from Lubbock, and the medical detachment from Plainview. The members were all West Texans. At Camp Bowie, they received further training and new French 75-millimeter field artillery pieces.

In September 1941 the 131st Field Artillery took part with other detachments of the Thirty-sixth Division in Third Army maneuvers in Louisiana. Shortly after the maneuvers ended, the Army high command decided to reorganize its National Guard divisions from so-called square divisions (four battalions, companies, etc.) into triangular divisions (three battalions, companies, etc.).* It completely abandoned the brigade concept and eliminated one infantry regiment and one artillery battalion from each division. As a result, it separated the Second Battalion from the Thirty-sixth and simultaneously sent it overseas to help form an additional Army division in the Philippines. If they wished, married men or soldiers over twenty-eight years of age could transfer from the Second. They were replaced by incoming draftees and volunteers from the First Battalion.

On Armistice Day 1941 the men of the Second boarded a train bound for San Francisco. After being inoculated and issued additional gear at Angel Island in San Francisco Bay, they sailed on November 21 to Hawaii aboard the USAT *Republic*. After a brief stay in Honolulu, the Second became part of a nine-ship convoy headed to the southwest Pacific to join the new division as reinforcement for General Douglas MacArthur's troops in the Philippines. On December 7 the convoy was a short distance east of the Gilbert Islands when Japan executed its sneak attack on Pearl Harbor. The next day Congress and President Roosevelt declared war.

The men of the Second Battalion, like those on board the *Houston*, expected the war to be brief. They imagined their enemy as relatively small people with buck teeth and poor eyesight, mechanically inept and armed with weapons that were inferior copies of Western technology. They believed that "Japs" made cheap toys, wore long skirts, and flew kites, and that the fighting would last at most six months and end in an American victory. Little did they realize that by mid-1942 those who survived would know that many Japanese military men were excellent warriors and often cruel and inhuman captors.

Because American forces lost control of the skies over the Philippines and the Japanese successfully destroyed Cavite Naval Base by bombing, the convoy sailed to Australia. Following a brief stop at Suva in the Fiji Islands, it docked at Brisbane on December 21. The Second Battalion unloaded its equipment and bivouacked at Ascot racetrack. Supposedly, Brisbane would

---

*According to Thaddeus Holt, the Regular "Army reorganized into the lighter but more flexible 'triangular' three-regiment structure first in 1937." Holt, "Relax—It's Only a Maneuver," *MHQ: The Quarterly Journal of Military History* 4 (Winter 1992): 31.

serve as a transit station from which Americans could send troops and supplies to General MacArthur's forces on Luzon. However, someone in the upper echelons of command must have decided otherwise. The Philippines, it was thought, had become a poor choice to reinforce. Thus, on December 28 the Americans boarded the Dutch transport *Bloemfontein* and sailed for Java to support Dutch, British, and Australian troops that were preparing to repel an expected Japanese invasion. One of the escort ships was the *Houston*.

After disembarking at Surabaja the unit moved inland to Camp Singosari, a Dutch airfield near Malang. Dutch commanders deployed the troops to assist fighter aircraft in defense of the field. Twenty-three members of the Second joined the Nineteenth Bomb Group when it arrived from the Philippines with fourteen B-17s; others served as support troops for the bombers. The unit came under fire for the first time on February 2 during an air raid on Singosari.

On February 27, twelve days after the British surrendered at Singapore, the Japanese invaded Java. By March 1 they had more than forty thousand troops ashore and were about twenty-five miles west of Surabaja. At this point the Nineteenth Bomb Group left for Australia, but the disheartened 131st Field Artillery stayed behind. As the only American combat ground unit in the Netherlands East Indies, some still expected the *Houston* to arrive and take them back to Australia. Of course, such was not to be the case. The Japanese had already sunk the *Houston*.

Some Americans were fortunate enough to get out of Java. The twenty-three members of the Second Battalion who joined the Nineteenth Bomb Group left the Dutch East Indies with it when that unit evacuated in early March. The 131st had received seventeen men from Headquarters Battery, Twenty-sixth Field Artillery Brigade, in late February. The brigade, which was from East Garrison, Camp Roberts, California, had gone to Australia with the 131st aboard the USAT *Republic* and then to Java on the *Bloemfontein*. At the time of the evacuation the majority of the battery's personnel, an additional one hundred men, avoided capture by returning to Australia. The unlucky seventeen did not, remaining in Java as part of Headquarters Battery, Second Battalion.

With a full-scale Japanese invasion under way, the Dutch ordered most of the Second Battalion to western Java to support Australian infantrymen fighting there. Battery E remained in the Singosari area to protect the airfield and Surabaja. In truth, the Americans provided little help. Allied resistance was crumbling, and on March 8, 1942, General Hein ter Poorten, commander of ABDA forces on Java, surrendered. Because his forces lacked air and sea defenses and because he overestimated the enemy on Java—he believed they numbered two hundred thousand instead of the actual forty thousand—General ter Poorten capitulated. The majority of the battalion was near Bandung when the end came.

Of the 557 men and officers of the Second, 531 became Japanese prisoners.* A few held out longer than the rest, hiding in the hills or making their way to the coast. Ultimately, they realized that surrender was inevitable, especially when it became apparent that the Javanese were eager to turn them over to the Japanese. Eddie Fung of Battery F expressed a common thought about surrendering when he said, "We had the feeling that we hadn't done enough, didn't do a good job. That hurt as much as anything." Uncertain of their future and undecided about Japanese treatment of POWs, they worried about what would happen to them. "I felt," Houston Tom ("Slug") Wright added, that the "Japs would kill us all and would decapitate the whole outfit."

Shortly after the majority of the Second's men were taken, the Japanese captured Battery E, which had separated from the main body of troops, in the Surabaja area. They held it there until sending most of its men on to Nagasaki and other areas of Japan. These Americans went by way of Batavia and Singapore in November and December 1942, meeting only a few of their fellow artillerymen at the famed Changi compound in Singapore while in transit. The Japanese held most of the Second Battalion with its commander, Colonel Blucher S. Tharp of Amarillo, at a racetrack in Garut, a town about thirty-two miles southeast of Bandung, and then at a tea plantation in the mountains nearby. From the plantation, where they met a few stragglers from the battalion, they moved to a bamboo grove nearer to Bandung. Unlike the *Houston*'s crew, they had full field packs or barracks bags with several changes of clothing, extra pairs of shoes, mess gear, canteens, toilet articles, and blankets. Better yet, after arriving at Garut, they did not come under close Japanese supervision; their own command structure was still in charge.

After about two weeks, however, Japanese support troops took control of the POWs, and their lives changed abruptly. They were herded on to a train bound for Tanjong Priok, and the guards kicked, punched, and slapped

---

*Two members of the battalion had been killed by enemy aircraft while aboard a B-17, and one died in a gunshot accident in Bandung before the unit's surrender. Thus the difference is twenty-six and includes the twenty-three men who transferred to the Nineteenth Bomb Group.

the Texans with rifle butts, their hands, and fists. Sergeant Luther Prunty, Battery F, admitted that this "was the first time in my life that I had a man slap me, and I didn't hit back. That was the hardest thing in the world. I didn't think I could stand it." He did. He also withstood rocks and rotten fruit and vegetables thrown at the prisoners by hostile Javanese.

Many writers have offered explanations for the cruel treatment visited upon POWs by the Japanese. The best explanations combine human nature, racism, and the Japanese soldiers' code of Bushido, or "Way of the War- rior." Believing that they belonged to the superior race, the Yamato, the Japanese viewed themselves as chosen people, descended directly from the gods. As such they conceived their and Japan's roles to be that of undis- puted leadership, while the proper place of subjugated Asians and their former colonial masters—the Dutch and British, and by association the Australians and Americans—was in absolute subordination and obedience to Nippon and their divine emperor, whom the conquered should feel honored to serve.

The aspect that had a more direct effect on POWs was the code of Bushido. As youths, and especially during basic training, Japanese soldiers learned that the greatest honor was to die for the emperor and that the ultimate shame was to surrender to the enemy. Capture disgraced the soldier and dishonored his family. If he died for the emperor, the Japanese people would worship him as a minor deity at the soldiers' shrine in Yasukuni on Rudan Hill in Tokyo. Naturally, the Japanese could not understand why the Americans surrendered. Adding to their disgust and disdain was the belief that by such actions POWs forfeited all right to self-respect or, for that matter, to life. Bushido also justified harsh treatment within the Japanese Army. Officers could and did abuse noncoms who in turn visited their fury upon privates. POW guards, many of whom were Asiatic but not Japanese, could hardly be expected to refrain from passing down the hierarchy the brutalities they suffered to the defenseless captives who were under their control. POWs were at the rock bottom of a social system that was harsh, punitive, fanatical, and often deadly.

Japan had ratified the Hague Conference agreement of 1907, part of which applied to war prisoners, and its delegate had signed the 1929 Geneva Conference agreement on principles and rules for treatment of POWs. Furthermore, Japan had approved the Geneva Red Cross Convention on the treatment of wounded, sick, and dead in time of war. On paper, fair treatment for American prisoners seemed assured. The Japanese promised to observe the Red Cross and Geneva conventions if they did not conflict with existing Japanese regulations, laws, and policies. Their regulations, which dated back to the Russo-Japanese War of 1905, were not particularly harsh. Indeed, early in World War II, Japan had established a Prisoner of War Administrative Division in the War Ministry and placed General Seitaro Uemura in charge. Uemura and his staff doubled as the POW Information Bureau, the source of official pronouncements about prisoners. Swiss officials assumed the role of "protective power" for the United States and handled matters relating to POWs.

Paper protections, however, were misleading. In fact, the Japanese had no standard of behavior toward captured Americans. Treatment varied according to the attitude or whim of the highest or lowest Japanese officer or enlisted man. Conditions differed from camp to camp and detail to detail. Punishment ranged from denial of certain privileges to immediate execution, either formal or in a fit of berserk passion. Human nature, whatever it may be, sometimes produces individuals who enjoy inflicting pain and suffering upon their fellow creatures, and the Japanese were not the only war criminals produced by World War II. Nevertheless, Japanese treatment of Allied prisoners was harsh. E. Bartlett Kerr, in his pathfinding study *Surrender and Survival: The Experience of American POWs in the Pacific, 1941–1945*, estimates that the Japanese took 25,600 Americans prisoner and that 10,650 of them died in captivity, many because of the brutal ways in which they were treated.

At Tanjong Priok, soldiers of the Second Battalion endured a fate similar to that of the crew of the *Houston* in Serang. The Japanese kept them in cramped quarters, four men to a six-by-eight-foot cubicle. They slept on filth-encrusted floors overrun with vermin. Open drainage ditches served as toilets and soon overflowed with human excrement. Rice, their staple, was often rotten and contained rat droppings and little white worms similar to common maggots. Over it the prisoners poured a watery stew made of chopped vegetables. Of the fare, Raymond D. Reed, a medic, said, "It wasn't a matter of picking out anything. You just looked that ol' worm in the eye and chewed him up. The weevils you'd just drink down. You soon passed the picky stage. It was food."

To avoid "corrective measures," the euphemism for punishment, the Americans had to learn an entirely new way of living. Saluting and bowing were necessary demonstrations of total respect of the Imperial Army. To the Texans, bowing was a form of deliberate humiliation, but they grudgingly learned to comply. It was during the first three months as captives that adjustments took place. Tom Whitehead, then a twenty-one-year-old member of Service Battery, summed it up concisely: "They were in power. We were at their mercy. So as a matter of survival, we tried to comply."

Without prior notice the Second was shifted by train and truck from Tanjong Priok to Bicycle Camp in May 1942. Captain Clark L. Taylor reminisced that "it was gorgeous—all the space you needed, and clean." There they met the oil-encrusted, tattered, dysentery-ridden sailors of the *Houston*. Houston Tom ("Slug") Wright remembered that "they were naked! They were naked! They had absolutely nothing!" Without orders, the soldiers, having come to Bicycle Camp with full field packs, shared their extra clothing. Army Lieutenant Ilo Hard said, "We became a group of American prisoners, so we split everything we had. An American was an American. We didn't draw any line, soldiers, sailors, or marines." Many from the *Houston* were also Texans.

Because of the exciting nature of the material, there is a tendency to want to write a narrative history about the men of the Lost Battalion, but that is not the purpose, nor should it be the purpose, of this book. This is their story, the POW experiences of the sailors of the *Houston* and the soldiers of the Second Battalion, 131st Field Artillery, who are or were members of the Lost Battalion Association. In preparing the oral history *Remembering Pearl Harbor: Eyewitness Accounts by U.S. Military Men and Women* for publication, the editors came to understand that nothing written by an outsider rings as true, or is as gripping, as accounts in the words of those who were present.

Although factual, these studies approach in drama the works of novelists, not because of the introductions and other material written by the editors but because of the vividness of the participants' memories. Nevertheless, the reader must remember that memory is fallible and that the interviews include information, such as certain anecdotes and the names of camp guards, that cannot be verified. Most certainly, there are mistakes made by both the survivors and the editors, and some opinions and accounts are included primarily to convey the thinking of the POWs about their experiences. The purpose of this oral history is to minimize the input of historians and to include as much as possible of what the POWs did say.

A few general observations do seem justified. First, the reader should remember that young men fight the wars that old men make. These POWs were mostly young men, nineteen to twenty-one years old, which in part explains why many survived. Second, the fact that the guardsmen were Texans, often from the same small towns, might explain their high survival rate. Many of the *Houston*'s crew also hailed from the Lone Star State, having joined because the ship bore the name of one of Texas's founders and one of its major cities. As Texans, they possessed a sense of community, a shared identity and common bond, not often found in POW camps, and they cared about each other's survival.

Like prisoners of the Japanese everywhere, these POWs became obssessed with food, talking about it constantly as their captivity wore on. "Without exception we thought about food," Roy M. ("Max") Offerle of Battery D noted. "All these young bucks, you'd think they'd talk about women. But when you have malnutrition you don't think about women— you think about food. We'd plan these elaborate meals we were going to eat." The second most discussed topic was liberation. When it became apparent that freedom was not soon in the offing, the prisoners began to live day to day. P. J. ("Pete") Smallwood of Service Battery remembered that he "did it one day at a time. I went to bed at night, and tomorrow was a new ballgame. It would be the last day we'd be there. I really mean that. I couldn't imagine being there another month. I just couldn't." In fact, they spent forty-two months in captivity, from March 1942 to August 1945.

Finally, the reader needs to keep in mind that many of the Lost Battalion members were Depression youngsters, unable to finish even public schooling. Thus, the reader will not always find perfect use of the King's English in their interviews. Likewise, Ronald E. Marcello conducted the interviews over a period of many years, almost two decades, twenty to thirty years subsequent to the experiences being described. Naturally, there are mistakes of memory, as well as the usual errors of perception. Inaccuracies may irritate some readers, but to us even this fault has its redemption. What men remember, albeit wrongly, often reflects an inner feeling that antiseptic truth cannot express.

The twenty-two oral histories excerpted in the following pages are from the Oral History Collection in the archives of the University of North Texas in Denton, Texas. More than 75 interviews with Second Battalion and *Houston* survivors exist, all but 2 having been conducted by Professor Marcello as the interviewer. In all, he has completed more than 174 oral histories with former prisoners of the Japanese in World War II. In conducting the tape-recorded interviews, Marcello followed guidelines prescribed by the Oral History Association. He interviewed each former POW individually and in private surroundings, and he directed a core of similar questions to each person, with more precise follow-up inquiries clarifying and expanding the various responses. He made certain that the tape-recorded interviews, after being transcribed and proofread, were placed along with one copy of the transcription in the UNT archives. He also had each interviewee sign the necessary release forms. The interviews presented here were chosen on the basis of the quality of information they give pertaining to the five chapters into which this book is divided.

As in the previous collaboration, on the topic of the bombing of Pearl Harbor, Robert S. La Forte edited the interviews and tried to bring order out of a jumble of recollections. He wrote this general introductory essay and the introductions preceding each chapter, the brief biographies of each prisoner before and after captivity, the epilogue, and the selective bibliographical essay. Documentation was drawn from the personal interviews, the POWs' hometown newspapers, works cited in the bibliographical essay at the end of the volume, and from sources already mentioned. La Forte used only those parts of each interview that pertained to the topic of the chapter in which it appears. He reduced these sections of the interviews by approximately 50 percent. Nevertheless, he made every effort to ensure that each presentation reflects the essence of the portion used. Relevant information has been provided about each person interviewed and presented here. Data regarding the individual's activities before enlisting in the military and since being released from captivity as a POW are included. Fortunately, the postwar activities of all twenty-two have been traced, even though several had died before this work was written.

In keeping with the book's purpose, introductory presentations have been severely limited in the belief that by providing only essential background information the interviews will heighten reader interest. The book is divided into five chapters based on what seems to be a logical way of relating the prisoners' experiences. The interviews in Chapter 1 discuss the individuals' capture and are followed by a chapter that concerns the uniting of the *Houston*'s crew and the field artillery battalion at Bicycle Camp. Chapter 3 focuses on the prisoners' transfer to the Changi prison in Singapore and the time they spent there. The largest number of interviews is found in Chapter 4, which details the building of the Burma-Thailand railway. The concluding chapter discusses liberation, the POWs' assessment of their experiences, and how these experiences have affected their lives since. There is also a brief epilogue.

Four of the survivors have published memoirs of these years. They are listed in the section on sources along with a selected number of remembrances by other nations' POWs who worked on the Death Railway. E. Bartlett Kerr's excellent study already has been mentioned and was used primarily as a reference point in the preparation of this volume. Kerr's thoughts regarding key elements that students should consider about captives were particularly heeded. Furthermore, his observations on prisoners, most of whom the Japanese captured in the Philippines, were compared to general observations possible about the men of the *Houston* and the Second Battalion.

Without qualification, one work that must be singled out by us is Duane Schultz's *The Last Battle Station: The Story of the USS Houston*. Schultz is a trained psychologist who writes interesting history. His dramatic account of the *Houston*'s exploits provided much of the information we have related concerning the ship. Schultz, as did we, made use of the UNT Oral History Collection.

In addition to the individuals already mentioned, other people helped in preparation of this book. They are in part responsible for that which is good in it, but in no way are they liable for shortcomings or mistakes that may exist. Thanks are due to our comrade and colleague, Professor Edward J. Coomes, who as always was a constant source of encouragement and help in a multitude of ways. Unselfish with his time, he read the entire manuscript, twice. Georgia Mann, a doctoral candidate at UNT, qualified further by newspaper experience on her family-owned Amarillo *Globe-News*, was another reader. SR Books' editor for this project, Peter Siegenthaler, smoothed rough places and caught careless errors and omissions. Betty Burch, administrative assistant in the Department of History, UNT, performed many clerical tasks associated with the preparation of the book as a manuscript. Sandra Weldin, graduate student and secretary, also provided assistance at a critical point. Shirley Dunnett, senior secretary of the Oral History Program, sought information for the volume at important junctures in the manuscript's preparation.

The following members of the Willis Library staff at UNT were also helpful: Richard Himmel, university archivist and assistant director for special collections; Perri Hamilton, archival assistant; Melody Specht Kelly, government documents librarian; and Beth Vaughn of the interlibrary loan department. Mary L. Nash, graphics artist, who prepared the maps for *Remembering Pearl Harbor*, prepared excellent maps for this volume as well. She was assisted by Ben Hight, computer graphics specialist in the Center for Instructional Study, UNT.

POW Camp at Tamuan, Thailand

Death Railway Train Negotiating One of Many Cuts along the Railroad

Prisoner Housing at Kanburi, Thailand

Aerial View of Phet Buri Prison Compound in Southern Thailand
(American Red Cross photo by George V. Enell)

Chapter 1

The Capture

Lieutenant Ilo Hard, the Second Battalion's forward artillery observer, expected that when Americans capitulated on Java it would be a lot like the popular image of surrender: "My position on being captured meant being overrun and probably out of ammunition or wounded or incapable of defense. We would be literally overwhelmed." He added that he never thought that the unit would "walk up and say, 'Here I am! Come get me!' " But he and most of his compatriots gave themselves up in just that way after General Hein ter Poorten, commander of ABDA (American, British, Dutch, and Australian) troops on Java, announced unconditional surrender on March 8, 1942.

Other artillerymen, such as Sergeant Roy M. ("Max") Offerle, of Battery D, from Wichita Falls, Texas, wondered what kind of treatment they would receive, whether the Japanese would shoot him and his companions. He worried, like Houston Tom ("Slug") Wright,* a twenty-seven-year-old private who had volunteered for the draft in 1941, that the "Japs would kill us all and would decapitate the whole outfit." A few troopers tried to reach the coast not knowing that the Japanese had sunk the *Houston* and the *Perth*. They hoped that the ships would ferry them to safety in Australia. Several, who actually made it to the coast, continued on to Madura, a small island off Java, where they surrendered. Still others contemplated going into the hills to continue resistance but after objectively assessing the situation gave themselves up as well. When the surrender became official, individual Americans kept most of their personal gear but violated Japanese orders and destroyed much of the Second's military equipment. Once the men accepted the fact that they were surrendering,

---

*Hard, Offerle, and Wright have interviews in Chapter 4, "The Death Railway."

speculation began about how long they would remain in captivity. At first they believed that their internment would be no more than six months.

The Japanese initially kept the main body of Americans at a racetrack near Garut, a suburb of Batavia, but soon moved them to a nearby tea plantation in the mountains. They next had them assemble at a bamboo grove in the vicinity of Bandung. During this period, which lasted several weeks, the Japanese largely ignored the unit. Unfortunately, this did not last; rear echelon Japanese troops took control of the POWs and herded them onto a train bound for Tanjong Priok. Weighted down by personal gear, the Guardsmen moved too slowly for the Japanese, who pushed, shoved, kicked, and slapped them during the train ride and while marching to the prison compound. To their surprise, the Javanese, who had been friendly with Americans, turned hostile, throwing rocks, rotten fruit, and vegetables at them.

Not all of the American artillerymen went to Tanjong Priok. A few were sent to a Chinese school in the center of Batavia and worked for the Japanese from there until they were reunited with the main body at Bicycle Camp. Their treatment in these early weeks of captivity was noticeably better than that of their fellows at Tanjong Priok. Battery E, which had been sent to help defend Surabaja, was captured haphazardly and separately by the Japanese, some after making it to Madura. They were kept at the Surabaja fairgrounds until October 1942 and then sent to Bicycle Camp, after the others had left. They stayed there until the Japanese shipped them to Singapore, en route to Japan, where they were imprisoned until the war ended.

Originally, the *Houston* sailors had it tougher than the soldiers. Their capture was more in line with popular opinion of what would probably happen when they surrendered. A few watched some of their buddies machine-gunned in the water. The Japanese took others of them prisoner while still in the strait, but most *Houston* survivors made it ashore, either to be captured by the Japanese or seized by Javanese, who turned them in, if they did not kill them.

Their first few weeks were horrendous. Seaman William J. ("Bill") Stewart* of Independence, Kansas, "had considerable doubts about whether it was worth trying to go on or whether just to forget about the deal and give up." He was badly burned during the sinking of the *Houston*. Covered with black oil, almost naked, and exhausted after battling the enemy and the sea, the Americans looked pitiful. The Japanese allowed a few of them to sleep

---

*Stewart still lives in Independence, Kansas.

and provided food. Others, with only brief moments of rest, endured physical and verbal abuse for three days as they pushed and pulled large carts, loaded with military supplies, inland for the Japanese.

The sailors wound up in a crowded theater in Serang with survivors from HMAS *Perth*, which had sunk moments before the *Houston*, or in jails at Serang and Rangkasbitung. In the theater, they sat for countless hours in cramped positions on concrete slabs. At Rangkasbitung the Japanese locked them in cells, with seven men in a space that measured fifteen by twenty feet. Their latrine was a wooden bucket for each cell, and the sleeping area was a large wooden shelf that sloped away from one wall. It had a four-by-four inch plank at its head to serve as a pillow. The food was miserable, and the men suffered from the shock of being prisoners. The situation at the Serang jail was much the same.

Conditions were a bit better for the soldiers at Tanjong Priok, but they, too, were crowded since in addition to the Americans, there were British, Dutch, Australian, and Sikh prisoners. The camp was bordered by the waterfront on one side and enclosed by barbed wire on the other three sides. The barracks were long, narrow, shedlike structures with cubicles, rooms that were six to eight feet square and used by the Japanese to house three or four prisoners. There were no bunks, but many vermin. M. T. Harrelson* of Service Battery remembered the rooms as "infested with body lice, chinch bugs [bedbugs], and cockroaches by the millions." There were no bathing facilities, and the Dutch-style toilets were overflowing with human excrement.

Nevertheless, under these circumstances the Americans began to adjust to captivity. They slowly resigned themselves to physical punishment inflicted by their guards—what the POWs called bashings. They began to learn the Japanese rules for camp conduct, some of which they found odd and inexplicable, such as bowing to their captors, or smoking cigarettes under peculiar circumstances. More annoying were the cramped quarters, restricted movement, bad food, and poor or nonexistent medical care that were to become their way of life for nearly four more long, dangerous, dreary years.

In this chapter two soldiers and two sailors tell their stories from the time of capture (in early March 1942) until the groups, members of the Second Battalion and the *Houston* survivors, were united at Bicycle Camp in May. Their stories reflect the varieties of experiences that the men endured and show how generalization about them belies the truth.

---

*Harrelson now lives in Mineral Wells, Texas.

Otto Schwarz
USS *Houston*

Otto Schwarz believed that growing up during the Great Depression helped the men of the Lost Battalion survive their years in Japanese prison camps: "The fact that we were children of the Depression and had been used to very little in the way of creature comforts made us not notice losing what we had. We didn't notice it as much and were able to survive it." Schwarz enlisted in the Navy from a Civilian Conservation Corps camp just outside Carson City, Nevada. He had joined the CCC after dropping out of high school in 1940. Born on September 6, 1923, in Newark, New Jersey, Schwarz said that he "had a typical life during the Depression. I didn't have any money and had holes in my shoes." He entered the Navy in January 1941.

After boot camp in San Diego, he shipped out to Pearl Harbor, where he was assigned to the USS *Lark*, a tugboat converted to a minesweeper. He sailed as part of a convoy carrying B-17s to Manila. After thirty-two days at sea the *Lark* went into drydock for a major overhaul in June 1941, and Schwarz went to the USS *Houston*. He said, "I was happy in the dungaree Navy,"* but he quickly learned to love the *Houston*.

By the time the United States went to war, Schwarz had settled into a routine as a seaman second class assigned to turret number one and the forecastle. His battle station was the forward powder magazine, where he spent his time during the Battle of the Java Sea and where he was when the *Houston* began to sink. "Being down where I was," he said, "we didn't know anything." He could hear "shooting like crazy" as the Japanese vessels cornered the *Houston*. Schwarz's description of the sinking and his capture follow.

"IT BECAME OBVIOUS that we were in trouble, and the ship started to lose speed. Down where we were, the next thing we knew we were given orders to abandon ship. All the hatches were battened down very tightly. I was stationed at the hoist, sending the powder topside, and then

_____
*"Dungaree Navy" refers to a working, noncombatant ship where the uniform of the day is dungarees and a blue denim shirt.

there was a group of people in the magazine behind us. I led the group up okay to the next deck, and we started to make our way up forward. I remember going up another deck and continued going forward through the compartments on the starboard side. A torpedo hit on the port side, and it knocked me off my feet. I was knocked unconscious. I came to in the marine compartment, so I knew where I was, and I quickly made my way up topside. Shells were exploding all over the place. Pieces of the teakwood deck were flying in the air.

"I went down on the port side of the bow. I knew that there was a boom, a boat boom, there. I went over the side and lowered myself onto the boom, and then I jumped into the water from the boom. I started to swim as rapidly as I could away from the ship. I remember the sensation. Shells were exploding in the water, and I remember my stomach hitting my backbone; it just kept bouncing back and forth. I remember that I only had one objective in mind, and that was to get away from the ship because the suction would take me down with it. I didn't even look back at it. I just headed out and kept going as fast as I could. I found swimming with the life jacket very difficult because they were not the new, modern Mae West inflatable ones, but these were the old-fashioned kapok canvas jackets that just envelop you.

"Anyway, I kept swimming, and everything started to quiet down. The ship had sunk, and the ocean was dark and silent again. I could hear occasional screams from some of the guys, and I embarked on an attempt to save my life by reaching land. We were not far from land. I could see the outline of a mountain or a hill in the distance. I knew that that was Java. I swam for hours, and I didn't meet a single soul. Sometime during the night, I heard boats going through the water; I could hear the engines. They were some sort of small craft. I could see searchlights in the water, and I could hear machine-gun fire. I saw a boat approaching me, and I became very frightened. I knew from what I could hear that the Japs were machine-gunning in the water, so I decided that the only thing that I could do would be to attempt to make them think I was already dead. I tucked my face up underneath the collar of my jacket and got an air pocket there, and I just bobbed up and down in the water.

"I heard the boat come up to me. They shut the motors down, just to an idle. I could hear them jabbering away. Then I had the strangest sensation. I could 'feel' a searchlight on me. I felt myself being poked with some sort of a hook or a pole, and I could hear the jabbering going on. I felt the searchlight go out. The boat started up and took off. I mean, you know, I was really scared, scared, scared! I prayed a lot, I mean, boy, I really prayed. I continued to swim, frightened the whole time, but with one thing in mind—

to get to land. I found that the life jacket started to cut my armpits very deeply, almost to the bone, but I was afraid to let it go because it was my last hold on life. It became a hindrance; it became waterlogged. So I was battling the ocean and the life jacket and everything else.

"Sometime during the early morning, I came across another *Houston* survivor in the water, a pharmacist's mate, and we started swimming together. But I developed very severe leg cramps, I suppose from my many hours at battle stations and lack of sleep and everything else. We could see on the horizon this outline of a mountain or a hill. The pharmacist's mate became a little angry at me because he felt that I was slowing him up. I had to constantly stop and try to work out the terrible cramps I had in my legs. I finally told him he might as well take off, which he did. He left me.

"Toward morning, I could start to see surf way in the distance; I could hear it. But everytime I would take one stroke forward, I'd go back two strokes because the currents were extremely swift. I just couldn't get anywhere. I couldn't go forward. This struggle went on for hours. Finally, just after dawn, a Japanese landing boat came up, and at that point I was glad to get out of the water. They pulled me out, and that's when I first met J. O. Burge.* He and I were picked up by the same barge. They didn't mistreat us. They just threw us down into the bottom of the barge. We didn't understand them. We just sat there wondering what was going to happen, and we were brought in to the beach. I still thought that I was being brought somewhere to be chopped into pieces. I just figured that we had bought it. But at that point we were so exhausted and so beyond any more physical endurance that that was it.

"They took us to the beach where we were united with several other *Houston* survivors—just a small group, something like seventeen or eighteen of us. The Japanese were unloading their supplies and personnel, and I'll never forget. I came out and got rid of my life jacket, but I just couldn't stand up I was so exhausted. I spotted a box laying there with Japanese writing on it. I didn't know what it was, and I went over and I sat down on it. When I did, a Jap came over and just started clobbering me. I wasn't supposed to sit on it. He just beat me. He came over and smacked me— knocked me right off the box. I wasn't mistreated to any great extent at that point except getting knocked off of that box. Whatever I did I apparently deserved it, but I don't know what it was.

"So then they started taking us one by one to a stand of palm trees. A Jap took me into the trees, and he pulled out a pistol and he held it up to my head.

---

*J. O. ("Jack") Burge's interview appears in Chapter 2, "Bicycle Camp."

In very clear, precise English he asked if I ever wanted to see my family again, and I said, 'Of course, I do.' He said, 'You will answer my questions correctly.' He asked me who I was, what ship I came off of. Then he started asking me questions about how many American airplanes were in the area, which was really a joke because if we had seen one American airplane we'd have been jubilant. Then he wanted to know how many American battleships were around, and he got belligerent with me. Of course, with regard to his questions, no seaman second class in the Navy would have known that. Anyway, he interrogated me for a while, and then he brought me back to the group.

"Then we started out on three . . . I believe it was three days and four nights of marching, pulling carts loaded with supplies and ammunition. What I gathered was that we had sunk the ship that held the little ponies that were to pull these carts. These were very large carts made out of tubular steel, like piping, with two large rubber-tired wheels on them. They were intended to be pulled by a small pony, from what I'm told. But one American equals one small pony in their minds. It was extremely difficult, although once you started they rolled fairly easily. They were maybe half the length of a pick-up truck bed and slightly more narrow. But to me they were quite large; I mean, it's not something that you would pull around in your backyard, you know.

"I was extremely weak, extremely hungry, extremely thirsty. We had not been fed at all. I had on a pair of pants, no shoes, no shirt, no hat, no nothing. A great many things happened on that march. Most of them are vague recollections that flash in my mind. The natives were very hostile toward us, and in some places they would run out and hit us with sticks and throw things at us.

"The carts were loaded with all types of supplies. One prisoner was put with each cart, in the front of it, and assigned a guard with a rifle and a bayonet. There may have been a few extra Japs around. I don't know, but there were enough. We started out going where I don't know, but we were on a macadam highway—eighteen prisoners and eighteen carts. I believe it was eighteen Americans. This trip lasted about . . . my recollection is a little bit vague because at times I was unconscious, but I think it lasted about three days and four nights, something in that area. The events are vague, and then I run into a period where I'm very lucid.

"There were long periods where, because of great physical weakness, we were absolutely at the end of our rope when we were picked up, and then to just get a couple of hours of rest on the beach, no food, and to be put into this situation, well, the only reason we were going on was because the guy was prodding us with a bayonet and making very free use of his rifle butt. Everytime you looked like you were staggering or stopping, you got hit on the head or the back or the back of the legs with the rifle butt, or you got poked with the bayonet.

"I remember that this went on day and night. We didn't stop. We stopped whenever the guards got tired. We stopped for five or ten minutes, and we'd go. They did not feed us; they did not give us any water. During the night I remember all kinds of military equipment passing us on the road—trucks and small tank-type vehicles. If there were a lot of trucks or something coming along the road, they'd pull us off the side and let us collapse. When all the trucks went by, whoosh, we'd go again. I remember one point where I lost consciousness completely, and my last recollection was that I was falling and the Jap was beating me with his rifle butt. I apparently passed out, but he got me going on my feet again because later in the morning I came up to my group. I had fallen way behind, and when they saw me, they said that they thought that he had killed me because they saw me fall, and they passed me, and then they heard a rifle shot. So they thought that he had done me in.

"I remember one point during the day, the asphalt highway would melt because of the extreme heat. We had no footwear at all. I remember once we came into a small town, and the Japs stopped to give us a rest and they took us into a small one-room schoolhouse. We went inside, and my feet were one blister from toe to heel. A little Jap came along, and I'm sure he was nothing but a private. He came by, and he made me put my feet up on the desk in front of me in this schoolhouse, and he took a pair of tweezers and ripped the soles of my feet off. Then he poured iodine all over them and ordered me outside. Outside the schoolhouse was a gravel path, and I had to walk over the gravel path to get to where the carts were. I've seen these Indian fire walkers, and I'm going to tell you that that smarts. Yes, that was really a horrible thing.

"Finally, our trip ended. We got to wherever we were supposed to go, I guess. My group was housed in a small schoolhouse alongside of a canal behind which was a larger house where there were some Japanese, a small detachment of some type. In our group by that time were the original Americans, two Englishmen that the Japs had picked up along the road who were members of a radio group, and one Dutch soldier. That was our prison camp.

"We stayed there for the entire period that the main group was in Serang theater and Serang jail, so that would be about five or six weeks. It was a small schoolhouse with nothing in it—it was bare—and we just slept on the floor. We were not seriously mistreated at any point. While we didn't eat well, we certainly didn't starve. The Japs gave us food when they got their rations—this little detachment of Japs. They also brought us a large snake one time—allowed us to skin and eat it. They wanted to eat it, too. Being born and raised in the city, I had never come within a hundred feet of a snake, let alone have one in my hand. So I became involved with preparing it, doing whatever the farm boys told me to do. I remember we skinned it, and I remember the Japs watching us skin it and actually cringing. They were repulsed by having to skin it and gut it. We cleaned it all up, and we cut it into little sections maybe two or three inches long and put bamboo slivers up through the spine. We had a fire from which we had removed the wood and just left the coals, and we stuck the bamboo slivers in the ground around the fire, slanting in over the coals, and roasted the snake and ate it. The Japs helped us to eat it. It tasted real great. It was really good. Under those circumstances, it was filet mignon.

"I had no problems with food. I'll never forget. Having come from the city, I wasn't used to some of the things that the old farm boys were used to. I'll never forget that the Japs gave us a couple of live chickens, and it was the first time I was taught how to wring the neck of a chicken. I did it, but it was a little repulsive to me.

"As I said, we were alongside this canal, which had little dams or dikes on both ends, and a duck was in the canal—one lonely, single duck. The Japs gave us permission one day to go get the duck. Well, if you want to see something, you ought to see a bunch of guys in a canal trying to catch a duck. We'd get near it and he'd go under the water and come up on the other side, and I don't believe we ever got the duck.

"Another time the Japs spotted a native on the other side of the canal with a couple of goats, and the Japs said to us, 'If you can go get one of the goats, go get it.' We went after the goat, and we got one. We almost got killed by the native; he was really going crazy. But by and large, the experience was not too traumatic. We were not abused; we were not worked. We were just there. If we got bored at that point, thinking, 'Gee, what the heck is this, just sitting around doing nothing,' it wasn't too long after that that we'd have been mighty thankful to go back to that boring experience.

"We were getting fed from whatever rations they were getting for that detachment. What apparently was happening was that the Japanese had come across all these prisoners now, and they didn't know what to do with them. They had no instructions or orders, and this was the period when they were deciding what to do with us. I suppose all these little groups were around somewhere. I said we stayed there the entire period. Excuse me, we stayed there a relatively short time, maybe a week or so. Then we were taken to a town called Rangkasbitung and put into a civilian jail. Rangkasbitung is a fairly good-sized little village, big enough to have a large masonry jailhouse. We were placed in this jail in cells. The jail was filled with civilian prisoners, but there were some empty cells, and they put us in these. The cells consisted of a slanted, wooden shelf that became your bed—everyone sleeping alongside of each other on this shelf—with a large board going along the top, which was your pillow. It had a bucket, a wooden bucket, in the corner, which were the bathroom facilities.

"Outside the cells was a nice courtyard, a little compound, and we finally convinced them to let us go out and walk around as exercise. We were not mistreated, but we were not fed well. We got a little rice a couple of times a day—slops. Just a small bowlful, that's all. They would come around with a bucket and scoop out a little rice, or sometimes it would be rice mixed with some kind of liquid. The army guys, the British, they had their mess kits. The *Houston* people had nothing. It seems to me that we had coconut shells and things that we had picked up along the way to use as bowls.

"Once that horrible march was over, we then were able to have time to start to think about our survival. During that week or two that we were in that schoolhouse, we were able to gather up whatever we could—a clay bowl or a coconut shell. Most of us, I think, had coconut shells that we had broken open. It became a matter of survival very rapidly. You wouldn't dream of stealing from your friend sleeping next to you, but, by God, if a Jap left a bowl of rice somewhere, or a native left a hand of bananas, you know, it was fair game. The Japs prepared our food for us at this point.

"We had some interesting things happen in that jail. Pinky King* was with me in my cell, and he was an extremely funny person. We always found a lot to laugh and joke about. Of course, at that time we were of the opinion that the Americans were probably landing on the island right now, and we'd be out of there in a week or so, so we weren't too concerned. We learned about everybody's childhood and their favorite dishes. Actually, if there were not cruelty and mental torture and illness involved, it's a great period of time for learning about other people—who they are and what they are, the English, the Dutch. I found my whole experience one of great value to me in that I think it helped form me into whatever I am now. I was young,

---

*Frank W. ("Pinky") King was a marine from Shamrock, Texas. He died of cancer on May 25, 1979, in Kingsland, Texas.

and this exposure to other people helped make me what I became later, good and bad.

"Not being forced to work, with plenty of time on our hands, we did a lot of talking and always looked for something to break the monotony, a practical joke or whatever. There was a fellow in my cell by the name of Red Krekan,* also a *Houston* survivor. He had been up the river, the Yangtze, in China for a while, and, of course, we always joked about the guys who were up the river; they were a little bit flaky and off the wall. Red acted as if he was, and I suspect he really was, to an extent.

"There were about eight, I think, or seven, something like that, in my cell. The two Englishmen were in my cell, and one of them was very feminine in behavior and also very timid and shy, so it was very difficult for him to use that wooden bucket in the corner in front of everybody. Red Krekan became aware of that very early, so Red took on the role of being a sex-hungry sailor from China. He started making passes at the Englishman just for the hell of it, and we had more fun over that. This poor Englishman, I believe he would have died if we didn't get out of there because he couldn't use our facilities too easily.

"I also remember the Dutchman, who could not speak a word of English, and I believe it was Pinky who taught him a few words of English. Now one of the jobs the Dutchman was given was the job of coming around in the morning to collect the wooden buckets and go empty them and bring us an empty. Pinky taught him to come around and say, 'Good morning,' and he'd hold up the slop bucket, and he'd say, 'America, shit-pot! Japan, flowerpot!' He'd give us our pot. Such was life in the Rangkasbitung jail for a month or five weeks or so.

"One day they came and took us all out in trucks, and as it turned out we drove to Serang, met the other group in the Serang theater and Serang jail, and then drove on to Bicycle Camp in Batavia. The others looked like hell. They had obviously been through something very different than what we had been through. We had been very fortunate, we found out later. While we were not fed well or given anything to do, we were not seriously mistreated. We did not have the dysentery problems that the guys in Serang encountered, and we were appalled to meet our group in Serang. They were in bad shape.

"Apparently, where we were the conditions were not that bad. We drank the water that was available in the wells and streams where we were, and aside from the runs, you know, a little diarrhea or something, we did not

---

*Albert F. ("Red") Krekan died on December 22, 1985, in Southfield, Michigan.

suffer any serious effects. We lost weight, but I think it wasn't a dangerous loss or a hardship loss of weight. I think it was the kind of weight that one loses when they lose the good life. You know, some fat goes, and you really get in better shape at that point."

Before Seaman Schwarz's ordeal ended he was about as far from "better shape" as a human being could be. Like his mates, he went from Bicycle Camp to Changi, near Singapore, and then on to the railroad near Thanbyuzayat in Burma. While working on the line he suffered bouts of dysentery and beriberi, which together landed him in the dreaded 80 Kilo Camp.* He miraculously survived 80 Kilo Camp and jungle ulcers, one of the main killers of POWs.

After the railway was finished, he followed a route that took him from Tamarkan, Nakhon Pathom, and Bangkok in Thailand to Phnom Penh and Saigon in French Indochina. He remained in Saigon and its environs until liberated, once falling into the hands of the Japanese *Kempei Tai* (secret police), but he emerged from that experience alive. Following liberation, Schwarz was transported to the 142d General Hospital in Calcutta; after a physical he was given $200 and sent into town where, he says, he "ate my brains out!"

He flew back to the United States across North Africa, landing in Washington, D.C., and taking a train to Newark. He had some trouble adjusting to "life" again. "You really don't feel like a human being anymore," he said, "after coming out of those jungles." He had to clean up his language and stop boozing. He spent three months going from bar to bar. His convalescence kept him in the Navy until June 1947. After that he became a postman. He is now retired and lives in Union, New Jersey. At the close of his interview, he said, "I don't want the world to forget this. I don't want people to forget what men can do to men, and I think it's wrong to let it die and not let people know about it."

---

*References to Kilo Camps are to work camps along the Burma-Thailand railway. Each camp's number was determined by its distance from the base camp, or railhead, at Thanbyuzayat, Burma. The 80 Kilo Camp was the hospital camp, also called the Death Camp.

Paul Papish
USS *Houston*

High blood pressure almost kept Paul Papish out of the U.S. Navy. Whenever he tried to volunteer, the minute the sphygmomanometer was strapped on him, his pressure would rise. This problem recurred several times when he tried to join in 1938, and, if his family doctor had not given him blood pressure pills and told him to take them just before being examined, high blood pressure may have kept him out of the Navy once more. But the prescription worked, and he was accepted in February 1939. He went to boot camp at the Great Lakes Naval Training Station near Chicago and then spent ten days at home before going to Bremerton, Washington, on Puget Sound.

Papish was born in Pueblo but grew up in Denver, Colorado, the son of Roman Catholic parents. Although a "landlubber," the world situation interested him in the Navy after his graduation from high school in 1937. Several times he saw the Movietone news report on the sinking of the USS *Panay*, and that event made him want to go to sea. He was assigned to the *Houston*, which was in drydock at Bremerton, and spent his first two weeks aboard scraping barnacles off her bottom. When the ship sailed it was to Long Beach, then on to Pearl Harbor, back to Mare Island in San Francisco Bay, and once more to Pearl. They finally proceeded on to Manila. Papish had joined the Navy to be an electrician but was assigned to the ship's storekeeper, where he served in the paymaster's office. Because of his interest in the *Panay*, he thought it odd that when war broke out he was at Iloilo on the Philippine island of Panay.

Papish's battle station was the after-battle dressing station in the ship's stern. The seamen there handled wounded sailors from the mess deck to the stern of the *Houston*. He was at his position the night the Galloping Ghost fought its last battle in the Sunda Strait. He described the battle as a "free-for-all": "You can't actually imagine in your mind what it looked like. It's indescribable. There is firing and firing. You could hear screams. It was just something. Then word comes to abandon ship." Below Papish describes leaving the ship, making it to shore, and being captured and interned temporarily in the Serang theater and jail.

""T HEY SAID THAT CAPTAIN ROOKS passed the word to abandon ship. 'Abandon ship!' You have practiced 'abandon ship.' You never expect to hear the words. Here I've been on the ship since June 4, 1939, and it's been my home for almost three years. My friends are here. 'No!' And then the second word comes to abandon ship.

"Painstakingly I sit up there on a bit* and take my shoes off; I tie them together and put them around my neck. I had flashproof clothing† on, and I had my helmet on. I had a life jacket on, and I look back and say, 'No! I don't have to leave! We're going to get through this!' The second word comes, 'Abandon ship.' I go through this whole routine. Somebody had gotten my life jacket, so I put on another life jacket over the top of the flashproof clothing. I sat there a while not thinking, but then I thought: 'It's time to go.' So I got over the life line and was standing there, and I pushed myself off the ship about fifteen or twenty feet into the water.

"Of course, the minute you hit the water, you're instructed to get away because there's going to be a suction as the ship goes down, and you'll go with it regardless of life jacket or anything. So I'm trying to make my way, and I thought, 'Well, to hell with this! I've got this flashproof clothing on!' So I spot a yellow life raft out there all by itself, one of the aviation life rafts. I crawl aboard and take my life jacket off; I tie it to the lanyard that's around the life raft so it doesn't get away. Then I proceed to take off my flashproof clothing. All the while I can see explosions and carnage taking place on the ship.

"All of a sudden I hear 'Zzzzing!' and 'Psshwish!' Machine gun shells have gone through the raft, and it's folding up on me. I thought, 'To heck with this!' I had to untie my life jacket and get it back on and get away from that raft. I'm not burdened down anymore; I'm down to my skivvies. I lost my shoes. Then I'm off swimming like heck. I heard voices in the water. I feel all this slimy stuff, oil, on me and everything else. I feel kind of hungry, and I pick something up in the water. It must have been a sea onion. It tasted just like an onion, and I ate it.

"Evidently, I found another life raft with people clinging to it. So I get by this raft, and I'm hanging on to it during the night. We're trying to get our bearings, and we go this way and that way. Anyway, then comes dawn, and you see land. You don't know which way you're swimming. Of course, you know which way the sun is coming up. That's the way I determined which

---

*A post from which a line is run to tie the ship to a dock, etc.
†Clothing treated to protect personnel against flash burns from exploding shells.

way to swim. The sun is coming up, so I figure the best way to swim is to the east, which is probably Java.

"I'm with this raft, and up comes the sun. You don't get on a raft if you're not incapacitated. The injured are in the raft. Immediately we're greeted by Zeros, and they're coming in, and they're machine-gunning. I'm thinking, 'Man, this is something else! We don't have any weapons; we don't have anything! What do they get out of this, machine-gunning people in the water?' One of my shipmates, Eugene ('Punchy') Parham* is on the raft. I looked over at Punchy, and I said, 'Punchy, if we're going to get out of this, we better get away from this raft because they're going to dive again on it.'

"So we strike out from the raft, and, fortunately, every now and then we would get into a squall, a little rain squall. It just seems like it's heaven sent. You're getting a little water on you, and you're hidden. I've been told that Ensign Nelson[†] had traded his Naval Academy ring to a native to go out with his boat and pick up survivors. Punchy was picked up by Nelson. But some of the people that were on the raft never made it into the prison camp. I think they floated out into the Indian Ocean, and that was it.

"Anyway, I made it ashore, and I figure it was about four o'clock in the afternoon by the way the sun was, and that figures out to about eighteen hours in the water. When I got up to the beach, and I could get my feet in the sand, I thought once you hit the beach, you get up as far as you can so that if you collapse, the tide that comes back up won't drag you in. So I got up on the beach, and I remember trying to straighten up and I couldn't. My life jacket was so waterlogged that I just collapsed right there on the beach, and I must have slept through the night.

"Through the night my side had been sore, and I thought maybe it was a stitch in my side from all that swimming. I didn't pay too much attention to it because it wasn't paining me too much. But it was uncomfortable. So the next morning, when I woke up, and I started to take my life jacket off, I looked down, and in the side of my life jacket, in the kapok life jacket, was a piece of shrapnel about the size of my fist embedded in the jacket right where I was hurting. Evidently, it had hit with force but had not penetrated, and it hurt something and caused me to vomit blood. I thought the onion I ate hadn't set too well with me. What has always amazed me is why I didn't notice the metal while I was in the water. When I woke up and looked around, there were several other guys around me.

---

*Parham now lives in Grand Prairie, Texas.
[†]John B. Nelson was from Orange, Texas, where he died on February 4, 1981.

"The sun was coming up again. Why I wasn't found, found by the natives or found by the Japanese, I didn't know. But looking at a map now, Banten Bay is up on the northern coast of Java, practically on the northern coast, near to the Sunda Strait. As near as I can figure out, I was on about the midsection of Java, between Banten Bay and the southern part of Java. Evidently, the soldiers were landing up in Banten Bay, and we were farther down the coast.

"So when I woke up, these guys were around me, and I think we had an officer with us. I think it was Ensign or Lieutenant Hamlin.* He got us all together; there were about eleven of us. So the first place we made for was this sort of house, a beach house. The house was deserted. Of course, we were looking for food and anything else. Here I am, in a pair of skivvies, barefooted, and that's the sum total of my possessions when I got ashore. So we found something to eat, and then we started walking.

"We were walking in for cover, and, man, it is cover! It's jungle. Anyway, we found a road. We were loose four days before we were captured—this little band of ours. We felt we were walking south where we understood they would be evacuating from —Tjilatjap and places like that. Well, little did we realize that we were walking in a circle. Anyway, we came to a deserted—what appeared to be—hospital hut. They had sheets and some of these cloth things, square cloth things. Somebody says, 'Oh, I saw one of those natives when I was on liberty wearing one of these things. They are sarongs.' So I immediately thought, 'Man, that's for me. All I've got on is a pair of skivvies.' So I get one of these blue sarongs, and I put it around me, and I feel a little bit more decent. But I still had no shoes. During these four days I don't know exactly what transpired, but from March 1 to March 4 we were loose.

"The fourth day of our trek, we had found a road, a macadam road. It's just like our tarmac or paved roads, the oil-paved roads. So we started following this. Evidently, we were going to the north, toward Banten Bay. The Javanese were around us, but they stayed away. There was no attempt to try to contact us. If we tried to ask them for food and things, off they'd go. How we subsisted for four days, I really can't tell, but there's a four-day interval that we were walking and sleeping and then walking.

"Then on the fourth day, all of a sudden out come these natives, and they had these sarongs on, and they had these bolos on their back. This old

*Harold S. Hamlin, Jr., accidentally drowned on May 20, 1978, at Lake Geneva, Wisconsin.

guy evidently must have been the chieftain of the lot, but he lays us down in the middle of the road on that hot pavement. It must have been at noon or close to noon, and this sun is bearing down on this hot pavement. He's making this band of eleven men lay down in the road on our backs. So I'm laying there, and he's giving a speech to the natives alongside the road. We're not knowing what kind of a speech or what he's talking about or anything, but every once in a while he'd utter a cry and put his ol' bolo up in the air, and they'd all say, 'Dodo!' or something like that. That's as near as I can remember what they were hollering back.

"All of a sudden, he jumps up in the air, he twirls around, takes his bolo, runs it down from my chin to my crotch, and I thought, 'This is it! This is where Papish meets his end!' So, lo and behold, he jumps off me, twirls around in the air again, jumps astraddle the next guy, and does the same thing. Well, he does this to all eleven, right down the row. Well, the last guy knows what's coming, so he's not worried too much. But me, I was first in line, and, my God, I tell you, you don't know what's going through your mind at a time like that.

"So he does this, and all of a sudden this sort of a panel truck appears on the road and pulls over to the side, and this guy gets out. He's got a turban on, but he's dressed western-style. This panel truck had a red cross on it, and this is where I start thinking, 'My God, the International Red Cross is on the scene already, and everything is going to be all right!' But looking closer, this red cross has been filled in to make a fire ball. It's, well, 'rising sun' is the word for it. We had other words for it, too.

"Anyway, this guy comes up. I'm there, and he looked at me, and he has this little silver pistol he's waving in the air. I'm looking here at the guy, and he started to talk real good English. He puts that gun to me, and he says, 'Did you steal or did you kill anybody for that sarong?' I said, 'No. We found this sarong up there at this hospital.' He shook his head, and then the rest of the guys said they had some of the other stuff, and he said, 'If you stole or if you killed anyone, you must pay with your life.' I said, 'No, I didn't steal it. I didn't kill anybody for it. I found it.' Well, he seemed satisfied with that.

"He got us in this truck and then took us to a compound down further. We found out later that this was probably near Pandeglang, Java. So they put us in a compound there, and I remember some Dutch women being in the compound, too, white women. They had some rice cooking there, and fried bananas, which later on I found out were plantains. That was about the first food we ever got, that those Dutch ladies fed us. Then they put us in there and said, 'Okay, you can sleep in there.' There are no Japanese around yet. See, this jail is not a jail, but a compound. I can visualize a fence around it, and then the huts that had dirt floors and pallets slanting down from the wall to about a foot or a foot-and-a-half off the floor, slanting. This was our introduction to the way they sleep. So we bedded down. There was about four or five of us in this one room.

"We go to sleep, and all of a sudden somebody's got me by the feet and pulling me off the pallet. He bounces my behind off the floor, on this dirt floor, and I'm thinking, 'This is a hell of a trick to play on a guy!' I come up ready to fight. Well, when I'm ready to fight, I get this gun and bayonet pointed at my head, and I'm thinking, 'Oh, my God!' Well, it was a Japanese soldier. This is my first introduction to the Japanese, my first introduction. All of a sudden I put up my hands, and he prods me outside.

"We weren't in contact for four days with the Japs, and then we came in contact with them with the rifle incident. This starts you to thinking. There was maybe a dozen or half-dozen of them going around to various huts where the guys were sleeping and rousting them out. There was no real physical contact except the harassment with the bayonet and the gun. I don't remember getting a rifle butt or anything at that time.

"They were probably some of the Japanese who landed at Banten Bay. They were of a small stature. They had sort of a beanie cap with a star on it. They were in a sort of khaki pants with their legs wrapped in leggings. One thing we noticed right off was the split-toed shoes, sort of tennis shoes with a split between the big toe and the next toe. It wasn't unusual to see a Jap standing at attention with his gun to his side and have a bayonet extending over his head. Some were real small.

"They took us by truck, a stake-body truck, and the next thing we know, we end up in Serang, Java. They just pushed you along with the rifle butt, but still no real aggressiveness, just the prod sort of thing. I was pretty lean, because I started out probably at 140 to 145 pounds, and by the time we got to Serang, with just a couple of meals under our belt, I guess we were feeling pretty hungry. Now other people had been taken from places and all gathered into this place we called the theater. It was actually a theater or movie house. One thing I recall is I managed to get a spot on the stage. A lot of guys had to make do with the seats and stuff which were very uncomfortable. The stage was at the foot of the theater, and there was an access of steps going down. I don't know whether there was a balcony. Anyway, in the back stood the Japs at each exit and entrance, and you couldn't move without asking. Being on stage, I had a view of what was taking place. I could see what was happening. Once you staked your claim where you were, it was honored amongst the rest of us. There was no encroachment into somebody else's territory, so to speak.

"One thing I remember is that one of our boys who was in turret two, which caught a tremendous amount of shell fire, was also on the stage. His name is William Stewart,* he was in the life raft, and that's the last time I saw him after getting off the ship. Then the next time I see him, he's in the Serang theater, and there's a pharmacist's mate taking care of him. Stewart was completely burned over his whole body. My God! I don't know how, but this pharmacist's mate was able to get water, which was a very precious commodity. There was an old sort of a piece of canvas or what might have been the theater curtain, and he kept Stewart wrapped up in this canvas and kept him constantly wet. Religiously, every morning while we were in that theater, he would unwrap him, and he would pull the dead skin off of his body. It got to a point where it was a stench. You got the stink of burnt flesh. Every now and then I can wake up at night, and this will hit me—the stench of burnt flesh and dead flesh. It never seems to leave. But he would religiously clean him, and he'd take this water and kind of keep him moist. Stewart's still alive today, but he was just one big blister then.

"We had no bathing facilities there, that's for sure. We had oil in our hair. I don't think I was encrusted with oil because I was in the water long enough, and I must have worked it off. Also, on the beach, in the sand, I remember rubbing oil off my arms with sand and then getting back in the saltwater, and it got too stingy.

"You entered the theater at ground level, and then you descended a little bit. It wasn't a steep descent, but kind of gradual. As you entered the theater, off to the left was a sort of courtyard thing, and this was our *benjo*, the Japanese word for toilet. I'd say it was probably no more than four or five feet by ten feet. Whenever you had to go, you had to get permission, or else you'd get slapped around. Now here is where contact began. Some guy would have to go, and he'd get up and start to go to the courtyard, and the Jap would come over and slap the living daylights out of him. Little did we realize that they do this to their own people. We didn't know that at the time. Their discipline was something else. You get slapped around quite a bit. When you get slapped around, and you see that nothing is really taking place, then you get defiant, and you figure, 'To hell with them! I ain't going to ask them!' And you get up and go. You take your punishment, but you feel better with yourself.

"These latrine facilities were adequate for us. There were Americans and Australians in the theater, as I recollect. I think there were more than

---

*William ("Bill") Stewart now lives in Independence, Kansas. He was sent from Java to Japan and so never worked on the Burma-Thailand railway.

200, maybe 210 or 215.* But let me put it this way—the *benjo* were adequate at the time because we hadn't eaten very much. I think that I went from the time I hit the beach until sometime in mid-April before I even had a bowel movement. Now that's going a month or so. I think most of the people were faced with that because I remember thinking, 'My God! I haven't gone to the bathroom except for urinating for I don't know how long!' But then when I did start, I mean that was it. I put it down to Serang and the raw meat and, of course, the condition of the rice balls. I was finally diagnosed as having amebic dysentery in the prison camp, but this was after Serang. The first indication of dysentery was when they transferred some of us from Serang into a jail.

"Another thing about the theater was the food: real raunchy, raunchy old rice balls, yellow in color, about the size of a baseball. There were things in it. Who knows what? I think they were worms and stuff like that, but I don't know. At the time we had no eating utensils. You ate your old rice ball like you were eating an apple. It was so old that it just stuck together, and it was so old you just bit it and ate it like an apple. I didn't get eating utensils until Bicycle Camp. This stuff would come in some kind of containers, and then they would start handing out the rice balls. You'd line up and get your rice ball. People were trying to buy food. I know some people came in with money, and some didn't. Then, lo and behold, one day the Japs came in and had some meat, and each man got a small piece of raw meat. They gave us this meat, and immediately we were going to build a fire and cook this meat.

"We thought we could go out in the courtyard and cook our meat. So some of our Boy Scouts got together, and they got a fire going. The fuel was probably one of the theater seats. So they start this fire and put a piece of meat on a stick, and they're kind of burning it and singeing it, and the Japs come in and see this. They think that it's just the *benjo* out there, and they won't go near it, there's just feces and urine out there. So a little of the smoke wafts in, and then they run out and start kicking this fire out. 'No! No!' We're not too well versed in Japanese, but you get the idea: 'No fires!' 'Well, how are we going to eat the meat?' 'You eat! You eat!' Believe me, you sit there, and you eat this raw meat. God only knows what it was—goat, dog, cat, or whatever.

"I don't know, but I think I must have been in the theater maybe two or three weeks when they sent some of us off to the jail. It was still in Serang. I remember this jail as being a regular jail with walls around it, concrete

---

*These numbers seem to underestimate the prisoner population in the theater at the time. See Lionel Wigmore, *The Japanese Thrust*, p. 533.

walls and so forth, with a big wooden door. It had sort of a high wall rounded at the top. If I remember rightly, it had jagged glass around the top. The wall was maybe ten or twelve feet high.

"I was one of the last that left Serang. We were in the jail when the rest were going to Bicycle Camp, and one morning we were awakened with trucks pulling up. We heard these trucks outside, and all of a sudden they opened these doors and in come these Japanese troops, and they've got machine guns. They came in and this officer is giving orders to his troops. In the meantime, they're going from cell to cell and rounding us up out of the cells, and they line us up against the wall. The troops were setting up the machine guns—one at each end and then one in the center. They set the machine guns up and lined us up against the wall, the prison wall, and I thought, 'Well, here it goes again.' So this is about the third time now that the 'end of Papish' is in sight.

"We're lined up against the wall, and this Jap officer comes up, and he says, 'Officer? Any officer?' in broken English. Mister Hamlin stepped up and says, 'Yes, I'm a naval officer.' Then he questions Lieutenant Hamlin, and when Mister Hamlin identifies himself as being on the USS *Houston*, the Jap says, 'Oh, Navy ship! No good! Navy ship sink hospital ship in Banten Bay!' Evidently, we also sank a pony ship that hauled their carts for them. The *Houston* and the *Perth* did quite a bit of damage in that area. He says, 'No good!'

"Then he says, 'Who's better man? Tojo or Roosevelt?' Lieutenant Hamlin says, 'Roosevelt.' So the Japanese officer hollered something back to the troops, he jumps back from Mister Hamlin, and the Japs start training the guns in on us. So then he steps forward again, and he asks Lieutenant Hamlin, 'Who's the better man? Tojo or Roosevelt?' The lieutenant says Roosevelt again. They start training the machine guns again. This happened three times, and finally he asked Mister Hamlin once more, 'Who's the better man? Tojo or Roosevelt?' Lieutenant Hamlin says, 'Roosevelt is my leader.' Evidently, this sufficed. He talked to the other Japs, and they broke the machine guns down and went out. Then they started lining us up to load onto trucks.

"When they were loading us in the trucks to take us to Bicycle Camp, I thought, 'Well, I've been first in line for too long and really have been catching the brunt of it. I'm going to stand back and see what happens.' Well, as each guy would get up in the truck, they had these bamboo poles, and they'd hit them across the buttocks, across the back, or across the legs when his butt was on the tailgate, you know, how you jump in a truck. They'd swing this bamboo, one on each side, and whale the heck out of guys. So I was looking the situation over, and I said, 'Hmm! They're not going to get Papish that way.' I was about last in line, and what I did was put my hands on the tailgate and boost myself up around and sat down with my butt on the tailgate. I caught a couple of bamboo poles right across the back and right across the side of the head. That's what the guys said when I woke up in the truck going to Bicycle Camp. I don't know how long I had been out, but they hit me with a force that pushed me into the bed of the truck, and the guys dragged me on in.

"The trip from Serang to Bicycle Camp in Batavia was another thing. I hadn't gone to the bathroom or had a bowel movement in about six or eight weeks. Going to Batavia is where our knowledge of Japanese came in. *Benjo* is about the first thing you learn. *Benjo* is 'go to the toilet.' Going down there in that truck everybody—I mean everybody—would holler, '*Benjo! Benjo!*' The Japanese driver would stop, and the Japs would jump out, and, man, I mean they'd disperse over to the side of the road. You weren't going to run away, the only place you were going to run to was where you were to squat and have your bowel movement. By that time things were settling in, and you'd get the cramp in your stomach, and you'd better go.

"About that period was when your thought of survival came in. I felt that in no way was I going to succumb to anything, or no way was I going to let anything get me down. I was going to do the best I could and live the longest I could under the circumstances. I didn't have any possession except my sarong, my skivvies, and my medal around my neck. I had a beautiful homeroom teacher, a nun, and she had given me a Miraculous Medal.

"I'm a staunch Catholic. I was not completely raised a Catholic until about the fourth grade when I started playing and going around with some Catholic boys in my neighborhood. They asked me, 'What are you?' I said, 'I don't know.' So I asked my folks, and they said, 'Well, you're a Catholic. You're baptized.' So the boys said, 'Well, if you're Catholic, you'd better go to church with us at Saint Filomena's,' which was a couple of blocks from where we lived. That was when the whole family got back into the faith, and we started going to Saint Filomena's, and I made my first Communion, and went to school at Saint Filomena's. I attribute my survival as due to my faith. I always had, you might say, my prayers to fall back on when things were getting rough. So I handled things the best way I could."

Things got rough for Paul Papish before his time as a POW ended. For three years he suffered amebic dysentery, and he had malaria and beriberi* for two years. Among his minor discomforts were crabs and bedbugs, periodically. He weighed ninety pounds. The beriberi had serious complications, and he ultimately lost all feeling in his legs from the kneecaps down. He also suffered stomach ulcers after the war. He said, "I can't understand and will never understand how a living human being can treat another living human being the way that we were treated. I don't know. It's man's inhumanity to man."

Liberation came for Papish on September 7, 1945, while working on a Japanese airstrip. A few weeks earlier he was thrilled when a Japanese officer assembled the Americans and told them of the atomic-bomb attacks on Japan. "They lined us all up, and this Jap officer said, 'America no damned good! America drop bomb on Hiroshima! Hiroshima, no more!' The next time the officer came around, he said, 'America no damned good! Nagasaki, no more!' At first Papish thought, "This guy is off his gourd," but a little later, after hearing of the A-bomb from other POWs, he knew liberation was near.

As a makeshift flag of the prisoners rose over the prison camp "it was something else, because the last time that I had seen Old Glory was when our ship went down. There it was fluttering at the mainmast, and the next time I saw the Stars and Stripes was on the day we were liberated."

Papish followed the route many POWs took home: two weeks at the 142d General Hospital in Calcutta, then a plane with stopovers through Karachi, Aden, Cairo, Casablanca, and Washington, D.C. He took a flight to Chicago and rode the Union Pacific's City of Denver from there. As the taxi stopped in front of his home in Denver his mom came running out and all she could say was, "My God! My God!" It was quite a homecoming.

When Papish retired as a chief petty officer in August 1959, after twenty years of service in the U.S. Navy, he was a chief storekeeper. His various assignments included a tour of duty with the Navy ROTC (Reserve

---

*Beriberi is a metabolic disorder resulting from a lack of thiamine (vitamin B1) in the diet. Two forms of the illness exist, labeled often wet and dry. In dry beriberi the nerves and skeletal muscles are affected, and symptoms include numbness, a burning sensation in the legs, and wasting of muscles. In severe cases, patients become emaciated, virtually paralyzed, and bedridden. Wet beriberi is more dangerous, causing heart trouble, which in turn leads to congestion of blood in the veins and edema in the legs and, sometimes, the trunk and face. Other symptoms include loss of appetite, rapid pulse, and breathlessness.

Officers' Training Corps) at the University of Colorado in Boulder. He has since worked for several industries: Emerson Electric, Litton Industries, and Joy Manufacturing. He currently resides in Colorado Springs, where he is "enjoying life to the fullest."

Luther Prunty
Battery F

One dollar made Luther Prunty join the Texas National Guard. That is what he received for weekly meetings, and he needed it. He also liked the two-week summer camp that Battery F, Second Battalion went on each year. It was not just the extra money that he got for the two weeks; summer camp meant a "vacation" at either Palacios, on the coastal bend of the Texas Gulf Coast, or San Antonio, where the unit bivouacked and maneuvered.

Born in Cundiff, Jack County, Texas, about fifty miles northwest of Fort Worth, on January 11, 1912, Prunty moved to nearby Jacksboro on his own to attend high school. He was in high school when he joined the 131st Field Artillery Regiment, which still used old World War I French 75-millimeter guns mounted on caissons and pulled by horses. He had served twelve years in the National Guard and was a sergeant and gun-section chief before President Roosevelt mobilized the Guard in November 1940.

Once the men of Battery F arrived at Brisbane, Prunty was put in charge of an American military police detachment. Later, following the landing at Surabaja, he left the Second Battalion in Singosari, going to Malang where he was provost sergeant for all of Java. On February 28, 1942, when the Japanese invaded the island, he rejoined Battery F and went with the majority of the battalion to near Bandung to support two Australian infantry companies. His battery fired twice, once for thirty-five minutes, stopping a Japanese advance.

When the Second surrendered on March 8, it was at a rubber plantation in the northern part of Java. Colonel Albert C. Searle,* the highest ranking

---

*Colonel Searle was the commanding officer of American forces on Java, which included the Headquarters Battery of the Twenty-sixth Field Artillery Brigade as well as the 131st Field Artillery. He was an old Regular Army officer. When it became apparent that Java would not be saved, the ABDA command decided that only tactical troops would remain on the island. That meant the 131st, which comprised the only American ground force in Java, would remain. When Searle heard of the decision he protested to General George H. Brett, commander of USAFIA, pointing out that while all Regular Army men had been ordered to evacuate, only the National Guardsmen were to remain to face the Japanese. Searle

American officer present, told them to lay down their arms. Although some of the unit left, trying to make it to the coast and freedom, Prunty did not. He felt "a responsibility to the bunch of kids that we brought." So the thirty-year-old Prunty stayed to be captured by the Japanese.

"WE HAD HEARD RUMORS of the way prisoners of war were treated, but we really didn't know. We were sure that all of our belongings would be taken from us, that any money we had would be absolutely no good. We didn't know. Hell, we thought some of us would be executed. There's a lot of thought, a whole lot of rumors, that go along with surrendering. But then you get to thinking that there's a chance the Japs would obey the Geneva Convention, that there were provisions made for prisoners of war; that we weren't completely disgraced by surrendering because we didn't decide that, and we had done all that we could do. There wasn't anyone afraid of dying. Well, there might have been an officer or two that showed a few signs of being afraid, but otherwise, as far as the men were concerned, they just decided to accept whatever fate brought.

"We were to turn over all the equipment in good order, and as far as it looked, it was in good order, but it was not in working order. The trucks, for instance, were in good order, except they had the motors burned out in them. We dismantled and disabled our guns to where they couldn't be fired. We took the firing pins out and threw them away and then depressurized our recoil mechanism. There's no way they could use them. The 75 millimeters would have had to go into ordnance to repressurize them. We buried our small arms and money. Some guys would light a cigar or a cigarette with $100 bills, no problem! We kept our mess gear, blankets, clothing, and personal items. I kept a little ol' .38-caliber pistol for a long, long time. The thing of it was, when the Japs took over, they didn't search us. The pistol didn't belong to me. It belonged to my gunner corporal, and he didn't know what to do with it. It wasn't Army issue. It was a little ol' Smith and Wesson .38. I kept it a long time. Then, I left it at Bicycle Camp because they were shaking us down.

"For maybe a week, we were at this racetrack in central Java, where we had left our equipment as instructed. Then we moved up to a tea plantation and stayed there a week or so. We didn't do anything. Exercised, of course.

---

therefore requested that he be allowed to remain with the 131st as the representative of the Regular Army at the surrender. His request was granted. See Walter D. Edmonds, *They Fought with What They Had: The Story of the Army Air Forces in the Southwest Pacific, 1941–1942* (Boston: Little, Brown and Co., 1951), 410n.

We held calisthenics. That was about the extent of it. We were just waiting to see what was going to happen. Captain Huddleston Wright,* the battery commander, saw that we kept military discipline.

"There were no Japanese there at all. They had come in to this racetrack, but the tea plantation was just on the mountain from the racetrack. They were operating from there. They had us up some two miles, I guess, high in the mountain at a beautiful mansion. It really had a view that was just unimaginable. Java is just a little miniature garden all over—all that I've seen. They irrigate the mountains clear to the top. I've never figured out how they get the water up there, but they do.

"We left the tea plantation then and went down to a sort of park. That's where I first saw the Japanese. They were Japanese frontline troops. I was shocked when I saw them. They were friendly. They wanted to talk. They wanted to talk to the GIs. They didn't want to talk to officers, just the soldiers. What they wanted to talk about was home. They were as homesick as the dickens. They were real nice fellows. They were clean-cut. I'd say they were in the neighborhood of six feet tall, possibly 170 to 180 pounds. We had always been told—through propaganda—that Japanese were real small of stature and wore horn-rimmed glasses and so forth. Not so. There wasn't a one of them that had on glasses; all of them were big, good specimens of men. They weren't dark; they were light complexioned. They were athletic looking. They were polite and just wanted to stop and talk. They had never seen an American and wanted to get acquainted with us. We thought: 'It's not going to be as bad as we thought it was.' That soon changed. Not with the frontline troops, though. Everytime we were in contact with the Japanese fighting troops, it was the same thing. They were very nice people.

"The Japanese were trying to drive some of the American trucks, and it was unbelievable to them that any American could just get in a truck or car and drive it. They wanted us to show them how to use the gears. They'd get those trucks, by the way, in low gear, and away they'd go. It was also unbelievable to them that there weren't more of us than there were. They thought that there had to be more people somewhere. That was the interrogation that went on. Not with the enlisted men. They didn't interrogate a single enlisted man.

"After a few days at the foot of the mountain, they brought their trucks and took us to a nearby railway station. We were put on a train there. We didn't know where we were headed, but they took us into Batavia. The

---

*Wright, of Battery F, died of heart failure at his home in Dallas, Texas, in 1991.

change in the people of Java had taken place. Prior to this, the native population had been friendly with the American GIs, but that changed immediately. The Dutch were real friendly, but the native population was bad! For instance, when we were going through Bandung, crowds gathered along the tracks and threw rocks and rotten vegetables and anything else they could throw at the train. Some of our guys, not thinking much about this, when we pulled in and stopped, had windows open to talk to the natives. We had gotten to where we could converse a little in Malay. For them this was to their sorrow because they got hit with first one thing and then another. It was like when the Fiji Islanders played "Marching through Georgia" to Texas boys.*

"Well, they took us on to a railroad station in Tanjong Priok. That's one of the places I went back to see three years ago [1983]. I went over there. The place hasn't changed much. That's the first place where we got acquainted with Korean guards and the Jap noncoms in charge. They were the occupation army. From the rail station, we walked to the camp. Hell, it must have been a hundred miles! Whew! That was when we learned about hiking in full gear. There were many, many loads that were dumped into the bayou as we went along, and everytime you did, you got a whipping for it.

"When we arrived at the railway station, the Japs told us that they wanted to count. Of course, we fell out in sections like we always had and dressed up and counted off. Well, that was fine for the officers that had told us in the first place that they wanted to count. Everything was just fine. We reported to our first sergeant, he reported to the battery commander, and he in turn reported to this officer, which was perfectly all right. Everything just went fine.

"Then there was another little, ol' . . . a three-star or whatever that is in Japanese. He was noncommissioned. He decided that he needed a count, too. Well, he wanted us to count in Japanese. There wasn't any way that we could do that. Dang it, he made all the section chiefs get in the ranks, and the commissioned officers had to fall in, too. He wanted a count, but there was no way. We didn't know anything about counting in Japanese.

"He told somebody to count, and they didn't count, and that's when they started doing a little fisticuff work. It was pretty bad. It was the first time in my life that I ever had a man slap me, and I didn't hit back. We had some pretty rough times out in the country in Texas, by golly. Some boys would come in from another town, and we'd get together, and you'd learn

---

*The 131st stopped briefly in Suva, Fiji Islands, on their way to Australia, and were serenaded there by the local military band.

how to take care of yourself. That slapping was the hardest thing in the world. I didn't think I could stand it.

"This was the occupation army. They were little. It was just awful, to have to stand there. I bet we stood there in that railroad station for three hours. One would count, and then the other would count. Then they decided that we couldn't count in Japanese, and they couldn't understand the counting in English, so they'd just have to count them all by themselves. One would count, and there'd be another come along behind him counting, and they'd gct different numbers. Oh, we had a time of it there in the station.

"Well, at the camp in Tanjong Priok, it was just an open field, near a sandy area covered with marsh grass. It was close to the coast. We weren't probably half a mile inland. It was very flat on a sea plain. There were some old barracks of stone that they put us into, and there was a barbed-wire fence. It was not a very substantial fence, just a few wires stretched up. These stone buildings, some had raised portions on the floor for your bed. They did shelter you from the rain. They had a tile roof. There was some electricity. I know that we made a coffee pot out of a water bucket and took two wires and put them in there for an element and connected it. By golly, we made one pot of coffee that was all right, but by the time we got around to the second one, it blew a fuse. We had all the camp down on us and all the Japs and Koreans. They were hunting for whatever it was that blew the fuse in the camp. They didn't find out.

"The sanitary facilities were nil. Like all of Java, there was just a slit trench—a ditch—some twelve or fourteen inches deep and six inches wide, and there was water running through it. Well, these ditches were there, but there wasn't any water running through them. Consequently, we had to dig garbage pits and slit trenches for a latrine. It was pretty bad. The water table is close there. You couldn't dig a hole very deep without being in water. The facilities were just bad and crowded.

"There was an old, partially fallen-down building that they put our kitchen in. They started some work parties out to clear the place up. In cleaning this old building, we were digging, and we found a bunch of cheese that, I guess, was all right, but to us it had been buried too long. I understand that they buried cheese so the worms would get in it, and it makes it better. Well, at that time we were still used to American food, which we ran out of and so had to start improvising on rice. We used that cheese, and it smelled worse than any Limburger cheese ever smelled. To a bunch of people who had never been used to eating stuff of that nature, well, it was just unclean. That's when the dysentery and other diseases started hitting us. We ate mostly rice and Chinese cabbage. We had money. Some of it was from our mess supplies, our battery fund. There was other money that was brought in by, for instance, Lieutenant Stensland,* who had come in with lots of money. Where it came from, I never knew. We all kind of got over the first diarrhea, dysentery, or whatever from the flies and so forth.

"The first rice that we had been issued was terrible. It contained not only dirt but worms, bugs. I don't know what you call them, but we see them here in the United States, here in Texas, in wood. They're kind of jointed-looking, and they'll eat into wood, and they've got a red head. They're white worms with a red head. The first number of days there, it got to where you sat and picked those worms out, but it finally got to where I'd have the worms look out for themselves. I didn't get to that until later! There were also weevils. And the cheese, I bit into a piece of cheese and had a half of a worm. It wasn't very appetizing.

"We had two meals a day at Priok. It was adequate for the kind of meals we were getting. That's where we had a little weight loss. Our cooks had no idea about cooking rice in a big ol' dish that looked like a disc off of a plow and about three times as big. It didn't have any hole in the center. I don't know what the official name of it was. We called it a 'wajan.'† That's what they cooked rice in. Either it would be just mush or it would be burned, one or another. But they finally got to where they learned how to pull their fire and cook the rice. But at Priok they didn't learn to. They were in the process of learning.

"Priok was terrible. It was terrible. Of course, being the first camp of that nature, it would have been. Our work wasn't hard. The work details went to the docks and rolled drums of gasoline around. There wasn't anybody in a hurry. It was just sort of a job. That soon came to a halt. But work details were voluntary. The first sergeant would assign people to go out unless somebody volunteered. In fact, you didn't go out unless you wanted to because somebody always wanted to go out and buy stuff and trade with the natives. I said, 'natives'; I mean Dutch people—women and children—they would always be giving you something or selling something.

---

*Roy Stensland was part of a mission dispatched with funds from General Douglas MacArthur's headquarters in the Philippines to the Netherlands East Indies. The mission's purpose was to buy food and charter vessels to supply the Philippines. During the evacuation following the Japanese invasion of Java, Stensland was reassigned to the 131st Field Artillery. See Edmonds, *They Fought with What They Had*, 373-4, 385. Stensland died on January 5, 1975.

†This is the Malayan word for "wok."

"I don't remember, but I think I heard we were at Priok about six weeks. It was such a shock that it seemed like we were there a year, but we were there just a short period. The big thing, I think, that we were learning at Priok was that we definitely weren't under our government, weren't under our own command. We were learning Oriental discipline, which we hated, but it had to be that way.

"The discipline in their army allows a buck private, if he out-rates or if he's been in a little longer than the next man, to literally beat the thunder out of him, and there's not anything the other guy can do about it. He just has to take it and try to do better the next time or tell him he will. They do it from the officers to the noncommissioned officers and down the line. That's their discipline. The Koreans* were under all the Japanese. They're right—well, I started to say they were right next to us, but they're not. The natives were in there between us and the Koreans. The Korean was on the low end of the totem pole as far as the Japs were concerned. They didn't think much of Koreans. Consequently, they put the Koreans where they could boss the natives around and beat them up. There wasn't any natives that ever beat up on us Americans, I don't think, but the Koreans sure did.

"They're sadists—the Koreans. Later up in the jungle, I saw a kind of a bamboo pen made up, and they had a pig in it. The pig had been brought up for rations. They took sharpened bamboo sticks and punched the pig to hear him squeal. They were standing around and having a ball. There's not a reason on earth why they did that but to hear the pig squeal.

"Of course, at Tanjong Priok I didn't see any punishment that I remember other than slapping. Later on it was different. They had rules. One thing you had to do, for instance, was that if one of them came in, you must bow, and that was a form of humiliation to us. If you salute a Jap that was understandable, salute their officers, especially. We knew military discipline. But this bowing, phew! And you must bow in the proper manner or get beat up.

"Well, after Priok we went into what they called—well, goodness, I've even forgotten what they called it now. Well, their history don't go back past 1947! Anyway, it was a Dutch military camp. Some of us walked to it, some of us went by truck. It was, say, six or seven miles from Priok. They

---

*The Australian official history says Korean guards were assigned at Bicycle Camp, about a month before the transfer of POWs to Singapore. The Americans do not all agree with this. Some think they first encountered Korean conscripts as guards at Bicycle Camp, while others maintain that the first contact was made in Burma on the railroad.

just told us to fall out with our full gear, that we were moving. The sick people and so forth and some of the baggage was taken by truck. They used those little three-wheel jobs for the sick, but the other people just walked. We were in good health other than what sickness we'd had at Priok.

"I remember Bicycle Camp, it was just a long boulevard. It had a fence on one side and buildings on the other, it was much like a college campus. The streets were real narrow. If a street was eight feet wide, well, that was real wide. They were paved with tile, and the buildings were tile. Yep, Bicycle Camp."

After leaving Bicycle Camp, Prunty spent a day again at Tanjong Priok and became worried that he would have to stay there once more. He said, "Lordy mercy, things looked really bleak." Things did get bleak for Prunty but not at Priok. On his voyage by ship to Singapore, he suffered from kidney stones and had to have them removed by cystoscopic surgery without anesthetic in Singapore. After several months at Changi he went north to work on the railroad, including time at Tamarkan, the site portrayed in the movie *The Bridge on the River Kwai*. He did not work on either the wooden or steel-and-concrete structures built there, but he watched B-29 bombers pound the steel bridge in 1945.

While working on the railroad he had amebic dysentery, malaria, and a six-to-eight-inch tropical ulcer,* which ultimately disabled him, eating through a tendon in the back of his leg. He managed to stay out of 80 Kilo Camp and asserted that he survived because of his "good fortune" in not going to the Death Camp. Prunty was liberated on August 27, 1945, and spent forty days at the hospital in Calcutta before being flown back to Walter Reed Army Hospital in Washington, D.C. He was operated on at Reed, having his "heel string—tendon—put back together."† He also had his left hand repaired, although it remained twisted and somewhat shriveled.

Prunty left the military in April 1946 with a chest full of medals, including the Purple Heart. Once back in Jack County, Texas, he stayed to himself out on the family farm for a year. Then, at the urging of his friends, he ran for and was elected to the office of county tax assessor-collector in

---

*A tropical ulcer started with a scratch or slight abrasion of the skin, which allowed a type of spore to enter the tissue. Unimpeded due to malnutrition and lack of medicine, the ulcer would develop often until a hand, foot, or leg became a purplish, cancerous, malodorous sore causing almost intolerable pain.
†Prunty undoubtedly means his Achilles tendon.

1947. He served in that office until 1962, when he became county auditor. He married, made wise investments, and retired in 1979. He now resides in the area of his birth, Jacksboro, Texas.

Raymond D. Reed
Medical Detachment

Ray Reed was twenty-one years old the day the Second Battalion landed at Surabaja, Java. He was born in Amarillo, Texas, on January 11, 1921, and had joined the National Guard in 1937. He was assigned to the 131st Field Artillery Regiment's Medical Detachment, a portion of which trained at Battery B's armory in Amarillo.* He joined for the money and because his friends, who already belonged, encouraged him. When the medics were mobilized, they bivouacked at the city's fairgrounds before shipping to Camp Bowie in Brownwood to join with the entire regiment. Reed was briefly detached from his unit and sent to William Beaumont Army Hospital near Fort Bliss, El Paso, Texas, to train as a medical technician, the only one in his group.

Reed was in San Francisco with the Second Battalion before he realized that he might be going into harm's way, and he was aboard the USAT *Republic* near the Gilbert Islands on December 7 before he "rudely awoke to the fact" that he would probably be involved in combat. "I had quite a few butterflies in my stomach," he said, "and I got extremely concerned over the fact that we weren't playing games. We were going to get serious."

Reed's first combat experience came at an aid station located on the airfield near Singosari, where the Second came under aerial attack by Japanese bombers. He attended the wounded, but "was so nervous that I couldn't hold the syringe to give a shot of morphine, and Doctor Lumpkin† had to do it." Although he was later assigned to a dispensary in Malang, he rejoined the Second when it moved to support Australian units near Bogor, called Buitenzorg by the Dutch. He retreated with the others toward Bandung, as the Japanese pressed in, and was at the rubber plantation near Bandung when the Dutch surrendered. Reed's interview begins at this point and

---

*Most of the Medical Detachment came from Plainview.

†Captain S. Hugh Lumpkin, M.D., was from Lubbock. He died of dysentery on August 1, 1943, at 100 Kilo Camp, Burma. His death was a blow to the POWs' morale, and he is mentioned in many of the interviews.

continues until he moved as a POW with the Second Battalion to Bicycle Camp.

" ALTHOUGH THE ISLAND HAD FALLEN, Colonel Tharp* said that we could go to the south coast to a place called Tjilatjap, where the USS *Houston* and HMAS *Perth* were to meet us and take us to Australia. Our purpose in Java had been served, and we could split up in small groups and make our way as best we could. Naturally, I thought my days were numbered, and I'm sure everybody else thought that, too. We had heard of the Japs' attacks in China and the Rape of Nanking. We had heard about the tremendous amount of damage and killings that took place in Singapore. We felt that our days were numbered unless we got off the island. We destroyed our vehicles and arms. We took the bolts out of all the rifles, threw away the pistols, dumped them and the ammunition into the river.

"After attempting to go to the south coast of Java and being blocked off, we finally decided that the best thing to do was to go into a little town there—I don't even remember the name of it—and take our chances with the Japs. We were still in radio contact with other guys around our own group. There were people on the coast; some had already reached the coast. We heard that either Rogers† or Stensland made an attempt to get a plane off of one of the airfields and was stopped by the Japanese. We were being advised by natives and some English that all the roads were blocked off, that you couldn't get through. We were told that if we could make contact with certain Javanese, they could smuggle us through during the night, but we never did make contact with any of these natives.

"Lieutenant Stensland had come in, I think, from Borneo in a Beechcraft—one of those old stagger-winged Beechcrafts—and he landed somewhere in Java. He didn't land in Malang, but he had found his way into our group and became a part of our group there in Singosari. He gained our respect for directing gunfire on the river. One of the tales that was told about him was that he would walk on the dikes of the rice paddies with Jap snipers across the river shooting at him. He would walk standing up and just keep walking back and forth using field glasses and directing fire without ever getting down to protect himself. His reputation for guts started about that time. It carried on quite a bit longer because he would stand up to the Japanese in prison camp and get the devil beat out of him.

---

*Colonel Blucher S. Tharp, the Second Battalion's commanding officer, was from Amarillo, Texas, where he died in a diabetic coma on November 12, 1954.
†Winthrop H. ("Windy") Rogers was an officer in Headquarters Battery. He now lives in Tacoma, Washington.

"Since I was a noncombatant I didn't feel ashamed of the way we surrendered. I can see where a combat soldier might. I was more afraid of the fact that the Japanese were going to shoot me on sight than I was ashamed of the fact that I hadn't done my part. I know when we walked into this town to see what was going to take place, we actually walked down the street, and there were Japanese soldiers walking down the street with rifles, there were Japanese soldiers directing traffic, and they didn't pay any attention to us. We even went into a store to buy something to eat, and there were Jap soldiers in the store buying something to eat, and we stood right beside them.

"We had gone to the store to buy something to eat, and the Jap soldiers were all around us. We walked out and tried to talk to them, and they wouldn't talk to us. We tried to talk to them in Malay, but they couldn't speak Malay. They couldn't speak English, and we couldn't speak Japanese. We kept walking along and asking, and finally found a guy directing traffic out in the middle of an intersection, and we asked him if he could speak American. He said he could a little bit. So he came over to the curb where we were, and we asked him where the Japanese headquarters were, and that we were trying to find someplace to surrender. We had given up the idea of getting to the coast. We had been told that all avenues had been blocked except for the smuggling, and we did not know that the *Houston* and *Perth* had been sunk, and there wouldn't be any rescue, anyhow. The group I was with, twelve or fourteen of us, decided escape was futile.

"Consequently, the Jap directing traffic told us where the head honcho's headquarters were, and we went down and there was a Jap lieutenant there. We asked him if he could speak English, which he couldn't. We told him we were Americans and that we wanted to know where we were supposed to go and what we were supposed to do. We finally had to speak to him in Malay to get him to understand. He left and told us to stay there and don't leave. So he left, and he was gone a couple of hours. Finally, he came back with a stake-body truck and told us to get in. The two Japs drove us up to a tea plantation way up in the mountains.

"We were the first POWs there. We got there, and there was a huge home and a guest house, swimming pool, and tennis court, but there was no one there. The Japs told us we were to get out there and take what we had with us and that they would come back and give us some food. I had a barracks bag with me. Most everybody lost their stuff in the Battle of Buitenzorg. I don't know if they call it that, but that's what we called it. There was a big home, beautifully furnished, swimming pool, tennis court. We were told we were going to get fed pretty nice, so we thought, 'If this is prison life now—if we are prisoners of war and this is it—we should have surrendered a long time ago!' We had it all to ourselves—every bit of it—and we had a lot of fun. We were enjoying the devil out of it.

"Periodically, the Japs came up with a truck and dumped food off there, mostly Javanese-type food or Chinese food, that they had picked up in that little town. I was completely confused about Japanese soldiers, because they seemed to ignore us; they seemed not to want anything to do with us. Having heard these stories of how murderous and vicious they were, we were really confused as to what type of people they were. Of course, they looked sloppy! Very sloppy uniforms! I don't recall them being dirty—they were clean—but they were very sloppy. Their uniforms didn't fit. They didn't look like they could fight their way out of a paper sack, to tell the truth. You wondered why in the world they could cover as much ground as they did, because they didn't look like they could hold their own against anybody. They were very short, and they were very quiet at this time.

"We were at the tea plantation awhile and in the meantime other members of the unit gradually gathered there. Well, one day they came up in the truck and picked us up. They told us that we were moving, to get all our stuff, and we did. We got in the truck, and we went down to this town. We came along outside the town itself, and they dumped us off at a place where the rest of our guys were. They were already there, along the railroad tracks. Doctor Lumpkin was there, and some more of our guys were there. They dumped us off there. They told us to just get off the truck and join the others, and that's what we did.

"Then we learned from the guys that were there that we were supposed to build us a place to live in ourselves. There was no information as to where we were going, or when we were going. I think the rumor was that we were going to stay there about a week. We were supposed to build something to get us out of the weather, so we proceeded to build a lean-to or a little hut-type thing and something to sleep on. The medics, we set up a medical aid station and treated people and doled out supplies of medicine. The Japanese would come around once in a while, but not enough to where we would even consider that we were interned.

"During that time, I remember one incident that stuck in my mind. There was a Javanese man that brought a very, very small two- or three-year-old girl up there. She had been severely burned, and I got out of the man that it was his daughter and that she had walked up to a wood-burning stove and put her arm up on the wood-burning stove and burnt herself all under her arm, all down her chest in third-degree burns. He wanted us to treat her, so Doctor Lumpkin turned to me and told me to go treat the girl. So

I went out there, and I looked at her, and I thought, 'Oh, boy, just a little bitty baby,' and that horrible burn that she had. I told him that I would treat the girl, but not to expect much because she was very severely burned. We gave her a very small shot of morphine to relieve the pain somewhat. Then I put tannic acid ointment all over the burns and wrapped her completely and told him to come back in three or four days, and I would look at it. I rather expected that we would be gone by then, and I wouldn't have to look at it anymore. I was afraid that she was going to die in those three or four days, and if she hadn't she was going to be very near death.

"He came back, and we were still there; they came just about dark. I gave her another shot of morphine, a small one, and I went to take off the bandages, and they were stuck—stuck just like they were on there with glue. I took a scalpel and cut the bandage off a little bit at a time to try to keep from disturbing the burns. Mosquitoes were eating me up, but I finally got it off. Somebody was helping me, I've forgotten who now. I decided not to use any more tannic acid ointment. I used tannic acid jelly, because it wouldn't stick. I put it all over her and wrapped her up again and said, 'Come back in three or four days, and I'll take another look at her.' Again, I expected her to be gone by then, and I expected us to be gone if she wasn't.

"They came back. I took the bandage off, and it was just pink, she was full of color. I did it again—wrapped her up—and told him that she was okay, and everything was lovely. She had survived, and how I have no idea. It made me feel pretty good. Then a couple of days after that he came back, and he had a great big wicker basket full of fruit. He hollered for me—for Reed: 'Where is Reed? Where is Reed?' I could hear him. I stepped out of my little place, and I looked down and saw this guy with his fruit, and he came up and presented it to me. I didn't get a whole lot of the fruit—it was distributed to the group—but I was thankful that he could think that much of me to bring it. I often wondered what ever happened to that little girl. She'd be quite grown now.

"It seemed to me like we stayed there two weeks, maybe three weeks. It seemed to me like it just went on. Every day was like, 'Well, we're going to be leaving,' but we just stayed on and on. Finally, we boarded a train for Batavia. We didn't know we were going to Batavia, but we boarded a train to go to Batavia. When we got there, that was the first bashings that we got. The Japs on the train were comparatively quiet; they didn't have much to say except to keep everybody seated and not milling around. Then when we got to the railroad station in Batavia, we were told to get off the train and line up in regular marching formation. This damn Jap officer along with these other soldiers were swinging those Samurai swords and dragging the ground with them, waltzing up and down, looking at everybody and hollering and screaming, stopping and slapping and kicking. I didn't get any at that time—fortunately. I don't know how I got missed. He wasn't bashing everybody, but he'd go about every tenth guy and give him a good whack.

"We left the railroad station and went to Tanjong Priok. We set up just like it was one of our military bases. There were all nationalities there. Indians—Sikhs—and Gurkhas were there, as well as Australians, English, Dutch, and Americans. It was a large camp. It looked like a picture of a typical Malay or Asiatic military base. It had little low huts with little verandas. It was dark. I remember that the buildings were dark, painted dark. I think it had been a Javanese army camp, that is, a Dutch army camp, which were mostly Javanese. It was a large area, and we set up just like we were in our old military base. My barracks was very much like the barracks had been at Singosari, except they had more wood in them. There were individual rooms and several of us, six, I believe, in each room that was ten-by-ten. I had a cot.

"We had regular toilet facilities; Dutch toilets, they're different. You have to squat down and wash instead of sitting on a stool. It was new, but actually, if you stop and think about it, it was about the most sanitary thing you could do. The water runs all the time, and you wash yourself after you've gone. It was a pretty good arrangement, under the circumstances. If I recall right, I think we took turns bathing. They had so many that could go bathing to the shower area—so many on certain days. About one bath a week. I don't recall if there was soap. We were all conscious of hygiene. As far as our bodies were concerned, we were very conscious of the fact that we needed to keep clean. Actually, the Americans never, in the whole time, deteriorated like the English to where they became extremely dirty and filthy and died from the result of it. The English were not clean; they were not clean people. The hospital section that I was in, where the venereal disease patients were, was forever trying to get things cleaned up, because we had people with open sores and open wounds.

"We stayed at Tanjong Priok quite a while, because I was put in charge of the hospital sections that had all the venereal disease patients in it. There were quite a few, going back to the period before we were taken prisoner. In other words, some of these guys that had gonorrhea and syphilis quite awhile by the time we got to Tanjong Priok were pretty well gone. As a matter of fact, we had fellows that were dying of venereal disease at the time I got there. There were about fifty men in the VD section that I was in charge of.

"The only thing we had to treat them with was sulfanilamide, and we did have some bismuth to treat the syphilitics with. We didn't have very much, but we had some to treat the very worst people with. It was rough trying to treat these particular syphilitics and the ones with gonorrhea because the facilities at the hospital were not as good as the regular facilities the guys were living in. The VD cases were having to lay on little bitty decks that we built up off the ground, or on the ground, or on concrete slabs. It was very dirty; it was a dirt floor. They had sores, called chancres, on their penises, and some had developed sores on the rest of their bodies, and we had to treat them mostly with sulfanilamide tablets ground up into powder. We had no oral medicine to give them for pain. The VD patients were very demoralized.

"I worked with them all the time. I had about four or five English corpsmen who worked with me, but I was the only American. I can't say that I didn't have pity or sympathy for them. Some I did. Some were very pitiful. The other guys thought they should have had better sense than to get venereal disease. They didn't want them to come around. As a matter of fact, they fenced off the area where we kept them. I think I worked pretty hard to try to make them as comfortable as possible. I didn't feel like they were ever going to be cured, because we didn't have the medicine or facilities to cure them. Some were so far advanced that they died from it, and you have to be pretty well advanced to die from VD.

"We had a main kitchen at Priok. The food wasn't as good as what we had up in the tea plantation, but it was not bad. We had the usual rice for every meal, stew, a little fruit. We didn't have any fruit or vegetables after that, or any bread. We would go to the kitchen to get the food at that time. We still had our own mess gear—American mess gear. I believe we ate two meals a day. I don't believe there was a sufficient amount of food at each serving, because I remember being hungry after I'd eaten.

"The Japs were very curious in Tanjong Priok. They didn't get real upset with anybody—well, maybe with a few. They made it difficult for some, especially officers. The Japanese would come over to our area and talk and give us cigarettes and candy. They would talk about what it was like in America and what it was like to be an American soldier and so forth. They weren't really very tough. It seemed to be that they were trying to be friendly. There was harassment, but it was only for the officers who they felt were not giving out the information they wanted, or if it was somebody who decided they wanted to go from compound to compound without permission. They got slapped around some. They gave us the rules, and if we didn't follow the rules we got bashings. The rules were mostly like you would have in a base, such as, lights out at a certain time, working parties will be prompt, no going from one compound to the other, no talking between prisoners of one compound to the other, no passing of notes. Such things as that.

"As far as I can remember, any bashings that took place, or any type of punishment, was because somebody broke a rule or talked back to a guard that came over to visit or said something dirty about him. I don't recall anybody that really went out of their way to beat up on Americans just to get a kick out of it like they did later on. If Japs came to you in your barracks, you bowed. If you went to their headquarters, you saluted when you went up to the guards and the officer that you were going to confront. In passing one of the guards or one of the Jap officers out in the open area, you saluted.

"In the Japanese Army discipline was extremely strict. It was so rigid and strict that we were aghast to the fact that they went to the extent that they did in their discipline. Even the English, their discipline was a great deal more severe than the Americans'. I can't say that the Australians were strict, but the English were. Then the Japanese, it was uncanny. For example, take a corporal. The private would bow and scrape to him just like an American private would to a full colonel. It was something else just to be a corporal. The sergeants were really something high up! Then the officers, they were absolutely untouchable as far as the enlisted men went. I can't say this is normal, but I've seen them beat each other until one dropped to the ground. That's pretty severe as far as one nationality to his own nationality. I don't recall officers bashing enlisted men, or, say, sergeants. There was an awful lot of bashing by sergeants of all the other enlisted men. Then that would filter down. If a private caught a good bashing, he would take it out on the prisoners almost every time.

"There weren't many bashings in Tanjong Priok. There were some but not many at all. They were so rare that they were quite a topic of conversation amongst everybody else if somebody got a bashing. If somebody got a bashing over in Bicycle Camp, it was just another bashing. It may be that way because I was in the hospital, and being in charge of the venereal disease ward, I didn't fare too bad. I didn't realize that it was really bad in Tanjong Priok.* Over in Bicycle Camp, although I was still active as a medic, there were so darn many medics and doctors and guys with more

---

*Portions of Reed's account concerning Tanjong Priok do not agree with most of the other POWs' accounts. He may be confusing aspects of Bicycle Camp with Tanjong Priok and vice versa. This seems plausible to us; nevertheless, his interview is included to demonstrate a variety of opinions among the American prisoners.

rank than I had that I didn't work much in the hospital or aid stations. I was mostly out on working parties."

At Bicycle Camp, Reed stopped working as a medic. He also got his first bashings there. Consequently, he complained about Bicycle Camp but found out later that there were Japanese prisoner-of-war camps far worse than it. While working on the railroad, he was disabled by three tropical ulcers on his legs; he was carried by his fellow POWs to a work site on the railroad where, as he put it, "You would lay and break rocks for ballast the whole time, and then they'd carry you back." His ulcers were treated by having five men hold him down and a rag put in his mouth to bite down on, while a doctor using a homemade, sharpened spoon dug out the dead flesh left by the infection.

Reed was at a camp near Bangkok when he was liberated. His group sang "God Bless America" upon release because they had forgotten the words to "The Star-Spangled Banner." He later gave depositions against his captors to be used in war-crimes trials. Asked why he survived, he credited faith in God, himself, and his fellow man, and being American. He said, "Being Americans, we came out of it. I say that not because I think Americans are that superior. I'm proud to be an American. But there were similar circumstances that hit, say, the English, and they didn't survive. They lost practically everybody in the camp. But the American attitude, . . . and I didn't know about this until Doctor Hekking* told me and the rest of us about the American attitude and how different it was from the other nationalities', even his own nationality's, the Dutch. He said that the American attitude was the greatest thing that he saw while he was in prison."

Reed had difficulty adjusting to everyday life, having lost his ability to take orders. It took time, but before too long he was attuned to being a civilian. He left the military in March 1946, attended college for a while, and finally settled for a career in display and design. He eventually owned his own design business. He and his wife raised a family of three children and now have five grandsons. He also served as a pilot in the Civil Air Patrol for more than twenty years. He recently lamented the fact that "we POWs did not have the vocabulary to tell people at home what it was like as Jap prisoners. The people probably could not understand any human living under those conditions."

---

*Doctor Henri Hekking was captured in Java while he was a physician in the Dutch Army. His knowledge of tropical medicine, the American POWs believed, was responsible for the saving of many lives. The interview in Chapter 4 with Houston Tom ("Slug") Wright deals in depth with Doctor Hekking's contribution.

Chapter 2

Bicycle Camp

At different times and without forewarning, in May 1942 the Japanese moved most of the National Guardsmen and *Houston* sailors by truck and train to Bicycle Camp, another former Dutch army installation in Batavia. In contrast to the previous experience, this camp would provide the best living conditions the majority would have during their years as POWs. Water and shower facilities were plentiful, the kitchens were well equipped, sanitation was adequate, and there was room for the men to stretch their legs. The two-story brick barracks in which they lived were typical of construction in the tropics—open-air, breezeway-type buildings with verandas and unscreened windows. Each barracks housed three hundred men, with three normally assigned to each cubicle or room. There were no beds, but abundant material was available for improvising one.

Much as earlier, the process of adjusting to life as prisoners continued. Bowing and saluting their guards became routine, although the POWs still found it repugnant. Lester C. Rasbury, whose interview appears in this chapter, put it cogently: "You have to go along with things and learn to live a different life. You've got to make up your mind: 'Well, that's the way it is, and there's nothing you can do about it.' If you want to survive, you've got to adjust because if you try to get rough with them, well, they can just get rougher. The best thing to do is just kind of go along. The way I always looked at it is to do what you're supposed to do. Still sometimes when you'd do that, you'd still get into trouble." Artilleryman Roy Armstrong* echoed this view, which was a common theme among the prisoners: "I just made up my mind that if they tell me to do something, I'm going to try to do it. If I can keep one of them off me, I'll go ahead and do what I'm supposed to do.

---

*Roy G. ("Army") Armstrong, of Battery F, lives in Jacksboro, Texas.

If they tell you, they're going to whup you, well, they're going to whup you. They don't bluff. They just come up and go to kicking and scratching."

Beyond the basic rules of the camps and the adjustments that the young Americans had to make, survival depended on the maintenance of military discipline. Group welfare was paramount to individual interests, and discipline was the ingredient that maintained this maxim. Colonel Tharp of the 131st Field Artillery, the senior officer present, was in charge. He headed a revised chain of command that included both Army and Navy officers. Noncoms and men in the ranks who showed extraordinary ability, and had the respect of their fellow prisoners, became part of the military hierarchy.

The Japanese camp commandant passed orders and organization for each day through American intermediaries. In the case of work parties, the Japanese assigned daily tasks to an American liaison officer, who determined which men and officers would do them. Although officers who went on work details did not labor, they performed a vitally important function. They tried to occupy the guards' attention as a way of minimizing bashings or allowing POWs to slip away on foraging campaigns. Lieutenant Ilo Hard said that "the only time we would go out of our way—I guess you would say fraternize—to any extent with the guards would be on work parties. At this time, around Batavia, we would try to get a Jap boasting about their conquests, with us standing there open-mouthed and listening to give him a good audience. The purpose was to keep the Jap in a good humor and keep him distracted so he wasn't pushing the work detail. It also gave the good thieves a chance to sneak off and do a little scrounging." Officers also saw to the maintenance of sanitary food preparation, latrine facilities, and enforced personal hygiene standards among the men. Their diligence helped ensure that no Americans died of sickness at Bicycle Camp.

Food became increasingly important, and even though its quality was better than at the previous places of imprisonment, the lack of it was a problem. To supplement the unit's diet, officers purchased food locally with money withdrawn earlier from a Dutch bank in Java. Captain Clark L. Taylor, who as supply officer handled the funds, discusses his role in helping obtain additional food in his interview in this chapter. Before the prisoners left Bicycle Camp, Taylor had spent almost all of this money, and the Americans had to rely increasingly on bartering or stealing.

A smattering of the Japanese language was another important way of coping with the rigors of captivity. The POWs tried to avoid the guards as much as possible. When they could not they discovered that if they knew Japanese commands they could often avoid bashings. The guards became infuriated when prisoners failed to respond to orders that they did not understand. The guards yelled commands in the usual manner of the Japanese military and expected the quick response that they got from Japanese soldiers. To know words such as *"Kiotsuke!"* (Attention!), *"Speedo!"* (Hurry!), and *"tenko"* (roll call) was essential. The Japanese issued each American a round wooden tag about the size of a fifty-cent piece and required him to carve an identification number on it. The POW retained the number throughout his internment, and if one forgot it, he was bashed on the spot.

By October 1942, after seven months as POWs, the Americans completed their accommodation to the new reality. They recognized the necessity of continuing their own military discipline and reluctantly accepted the need to follow Japanese rules and adjust to their captors' mentality. These accommodations played a vital role in carrying them through their three-and-one-half-year ordeal. Those who would ultimately work on the Death Railway were ready to leave Java but unprepared for the crucible that lay ahead.

J. O. ("Jack") Burge
USS *Houston*

After Jack Burge was captured by the Japanese he stayed as close to his guard as he possibly could; he was understandably afraid of the natives. He said, "I found out that there was probably a lot more survivors off the ship, but there was a price on our head. The only way you was going to survive was to stay with the Japs, because these natives'd cut your head off or your ears or something—part of a white person that could prove that they had killed you—for twenty-five guilders or whatever the price was. So the only safe place was with the Japs. Sometimes the natives'd come up and try to get the guard to let them take you off in the jungle. Well, no way; he'd keep you with him, because he knew what would happen, and then he'd have to pull the cart." The carts he speaks of were the same as those described by Otto Schwarz in his interview (see Chapter 1), the carts Burge, Schwarz, and about twenty other American seamen pulled after being captured by the invading Japanese.

Burge was born in Beckett, Ohio, on August 9, 1918, and joined the Navy in October 1938, after graduating from high school and spending a brief period working in construction. Since he was over six feet tall, he was assigned from boot camp in Newport, Rhode Island, to the Navy's New York World's Fair detachment. He disliked the frequent and lengthy drills required of the "show troops" at the fair, so when the opportunity arose he transferred to the *Houston*. At the time she was at Charleston, South Carolina, having returned President Roosevelt from his 1939 cruise.

Three years later, in February 1942, when the *Houston* fought its last engagements, Burge was at his battle station with the aftermidship repair party in the after engine room. His experiences from the time of the sinking until he went to Bicycle Camp were very much like those of Schwarz, whom he met in the Japanese landing barge that fished them out of Banten Bay.

"THE JAPS LOADED US ON TRUCKS and took us into Batavia to Bicycle Camp. It was as uneventful a trip as could be on six miles of muddy roads that bounced you around a little bit. The guards were as scared of us as we were of them, you know. They kept you pretty much under surveillance with the end of their guns and bayonets. They were scruffy-looking. They had belly bands,* and one size shoe fit everybody—tennis shoe. They'd tie a string around their pants leg to keep the dust out. It was a different army than ours, but they'd had a rough row. They'd been marching. I've seen them, though, even if they had to wash their clothes in a mudhole, wash the sweat out of them before they'd go to bed at night. They carried drums—regular oil drums—and had a wooden platform built. If they had time they'd fill them up with water and light a fire under them. They'd all get in—to me, it was boiling water—and take them a bath. They were cleaner than a lot of people gave them credit for; they tried to be under the circumstances.

"Well, Bicycle Camp was another world after where we'd been. It was a Dutch barracks and had cubicles in it. The Dutch Army was, you know, native soldiers, Javanese. These were native quarters. The way I understand it, their families could live with them. It was dry, and we all eventually got rice sacks and made us bunks out of them on the walls. So everybody had an individual bunk, and it was about six people to a cubicle and guards at each end. When a guard'd come through, why, you had to holler '*kiotsuke*,' that's 'attention' and all that stuff, you know, get up and bow. You had to bow to them. I think the guards were still Japanese in Batavia. If you smoked, you had to have a bucket with you all the time—something to put your cigarette out in. You had to carry that on your belt. You had to bow to them all the time; anytime that you seen them, you bowed to them.

"Some of the ol' boys, if they didn't bow to them or got caught swiping something, look out. If you followed their stupid rules—which seemed stupid to us—you got along pretty good there. The Japanese guards weren't anywhere near as ferocious as the Korean guards we got later on. They'd take guys and make them kneel with a bamboo behind their legs; face the sun for ten or fifteen hours, you know, as long as the sun was shining and maybe stay that way overnight. They'd slap us around some. Some of this was done at Bicycle Camp.

"As a rule they kept those who violated rules around the guardhouse. They'd hold a rock over their heads or kneel with this bamboo stick behind their knees or something like that. What we called bashings weren't too frequent by the Japs. If you'd been told that you'd have a can with you all the time if you're smoking a cigarette, or that you'd bow to them when you

---

*The so-called belly band was a cloth wrapping around the abdomen to keep the stomach warm.

see them, that stuff, you complied. If you didn't, their form of punishment was beating and kicking. If you got a little careless in any respect, why, that was their way of getting your attention. It got your attention. It didn't take you near as long to learn *benjo* for restroom and *mizu* for water and things like that, you know.

"It's that way in their army. If you see a colonel slap a captain in the morning, you know that one of you is going to get it before night, because each one of them will save face. The captain gets the lieutenant, and the lieutenant gets the master sergeant, and the master sergeant gets the sergeant, and the sergeant gets the corporal. When you see a little 'no-star'* out there get it, why, he's going to look around until he finds a prisoner someplace doing something wrong, and he can beat on him before he goes to bed. That's the way they save face.

"It wasn't near as bad in Bicycle Camp as it got later on. There seemed to be lots of Japs there. They was everyplace you looked. We tried to ignore the Jap guards like the plague, because they were so easy to misunderstand and then you was in trouble. The best thing you could do was just stay away from them. I never had much to do with them there. They had their rules, and they was going to knock you around if you didn't obey them; so the best thing to do when you did come in contact with them was to do like they asked and go about your business. If you got a little lax or got caught doing something you shouldn't, you got the punishment.

"They were liable to walk through the barracks anytime; they walked through at regular intervals. There was one boy off the ship that had an epileptic fit one time. He was a big ol' boy. He was bald-headed, and the soft spot had never healed in the top of his head; you could see his heart beat. He threw one fit, and it took a whole bunch of us to hold him down, because he was a big, strong ol' boy. The Japs came rushing in there with their rifles; they didn't know what was going on. When they seen his pulse beating in the top of his head and the antic he was going through and frothing and so on, from then on, when they heard a commotion like that, they didn't come around; boy, they'd just stay gone. They were scared to death of him.

"If the Japs made some stupid rules, they'd tell the American officers and the officers'd call us together and tell us, 'Don't forget it!' It was just that simple. If you did what they said, they let you alone. Once the word was passed down, 'Go sign your name,' or sign somebody else's name. This was when the Japs was going to first get a record made of us, and we'd promise

*"No-star" refers to the lowest ranking enlisted man, undoubtedly a Korean conscript, in the Japanese Army. He was so designated because he did not have enough rank to rate having a single red star sewn on his uniform sleeve or hat.

not to escape. It didn't mean anything.* Why get out there in the sun and get beat on for three or four days and then sign it anyway? You told each other, 'Now I'm going to sign it, but I'm lying. My word's no good to these people.' It was just a way of getting it over with, you know. We'd sent a postcard one time.

"It's been a long time ago and I'm trying to keep this honest, but it seems to me like we did get to send a postcard in Bicycle Camp. It just keeps coming back to me that we did get to send one that was already made up. You had to say, 'I am well,' and 'I am a prisoner of the Japanese Imperial Army.' The only thing that they'd let you do was put down one sentence, 'I am with so-and-so friend.' So I put down that I was with Albert Kennedy,[†] and Albert Kennedy put down that he was with me, because our parents knew that we knew each other, see. So by getting one from him, they in turn could call my folks and tell them that I was all right, but none of these cards ever got back. I don't know whether it was just to make us feel better or what. I think it was in July of 1945 that I think my mother got the first card from me.

"When we got to Bicycle Camp I believe that the 131st was already there, or they brought them in about the same time.[§] I don't know; there was so much confusion and newness to it all. There was some Aussies already there; they were pretty well set up. They brought everybody there—Aussies, English, and Americans—131st—and all. I imagine the *Houston* crew were about as scruffy as anybody they'd ever seen. I was fortunate in not having any fuel at all hardly on me after swimming through so much of that diesel oil. But it burned some of them to where they'd peeled. It went two or three layers deep; they was a pretty scroungy-looking bunch of dudes.

"Well, we just got together with the 131st and talked and found out their experiences, and they found out ours. We didn't know they were there, and they didn't know we were there, so we had a lot to talk about. We talked about battles we'd been through. We talked about Texas. Before I got out of there, I could go from Jacksboro to Decatur or anyplace. I knew every side road; I knew all about it, because they—the majority of them—were from

---

*On July 4, 1942, the Japanese demanded that all POWs sign a statement promising loyalty to the Emperor and pledging not to escape. At first the Americans refused to sign, but after Japanese beatings and threats to kill the officers, the POWs signed the statement, rationalizing that it meant nothing since it had been obtained under duress.

†Albert ("Al") Kennedy, of the USS *Houston*, now lives in Arlington, Texas.

§Burge's memory is incorrect. The 131st got to Bicycle Camp after the arrival of the *Houston* survivors.

within a hundred miles of each other. You knew everybody's girlfriend; you knew all the back roads; you knew old John Farley's barn down there; and you knew where to turn and go down that road to get to somebody else's house and stuff like that, you know. Of course, the main topic was probably food. We didn't have dream menus yet; that was later on, after Java.

"What gear the 131st could spare they shared. I mean, they had to look out for theirselfs, you know. They didn't have too much. They weren't outfitted like a regular army, you know. They just had maybe one or two pairs of shoes and so on; they didn't have enough to go around. I didn't get anything right then. Some did, but I was comfortable; I mean, I didn't need clothes, really. Then when we got up in the jungle, they were getting so low that about all of us was wearing G-strings.

"Well, we Americans stuck pretty much to ourselves. Now some of us socialized with the Aussies; they were fine people. The Australians at that time, in my mind, was an American about thirty years before. They were a little behind, you know, but they was good ol' boys, all of them. The camp just had one fence around it. You could go visit back and forth to the Dutch. There wasn't too many English there; we really didn't get the English until we got to Singapore. We all had separate barracks, as far as I can recall, across the compound, maybe sixty or seventy feet then there was another barracks. Soldiers were over there, and the Australians somewhere else. There was no animosity or anything among the groups, but we just, well, we just knew one another. We really didn't try to ignore each other.

"It was in Java that they took the officers and nonrated men and separated us, and then the rest of us got more integrated, you know. It took awhile to get acquainted. I mean, it does in big groups like that; the sailors stick to theirselfs, the soldiers stick to theirselfs, the Aussies stick to theirselfs. But as time wore on, everyday you met somebody else and got more integrated and so on, you know. There's a certain amount of security in being around your own group.

"Well, the food wasn't too bad. It was rice. It wasn't our diet, but we'd have rice and some kind of stew or something. I got yellow jaundice there, and the doctor said it was the grease off of pork that caused it. To the Japs a hog is the hams and shoulders, and they'd just skin it out. So they was letting us have the rest of it, and we'd put it in these drums and boil it up, you know. Naturally, there's an awful lot of fat on it, but we figured we needed anything we could get, so you just put it on your rice and eat it.

"We had plenty of food, such as it was, in Bicycle Camp. I don't remember being hungry. They didn't feed you that well or that often, but still you got a big dip of rice and a dipper of whatever they had boiling in the barrel. I used my coconut as a dish for a long time. Finally, we'd find tin cans and half-gallon or gallon buckets and stuff like that to use. Everybody learned to scrounge. Whatever you'd run across belonged to you, you know. It could always be made into something, or somebody would trade you an egg for it or something. Nothing went to waste. If it was cloth, why, you'd make a G-string out of it. If you had enough for two, why, you'd give one to your buddy and so on like that.

"I believe the 131st took care of the cooking. It always tasted good to me. But we had a cook off the ship—he's dead now—and he was an old China hand. He cooked the rice in what they called 'big Y-johns.'* They were about three feet across and maybe a foot deep, kind of hollowed out. You'd cook your rice in there with a big wooden cover on it. They made good steamed rice. The best of it was what stuck to the bottom. When they'd take the rice out, you know, then you'd get that burnt rice, and that was good.

"When we got up in the jungle, the rice got to be half rocks and worms, but down there it wasn't bad. When I had that yellow jaundice, which is hepatitis now, all I could have to eat was the water from the first washing of the rice and a pound of granulated sugar every day. I got well, so I guess that's why. You know, the water would be real starchy from where they'd wash the rice, and there was trash in it. It was very unpalatable, but I wasn't going to get anything else. The doctor said, 'Drink it,' so I drank it.

"I hadn't been there maybe a couple of weeks when I got yellow jaundice. I did eventually go on sick call, because I was starving to death. Everytime I'd get up there and smell that stuff, I'd get sick. I couldn't face going through the chow line. When it gets so you can't eat at all, well, I made sick call and told them how I was. Of course, by that time, I was yellow and my eyeballs were yellow and everything; it wasn't hard for them to tell what I had. But we had no medication, so that's when they gave me this diet of rice water and granulated sugar. I don't know where they got it in the hospital. We didn't have sugar on the mess line or anything, but they had it there.

"In the hospital we just had a makeshift bunk and nothing to go with it, you know. There wasn't any such thing as aspirins or bedpans or anything else that I know of. They just put you off here in this room so that you didn't spread what you had. It was isolation; I guess you'd call it that. You sat there and stared at the wall until time to drink your rice water again. I was there just four or five days. It was American doctors and Dutch doctors, so the

---

*He must mean *wajan*; other POWs use this Malayan word for "wok."

Japs didn't have anything to do with us in there. The POWs' health was pretty good for what they'd been through. Like the group I was in, their feet was peeling, and their wounds made from the oil where it'd peel off with the skin, and from pulling the carts. Some of these ol' boys were getting over the filth and stuff from Serang. But their idea of toilet tissue was a bottle of water. The Dutch commodes are just a hole in the floor with two foot tracks in concrete up there. You'd squat down there, and then they had these bottles of water lined up there, and you'd wash yourself off with it. It was different, but you get used to anything, you know, when there's no other way.

"I guess they had showers someplace there, but I don't recall them. The bad things you don't remember. Now when we get together at our conventions, I'll run into somebody like [Otto] Schwarz. He didn't remember us being interrogated when we got to the beach in that landing barge. Just a few years ago, I was telling him about it one time—if he remembered it—and he didn't remember it. When I told him, it became perfectly clear to him. That's the way with our shower stuff. It wasn't too bad, or I'd remember it, see. But there are some things, you know, any day you'll talk to somebody, 'Do you remember this?' 'No.' Then they'll ask me do I remember that— 'No.' But when they tell you about it, it'll all start to come back to you.

"Well, there were spigots here and there in the camp with running water in them, and it had a high sulfur content. I got an ulcer started on my leg, from scratching a mosquito bite, I guess. Anyway, it was a break in the skin, and it got about as big around as your little fingernail. I just started letting that water run in it, and it cured it up. Well, it tasted like sulfur, you know, brackish and sulfurish. I just remember this one spigot that I always used; it stuck about three feet out of the ground on a pipe. But they never shut the water off or anything.

"We had some work details there. I don't remember just how long we were there. But I know they'd take us out in trucks; it wasn't very far. There were so many people with guards. We'd have different jobs to do. I don't really remember much about the outside details until we got to Singapore. People went because they were bored and might be able to steal something or pick up something someplace, you know, to better yourself.

"I get going on work details confused with Saigon, but I believe there was a Dunlop Tire and Rubber Company there, and we'd go out and inventory tires and motor spare parts and stuff like that. It wasn't too much of that pick-and-shovel work. There hadn't been much war damage at the time in Batavia, I don't think. But the Japs were collecting their loot, you know, they wanted to know how many truck tires were in this stack and how many of these spare parts over there. Of course, we would sabotage them when we could. We'd break the seals on spare parts to where air could get to them. Maybe if they wasn't watching too close, you'd take a leak over a bunch of them where they'd rust quicker. Or you'd get down inside these stacks of tires and try to cut them with a nail or whatever you could find, to mess them up. But there again, we didn't figure they were going to use them, because we was going to get liberated at anytime.

"Although it was real hush-hush, we had a radio, and we got news from some of the Dutch allies. It just filtered down, by word of mouth; I don't know how. I didn't want to know where the radio was. I wasn't a radioman. If they needed a part and I was on a working party around a radio station, I'd picked up any piece of wire, tube, anything electrical. You just brought them in and gave them to the CO, and that was the last you seen of them, you know. Most of the news we was getting was Japanese-oriented. I think once a week they listened to some station on the West Coast [of the United States], if they could pick it up under certain weather conditions. I didn't really know too much of what was going on in that respect, because it didn't make any difference: 'Just keep your nose here, and in three or four months we'd be going out, anyway,' you know. That was before it really got serious with me.

"Bicycle Camp was for me the most restful place as a prison that we'd been. It was about the best place. Of course, when we got in Saigon, it turned out to be all right; but the trip through building the railroad and stuff had taken so much out of you. If you'd just stayed in the Bicycle Camp, it would have probably not have been too bad. I think we were there about six months. We left in September or October.

"The strangest thing about this, I don't remember when we went from one place to another. But my mother knew the year that I went from one country to another. She's got that ESP or something. When I came home, and she said, 'In such-and-such a year, where did you go? I know you went from one place to another. I knew you was still alive, because I felt it when you moved.' It was still confused in my mind.

"The only thing that I remember when we left Java—and don't ask me why they did it, but they did it each time you went from one country to another—they took a glass stir rod for a mixed drink, like that, like a swizzle stick, and they'd wipe it across your butt and put a smear on a piece of glass. Then they put it in an envelope with your name on it. What went on from there and what they were trying to find out, what kind of disease they determined from that or what, I don't know. But I know that no one was stopped from going out of the gate when you got ready to go.

"They divided us up, then they shipped us out. I didn't know where we were going, our next destination, when we left. I guess it was the fear of the unknown, you know, you don't know what you're going into when you leave. So if you're surviving all right there, why take a chance. Well, it was unsettling to leave. I gathered up what I had, a G-string, tin can, coconut spoon—that's all I recall. Oh, I'd hung on to the coconut bowl. It didn't take me long to pack. They just took us down there and put us on the ships and away we went."

Burge followed the route taken by the other Americans who worked on the railroad, but, unlike many, he was fortunate in never having jungle ulcers or a bad case of dysentery. He did have trench foot and boils on his legs; those, plus malaria, which everyone had, were his worst diseases. His cure for trench foot is interesting:

> I'm standing there trying to walk, it was morning, and an ol' Aussie comes by. He said, 'Boy! Mate, you've got a bloody beautiful case of trench foot there! You got any shoes?' I said, 'No.' Well, he said, 'You bum, beg, or steal any old rags or anything you got and wrap them around your feet. Everybody going to that latrine, you have them piss on them.' I said, 'What?' He said, 'It's bloody terrible!' He was an old-timer; he was in the trenches of World War I, and he said it was a sin to urinate on the ground in those trenches in France. He said if you didn't have trench foot, you used your buddy's boot.
> Well, they told us quite a few things that seemed farfetched that they learned through hard knocks. I did what he told me, and, man, it was a stinking mess! The next morning, well, I took off them rags, and there wasn't a mark; the swelling was gone; all them little cuts had healed up. It's that tannic acid in the urine that cured that trench foot. Them ol' Aussies, I looked up to them quite a bit for their homespun learning, you know.

Burge left the jungle in October 1943 and spent time in Tamarkan, Thailand, and Saigon, Da Lat, Nha Trang, and Thuy Moa in French Indochina. It was in Saigon that he awoke one morning and found the Korean guards were gone. Later in the day an American plane flew over dropping leaflets that said, "Stay where you are. The Air Force will be in to get you out." Five days later he was repatriated, and followed the usual route through Calcutta back to Washington, D.C.

Burge found life boring at home and decided to stay in the Navy. He helped sail the new USS *Houston* into the port of its namesake city and spent twenty years in the service before retiring on December 23, 1958. He had served aboard the destroyer USS *Thompson* and the aircraft carrier USS *Essex* and fought in the Korean War. After retiring from the Navy, he worked for three years as a powerhouse operator for Ohio Power in Beverly, and then moved to Grand Prairie, Texas, where he spent more than fifteen years in the same occupation working for Ling-Temco-Vaught (LTV) Corporation. He retired in the 1970s and now lives near Fort Worth in rural Azle, Texas.

Lester C. Rasbury
Headquarters Battery

Lester Rasbury was born in Decatur, Texas, on May 31, 1917. Although his parents stayed in the area, they moved frequently, and as a result Lester left school in the eighth grade. In his words he "quituated" from school rather than "graduated." For the next nine years he worked as a farmer, grocery-store employee, service-station attendant, and in a creamery before joining the Texas National Guard in October 1940. He and several other Decatur boys had tried to enlist in the Navy, Air Corps, and Marines, but for a variety of reasons were rejected. In fact, the National Guard was "full up" when he first tried to enter, so he had to wait until it was federalized on November 25 before being taken.

Rasbury was placed in the radio section and served there during training in Decatur, at Brownwood, on maneuvers in Louisiana, and finally in Java. During the Louisiana exercises he was attached to a group headed by General George S. Patton. While on the USAT *Republic* heading for Australia, the ship crossed the equator and the international date line, and Rasbury was initiated by the Shellbacks of the Sons of Neptune and members of the Court of the Grand Dragon. He became a Shellback, as well as a member of the Realm of the Golden Dragon. His initiation was so rough that medics had to use two stitches to close a gash over his left eye.

When the Second Battalion reached the Dutch airfield at Singosari, near Surabaja, Rasbury was placed in charge of the post exchange, which was bombed during an air raid while Rasbury was outside in a foxhole. After the Second confronted the Japanese near Bogor (Buitenzorg), he was part of a patrol that went on a "sniper hunt," but did not find any Japanese marksmen. At about noon on March 8, while close to Garut, the battalion learned of the Allied capitulation. Rasbury considered going into the hills, but then thought, "How can you survive? If you run into a patrol, then you're in trouble without much ammunition or anything." Like others he felt ashamed of surrendering, but found out later that "we did what we were supposed to do; we were just sacrificed. I think after that most of us had a better feeling about the situation."

His experiences at the racetrack, the tea plantation, and at Tanjong Priok were typical of the unit's overall circumstances. From Rasbury's perspective not much happened at Tanjong Priok that was worth discussing, but experiences at Bicycle Camp were different. There he demonstrated an entrepreneurial ability that would serve him well as a prisoner. In fact, in a minor way his career as a POW reminds one of the character played by George Segal in Bryan Forbes's *King Rat* (1965), a movie adaptation of James Clavell's novel of the same title, which concerned a World War II Japanese POW camp. The camp depicted in the movie is Changi, Singapore, late in the war, where Clavell was interned. Other interviews, presented later in this book, suggest different members of the Second Battalion as the model for the character portrayed by Segal. In the following pages, Rasbury discusses his adventures and misadventures in Southeast Asia.

"WE WENT BY TRUCK, and it didn't take us long. It wasn't too far, just an hour or something like that to drive. Bicycle Camp is in Batavia, and Tanjong Priok is part of Batavia, which is now called Djakarta. It's just the docks.

"Well, when you first looked at Bicycle Camp, you couldn't tell too much, because it was a long camp that went way back. You know, it wasn't wide. You'd just see these barracks, and you'd go in by the guardhouse. I don't know why they saved the front barracks—right in the front—for the Americans. The English and Australians probably had something to do with that. The Dutch were over by themselves; they didn't mix us in with the Dutch at that point. It seems like there was a rock wall up around the front, and then there was barbed wire at the back and the sides, because the guards would walk around the outside of this barbed wire.

"I think if the Japs had thrown us behind barbed wire right away it would have bothered us. Some of the sailors had encounters like that; I think they had it worse than us. As soon as they hit the island, well, the Japs picked them up and threw them in jails, behind barbed wire, and they didn't have freedom like we did. It seemed like we just gradually adjusted to this life; we didn't have barbed wire around us at first, but we couldn't go anywhere. Well, some did, but you weren't supposed to. We were a lot better off than those Navy boys.

"We had a long barracks with porches. I wound up out on the porch, because I never liked to be crowded inside. After a couple of days of getting adjusted to a new place, you know, finding your way around and having new friends—this is where we got together with the sailors off the

Houston—well, when all the excitement of talking and finding out new and different things died down, then we started to settle down to living. They put me to work in the carpenter shop with an Australian. They had to have a carpenter's helper on the woodwork detail. I had done some of that, and they knew it, and they sent me up there. I worked for the Australian for a long time there. What we were doing was building beds out of doors off of buildings and making bunks for hospitals. I made me a frame and put a rice sack on it. That was a lot better than sleeping on a concrete floor. I always came up with some kind of sleeping quarters. I just didn't like sleeping on the hard floor. So I took two boards and two-by-fours and made a framework and put the sacks over it and made a hammocklike bed.

"Of course, I've always been a merchant, making money, surviving on my own all my life. As prisoners we didn't have much money. We were working for twenty-five cents a day,* I think that was it, when we went out on details. But if you didn't go out, well, you didn't get anything. Well, I wasn't going out. I was working in the carpenter shop. They had a canteen where you could buy stuff, and I started making fudge candy. You could buy this sweetened condensed milk, and it had a recipe on it. So I started making just plain fudge from the recipe, you know. It sold pretty good. So other people decided, 'Well, if he can do it, so can we.' So they decided they'd do it, too. I would do this at night after I got off from work. They'd let us build fires out in the camp in certain areas where you could cook stuff and things that way. So these others started and narrowed my sales so that I had to do something else.

"Well, I went to the canteen and bought all the chocolate they had. They only bought supplies once a week, and I knew that I could last a week on all the cocoa they had. So I had chocolate fudge where the others just had plain old fudge. Well, my next move was when they got chocolate. Then, I bought all the peanuts up and put peanuts in the fudge.† Well, this went on for a couple of months. I had two or three guys shelling peanuts and helping me make candy and sell it. It was just a little business, you know, right inside the camp.

"I'd go out on other details if my time came, but most of the time I worked in the carpenter shop. The last job I did before I quit was help put a door on a room in the guardhouse. When we got through, the Japs wanted us to put a lock on it. Then they told us to go in another room where they had ammunition and move the ammunition out into the locked room. They

---

*The Japanese paid privates and corporals in occupation currency the equivalent of ten cents and noncoms fifteen cents per day, with payday coming every thirty days.
†The POWs called it Rasbury's Finer Fudge.

wouldn't let the guards have but one clip. They got a bunch of Korean guards in there, and they didn't know anything about rifles. They'd shot the ceiling nearly out of the place—letting their rifles go off. The Japs wouldn't let them have much ammunition; they just issued it to them when they wanted them to have it. So, they kept the ammunition locked up. That was the last job I did with them. I guess I worked there probably three months.

"When I wasn't doing anything, I built me a desk, sort of a draftsman's desk. It was about three feet long and about two feet wide. It was hinged but had no metal screws; it was put together with pegs. This Australian carpenter, boy, he was one of the best. He really knew how to carpenter. I learned a lot about carpenter work from him. But they really didn't have enough work to keep us busy, and I wanted to get outside and see what was there. So I started going out on details. We went to a golf course and stacked barrels. We'd go down on the docks, and we went to another place where they had car parts. We'd straighten them up and separate them. It was just boxes of stuff. They were shipping most of this stuff to Japan or using it on their vehicles and things there.

"There weren't too many rules in Bicycle Camp. The first time I got hit by the Japs was for not bowing. If you were bareheaded, you bowed to them; if you had a cap or a hat on, you saluted them. That was the main rule. It was kind of funny how I got it. I never did like oatmeal; I'd never eat it. But that morning we had oatmeal for breakfast, so it was either eat oatmeal or not eat. So I ate it, and it was good. I heard they had some more, so I went back for seconds. But they'd run out just before I got there.

"I was going around the back to go out, and there was a guard standing behind a gate that I went through, and there was a sack hanging on this gate. Well, I didn't see him. He steps out from behind the sack and hollers at me. Well, I had my cap on, because I didn't like to bow. I always wore my cap. I saluted him, but that wasn't good enough. Before I knew it, he'd bopped me up side the head and then made me go around behind the kitchen. There were about four other guys there. The only one I remember for sure was Crayton Gordon* from Service Battery. They were standing with their arms straight out at attention. Well, we stood there awhile and were about to give out, when this Jap came out of the kitchen and told us to go home. We started out, but we met this other guard around the corner, and he put us back at attention. These two Japs got into an argument, so old Crayton said, 'Well, I believe we're gonna get bashed either way, whether we stay or go!' I said, 'Well, you all can stay if you want to, but I'm going!' I took off while

---

*Crayton R. ("Quaty") Gordon's interview is in Chapter 4, "The Death Railway."

they were arguing, and the others took off, too. We never did hear any more out of it. But we heard the two Japs got in a scrap right after we left; they really tangled.

"They'd let you buy writing stuff, you know. Bicycle Camp is where I bought a couple of books that I kept all my notes in. They didn't care if you had your pocket knives or anything like that, either. Of course, if they caught you with a gun, they'd probably take it away from you. Then, they were really strict about smoking and smoking areas. You'd better have something to snuff out your cigarettes. You'd better not let them see you throw a butt on the ground, because they were really scared of fire. I didn't bring a radio in, but someone did and set it up. I never saw it after that first time.

"Once in a while the Japs would pull sneak inspections. In fact, they changed guards there one time, and we got a bunch of Koreans in there that were really rough. One they called the Brown Bomber; he'd just be sitting around out there on guard kind of getting bored with everything, and he'd just grab his rifle, put his bayonet on it, and here he'd come. He'd walk down through there, and you didn't have to do anything; if he didn't like your looks, well, boy. If you were too tall—he was really short—he'd make you get down on your knees where he could slap you a few times. It just aggravates you to go through that. He couldn't hurt you—they couldn't hurt you—but they hurt your feelings.

"About the best way I can describe the Korean guards is that they'd been under the thumb so long, when you'd give them a little bit of authority, boy, they took advantage of it. They thought authority meant to beat people, I guess, because they sure liked to. They had some treacherous ways of punishing people. Maybe they caught people with some things—nails to fix their bunks or something to eat. They'd shave their heads and put them out in the hot sun and make them get on their knees and put a bamboo stick behind their legs, in the fold. They did this in the evening, and the people were still there in the morning with a big sign saying, 'These men have stolen.' Well, some of the men passed out and were turned loose the next day. They were there nearly forty-eight hours. The Koreans were sadistic.

"It's the same old story that I said before. If they caught you doing something they didn't like, they'd punish you for it. We all knew that, but sometimes we took a chance. It was according to what was involved whether we'd want to take a chance or not. It was according to how hungry you were or something like that. The one I most remember was the Brown Bomber. Boy, when he'd come through the barracks, he really knocked heads. You didn't have to do much for them to do some bashing. There in that camp especially, if they decided they wanted a little exercise, they'd just take off and go down through the barracks. You didn't want to fall while they were bashing you because that's when they'd start stomping you and hitting you with the rifle butt. You wanted to stay on your feet the best you could. But one time, the only time, I was hit by a Jap.

"I saw Lieutenant Stensland hit a Jap there in Java. We were out on a park just leveling it, just something to be out of the camp. There was a Dutch lady who brought some bananas on a bicycle; she stopped and held them up. There was a guard who came up behind her and hit her. She didn't see this guard, and he hit her and knocked her down, bicycle and all. We were across a kind of ditch, and Lieutenant Stensland, before you knew what was happening, was over there, and he knocked that Jap down. The Jap went one way, and the rifle went the other. The lieutenant helped the lady up, and, boy, that Jap picked up his rifle and ran. He got out of there, and he didn't do anything about it. It scared him, I think.

"I saw one other case after we got up in the jungle—a guy named Hugh Faulk,* a Marine. We were working on this cut, probably three or four feet deep, and the guard was standing on the bank. He didn't think Faulk was working hard enough, so he hollered, 'Speedo! Speedo!' Ol' Faulk said, 'You and the Dutch are the same! You just jabber all the time!' He made the guard mad, and he jumped in there. The first thing you knew Faulk had hit him. Faulk let him have it good. Boy, the guard jumped up, grabbed his rifle and put a shell in it. I thought for sure he was going to shoot Faulk, but he didn't; he backed off. Evidently, they had orders not to shoot, or I believe they would have a lot of times.

"When we got to Bicycle Camp, the *Houston* people were already there. We were sort of embarrassed, since the Australians and all were there as well with them. The *Houston* people didn't have any clothes and were running around in G-strings and stuff like that, you know, and eating garbage. Of course, they were eating with the Australians, you know, and, boy, they'd just eat anything they could get hold of. The stuff they had to eat out of: one guy had a hubcap off an English V-8 Ford, and another one had a small night pot, a baby pot. They didn't have spoons, knives, or forks, nothing that way. So when we got there, well, we fitted them out with everything that they needed.

"They didn't have anything, because they'd lost it on that ship. They were even lucky to get ashore. Some of them had been in the water a long

---

*Joseph Hugh Faulk, of the USS *Houston*, died in a farm accident on September 23, 1971, in Milburn, Oklahoma.

time. The tide would bring them in and then take them back out; they were so weak they couldn't swim. I don't see how as many of them survived as did. Well, we just all mixed in; we were all Americans. When they started sending them out on details, they'd mix us up.

"The food wasn't too bad, because the officers took money and bought supplies and channeled them through the kitchen. It was battalion money. The last month that we were supposed to get paid, they kept it. They thought it would be more beneficial to us that way instead of paying us off.

"Talking about food, there's one thing that happened to me. This friend of mine was real sick, and I was doing all this work and selling candy and trying to keep food for him to eat, like peaches and cream and stuff that way. Well, when they decided to channel all food through the kitchen, they wanted us to turn our food in. They wanted us to stop buying it, because that way they could buy more for the kitchen. Well, I didn't turn mine in, so the major came to talk to me about it. I said, 'Well, sir, I know I'm supposed to, but I've bought this food. I know you're going to pay me for it, but I got this as much for Chumley* as I have for myself on account of him being sick.' I said, 'If you will set up some sort of a kitchen for people like him that need a little something extra, then I don't want to get paid; I'll just donate my food.' He said, 'All right. We'll just do that, and you're in charge of it.'

"I didn't know that it was going to be work for me, you know, but I went up to the kitchen and got me a room in this little building for the sick people to eat in. We had tables. I got all the soup. I didn't get all the fruit, but if they were short on fruit, why, I still got all I needed. If somebody was sick and was in for days or so, like with dysentery and stuff like that, well, I had a special diet for them. I fed quite a few people through there.

"I didn't have close contact with the officers in Java. But there were some of the officers that ate a lot better than the men, because the officers bought their own. They had the money to buy it. The officers had a little more money than the men. They were paid. I think they were paid. Oh, I'm not sure of the amount, say about $200 a month.† The Japs'd hold out so much for clothing, which the officers didn't get; and they'd hold out for lodging. They'd give them five to twenty-five dollars at a time—whatever it was—and the rest went into the bank in Tokyo. They paid them according to the books. They paid them as much as they did their own officers, but the

---

*Horace E. Chumley, Headquarters Battery, now lives in Decatur, Texas.
†Officers were paid the equivalent of twenty-five cents per day in occupation currency.

Americans didn't get it. In the camps I was in, the officers were in charge of the groups. But there was an officers' camp where they'd work.

"I believe it was at Bicycle Camp, but I'm not sure, that the colonel put out an order—and it was passed down—that since we were at close quarters, saluting would be stopped. Because it was a pain for them as much as for us, you know, because of close quarters. As far as military discipline and everything, it was carried on as well as military organization and everything. I think the Japs requested that. But the little formalities, that type of thing, didn't have to go on, because we were too close together.

"I don't think anybody was ever overworked. They didn't have enough work for us all to do at Bicycle Camp. It was just more or less to get out of camp that we worked, and everybody would more or less volunteer to get out. Once in a while down on the docks it was pretty heavy work, you know, like loading stuff, but most of the time it wasn't. I don't know how many people were there, but I'd say there was at least three thousand to four thousand in the camp. We got on with the Australians, especially the Australians. We got along better with them than either the Dutch or the English—either one. I think the Aussies are more like us. They just talked different. I think if their country was a little bigger, why, it might be another United States of America.

"Well, sir, a typical day at Bicycle Camp was, oh, I'd say we'd get up around seven o'clock, because they didn't usually go out on details until about nine. The Army had a bugler, and then the Navy had a bugler. They used the Navy's most of the time. He'd blow reveille or whatever they wanted him to blow. Then, we'd all go to breakfast and come back and get ready to go out on different details or whatever your work was for that day. We had roll. I believe the roll call was the first thing they did, first roll call and then go to breakfast.

"Each organization, each battery, called their own roll. Then they took the report to the Japanese. Sometimes we'd have a Japanese muster, and then they'd do the counting; we wouldn't do any. That's when we had to learn to count off in Japanese. They'd count how many back this way, and then we'd count across. Boy, they'd walk along and see that nobody got out of line that way. We'd count off, and then they'd multiply it by that many. They'd have these things with beads on it, you know, an abacus or what-ever, and they'd go across and then figure it up right quick.

"Out on details they'd usually bring lunch to us, or if it was someplace where we could, they'd let us buy our lunch. In Java, we'd usually knock off around three or four o'clock or something like that—kind of early—because we'd come in and have a lot of time from then until bedtime. We'd go up and visit with the Australians and visit with each other and talk about things that happened out on the details that day and stuff like that—about something to eat, what they were going to do when they got out, or about girls—just like if it was a normal way of life, you know. Eventually, you get to where it's just a regular routine.

"Bicycle Camp wasn't too bad. Horace Chumley was one that stayed there all during that time. I don't think he ever left. I never knew him until I got into the service, even though he lived at Alvord. Well, we got together in Brownwood; we were sleeping in the same tent. We got to running around together, and we just sort of became real close friends from then on. He never did leave there.* There's one thing I'd have liked to say on this Bicycle Camp when we were talking about the Navy boys. See, there's a lot of things that happened like this probably that I overlooked. It's funny now, but at the time it happened, it could have been serious. I was out on a detail, and I went down to get some water at a little ol' place. We were cleaning up the camp. I don't know whether it was for the Japanese to move in or more prisoners or what, but we were cleaning this place up. I went down to this building, and there sat a box full of silverware—knives, forks, and spoons. Well, the first thing I thought was, 'Now how can I get some of that stuff back to these Navy boys?'

"Well, I studied about it and went back about my work and kept thinking about it. I thought, 'Well, I'll just go get them and put them in my pocket.' I had loose coveralls on, and I thought, 'Maybe they won't even think about looking in my pockets and checking us.' So I went back and I got forks and spoons. I knew they could do without knives. I don't know, I guess I got about a dozen of each. I had them in those big ol' coverall pockets.

"Everything was working out just fine. We were getting ready to go; they lined us up to count us and everything. They counted the tools, and there was a chisel missing. Of all things! If it'd been a pick, you know, it would have been all right, but it was a chisel. They shook everybody down. Man, they was coming down that line getting closer and closer, and I thought, 'What on earth am I going to do? They're going to find all that silverware in my pocket.' So I had my canteen on my gunbelt, and I thought, 'Well, I'll just put them under my belt; I'll try that.' I told an ol' boy, 'Kind of cover for me here a minute.' I just stepped back behind the truck where they couldn't see me, and I took the silverware out and put them under my

*Chumley remained behind when the unit left because of jungle rot on his feet and stomach problems.

belt because it was real tight, and then I buttoned my coveralls back up and stepped back in line.

"Well, they were coming down through there, and they shook my pockets and those things rattled, see. He got about three men down from me before it dawned on him that he heard something. He came back, and if he'd done the same thing, it would have rattled again. But he took and felt on my pockets real gentle-like. Of course, nothing rattled. Boy, I just knew I was going to get caught, but I didn't, and that's the way I got the spoons and forks. It was Dutch stuff, Dutch silverware.

"The first people that started leaving Bicycle Camp were technicians, and they were supposed to go into Japan. Because when they came around, they let everybody make up their minds whether they were a technician or whether they were something else. Since I was a radio operator, well, some of the boys thought, 'Why don't you go on to Japan? It might be better there than it would be in the jungle.' Of course, we didn't know where we were going. I told them, 'No, I'll just take my chances elsewhere. I didn't even want to let them know that I was a radio operator or that I knew anything about radios. What I turned in was that I was a creamery operator, so they didn't know what I was. I stayed behind and went with the next bunch.

"A lot of people think it's silly, but I believe in fate. It just seemed like I had something guiding me along the way. Like, when we were eight days out of Honolulu, then we went south. We went down to Australia; we didn't go to the Philippines. Just like the day the Japs bombed my PX, why, I didn't stay in there. I could have, but I didn't. I just sort of let things happen as it will. I just played my hunches and listened and took the best course that I thought I could, if I had a choice.

"At Bicycle Camp I started a book of rumors. It got to be so much that I didn't have paper enough to put them all on. One of the first rumors that I remember in Bicycle Camp was that the 'Fighting Texans' were still fighting. We heard it on the news that came back by radio, that the Fighting Texans were holding out in the hills of Java. Shoot, we'd been prisoners for over a month. But, you know, that's how things like that started. So I kept a book of rumors, and there were really some good ones. But I didn't keep it up, and I guess I lost it somewhere; I don't have it anymore.

"We knew a little bit before leaving that we were going, and we had time to prepare and get things ready. In other words, we knew we wouldn't see people for a long time, if we ever saw them again. We just sort of celebrated with each other and things that way. This friend of mine, Chumley, he was sick and couldn't go. He had some bad feet or something and couldn't wear his shoes, so they wouldn't let him go. I gave him all the money that we had—what little there was. I kept thirty-five cents for souvenirs and that's all, because I didn't know whether money would be any good where we were going. We weren't sure of anything at that time; it was more or less just rumors.

"I took my mess kit, my eating gear, and water bottle. I carried a couple of blankets, a shelter half to roll it up in, and my barracks bag with a few odds and ends in it—not much because I already made two of those road marches, and I didn't want very much. They carried us in trucks, because it was a good ways to the docks. They carried us down there and put us on a barge, and then we got off the barge onto the ship. It was a scary feeling."

Rasbury went to Changi and became active in trading commodities and exchanging money. After he had worked on the railroad for a while, the Japanese allowed American officers to have orderlies, one orderly for every four officers. Lieutenant Isaac Alvin Morgan, Captains Clark Taylor and William ("Ike") Parker, and Doctor Lumpkin,* also a captain, chose Rasbury. The American officers used orderlies (the Japanese called them *toban*) to get additional enlisted men away from working on the railroad. Rasbury washed the officers' clothes, got their food, made their beds, cleaned their areas, and performed other such services. At various times he suffered dysentery and shingles and, after going with the railroad crew to Tamarkan, was disabled briefly by malaria, dropping from his usual weight of 150 pounds to 100 before recovering.

In late 1944 and early 1945 he was sent to Camp Tamajao on the Burma-Thailand border, near Tamarkan. He was first a woodcutter and then a tinsmith. He regained his lost weight, but came near to losing his life: "There was a Jap guard there, actually one of the Koreans who claimed to be a Christian, who told us that they planned to machine-gun us and burn us. He showed us the machine-gun nests up on a hill. He said, 'They're going to run you in there and pour gasoline on you and burn you during an invasion.' He said, 'Don't go in that hole!' He told us where to meet him. He said, 'Meet me at that fence, and I'll take you out of here.' But it never did come to that. I left the camp before the war was over. I guess I left about two months before the war ended." What Rasbury described occurred under

---

*Morgan was in Battery D. He now lives in Marshall, Texas. An interview with Taylor is included in this chapter. William ("Ike") Parker died of a stroke on September 7, 1970, in Ozark, Alabama. Doctor Lumpkin has already been identified; he and Parker are discussed by several POWs whose interviews are included in this book.

different circumstances on the Philippine island of Palawan, where about 139 American prisoners were massacred by the Japanese at the war's end. They were burned by flamethrowers and machine-gunned as they emerged from air-raid shelters at the Japanese air base on the island.*

Rasbury was at a smaller camp in the jungle building a railroad spur when the war ended. The Japanese took him and his crew to a town south of Tamarkan and freed them. After several days the Americans were moved again to Phet Buri, on the Gulf of Siam, southwest of Bangkok, and flew from there, via the hospital in Calcutta, to a posting near New York.

Back in the United States, Rasbury, at first, did not want to leave the area or call home. Finally, however, he went by train from the East Coast to McKinney, Texas, where he stayed intermittently at another hospital for several weeks. Unable to remain at the family farm near Decatur, he applied for a ninety-day furlough and began "running around." He found it impossible to remain in one place long, and says, "I'm still that way; I've never got over it." Rasbury was separated from the service in May 1946, working as a security guard, commercial photographer, and electrician until his retirement. He now lives in Fort Worth, Texas.

---

*See Kerr, *Surrender and Survival*, pp. 212–15.

Clark L. Taylor
Headquarters Battery

Clark Taylor, born at Iowa Park, Texas, in 1915, was only thirteen when he convinced recruiters for the Texas National Guard that he was eighteen and eligible to belong. He enlisted for the dollar that guardsmen were paid for Sunday drill, and for the camaraderie and excitement of bivouac and maneuvers. Through the years he rose in the ranks, holding the rank of first lieutenant when the Guard was federalized.

Taylor was firing officer in Battery D, Second Battalion, at the time of mobilization but became liaison officer on the regimental staff and then Second Battalion S-4, or supply officer. As such, when the unit landed in Australia and later Java, he was the chief procurement officer, spending little time with the gun batteries but moving around to buy supplies. In control of a 1 million-guilder line of credit at a bank in Bandung just before being captured, he withdrew 150,000 guilders and gave some of it to individuals in the unit, while keeping a substantial part for purchases by the battalion.

When the Second left Singosari for Tjilatjap, Taylor was with the group, under orders to disembark for Australia. Before they got to Tjilatjap, however, their orders were changed, and the gun batteries were sent to support Australian infantrymen. From the time of surrender in early March 1942 until the move to Bicycle Camp, Taylor continued as S-4, but did very little in that capacity. Here, he provides some of the best and most reliable information available about Bicycle Camp.

"WE WENT BY TRUCK to Bicycle Camp, as I recall. Well, it looked gorgeous! The streets were paved with asphalt; the quarters were well-built. It was a Dutch barracks, so it had just about everything you would want: showers, all the space you needed, real clean. It was quite a relief, although the facilities for keeping people out or keeping them in were better than what we had been in. As I recall, it seemed to me like they had a wall around it, not too high. Of course, no one thought of escaping. There wasn't anyplace to go.

"The barracks were stuccoed, with cement floors, tile roofs, running water. I don't know whether the water was hot and cold or even if we needed hot water. The cooking facilities—I believe we were still using our field equipment to cook in. What was beautiful was that we could get food from the outside. We had drawn money in Bandung, and we started buying whatever we felt that we needed. I believe Windy Rogers headed a little group to go out in the open market and buy what he could buy. Most of the time it was canned goods, beans, those good ol' pinto beans. Our kind of food, you know, beans, peas, dried fruit, or anything like that, and canned goods. Down in the basement of the officers' quarters, we had collected a good amount of rice and canned food. We had a nice collection in this basement warehouse. We had Chinese cabbage; the Chinese off the *Houston* taught us how to cook Chinese cabbage, and it was pretty good eating, darn good.* We had good food in Bicycle Camp. Plus we had our own canteen where we bought cigarettes, bananas, maybe a coconut, eggs, to where a man could supplement his own diet. We stocked the canteen. Captain Ike Parker took charge of it. We had so much money to spend, and he would buy goods. We had a fund to buy with, and we got the money back by selling.

"The Japanese asked us if we had any public funds, and if we did, we were to turn them in. Colonel Tharp told them we'd run out of public funds a long time ago. They took his word, and that was it, although we still probably had around 90,000 guilders to use to buy stuff. We kept it in the basement there. I'm sure some people resented it, thought that the officers were living better. You'd get that, but we were going to eat with our own units. As far as I remember, there wasn't much change in our eating. We were going through the same line that the men were going through. They might have thought we were eating chocolates or something, but there wasn't anything like that. The food that was in the basement warehouse was being distributed among the various units.

"We had a cooking unit, which comprised all batteries, and a couple of different serving lines. Most of the time we probably had two or three stations set up to where we would eat. The men who were cooks in our battery were in the cooking unit, but our battery didn't have anything to do with the cooks and their job. At Bicycle Camp we had good rice. So you had rice to eat, and you might have some cabbage, beans. We were

---

*Aboard ship, the *Houston*'s officers had Chinese cooks, some of whom survived the sinking and continued to cook for the officers' mess in Bicycle Camp.

supplementing our diet that they were giving us. Some meat might be in our stew. Not big chunks of meat, but there would be meat in it, and maybe some kind of fish. Java still had a lot of food out there to buy. It wasn't like that later when we got in the jungle. The stores in Java had food in them.

"This Japanese captain, when we first came there, lined us up and spoke. He had worked for GMC, General Motors. He spoke perfect English. He had been to America many times, he said. He told us, 'This war, like all wars, will come to an end one day. You're going to run into some good Japanese and some bad Japanese. Treat them on an individual basis. Don't think of every Japanese as being like any particular one. Make friends. Those that you get along with, make friends with them, because this war will be over one day and then we're going to want to be friends after it's over.' That speech always stuck in my mind. What else could you ask for?

"The way we were treated by him, I would say, was a real blessing. It was a real blessing to get in that camp. He allowed volleyballs to be brought in, boxing gloves, band instruments, to where we could entertain ourselves. We had work parties going out of our camp. It seemed like we still had time on our hands, so we played a lot of volleyball, had a boxing tournament, an all-nations tournament. It surprised me to see that I had so many good boxers in my outfit. I didn't know that Zip Zummo* had been a Golden Gloves champion. I remember that to win the tournament he fought an aborigine from Australia. That Italian sure had a killer's look on his face when he went in the ring there. He was the heavyweight champion. We had an international officers' volleyball tournament. We got pretty good at playing volleyball.

"When we arrived we displayed our equipment for them to have a look at it. Within that equipment was a complete radio, disassembled, that would be put back together later. At the time we weren't using it, as far as I know. I believe Headquarters Battery had it, and they scattered it out among their noncoms, and they pretty well concealed it. The Japs didn't go through our equipment physically, looking into and under everything. They never laid a hand on a person to search him.

"At Bicycle Camp we had Korean conscientious objectors† guarding us, and they made things a little different. They didn't smoke, they didn't drink, and they thought we were bad because we did. Anytime you came through that place with a book that you may have picked up someplace like

---

*Vincent ("Zip") Zummo, of Service Battery, now lives in Port Arthur, Texas.
†Given the nature of Japanese military thought this statement seems difficult to believe.

a school—we did some work at schools—we'd tell them it was a Bible. They would say, 'Okay,' so we could bring it into camp. They weren't good soldiers like the Japanese. They were conscientious objectors. They had been given some training, but they were never part of any fighting force. They were a different breed of cats. We were with Japanese fighting men, then here come the conscientious objectors.

"You hear the Koreans were cruel, but they were individuals, too. Some were worse than others. You had cruel guards in American prisoner-of-war camps. You would find somebody who would enjoy beating up on someone else for the least little reason. The Koreans could have been easier, but we were to have to live with them from then on. That was it. I would have rather had the Japanese as guards.

"I can remember a couple of occasions of cruelty. The Koreans would like to talk about boxing and such things. I think it was Sergeant Ellis Schmid* who had committed a small infraction, and this short Korean couldn't reach up to him. I remember he had Schmid come over to a lower place where he could reach and hit him. Instead of just slapping him like they usually did, he doubled up his fist and hit him. Well, it didn't take long to get over there and put a stop to that, but what the guard was trying to do was to see if he could knock Schmid down. This is the guard that was later hung, you can be sure. His name was Makan.† Nearly all these guards were hung as war criminals, and their commander, too.

"One thing that happened one night was I heard a god-awful commotion going on over in the next barracks, and I went over there. It was Makan again. This was right when they said lights out, nine o'clock, or when we went to sleep. There was a sailor whose name escapes me now.§ By the time I got there, Makan had slapped him enough to where some blood was coming out of his ears. I said, 'Wait! What's the matter?' He said, 'He was smoking.' I asked the sailor, 'Were you smoking? If you were, it's better to say yes, otherwise you maybe will get another smack for making him out a liar.' That's what the seaman was doing, but I didn't know it. Anyhow, Makan took him outside—his name was Hendricks—and put him up against a tree and drew the bolt back like he was going to shoot. He wanted Hendricks to say that he had been smoking, but he didn't, he kept saying,

---

*Schmid, who was in Service Battery, died of a heart attack on July 7, 1977, in Slaton, Texas.
†"Makan" is the Malayan word for eat, meal, food, consume. According to other POWs, Makan loved to eat—thus, the nickname.
§Elsewhere, Taylor identifies the sailor as R. H. Hendricks of the USS *Houston*. Hendricks died of dysentery on December 30, 1943, at Kanchanaburi, Thailand.

'No!' The little Chinese guy, Su Suomi,* came over there, and between Su and me, we persuaded Makan to leave Hendricks be. We said that he was sick in the head. Makan finally stomped off.

"I told this to the OSS in Calcutta, and when I got back home they sent me a picture of Makan and asked, 'Is this the man you were talking about in Calcutta?' I answered, 'Yes.' Then a man named Milner[†] came through later getting stories from POWs. He was going to write a book. He said, 'You know that your story was the one that they hung Makan on?' I said, 'No, I didn't. It wasn't a hanging offense.' Hendricks had told me the next day that he had been smoking. I put that in my report, too. Later on, Hendricks died, before we got out, but not from the beating. He was sick already. But Milner said that they hung just about all of the guards. It is awfully hard to hate somebody who has been hung. Give them five years of hard labor like we got, but don't hang them.

"Well, when we got to Bicycle Camp, the *Houston* sailors were so glad to see us because we had extra clothes. They were without clothes and mostly without money. Some of them had American money, and we exchanged it for them. Later on, we had a payroll, and then they all got a little money. I wish I could remember how much. It seems like it was fifty guilders a man. I don't know exactly how much, but they signed for the payroll in Bicycle Camp. Yes, the *Houston* survivors were kind of cruddy.

"Another incident at Bicycle Camp that I remember was the one leading up to the signing of a pledge not to escape. I'd been out on a work detail, and I can't recall what we did, but I came into the area and the officers were all lined up. The Japanese yelled for them to come to attention, and everybody came to attention and bowed, and all of them had had their heads shaved. I said, 'How come? What's the big deal with the shaved heads?' The Japs could hardly wait to get me sheared, real quick. It was the funniest thing, seeing all the marks and scars on the officers' heads. Then came the matter of the pledge.[§] We still didn't know what it was all about.

---

*Sulo W. ("Su") Suomi, of the USS *Houston* and in fact of Scandinavian origin, now lives in Alameda, California.

[†]Samuel Milner was planning to write on the Lost Battalion but has not completed the project. Milner is the author of *Victory in Papua*, which is part of the series titled The U.S. Army in World War II (Washington, DC: Office of the Chief of Military History, 1944–1981).

[§]The July 4, 1942, pledge is discussed in the interview with J. O. Burge earlier in this chapter. Taylor undoubtedly felt ill at ease when mentioning it, but he provides a fair account of the events.

"They shaved us as preparation for a sea voyage that we didn't know about at the time. I didn't know about it. Then came the deal where they said that they had a pledge for us to sign for non-escape, and that they were going to start paying us. I think it was either ten cents or twenty-five cents a day. We put up a token resistance. It was planned ahead of time by the colonel and General Black* what we were going to do. It would be a token resistance. We would just sit there. I believe we finally got in a squatting position. The guards would come by with their bayonets and get real close to your nose. I would say that this went on for something like an hour.

"I don't know how the Japanese worked it out. I know they had Captain Black,† Lieutenant Stensland, and somebody else in the guardhouse. They had them sitting on bamboo between their knees and on their calves. It was a tough deal. Every now and then they would get a slapping around. Finally, the general and Colonel Tharp said, 'Okay. Turn them loose. We'll sign.' The colonel said to us that our signing it didn't matter a damn thing. Anytime you sign under duress—and that's what we said when we told the men to sign—it doesn't mean anything. You can't escape, anyway; you didn't have anyplace to go. So, why not sign and have some pay? They had brought out machine guns that day and lined them up. I'd forgotten about that, but they sure had.

"My job wasn't much at Bicycle Camp. I took care of my own stuff and shelled out the money and kept track of it. Men under me issued the money out. I kept track of whatever we did. We still had pencils and paper, and everything was signed for that we issued. I can't remember being on but one or two work parties outside the camp, because there were too many officers there. Four or five work parties went out a day with maybe thirty or forty men to a party. Well, with an officer in each group, you still had many left over. Mostly, I engaged in recreation. I played volleyball and bridge. That was about it. Of course, we talked. We talked about the Navy's version of

---

*Brigadier A. S. Blackburn, an Australian officer, commanded the so-called Black Force on Java, which was a composite Allied force consisting of the Australian Second/Third Machine Gun and Second/Second Pioneer Battalions, two British antiaircraft units and a light tank battalion, and the American 131st Field Artillery. See H. P. Willmott, *Empires in Balance: Japanese and Allied Pacific Strategies to April 1942* (Annapolis: Naval Institute Press, 1982), 357.

†The only American POW named Black was a *Houston* seaman, Arthur Black, whose whereabouts since liberation are unknown. The Captain Black mentioned here may have been an Australian or British officer or Lieutenant Colonel C. M. Black, who commanded the first group of POWs, including 191 Americans, sent in October 1942 to Burma to begin work on the railway.

what happened at Pearl Harbor and our version of what we thought about it. It was later on, when we got to Singapore, that we saw a *Life* magazine which was published before the war and outlined exactly how the attack was going to happen. This was the Japanese *Life*. Their version of *Life* magazine. They had, I believe, a picture of the darn ships—the way they were lined up. That gave us a lot to talk about.

"I was going to tell you. I was close to Doctor Lumpkin one day, and a Japanese came up to him and told him that he had caught syphilis. The guard had some medicine he had gotten and wanted Hugh to give him a shot. I forgot what they were using in those days, but it wasn't penicillin. He was afraid that if he went to a Jap doctor for treatment that he would be in a helluva lot of trouble. He would have. That was a big offense for them, to have sex outside of their traveling sex group. You see, they had their own geisha girls. A private or anybody got rewarded, if he was a good soldier, by getting to go to the geisha house. They kept them sanitary. If a soldier got syphilis on the outside, boy, he better not let a Jap officer know. He would be in real bad trouble for it. I guess about once a week that guard would bring his shot, and he'd always bring something to eat. Hugh would say, 'Here come my little ol' friend. I'm so glad that son-of-a-bitch has syphilis!'

"There really wasn't a lot of sickness among us. The Navy had what we called jungle rot. They had picked it up, but they did have medicine to treat it. It wasn't long before most of them were over it. I would say medicine wasn't a problem then. It would have been nice to have spent the war in Bicycle Camp. Java is one of the richest places in the world in food. They don't eat their long rice. They grow a real long staple and ship it out for exchange. Like I said, Java's the richest place in the world: quinine, bananas, coconuts, maple sugar, palm sugar. It's rich. The rice grows plumb to the top of the mountains, all over the place.

"The Dutch were terrific colonizers. Their trains ran all over the island. They were like the electric trains we had back home. Most of them were electric. The Dutch were good at utilizing their people. There were close to fifty million people in Java at the time. They didn't have electric warnings on their railroad crossings. They had a man to warn you and put the gate down. They signaled by drums. You would know the train was coming by the drumbeat. They did the same thing for an air-raid alarm, by drums.

"Life was a day-by-day situation. I don't know if we were getting news on the war. We made up our minds that it wasn't going to be over as soon as we first thought. We had one or two discipline problems at Bicycle Camp. Somebody stole food. I've forgotten just how that happened, but we had an ironclad rule: you do not take food or anything from your buddies. We said, 'Don't steal the rations! If you want to steal, steal rations from the Japanese.' So, we had a sergeant that stole. You might say he was tried and busted. Other than that I don't recall too much of that sort of thing happening.

"We kept records of everything. I have some records of money to the exact penny spent. I probably have the only records of that. They came back in the last trunk. We still had typewriters and could work up orders and that sort of thing. I remember from my records a copy of the final order issued by our command as prisoners. I got back home with that thing. I can't remember much other papers, however. Anyway, I don't want to get too far away from talking about this camp now. When we had men die, when we promoted men, we had their handbooks—little ol' service records—and we'd make notations in them. I don't know whether other parts of the battalion did or not, but I know that we did.

"I'm sure that they asked for a list of prisoners of war from the colonel. They probably told him, 'Give us a list of the men,' and that's what happened—he gave them a list of the men. That would have been done through the adjutant's section. I'm sure that they had a list of us, probably our serial numbers, rank, and the whole works. We wore our own uniforms and rank. I was never questioned by the Japanese individually. I don't know anyone who was. I'm sure we had our own bugles, blew our own reveille. Everybody got up at the same time and took care of their toilet or whatever, shave, brush their teeth, et cetera. Everybody shaved everyday. By then it would be breakfast time. Then, I'm sure we were accounted for, at least once a day. They insisted we count off in Japanese, so we learned to count in Japanese.

"When we left, the first group that they collected were technicians—those who had any technical skill. Humble* worked for the telephone company, so he went in that first group. Some other mechanics or technicians went to Japan. I don't know that they told us they were taking them to Japan. They just wanted those with skills that they could use. I don't think they knew that they were going to take them to Japan until later. Now, when that group left, they took their share of all the rations. You might say they had all they could carry. The money was also divided. Medicine or whatever was divided out, too. The colonel didn't go with the first group.

"It wasn't too long after the head-shaving incident and the signing of the pledge that we were told that we were leaving. I don't know whether

---

*Maxwell F. Humble was a lieutenant in Service Battery. He now lives in San Antonio, Texas.

they told us where we were going, just that we were going. I think that we were leaving, is what the signing of the non-escape pledge was all about—the escape bit—they were afraid that we would jump overboard into the sea. Anyway, we divided up the food, beans, rice, whatever, and we had everybody carry a share of it. We were in pretty good shape with food. We left there with quite a bit of canned goods. I would say there were at least two or three cans of food per man. Milk, maybe salmon, corned beef, coffee—whatever we could buy to eat that was canned or cooked. Just about every man had three or four cans.

"The first group to leave was the Fitzsimmons* group. I went with the next group. We went down to the docks by truck and got aboard the *Dai Nichi Maru*. We were packed aboard the *Dai Nichi Maru*. You couldn't stand up, not enough room, we were *really* laying next to one another, but we had to stay that way until we got out to sea."

Captain Taylor ultimately worked on the railroad in Burma and Thailand, not actually laboring on the line but doing chores in the prison camps. His health deteriorated drastically. He went from 155 pounds in weight to 90 pounds. He had dysentery, ten attacks of malaria, dry beriberi, and scurvy. Malnutrition, however, was his deadliest enemy; it slowly affected his sight, leaving him with 20/200 vision.

He has attributed his survival to help from two members of the 131st, Jack ("Doc") Cellum[†] and Lieutenant Eldon Schmid.[§] Schmid, the twin brother of Sergeant Ellis Schmid, who was mentioned at the beginning of this interview, was a member of Service Battery, Second Battalion. He had been saving a can of condensed milk, which he gave to Captain Taylor at a critical point in Taylor's illness. "It was," Taylor remembers, "that real thick stuff, *gorgeous* stuff." Cellum had stolen canned salmon from the Japanese and gave a can to Taylor before being caught and punished. Weeping as he related the story, Taylor said, "He was sharing, and they caught him. They put him in front of the guardhouse at attention. They had bamboo, and every now and then they'd whop him. They kept him there at least twelve hours, and I prayed every time they hit him. He came through it like a man."

---

*Captain Arch L. Fitzsimmons, commanding officer of Headquarters Battery, was the ranking American officer in the first of the two groups to leave Java in fall 1942 destined for work on the railway. Fitzsimmons died on November 11, 1983, in Albuquerque, New Mexico, of Alzheimer's disease.

[†]Cellum, a member of Battery F, now lives in Lubbock, Texas.

[§]Schmid died of a heart attack on May 25, 1970, in El Paso, Texas.

In addition to suffering his own physical decline, Taylor had to watch his best friend, Doctor Hugh Lumpkin, die on August 1, 1943, at 100 Kilo Camp:

> I remember Hugh got so sick. He had malaria and dysentery at the same time. He dehydrated so bad. We cut a hole through the floor, so he could put his bottom in it because he was going ten, twelve, fifteen times a day. Everytime he'd drink water, it would go through him. He wanted a Dutch doctor to boil some water and put it through his veins. He felt like the only way to save himself was to get some water in him. That's a treatment for cholera and dysentery. He had been making autopsies, looking for cholera, because a cholera scare had come up the river. This Dutch doctor was afraid to do what Hugh wanted, afraid he would kill him. He thought he would go too fast and get air in the blood vessels.
>
> Well, Hugh died. He was a beautiful man. We buried him good, said some prayers over him. I believe Colonel Tharp read the sermon. When a man died his captain read the sermon over him. I'll tell you, it was hard to come to the realization that Hugh wasn't there anymore.

When the war ended Taylor was on a train to Bangkok, Thailand. He was being shifted with a number of officers who were kept near the fighting. He went from Bangkok to Rangoon, Burma, and then to the hospital in Calcutta. He returned to Texas in November 1945, but spent the next two years in and out of hospitals in Texas and Pennsylvania. His eyesight never improved. He drove to his interview using field glasses so that he could read street signs. When asked why he made it through this ordeal, he said pride in country and the military were the reasons.

Clark Taylor had planned a career in the United States Army, but after his POW experience he left the service to sell insurance in Waco, Texas. He died of cancer at the Veterans Administration hospital in Temple, Texas, on August 24, 1986.

Chapter 3

The Road to Burma

The trip from Bicycle Camp to Singapore was one of those unforgettable experiences endured by the survivors of the Death Railway camps. Although many other details have faded from their memories over the years, the voyage of the second contingent on the *Dai Nichi Maru* has never left them. The Japanese crammed them into hot, filthy, smelly quarters using gun butts and bayonets as prods. Each man had thirty square inches of space and no more in the bowels of the rusting old freighter. Roy M. ("Max") Offerle, at the time twenty-one years old and in Battery D, said that "sardines had more room in a can than what we had in that ship."

The movement, which would eventually take the Americans to Burma to work on the railroad, occurred during the first two weeks of October 1942. About 2,000 men—at least 668 Americans, nearly 375 Australians, and approximately 1,000 Dutchmen—left in two contingents, one on October 2 and another on the eleventh. In the first and smaller group, commanded by the Australian Lieutenant Colonel C. M. Black, were 191 Americans under Captain Arch L. Fitzsimmons, commander of Headquarters Battery. Colonel Tharp headed the second and larger body of men, which included about 477 Americans.* The *Dai Nichi Maru* carried the

---

*The reason for the indefinite numbers stems from uncertainty about how many Americans remained at Changi and thus never worked on the railroad. At least twenty stayed behind because of illness. We know that between thirteen and nineteen left later in May 1943 to work on the southern portion of the railroad and that a few Americans remained at Changi for the duration of the war. It is unclear how many members of the battalion who were being shipped from Java to Japan were sent through Singapore and assigned to go farther but never made it. Among technicians drawn from both the *Houston* and the Second Battalion, and with Battery E of the Second, were men who stayed in Singapore despite the Japanese military's original intentions.

Tharp group. To those familiar with America's slave-trading past, the comparison between the *Dai Nichi Maru* and the eighteenth-century ships of human bondage was easy to make. Distress aboard the *Kinkon Maru*, the vessel that carried Fitzsimmons's troops, was not as great.

The hold of the *Dai Nichi Maru* was divided into three tiers of wooden platforms with only three feet between layers. The Japanese forced each prisoner to sit cross-legged for most of the voyage. Although the following interviews describe in detail the agony the prisoners endured, Lieutenant Julius B. Heinen* of the 131st has best explained how the POWs were crowded on board:

> As the Japanese filled the bottom, they started filling the center, and then the top. When all that was full and you thought you were cramped, there were still men with no place to put their bodies and who still had to get down in that hold. So the Japs made space. They just took a rifle butt and jammed it at the guy who was closest. Well, his reaction was to try to get away from the rifle butt that was coming at him, so he moved backwards with as much force as he could generate. That left another space where another man could get in.

To make matters worse, the Japanese had hauled horses in the vessel, and some of the prisoners suffered from dysentery and were unable to reach the jury-rigged toilets that hung over the side on the main deck. Thus, a combination of human feces, body odor, and horse manure fouled the air, making it "so bad that you could cut it down in the hold." The men lacked water. Houston Tom ("Slug") Wright of Battery F declared, "There's nothing worse than being thirsty. You dream crazy dreams in a kind of haze, and you think of meadows and flowing fountains and springwater. You torture yourself." Fortunately, the trip was only a few days.

After arriving in Singapore the Americans were put in Changi, the famed British camp, which was located at the northeastern tip of the island and was being used as a prison compound. The camp already housed over sixty thousand British and Commonwealth POWs, most of whom had surrendered when Singapore fell. Although the ordeal that faced the Yanks in Burma would be greater, they never reconciled themselves to the short period spent at Changi. Most developed an instantaneous and abiding hatred of the English—"limeys," to use their word—especially the officer corps. They resented being "bossed" by the British, who effectively controlled life in the camp, and they felt cheated by not getting what they believed was the American share of Red Cross packages.

---

*Heinen, a member of Battery D, now lives in Dallas, Texas.

Fitzsimmons's group stayed at Changi for only two weeks, while members of the other Lost Battalion group remained about two months, with a few staying even longer. The unit briefly made contact with Battery E, Second Battalion, which came through Singapore on its way to Japan. Battery E had been detached from the battalion at Singosari, Java, staying behind to help defend Surabaja. Until this encounter at Changi, it had been the "lost battery" of the Lost Battalion, having been housed in a warehouse compound near Surabaja to perform salvage work before being transported to Japan.

Sometime between late October 1942 and January 1943, Americans, Dutch, and Australians went by train and ship from Changi, via Rangoon, to Moulmein, Burma. The voyages were not as uncomfortable as the first trip for the majority, but one trip was deadly for a few Dutch and many Japanese soldiers. In January 1943 when a convoy of three vessels, two of which carried the larger group of Americans, was one day out from Moulmein, four American bombers attacked, sinking one of the ships. No Americans were injured; indeed, they stood on the deck of their transport "hooting and hollering" for their countrymen to "sink the bastards!" Ironically, most of the men killed were Japanese soldiers being sent to Burma. A few Dutch POWs also died in the attack.

The POWs knew that they were bound for Burma to work on a railroad that would connect Rangoon to Bangkok, Thailand. They had no idea of the misery that lay ahead. Most stayed overnight in Moulmein, across from the pagoda made famous by Rudyard Kipling's poem "Mandalay,"* but were moved to the railroad base camp at Thanbyuzayat, Burma, the next day.

---

*Most of the men interviewed were familiar with Kipling's verse, which was published as part of his *Barrack-Room Ballads and Other Verses* (London, 1892). Reference to the pagoda is in the first and last stanzas. Some of the survivors quoted the last passage as if it forebode what lay ahead of them: "For the temple-bells are callin', and it's there that I would be—/By the old Moulmein Pagoda, looking lazy at the sea;/On the road to Mandalay,/Where the old Flotilla lay,/With our sick beneath the awnings when we went to Mandalay!/On the road to Mandalay,/Where the flyin'-fishes play,/An' the dawn comes up like thunder outer China 'crost the Bay!"

Donald C. Brain
USS *Houston*

Even before Don Brain was transported to Moulmein to work on the railroad, he had been to Burma. In fact, he was well traveled long before he joined the Navy, having been to many places in Southeast Asia where the Japanese would later send him. His father, who worked in the oil fields, regularly went overseas for employment and took the family with him; they went first to Kirkuk, Iraq, in 1926, then later to northern Pakistan, Rangoon, Singapore, Shanghai, Java, and, once, even to Japan.

Born in Long Beach, California, on October 27, 1922, Brain had minimal formal schooling until he was about fifteen; his mother or his travels provided whatever education he attained. When he was young, he spoke only Arabic, but he later learned English and became tolerably proficient in Burmese. After his junior year in high school, he quit school, joining the Navy in November 1940. At his request, he was not accepted until after New Year's Day. He chose the sea because he knew "the Navy feeds pretty good and [he] didn't particularly relish the thought of sleeping on the ground or walking in mud and stuff." Following boot camp at San Diego, he was assigned to the USS *Dewey*, a destroyer. When the opportunity arose, he volunteered for the Asiatic Station and was sent to the Philippines, where he joined the *Houston* in September 1941 at Iloilo.

When World War II opened a few months later, Brain was working in the ship's scullery and had a battle station as ammunition handler in the after part of the vessel. After the *Houston*'s sinking, he spent thirty-six hours in the water before making shore. Clad only in a T-shirt, he clothed his lower body with a sarong given him by a native woman. Brain was held a few hours by Javanese officials before being turned over to the Japanese. He was put in the Serang theater and later transferred with forty other sailors to the Serang jail.

At Bicycle Camp, Brain was one of the *Houston* survivors given a pair of shoes, pants, and a shirt, courtesy of the Second Battalion. Like others, he applauded the soldiers' generosity. He also praised Dutch women who helped the Americans during their time at Bicycle Camp. And, although he liked the camp, he said things about it not often discussed by other POWs.

For example, he commented on fights over food, while pointing out that such fights were more frequent later: "I would say that probably 99 percent of all fights that broke out in prison camp were based on groceries—most of them that I knew of. Somebody was always saying, 'Well, I bought this, and I said I would share it with you, and you took a bigger bite' and then it was, 'You son-of-a-bitch,' and then that's all it took. Tempers got pretty short there, too, but they weren't too bad at Bicycle Camp."

Brain left Bicycle Camp with the first group to go, the so-called Fitzsimmons contingent. His account of the voyage to Singapore, the internment at Changi, and the trip to Moulmein, Burma, follows.

"OUR OFFICERS RECEIVED WORD that the Japs wanted X amount of people to be transferred out of Bicycle Camp. The officers took the roster and started picking names, and they chose us. I happened to be in the group selected, and I was not aware of where we were going. I went with mixed emotions. I thought, 'Well, are we going to go someplace better than Bicycle Camp, or is it going to be worse?' I still had memories of Serang theater and Serang jail.

"Then we got the word that we were going to Singapore, and I thought, 'Well, gee, this ought to be a lot better, going to Singapore.' Having been to Singapore several times in my youth, I thought, 'This is going to be beautiful.' We got down to the boats—they came and picked us up and counted us all out to be sure that we weren't taking too much with us, and then we were given some rations to take with us.

"The 131st supplied the rations. There were cans of beef stew and, oh, I forget what. But there were maybe two or three guys assigned to a can of this, that, and whatever. So we got our buddy system* set up again, and they loaded us up in trucks out of Bicycle Camp. I didn't fully understand we were going to Burma until I got to Singapore. They put us in this transport that was just unbelievable, the conditions that we traveled in. There were two ships that left at the same time, and I don't know if there were people on the other ship. I seem to have the idea that there were, but I don't remember the name of either one of the ships. They left from Tanjong Priok, and we headed to Singapore.

"They put us down in the holds. I don't know what, but they had hauled grain or some darn thing in it, and rice. I was part of one of the first groups

---

*"Buddy system" refers to a support group of three or four POWs who shared extra food, provided medical care, and performed other functions to ensure survival. All agree that such organizations were essential to getting through the ordeal, especially while working on the railroad.

to go aboard, and, of course, we had to immediately go to the very bottom. There were sacks of grain and stuff down there, and it had gotten damp and started to rot. It was hot down there, damp, and stinking. There were three tiers and three deck levels in this hold, and between each deck level they had wooden bunks or platforms, and each guy had probably a width of two feet. I would say two feet at the most and probably a length of five feet. There were platforms put in between the decks. The average guy could get on his hand and knees and crawl up into a bunk. It was a very narrow space. These were in the upper level, but we were down at the bottom where the ship starts to come in toward the keel. There was a little bit of water down in there. Over at one side they had a bunch of bunks, but most of us slept on the rice sacks or just laid around where we could down there. Along about this time people were starting to feel ill. A few people had picked up dysentery, and the sanitation conditions down there were just horrible. After we went on the ship, it seems to me it took about three days to get to Singapore. This was the very first of October, as I remember correctly, when we left.

"The Japs would pass wooden buckets of rice down to us. The first day we were fed aboard there, when the first bucket of rice was sent down, not everybody got some. A portion of the guys got a pretty good ration of rice, and we thought there would be another bucket coming down. There wasn't. Come to find out that was it. In the end if everyone had gotten a share, you would probably have gotten maybe a tablespoon-and-a-half of rice. That was all, and that was if everyone had some rice doled out to them.

"There was some complaints made. The next day we received the same amount of rice, so we took precautions to see that everybody got some this time, the same amount. There was a guy designated with a measuring cup, and he'd just scoop so much out for each person. Of course, we had some of the canned rations we brought, so we supplemented that with the rice, the cold stew, which helped out considerably. The day or so before we arrived at Singapore, we did get an extra ration of rice one evening, and it seems to me we got into Singapore the next morning. It was in the daylight hours when we disembarked. The humidity down there in the hold was just stifling. It was muggy and very hard to breathe. Then, with this pungent odor, this grain and rice down in there in the process of rotting, it put off a sort of gas. I think they called it a methane gas.

"There was one light bulb, that they dropped down on a cord, hanging in each level of the hold. We had one, and it was probably equivalent to a seventy-five-watt bulb, and it hung right in the middle of our area. Back in the corners you couldn't see a thing. It was totally dark back in there. A few of the boys complained of rats being in that area, but I didn't come in contact with any of them. I didn't see them, but it was common knowledge that on most of these type of freighters, there were rats. So you suspected it, but I didn't see any. Some of the boys said they did.

"They had a latrine on the topside that was jury-rigged timbers mounted over the side of the ship, and you could go into this area to relieve yourself over the side of the ship. Like I say, we had a few people who were developing diarrhea at this time, and there was a bucket that was used, and it would be hoisted up on a rope by other prisoners. We had no problem with the latrine bucket at this time, going from Java to Singapore.

"When we got to Singapore, we got unloaded and put on trucks and went through the town—a portion of the town of Singapore—and I was just appalled at the damage that was done there. I couldn't believe it. Then, of course, as most people know, Singapore itself is on an island, and we went around on the eastern northerly side to an area called the Changi barracks, the Changi area, and that is an army installation. The area we went to is where they kept native troops, and the quarters were very similar to what we had in Java—the same configuration: concrete floors and a very poor grade of plaster for walling, all open, no windows. On the main road going to this area, we went by the Changi prison, which became quite famous later on, and we stopped there for a few moments. Nobody got out. We were in trucks at the time.

"My first reaction was, 'Good Lord, we're not going to go in there! I hope not!' Basically, it was a prison the British had built for the natives. It was old. I had been acquainted with the type of prisons the English had built in their colonies all through the Near East, Far East, Asia, and I felt real low about this time. Then all of a sudden, why, with a little bit of conversation among the Japanese officers that were there, the trucks moved out, and we went on down the road quite a way and kind of came to, it looked like, a staging area. We were off-loaded, and there were some carts and some rickshaw-type carts, and we unloaded everything off the trucks and put it on these carts. I guess it must have been the better part of a mile-and-a-half, two miles, that we had to push and pull these carts with all the gear on them. We were designated to occupy some buildings, which we were billeted in, on the side of a hill up from the roadway. Directly across the roadway, about a quarter of a mile down, there was quite a big installation. There were buildings down there that housed mostly Japanese guards.

"Most of the British forces were intact at Changi. The Japs seemed to have left the British commanding officer there with them. I don't know what he was—Brigadier General Wavell* or something like that. I don't know whether I am pronouncing it right, but he was in charge there, and he seemed pretty well to be running this old Changi fort, this old British installation. Of course, he got orders from the Japs for how many people they needed for different working parties in the area, and he was given a certain amount of details to do within Changi. But it was run by a typical British officer with his swagger stick and his ribbons and his pushy mannerisms.

"I didn't develop any relationships with the British, myself, personally. I did not think they were good people; however, when I say the British, a lot of people get confused. They think of the troops from India, the Australians, the New Zealanders, the people from Britain proper, and the Scottish as all British troops. I single those people out, and I refer to a Scotsman that is in the British Army as a Scottish trooper and the Australians as Australians and New Zealanders. The actual British soldier himself, as an individual, there are some fine people there, but as a group I had just as soon not be involved with them, and especially with their officers because of the caste system that they had developed. I think my dislike began when I was six or seven years old, being amongst them, and later on in life being involved with them in foreign countries.

"When we got there, there was no two ways about it. Our officers were informed right away that they fell under the command of the British, that they were A-1, and that what they said was law regardless of what the Japs said. If our officers wanted to talk to the Japanese or complain about anything, they had to go through the proper chain of command—through the British command that was there. Then if the British felt that it was warranted, why, they could do so.

"As a group, the British were quite arrogant toward the natives in whatever country they happened to be stationed. They felt above them, and any of these natives was to be treated as a serf or a slave—commandeering them for anything that they felt like they could get away with. The British were anything but clean. They lacked sanitary behavior or education or whatever you want to call it. They weren't quite as sanitary as even some of

---

*Brain confuses General Wavell, the overall British commander in the area, with Lieutenant General Arthur Percival. Percival was blamed for the defeat of 130,000 British forces in one week—culminating in the surrender of Singapore on February 15, 1942—by the Japanese General Tomoyuki Yamashita. Singapore and its Changi Naval Base were often referred to as Britain's "Gibraltar of the Far East." Their ignominious loss was described by Winston Churchill as the "greatest disaster and capitulation in British history."

the natives, and my detail, my labor task, was to dig latrines for the British! With complete confidence I can say that the Britishers' biggest problem, their biggest downfall through their whole ordeal as prisoners, was their lack of cleanliness, sanitation. Sanitation and hygiene were one of the essentials to survival. You didn't get to take a bath as often as you should, but regardless of whether you had soap or not, you would use something to try to rub your skin clean: sand or a piece of sandstone or something of that nature.

"To my recollection, I was at Changi two weeks. I never developed any roots there or any comradeship with anybody outside of the immediate group I was with. We tried to clean up the barracks that they had put us in. They were more like horse stalls with a passageway to one end of the building, but I assume they must have had some type of Malaysian troops in there because this is where we first contacted body lice and bedbugs.

"Once the lice got attached to your clothing, you had no means of completely destroying them. The live ones we could destroy, but the eggs, we just didn't have the facilities to destroy, so we were constantly trying to get rid ourselves of these animals that lived in our clothing and in our hair. This is where I finally shaved all the hair off of me that I could possibly shave except for my eyebrows. Of course, the bedbugs were a different matter. We had these little rolled mattings; I forget where we got them—if they were issued to us or whether we had stolen them—but, anyway, we had them in our possession. I had to get rid of mine because it was just so full of bedbugs. They got so interwoven in this matting, bamboo stuff, that the only way you could get rid of them was to burn it. So when we left there, I just left mine there; I didn't take it with me, and I hoped I would get one later.

"One morning there was a bunch of trucks that came down, and they said that all Americans were going to be transferred, that we were going to go on a boat. That is when we got the word definitely that we were headed for Burma. Immediately, I thought, 'My God, where in the hell in Burma are we going?' My mind just thought at first that we were going to the northern part of Burma to work in the mines. That was the first thing that cropped up, and then I thought, 'Well, are they going to take us up to the southern part where it narrows down into Malaya, and are we going to be in the rubber plantations doing that type of work?' My mind just wandered all over. I thought, 'Well, maybe we are going to go to the Irrawaddy Valley and work in the oil fields there.' Then I got to thinking, 'We really don't have any technicians who actually have the expertise to work in an oil field.' My mind just wandered and wondered about what type of work we were going to do, and finally there was a whisper around that we were going to work on a railroad. I thought, 'My God, where on a railroad are we going to work? Are we just going to maintain one or what?' I wasn't privy to getting first-class information. It was all hearsay, rumors.

"I knew the British had tried to build a railway, but when you're on a lean diet, your mind doesn't seem to function too good. After we got to working on the railroad, then things clicked, and we even ran into some of the old survey markings for the old right-of-way. The Japs kept pretty close to them for quite a while. Anyway, they loaded us aboard a bunch of trucks this one morning, and we left Changi and went down to the docks and got loaded on a pretty good-sized Jap freighter. There were about four or five freighters, pretty good-sized ones, tied up to the dock with a couple of smaller ones. If I remember correctly there were four of them. One, just from the looks of it, seemed to be European-made. I have no idea what it was. I never did take the time to learn or pay attention to such things, but it had an old design.

"Anyway, we got aboard these transports, freighters, and the conditions there were just as bad as they were coming from Java to Singapore on the first run. Then after we got all aboard, I ended up down in the bottom hold again for some darned reason, but that's where I was with a few people. Our rationing was a little bit more scheduled than it had been coming from Java to Singapore. The quality was not improved at all, but we did get a little more rice, regularly. We were still getting basically nothing but rice.

"I think down there in the bottom area where we were, there were probably between thirty-five and forty of us. Then, of course, we had a few more sick people with us this time. Some of the boys seemed to get a bit sicker in Singapore because the British weren't too willing to share their rations that they had. The British all looked well; they didn't look like any of them suffered from malnutrition. Of course, the British Tommy didn't eat too well, anyway. His basic ration was hardtack and corned beef or salted biscuits and corned beef. But we didn't eat well either. Everything was more or less makeshift when we first got to Singapore, so a few of the boys started to slip a little bit.

"Well, we got on these boats, and we went to Rangoon. We went up one of the estuaries on the Irrawaddy River to Rangoon. That's back up in there about forty miles. I was at the railing with a few people when we pulled into Rangoon, and there was a lot of speculation about where we were and what town this was. I mentioned to a couple of guys next to me, I said, 'Hell, I know where we are now. This is Rangoon, Burma.' Someone made the remark, 'Well, you're a smart-ass sailor! You don't know where we are! Blah! Blah! Blah!' So I just let it go at that; I didn't want to push the issue.

"We got transferred off this boat and put on a smaller one, and I don't know if this smaller boat had been in our convoy or not, but, anyway, they had it unloaded. There wasn't too much stuff on it. Then they really packed us in. If my memory serves me correctly, it took us all afternoon and the whole of the following day to get to Moulmein. It was just about dusk. I had thought that if we could just get to Burma, then I was going to be in a far better position than in Java or Singapore.

"When we off-loaded, we were put up in this prison that had been built in the 1700s, maybe the very first part of the 1800s, and it was quite dilapidated. They had a lot of Burmese in here. Anyway, the Japs left, so I went over, and I asked a native, 'Is this honestly Moulmein?' I was speaking to him in Burmese. He said, yes, it was Moulmein. Well, this Britisher that was there was astounded. He says, 'You're not British. What are you? Canadian?' I said, 'No, I'm an American.' He says, 'How in the bloody hell did a Yank learn to speak Burmese?' I went on and talked to him. He was a planter. He had been a planter and had joined up with part of the British forces, and they had been captured. He was with the British troops being held in the prison.

"So talking to him and the Burmese, I found out that this area where we were is where they had impounded lepers. I said, 'Just a minute. I'll be back.' So I hotfooted it to one of the officers. I believe it was Jimmie Lattimore.* He was a lieutenant. I said, 'Lieutenant Lattimore, sir, this is a leper area,' and he said, 'Somebody else told me that.' He said, 'I don't recall where I got the information. How do you know that, Don?' I said, 'I was talking to a British planter and a native down there.' He said, 'Oh!' and there was never any more said about it.

"After we had cooked some stew and eaten that and some hardtack—I believe it was hardtack—I went back down there and tried to find this planter again, but he wasn't there. But the Burmese that I had talked to earlier called me over and wanted a smoke. I told him I didn't have anything to smoke, and it took me a little time to recapture all the Burmese I had learned earlier. Of course, he didn't know any English, but by drawing a few pictures and one thing and another, I found out that we were going to build a railroad."

Brain's ability to speak Burmese benefited him somewhat during his later captivity. He first worked on the railroad with other *Houston* survivors, but

---

*James P. Lattimore, of Battery F, died of cancer in Levelland, Texas, on June 16, 1989.

the Japanese needed an interpreter to converse with the natives, and they used Brain. Since he could talk to the natives he was put in charge of the cattle herd, which accompanied the work crews and served as part of their food supply. These jobs put him in close contact with the Japanese, who bashed him with some frequency. Nevertheless, Brain believed that he "probably got along better than any prisoner in Burma." His good deal did not last. He was returned to work on the railroad with a maintenance crew and suffered the usual maladies that befell the POWs: tropical ulcers, dysentery, malaria, and pellagra; bedbugs, lice, and leeches. At times his diet differed significantly from that of his fellows. He ate native foods, including a variety of bugs and beetles.

Toward the end of his imprisonment, Brain was separated from Americans and worked mostly with Australians and the British. When the war ended he was near Phet Buri; only four other Americans were in the work crew. He was flown to Calcutta and put in the obligatory time at the 142d General Hospital. Returned to New York, he spent two weeks at St. Albans Hospital before going home to Long Beach. He stayed some of the time in a naval hospital there while undergoing tests. Don Brain had expected to make a career out of the Navy, but three months after getting back to the United States he requested and received his discharge from the service.

He believed he had less trouble than most readjusting to freedom and being a civilian. "Some people may have thought I was goofy," he said. He craved three kinds of food: rolled oats, lettuce, and milk. Actually, his wife, Polly, thought his problems went deeper. She said, "He covered up his true feelings about being a POW by making fun of it. He was embarrassed by the scars his tropical ulcers left, and he was never really well, always nervous." He never did get over his dislike of the English and Koreans. After Brain left the military in 1946, he ran a vacuum truck business in the oil fields of California. He died in Seattle, Washington, on June 23, 1986.

Seldon D. Reese
USS *Houston*

Seldon Reese was something of a romantic, joining the Navy in September 1940 because he liked the cut of the uniform sailors wore. He paid a yeoman twenty dollars to arrange a transfer from Pearl Harbor to the Far East because he "loved Asia." At times he lived among Filipinos in the Los Angeles Chinatown. Given the circumstances of his birth and upbringing, his interests seemed unusual. He was born of an old East Texas family in Bronson on June 19, 1922. His family had moved into the area before the Republic period and had its own cemetery, which was later included in the Angelina National Park, about one hundred miles north of Beaumont-Port Arthur.

Reese was assigned to the *Houston* three weeks before the Pearl Harbor attack. He was on a 1.1-inch gun in the Sixth Division, the part of the vessel that included the Number Three gun turret. When the turret was destroyed by a Japanese bomber, he was part of the cleanup crew. He said: "I worked for about three or four hours—time was kind of indistinct—carrying up bucketsful of blood and brains and arms and legs and hands and feet out of the compartment."

Following the sinking of the *Houston*, Reese was in the water for eighteen hours before being picked up by a native sailboat. He kept free of the Japanese for several days, during which time he watched a Malayan village looted and its people massacred by bandits, who stole most of his possessions. Turned over by the Javanese bicycle police to the Japanese, he was placed in the Serang theater and then Bicycle Camp. At the time he had only a sarong for clothing, something he wore until he arrived at Changi. He believed that "on a personal basis, the Australians were actually more sharing than the 131st," a minority opinion among the POWs.

Reese's interview is among those whose tellers are capable of embellishing their story with the kind of excitement lost in some accounts. But, as with all of the survivors, there were times when details were forgotten or difficult to conjure up.

"I LEFT JAVA on the *Dai Nichi Maru*. You know, the funny part of it is, we thought when we got to Burma it would be better. We were actually looking forward to it. We just knew that in a working camp they'd feed us better, and we'd have a better life. But that's where the shit hit the fan! At Bicycle Camp we were just told we were going to move out, and we went on the *Dai Nichi Maru*. I still had my sarong, and I had an Australian canteen and an Australian mess kit, and that was about the size of it. If I had anything else, I don't remember.

"Aboard the *Dai Nichi Maru* conditions were pure hell. They don't transport men in comfort like Americans do. Again, their own men, as well as ours, were treated this way. In other words, the *Dai Nichi Maru* was the *Dai Nichi Maru* whether it had Japanese aboard or Americans. Well, about three feet above the bottom of the ship they had a shelf, and about three feet above that shelf, they had another shelf; we got into or onto those shelves, and we laid down in there. You couldn't even sit up straight. You could half-incline, but you couldn't sit up. We came out when we wanted to go to the *benjo*, and that was about the size of it. It was hotter than holy hell, and it stunk! God, that place stunk! The stink was body odors and just the stink of a rotten, old Japanese steamer. It was about a hundred years old and was a coal burner. Dysentery wasn't really too bad yet. It was the stink of an old ship and so many bodies so close together, and it had carried those bodies many, many times before to many, many places. It was just a stinking, rotten mess.

"The food and water situation was terrible, terrible, terrible! We had practically no food and water, just barely enough to sustain us until we got to Singapore. I can't for the life of me remember how we were fed or when. All I remember is that that ship was hell—holy hell! I don't think I got up on deck more than once the whole trip. Of course, it's not a very long trip from Batavia to Singapore. Oh, maybe two or three days. It's a very short trip. I think I got up on the deck for a few minutes—a very few minutes—to go to the *benjo*.

"Well, when we got to Singapore, Changi Village was not bad. I know the moving picture *Changi Village* made it look terrible. That movie was fiction from one end to the other. There wasn't even a basis of foundation for that picture. Changi was beautiful from a physical standpoint. It was built up in the hills above Singapore. Of course, Singapore was really a hot, dirty, filthy city at that time. Changi was clean and up in the hills—it was cool—overlooking the straits between Johore Bahru and Singapore. There were monkeys all around. It was really beautiful from a physical viewpoint.

"The barracks were British military barracks. They had the red tile roofs, and they were stone. They had verandas. There was a shower area in every barracks. I had rice bags that I used as blankets and carried what little gear I had in them. One thing I remember, the sun at Changi Village was extremely hot, but if you got in the shade, the wind was extremely cool. It was either one way or the other.

"Now the English had some Red Cross food there that the Japanese had allowed them to have, but the English said that since the food had been sent to them, it was strictly meant for them and nobody else, and the Americans and Australians got none of it. The English kept it all. We figured that we were fighting the same war, and we deserved the Red Cross goods as well as they. I mean, you would have thought they would have given it to the Australians, but they didn't. They told the Australians that this stuff was sent to the English and 'Damn you!' There were some 80,000 British and in the vicinity of 1,500 Americans, I think it was, and I don't know how many Australians, but I guess about the same number as Americans. The British did everything on a percentage basis—twenty-nine Australians and one Englishman, and twenty-nine Americans and one Englishman for all the hard work. A real percentage basis!

"There were work parties, but like at Bicycle Camp, the work wasn't really too hard. We cut out an area that had been a rubber plantation and started a farm there. We didn't finish the farm; we moved on before the farm got started. The work that I did was cutting out the rubber trees. The Japanese were trying to make the camp self-sufficient. Cutting rubber trees wasn't too hard; they didn't rush us too much. We cut the trees and dug up the stumps. Digging up the stumps was pretty hard work, but they didn't rush us all that much, so it wasn't too bad. Besides, I was in great condition. Now some of the guys—a very few—started getting sick at Changi.

"The food was about like Bicycle Camp. It was rice with a very, very thin soup. The English had some ducks. I know one American stole a duck from an Englishman one time, and, boy, they raised holy hell about that. The Americans, Australians, and Dutch thought nothing in the world of stealing from the English after the way they acted about the Red Cross goods.

"I was involved, standing and watching, in the business called the 'stealing of the King's coconuts.' This Dutchman went up a tree, and he threw down four coconuts. As a matter of fact, he gave me one of the coconuts. Now, I'm going to do some plain talking, all right? Well, these two military policemen came up, and they told him, 'Man, you can't steal the King's coconuts!' And he said, 'Well, fuck the King and the Queen, too!' So he came down, and he and I ran the military policemen away. Another Englishman walked up, and this Englishman asked the Dutchman if he had a cigarette, and the Dutchman said, 'No!' and then he pulled a pack of cigarettes out and offered me one. The Englishman said, 'You just told me you didn't have any cigarettes!' And the Dutchman said, 'For the English, I have nothing; for the Americans, I have everything!' I was right there, and that's the 'King's coconuts' bit. I tell you, if something was the King's, then it's the King's. You don't dare touch the King's possessions.

"In some cases, you didn't have to have passes to move from one section to the other.* I don't know whether you could move around freely or if you had to have a pass to go to the English part. I never did attempt to go to their section. We stayed away from the English; we did not like them. Later on, I did meet some very nice Englishmen, and we got to be good friends; we got to where we could understand them. But at that particular time, the Red Cross goods deal caused a lot of animosity, and we didn't like them. I personally stayed away from them. But we were in close contact with the Australians and the Dutch. The British weren't clean, but that was true with the Indonesian Dutch, too. Still the English were the worst. We worried a lot about hygiene and that stuff. I mean, with all the hunger you knew disease was bound to get started, so we were careful. This concern is the reason we were looking forward to the Burma railroad bit, because we figured we'd get more food there and be strong.

"The individual British soldier was pretty well defeated. But the British had as high spirits about the outcome of the war as we did, and so did the Dutch. As a matter of fact, I made the statement that no two countries could defeat the entire world, and this Dutchman said, 'America could.'

"The Japanese weren't too bad at Changi. We hadn't run into the Koreans yet.† In fact, we never saw many Japanese. Mostly, the guards we saw were Sikh Indians that had turned on the British. The only thing I really know about the Sikh is that their religion requires them to be homosexuals. You know, Sikh to them was like Christ to us, and he was going to return to them as Christ will to us. But women are far too unimportant for Sikh to be born of a woman, so Sikh is going to be born of a man, so they all go around 'switchy-swapping' or 'buggering,' because each one of them wants to be the mother of the new little Sikh when he's born.

---

*Changi was divided by nationality. A pass was necessary for movement from one section to another, and each entrance was supervised by Sikh guards.
†He may be wrong. Korean guards were probably at Bicycle Camp.

"Well, the Sikhs in India are about the most vicious bunch there, and incidentally, I've read the history of India. I'm pretty much of an historian myself, although I don't have any degrees in it, but I've read a lot of history. The Sikhs in India are known as great fighters. They are very sneaky, but they are highly respected as fighting men. They stay away from the Gurkhas. Now the Gurkhas are the really respectable people. Incidentally, the Gurkhas and the Maori were the only native troops in the British Army that received the same pay as the British. They were integrated, not in British outfits, but they went to church with the British, and they went to British nightclubs, and so forth. The other Indians were not allowed to do this.

"Well, we were looking forward to leaving Changi and going on to a job, because we figured when we worked more, we would be fed more. We didn't know even if we were leaving; we just believed we were. As it happened we were in Changi about three months. We wouldn't have been there that long except—according to what I heard; it was strictly rumor—that American submarines had been giving them hell. So they delayed our leaving Changi, and, as a matter of fact, we didn't leave Changi by ship. We went down through the Malay peninsula, and I can't think of the name of the town now. It's way down on the tip of the peninsula. Oh, yeah, I think it was Penang, where we boarded the *Dai Moji Maru*.

"I didn't know in advance when we were to leave. We went to Singapore, and we were put on a train, in freight cars. Again, we sat cross-legged, Indian fashion—crowded in just as many as you could get into a car. They weren't completely closed-in cars, because I sat on the train for about two hours looking at a Chinese girl on a passenger train, and she was the most beautiful girl I ever saw in my life. I'll never forget what that girl looked like; she was mandarin, and, oh, I wished I had been free.

"The *Moji Maru* was not nearly as bad as the *Dai Nichi Maru*. The captain, for one thing, was a really great guy. He allowed us on deck more. As a matter of fact, I talked to him personally. He spoke English. He told us before we left Penang—he told me—that if we got to Moulmein, it would be a miracle, and he knew if he got there, he would not get out. He was very talkative, friendly. He wasn't a bad guy at all. He was a little more educated than most, and, of course, he was a sailor, and he had been around the world; he knew the world. You know, most of the Japanese didn't know much; even their officers didn't. As a matter of fact, I've had Japanese officers tell me that they would eventually starve America out, because they had taken a majority of the rice-producing countries of the world. They just couldn't imagine anyone living on anything except a vast amount of rice.

"The *Moji Maru* was bad, but the conditions were not nearly as bad as the *Dai Nichi Maru*. The shelves weren't nearly as close together, and the ship didn't stink nearly as bad. We got better rations and better treatment from the Japanese all the way around on the *Moji Maru*. And, of course, on the way to Moulmein we got bombed. There were two ships.* I don't know the name of the other one, but it had Japanese and Dutch on it. The *Moji Maru* had English, Australians, Scots, and Americans. It was four B-24s.† They sunk the other ship that was with us. They hit a lifeboat on the *Moji Maru*. They had an old field artillery piece set up on the fantail of the *Moji Maru*, and they tried to fire a shot at the planes, but the gun blew up; there was a big cloud of smoke that came up from the gun, and a bunch of machine-gun ammunition went off on the bridge. One American got some shrapnel in his back. I don't think anyone else was hurt except some Japanese officers on the bridge. There was smoke piling up from the fieldpiece, and the Japanese captain showed his intelligence there again. He ordered everyone to the starboard side that could possibly get there, which gave the ship a list. Then he gave the ship a hard right rudder, which started it going in circles in the water. The Americans in the B-24s honestly thought it was going down, too. He fooled them.

"A strange thing about the bombing was that the other ship got sunk, but the four bombs that were put into it were all in the hold that the Japanese were in. There were something like thirty or forty Japanese survivors, and there were something like thirty or forty Dutch killed. We picked them all up on the *Moji Maru*—what we could find—and went on into Moulmein. During the attack every one of the Americans was screaming, 'Hit the son-of-a-bitch! Sink the bastard!' I was still down in the hold, but I was looking up out of the hold, and I could see the planes, and I was screaming just as loud as anyone else. We wanted it to get hit and sink. I can honestly say that. Later, the Japanese captain told us that he would never get out of Moulmein, and I know that for a fact. I was on a working party that unloaded the ship of the food supplies and rations and the things that it had brought with us. It got underway while we were still on the docks, and some bombers hit it while he was still inside the bay or gulf or whatever.

"They put us in a Burmese prison for a couple of days, and it was like hell! We got issued one quart of water a day to bathe with and one quart of very hot water that had been boiled to drink. The food was bad. But we knew that we were in transit, and we knew that we weren't going to be there

---

*Witnesses to the attack report that there were three Japanese ships in the group.
†Witnesses report that three of the planes were B-24s, and one was a B-17.

long. As a matter of fact, the couple of days we were there, we watched the chain gangs leave out with chains on their legs to go to work.

"That chain gang stuff worried me, but the one interesting point of it was that I could look right from the prison and see the old Moulmein Pagoda. Well, you know, in the American schools back when I went to school, Kipling was one of the main authors that they stressed; as a matter of fact, I could say 'Mandalay' by heart. I was very interested and spent a lot of time looking at the old Moulmein Pagoda. I was there one, two, or three days—something like that—and then we went to 18 Kilo Camp."

Reese worked on the railroad in Burma, but spent a great deal of time in the hospital—a total of nine and one-half months. Although he also had beri-beri, malaria, neuritis, colitis, and jungle ulcers, a terrible case of dysentery landed him there for three of those months. He went from 168 pounds down to 90 pounds before the infection was checked. When he was sent to the hospital for a second time, as the group he was with arrived at 80 Kilo Camp (Hospital Camp), the Japanese told them, "You're no longer any good to us, and we have brought you here to die." Even though the Japanese called 80 Kilo Camp the Death Camp, Reese survived and proved them wrong.

At Hospital Camp, Reese served on the burial detail. He describes a typical burial as something done with a minimum of ceremony: "You took all the clothing off the man—if he had any clothing—and you wrapped him in a rice bag, and you dug a hole barely deep enough to cover him, and you threw him in and covered him up. Then you went straight to digging the next hole for the next guy. There were about twenty-five to forty deaths a day. You just threw them in and covered them up, and then dug the hole for the next guy."

Fond of Asians—Reese considered the Burmese "the most civilized people in the world"—he hated the Korean guards, claiming that he helped kill at least one during confinement and "worked several over" after liberation. Although most of the men spoke well, if not highly, of Colonel Tharp, the Second Battalion's commander, Reese, a Navy man, did not. He had a disagreement with Tharp, who disapproved of Reese selling a Dutch coat and shoes he had been issued:

I sold the shoes and coat to buy food. When I came back in, a military policeman caught me, and he carried me before Colonel Tharp. Well, I was still pretty sick, so he looked at me up and down, and he said, 'Well, I can't do nothing to you, but I'll tell you, by God, what I will do. If I catch you doing that again, I'll turn you over to the Japanese!' I told him, 'You Goddamned, old motherfucking son-of-a-bitch, you turn my ass over to the Japanese if you want to! But when we get back home, your ass will be tried for high treason, and don't you never Goddamn well think it won't!' He said, 'You're dismissed!' From then on, my hatred for Colonel Tharp increased bountifully.

Reese was at a camp in southern Indochina when the war ended. The Japanese trucked him to Bangkok, and the Americans flew him first to Calcutta and finally to a naval hospital in Albany, New York.

After some time in hospitals, he was released. He performed shore patrol in Houston and Galveston, but mostly he took his back pay and invested it in "houses and lots," and said he didn't "regret a single minute of it, because I was making up for lost time." The investment was in "whore *houses* and *lots* of alcohol." In time, of course, a degree of readjustment came, and Reese married and raised a family. He became a workman for Union Carbide in Texas City, Texas, and later for Union Oil of California in Brea. Seldon D. Reese died on January 15, 1988.

Garth Slate
Battery F

Born in Bagwell, Texas, in 1921, Garth Slate left Texas for the first time destined for Java and captivity. He had joined Battery F, Second Battalion in May 1940, but his relations with that unit went back much further. As a boy in Jacksboro he rode the horses used by the local National Guard outfit, Battery F, to pull its caissons and limbers. Memory of those days and knowledge of an impending war caused him to enlist. He reasoned that he would soon be drafted and might as well serve with men he knew.

Just as Slate was not the only Texan in the 131st to be leaving the Lone Star State for the first time, he was not the only one to be seasick all the way from San Francisco to Hawaii. "I was doing all right," he said, "until a Reserve Navy chief who had been called up got upwind of me and got sick. That made me sick. So for the next two days I was whoosey. I couldn't eat." His bout with mal de mer was long since forgotten when the announcement that Japan had attacked Pearl Harbor was blared over the USAT *Republic*'s loudspeaker. "This thing won't last long," he declared. He was an "eager beaver" to meet the Japanese—"those little short guys, slant-eyed, shaved heads, in slouchy uniforms, who couldn't see too good." He adds, "I found out later they can see pretty darn good."

In February 1942, when the Second Battalion moved from the airfield at Singosari, where they had encamped after coming to Java, Slate thought that they were going to the coast to be transported back to Australia. Unfortunately, such was not the case, and after being separated from the main body of his troop, he and another member of Battery F managed to rejoin the Second Battalion in time for Slate's twenty-first birthday on March 8, the day Java fell to the Japanese.

After helping to destroy the battery's equipment, he went to the tea plantation and then to the racetrack at Garut. He avoided Tanjong Priok, having been placed with twenty-two others as a member of an advance party to ready a camp for the POWs. Actually, they were sent to a Chinese school in Batavia. They never prepared a camp, but for the next six weeks he worked out of the school on various details assigned by the Japanese.

Slate's interview illustrates that in some ways being a prisoner was not a great deal different from Colonel Harry G. Summers, Jr.'s, definition of war: "primarily sheer boredom punctuated by moments of stark terror."

"W HEN THE RUMOR started floating around that we were going to be moved—I don't remember whether the rumor was to Singapore or not, but I think it was—they had a place at Bicycle Camp where the Japanese had set up records for all POWs. One of the guys, Robertson,* our battery clerk, was working over there. He said they were going to need a couple more guys to stay there to take care of all the records.

"I decided, 'Shoot, they're going to move them off up to Singapore, and I don't know what's going to happen.' The Japanese were going to keep the prisoner headquarters in Java, and so I tried to get a job at the place, keeping records. Somehow my application fell through, and I didn't get to stay. I worked over at the records place two or three days, and I talked to the Jap in there. He spoke good English, and he said, 'I'll see what I can do about getting you left here.' The last day I was over there, he said, 'Well, I put in the request, and if they're going to let you stay, they will tell you in the morning, at camp.' Well, the next morning, I had my bags like the rest of them—headed for a boat—and I wasn't told to stay.

"The first thing the Japs did before this was come through the camp and take people like mechanics, technical people, take them and ship them out. Then they broke us down into groups to ship to Singapore. We were told that they would do it, and they did; they broke us down into groups of about two hundred people. They took one group out, and I was in the second group. They took this first group out and put them on a ship. We stayed awhile and followed the same usual routine, and then they set a date for us to leave. If I'm not mistaken, we left about two weeks or maybe a month after this first group. I don't know if it was that long. It was somewhere in there—maybe three weeks later.

"The officers made sure we had certain clothes to wear, and then we could take anything we could carry. That was one thing they explained: if you can't carry it, the Japs are not going to haul it for you. They also told us we were liable to do a lot of walking, and we'd better not have anything that we couldn't carry a long ways because that's one of the first things that people started doing, getting rid of stuff when they'd have to walk a long ways. So the only thing I had was what I could carry in my bags. The main

---

*William F. Robertson, Battery F, died of cancer and cardiac arrest on November 8, 1974, in Greenville, Texas.

things I kept were my blankets and clothes. A lot of other stuff I got rid of. I had my mosquito net, and I kept it. I had a raincoat, but that thing weighed too much, and it didn't get cold out there; and if you had the raincoat on and it started raining, you'd start sweating and get wet anyway. So I threw away my raincoat. I just carried essential things. I had eating utensils and a few personal items that didn't weigh much—stuff that the Japs wouldn't raise Cain about, things you weren't supposed to have.

"I didn't want to leave. We kind of got into the routine, and we didn't know what we were going into. Actually, it wasn't too bad at Bicycle Camp. Leaving it, well, you'd say, 'What in the world am I going to hit next?' Going to Singapore! I had heard rumors and had been told that we were moving into a big, permanent English camp and that a lot of Englishmen were already there. Well, they put us in trucks and took us down to Tanjong Priok. They put us on an old ship, but I don't remember its name. It was an old freighter. I remember that it had toilets that were built so that they hung over the side of the ship. Everytime you went, you looked down, and there was water, and you'd hope to heck that those things didn't fall off because it didn't look like they were on there too good.

"I was put in a hold way back in the back. If I wanted out, I had to crawl over everybody to get out. It was the same thing going back in: you crawled over everybody. I think I had to crawl over four people to get back to where I was put. You couldn't stand up. The space between the wooden platforms you were on wasn't over, I'd say, about thirty inches. You could sort of sit, but as far as standing up, you couldn't. A lot of times when you were crawling, you'd hit your back on the top of a platform.

"When you slept, you would just stretch out, but down in this hold there was no air circulation. It was awful hot, so you'd stay in there as long as you could, and then you'd get out. You always had to make a trip to the *benjo*. If there weren't too many going, the Japs'd let you stand on top, and at least you were getting fresh air. There was a steady line out of the hold getting a little fresh air. During the day, you'd stretch out where there was a little air, in the center of the hold, and sleep, because at night, at times, it would get so hot that you couldn't hardly stand it, when everybody was there, and it stunk.

"You lived down in a hold that'd been fixed up probably to transport Japanese troops in it. To eat, you'd come out on deck with your mess gear.* They'd let out so many at a time, and you'd go through the line. Usually,

---

*The vast majority of POWs remember that food was lowered into the hold in buckets and then was distributed there.

they'd fill my mess kit full, and that was it. When they'd start, they'd want to get rid of you in a hurry. They made sure you kept going. You'd go back down in the hold to eat, and they'd let you up to wash your mess gear out when you got through. Sometimes, if I remember right, there was hot water there, and sometimes there wasn't. They did have, I think, a few Americans that helped them with the meals, but the Japs done the cooking out on deck. This was the first time we'd run into a little different type of food. They gave us a kind of rice and a boiled barley, but they cooked it for us.

"It wasn't exactly a comfortable trip—it was uncomfortable because they had you crowded up so—but it was a short trip, not too long. I think it was a week that we were on the ship, and time passed pretty good. The main thing was trying to stay cool. You were beginning to get used to spending time, and one day didn't mean a whole lot to you because you weren't going anywhere, anyway. But I was glad to get back on land again.

"We docked in Singapore, and we were told that the Japs were going to move us to an English camp. We were going to have trucks to go out there. For some reason they killed time before we finally got off, and the only thing I ever figured out as to why is that diplomats that they were exchanging were being loaded on the ship in front of us. They didn't want us out on the docks until they got all those people in. I saw several people going aboard. They could have been English. They were white. We found out later, in talking, that they were exchanging the diplomats. Where they sent them from there, I have no idea, but that's why we were delayed.

"Boy, it was unbearable waiting. If I remember right it was several hours. Everybody had all of their stuff ready to get off because when they said, 'Let's go,' you had to be ready to get off. And then we just kept sitting there. And you wanted to know when: 'We're here! Let's get off!' We were beginning to wonder if we were going to have to spend the night on the ship.

"Well, we did get off and they put us on the trucks, and we started the trip to Changi. We passed this big prison, Changi jail. At first, that's where we thought we were going. But we passed it, and they took us to Changi camp. They took us to a certain point and checked us into the camp. We got out and got counted again, and then we started walking because the trucks turned around and left. The barracks that we were going to stay in, I thought we never would get to them.

"When the Japanese took Singapore, they captured 115,000 English prisoners, and most of them were still in the camp, so it was quite a large 'garrison,' as the British called it. The Japs said that the barracks they were giving us was way off on the side of the camp. Actually, we had a good view. We were up on a hill looking out over the channel or canal that went around Changi.

"We were put in three-story barracks, concrete, but there were no bunks in them whatsoever—just bare barracks and four walls. Everything had been taken out. So we went in and were assigned a spot on the floor, up against the walls. The Japs said, 'Now here's your spot, and here's your spot,' and that's the way they figured out where we were going to sleep. My spot was where the posts were down the middle of the barracks. They said, 'You can put your bedroll here and sleep there.'

"Well, that's what we did, and then everybody started looking for something better than the floor to sleep on. I've tried my best to figure out where I got a canvas cot, but I managed to get me a canvas cot, and I moved that thing in, and I put my mosquito net over it. I set the cot in little cans of oil. We used any kind of oil we could get, and we oiled the strings of our mosquito nets to keep bedbugs from crawling on you. They would crawl across the ceiling and drop on you, because that place had more bedbugs than any place I ever saw in my life.

"During the day you'd put your stuff out in the sun and pick bedbugs out of it any way you could. The sun normally would kill them. But that night, they'd be right back. They had some peanut oil I got hold of and put on all my strings, so I kept them out pretty well. I didn't have too many awful bites. They wouldn't cross the peanut oil. They wouldn't cross water, but water evaporated too fast, where the oil wouldn't. But once a week, you'd make sure you had plenty of oil, or you'd check every day in case somebody knocked your cans off and spilt your oil. You'd oil the strings holding your mosquito net about once a week. You didn't let anything touch the floor, even the mosquito net. When you let it down, you tucked it in to where it wouldn't touch the floor, the main reason being to keep mosquitoes out, too, because they were awful bad.

"To start with we wanted to be friendly with the British, but they came up, and the first thing they let us know was that everything on the island belonged to the King, and they were protecting the King's property. We had heard on the way up there that we had Red Cross supplies in Singapore. So when we got there and the deal came up over the Red Cross supplies, they said our supplies had already been sent to Burma. There was so much Cain raised about that, well, all of a sudden they found us some. But then things started deteriorating between us and the British because everything belonged to the British. They got out and drilled everyday, and they polished their boots everyday, and according to them, their officers were making them 'soldier' everyday. Well, we just didn't go for all of that, and especially that everything belonged to the King.

"The British were living pretty good. In fact, down below us, there were some British sergeants who got hold of generators. They had lights at night. Well, we didn't have any kind of lights in our barracks. The English officers had a good setup, eating good food, and they had people—I think they called them 'batmen'—wait on them. So we just got to scrounging around, and we'd go steal the officers' chickens.

"The Japs took us over to clear out an area, and they said they were going to make the camp self-supporting, and we were going to plant a garden. So they told us to clear so much land. Well, we started cutting down coconut trees, and the British started raising Cain because they were the King's trees: 'You can't cut them down!' We said, 'Well, the Japs said to clear this out,' and they said, 'Well, oh, no, they didn't say cut the coconut trees down!' But the Japs said, 'Cut the coconut trees down,' so we cut the coconut trees down, and the British didn't like it, but there wasn't anything they could do about it. English officers came around once in a while to tell us, 'Well, you're not supposed to do this, or you're not supposed to do that, because all of this belongs to the King, and we're preserving it.' Well, I figured that if the King wanted to preserve it, he wouldn't have let them lose it in the first place, anyway. So we didn't get along too well.

"Most of the English were still in their same barracks. They still had their same uniforms and everything, where we had already gotten rid of most of our stuff. The old deal always came back to our situation at Malang, trying to get our footlockers out of there, which we had to leave stored there when we left. Well, the British had all of their stuff with them, when we'd got down to either one or two changes of clothes.

"We seldom ever saw a Japanese guard. If you went from the part of the camp where we were to the hospital area, you had to get permission, and you had to pass some Sikh Indian guards. These guards would make you stop and get permission, and then you had to salute them as you went through, and then you had to do the same thing coming back. I don't think I made that trip but twice. I went one time because I heard I could buy something over there in their little ol' PX. But I didn't make many trips there. Changi was another place where there was no place to go. On one side they had patrols, but the English used to go to town. They'd watch a patrol pass, go under the fence, and go on, but they'd always get back before daylight. It was a long way—too far for us. I never thought anything about going to town. I didn't know where I'd go after I got there.

"In the mornings they'd want work details and take you over to clear this land where they were going to plant this garden. You actually didn't have anybody supervising you. The ones that took you over told you what to do. We halfway did the work of clearing it, and we stood around and talked most of the time. We'd cut the trees down to agitate the English, that was the big thing. Supposedly, we were doing it for us. We were going to raise our food, at least that's the impression I got. We'd cut the trees down, and then we'd have to haul them off. So over a period of time, we got the area pretty clean.

"We had some 'horseless carriages,' vehicles with no engines, to haul the stuff in. Somebody'd get up in it and guide it, and the rest of us would push, and that was our truck. The engines had been taken out to lighten them up, but you'd haul everything around with them. One guy'd get to sit up there and guide, and the rest of you'd get behind and push. We had lots of fun with them, lots of races. We'd race here and there. The English couldn't understand this at all. They couldn't understand our whole attitude. They said we were too happy-go-lucky. Well, you might as well make the best of it, have a little fun along the way, because, as I said before, you weren't going anywhere and worry wasn't going to help you a bit. So we just made a little fun out of the horseless carriages and went on and done part of what the Japs wanted done.

"The English had control of the food. And that caused trouble. We didn't think we were getting our portion of it. They kept saying, 'Well, you are,' but then they were dishing it out, so how could you fight them? They made distribution to our cooks. I don't know how many supplies the cooks'd draw at one time, but they'd draw all of it, and they'd have to go down and get it from the English.

"Our cooks were good at not wasting food. They would cook what they had to feed all of us and not waste anything because there was no such thing as throwing stuff away. The English would give them, say, a hundred-kilo sack of rice, say, for three meals. Well, they'd cook about a third of it this meal, a third the next meal, and that was about all they could do. For breakfast they finally got around to cooking the rice with a lot of water in it and all, and that would make more for the dinner and supper meals. We called this breakfast rice pap. The vegetables they got for the stew, well, that had to be broken down to make sure you had enough to more or less flavor the rice the same for each meal.

"The cooks, I'll give them credit. Most of the time, they did a good job, and they had a thankless job, anyway. People would give them fits over why they didn't do this and didn't do that, but they didn't have much to do with. People were always accusing them of getting more food to eat. But the cooks didn't weigh any more than we did or get any fatter. But, let's face it, if you're cooking, you're going to get a little bit extra. I knew that, and the rest of the guys knew it, too, I think.

"Everybody would go by and see if they could get a big handful of the burnt rice, the crust at the bottom of the pot. It was something hard, crisp— a little treat—where everything else we ate was all soft. And another thing, charcoal was good for your stomach, and I ate a lot of it that was burnt black because the doctors had told us that this was good for us, that it would help keep dysentery away. Well, I ate it, and sometimes I'd even get a piece of burnt-black wood and just eat the charcoal off of it. A lot of guys said, 'You can't get me to eat that,' and I said, 'Well, they said it's good for you, so I'm going to eat it.' I give that credit for keeping me from getting sick a lot.

"We got rice, we got stew, and then they had some Red Cross rations that we'd get mixed with it. I was told that the English took a lot of the individual packages and rather than give them to an individual, they'd issue it to the kitchens. So we got a little of it through that way, but not much. We usually got the other run-of-the-mill stuff because the English kept telling us that they sent our supplies up into Burma. We got mutton from them one time that I remember, and it was so raunchy and bad that I don't know if very many ate it. You could smell it a mile away. It came out of freezer plant from somewhere, and it had been in there so long until parts of it already started deteriorating. It was dry and didn't taste very good.

"Battery E had been separated from us in Java, and it came through Changi. They were in a different area from us. I was on one of my trips to the hospital, and I got to see a couple of the guys. They had them over at another place, and they said, 'We're not going to be here long.' I knew they were coming, going through, but I didn't get to see any others. It was one of those deals where you were all in the same camp, but you couldn't get over to see them or to see what happened to them.

"Morale was low at Changi, and the British morale was the lowest. One thing: I got to where I'd talk to a couple of British. They didn't like the way their officers were treating them and running the place, trying to keep it a garrison. The British officers had even court-martialed some of their own people. So their morale wasn't too good. They would be thrown in the stockade for different things they'd do. But the Scots, now they were something else. They would come up and talk to you. They called us Yanks. They thought we were something else. They liked to come up and sit around at night and talk. They'd bring books so we'd have something to read. We just did lots of sitting around and talking to them. They'd always bring tea. To show how much they had, you'd go down there, and they had tins of milk to put in their tea. We didn't know what a can of milk was along about then, but they had it. They didn't care too much for the British either, and they were glad we came in there.

"The Scots'd share more. They brought a lot of stuff to us that they got hold of. They had more than they knew what to do with, so they would share with us. They would tell us where the stuff was if we wanted to go get it, which we'd got to scrounging pretty well. They told us where the British officers kept their chickens and where we could probably go steal some of their eggs and where they kept their supplies. They were kind of hard to get to, but the chickens, we could steal them. If they hadn't gathered their eggs, we could steal eggs, too.

"I was out a few times at night to steal a few chickens and liked to got caught several times. We stole some of the English noncoms' cream. They had them a little patio built, and they had these cans of milk setting out, and their sugar bowl and their teacups and all of that. Well, we didn't want the cups or nothing, but we'd steal the sugar and the cream. But they finally decided that the Yanks were stealing everything, so they started moving it in and hiding it. But some of the English liked what we were doing to the officers and noncoms. It kind of lifted their morale.

"Some of the English had come right out of Dunkirk, went back to England, and then went right on to Singapore. A lot of them didn't care anymore. There were a lot of Englishmen that were married, but their families were back in England. One of them told me that he came out of Dunkirk, and they got him to Singapore so fast that he didn't even get to stop long enough to see his family.

"Well, when we got ready to leave, to go get on the trucks to go catch the train, here come the Scots in their dress kilts and their bagpipes. They piped us out, which, I understand, is the highest honor that they can give you. So they piped us all the way down to the trucks until we got on the trucks and left. I talked to an Englishman later, and he said he'd never known of an English outfit that the Scots ever piped out of anywhere, but he said, 'They piped you Yanks out.' I said, 'Well was that good or bad?' He said, 'That was good because that shows what they think about you. If they hadn't liked you, they would never have done it.'

"Well, the Japs took us and put us on a train, and then we went to George Town, or Penang. I think they're right next to each other or something, and that's where they took us. The trip wasn't too long. I don't remember much about it. It seems like we were crowded in what were cattle cars with open sides, I mean, slats. We had air flowing and hay on the bottom to sit on or sleep on, on the floor. They'd stop the train at different places to feed us. They had feeding points. Actually, it was kind of an uneventful trip.

"We boarded the *Dai Moji Maru*, and in comparison to the first one, the one to Singapore, this second ship I got on was not crowded. We had plenty of room, and we were allowed more freedom on deck. In the hold, you had plenty of room to stretch out, and the food was not too bad. Of course, the sailors were cooking it. It was kind of like you were taking a cruise to start with. Things were pretty easygoing.

"After we were underway, when we got a day out of Moulmein, we got bombed. There were two ships in the convoy plus a little escort. Well, I'd gone up on deck because while I was in Singapore, I got hold of some saltwater soap, and the Japs'd let you go up on deck and use one of the deck hoses to take a bath. So I was trying out my soap, and I was all soaped down, and all of a sudden, I heard this drone. It was about noon.

"The sounds between the American airplanes and the Japanese airplanes were different because on the American airplanes, the motors were synchronized and the Japanese weren't. They had a kind of, oh, a rumbling sound to them. You could tell that their different motors weren't synchronized to fire at the same time. But I heard this steady drone, and I looked up, and all I could see was four motors going over me. I knew the Japanese didn't have any four-motor planes, and I could see these little black dots coming out from under the plane. And I knew, I could stand there by the superstructure and look up, see the bombs coming from the plane, and that they weren't aimed at us. They were after the ship behind us, the largest one.

"Well, I grabbed the hose to get the soap off of me, and about that time the bombs started hitting the other ship. I could see one hit the front, and all of a sudden all you could see was big, black smoke. The guard started getting 'bent out of shape' at me and wanted me back in the hold. Well, I didn't have my clothes back on, and he was trying to rush me. I didn't want to go in the hold, so I was trying to kill time and to get the rest of the soap off of me, and he was trying to watch the plane and get me back in the hold. There were some other guys there that he was trying to run into the hold, and they were just standing and watching.

"All of a sudden a plane came across us. I was looking up, and I saw the bombs coming, and I said, 'Boy, they're bound for us!' because they were just about far enough out. When I heard them whistling, I hit the deck, and the Jap guard hit the deck with me. The bombs hit on each side of the ship, and it was just like the ship raised up out of the water and then just dropped back. I couldn't hardly breathe because that jarred all the dust loose on that ol' ship. Then I started getting into my clothes in a hurry because I knew that if I wound up in the water, I didn't want to be in the water buck naked. I wanted some clothes on. So I got my clothes on, and by that time the Japs had brought some people out of the hold. I know they came up because on one side of the ship a bomb had knocked some holes in it, and the Japs were trying to figure out what the damage was, because the pumps started working.

"I recall during the attack that the Japs fired at the planes and hit the ship's superstructure. Well, I don't know what they were firing at, to tell you the truth; maybe somebody accidentally set the gun off and it fired. I know the Japs panicked. They started a small fire there, and they got it out in a hurry. Then things started happening awful fast. I saw the other ship go down, and then we started circling. It wasn't too long until these Japs came running from up toward the bridge, and they went to hollering to us, 'Come here! Come here!' So we were throwing these nets over the side, and we started picking up survivors. The survivors coming up the nets, some of them, you had to go down and help up, and some could make it all right. One of them come up carrying a big fish. They didn't have life jackets issued to them, but in the front of the ship, they were transporting a thousand Jap soldiers. Well, we picked up 950 Dutch prisoners and 50 Jap soldiers, because the bomb hit in the hold that the Japs were in, and it didn't hit the Dutch.

"Well, all the time this was going on, the Japs weren't saying too much. The ship was circling, and there was an officer up on the bridge who was more or less directing things, and they would point to these people in the water, and they kept picking up survivors. In fact, I think we stayed there around six or seven hours, and we were wondering why in the heck they didn't get away, get somewhere, because the Americans might come back after us. I'll say one thing, that ol' Jap captain stayed right there, and this little corvette kept circling, and he picked up some, and they brought them over and put them on our ship. But the captain stayed and picked up everybody that he could.

"Then we started underway, and now the ship was crowded. If you could find a place even to squat, draw your feet up under you and sit down to sleep, you were lucky. But we got all of the people out of the water, anyway. Then we started underway again, and I know we were underway all night, because I had to go up to the *benjo* late in the night. It was pretty moonlight—pretty light—and I could see we were passing through a convoy that some planes had bombed earlier in the day, before we were bombed, and nearly every one of the ships had burnt up, been destroyed. Some of them were still burning. Some of them were like a silhouette of a hull with the whole superstructure gone. I believe it was the next day that we started into the harbor at Moulmein.

"Going into Moulmein, there was one of these little Jap Betty bombers that came down the river, and there was some Jap officers sitting on the boards across the hold. They were open, but the support was still there. This one Jap officer got so scared that he jumped off into the hold and broke his leg; and another one jumped off, but he didn't break his leg. Just that Jap plane coming down through there, man, they thought they'd had it again. Then, after we docked in Moulmein, they took us off, and we were sent to a native prison, right under the hill from the Moulmein Pagoda. When we found out what it was, the first thing that we started asking each other was, 'Is that the pagoda that Kipling wrote about?' It was right in sight of us. You could see almost the whole pagoda. The side of this prison I was in, everytime I walked out of this cubicle, there the pagoda was, just staring you in the face setting out on the hill.

"You could tell where we were was a regular prison camp, but they didn't lock the doors on us; I mean, the doors stayed open. They said, 'Well, you're not going to be here long because we're going to move you up to the railroad,' which, I don't remember, I think we weren't there too long—five days—before they decided that it was time for us to make our little walk up to the railroad, to the camp we were going to. It took us almost a day to walk from Moulmein to Thanbyuzayat."

During Slate's time working on the railroad, the part he hated most was helping to build bridges, which required long, hard toil, often in water, for extended periods of time. He was fortunate that much of his duty on the railroad gangs was spent cutting timber, allowing him to avoid many of the illnesses suffered by others. He did not have dysentery and only a small jungle ulcer for a day or two on his foot. He did have malaria and contracted pneumonia, which almost killed him. He lost weight, dropping to ninety pounds.

After work on the railroad ended, he was placed with two hundred other men to be sent to Japan as "show prisoners." Assigned to Kanchanaburi,* they were kept separated, well fed, and clothed in Dutch army uniforms.

---

*In most of the interviews and in writings about the Death Railway, the camp is referred to as Kanburi and the village as Kanchanaburi. However, these names may be used interchangeably.

They spent three months playing cards and mah-jongg, but because of the perils of travel by ship were never sent to Japan. In April 1944 he was transferred to Saigon, where he worked on the docks, at Tan Son Nhut airbase, at a Dunlop rubber plant, in an ammunition depot, and erecting long-range radio antennas. He also engaged in sabotage that may have gotten two Japanese soldiers executed. As he remembers the events:

> We were putting aviation gas in this big tank where they would back their truck up to load it. Somebody came up and found a fifty-pound sack of sugar, and we dumped it in that aviation gas. That didn't do the fighter planes too good the next morning when they took off. In fact, six of them cracked up. We don't know whether our sugar did it, but it was actually a hundred-kilo sack of sugar that we put in about five hundred gallons of gasoline. But they caught two Japs that were sabotaging their own planes out there, too, about two or three days later, and they shot them on the side of the runway. So I don't know whether they blamed that on the Japs, but they told us that these guys were sabotaging their own planes.

While in Saigon, Slate witnessed a major air raid described by many POWs who were sent there:

> From our camp we could see out over the airport. All of a sudden, the sirens went off, and we started looking around, and the sky started filling up with planes, and they didn't have the Rising Sun on them. Then the Japs were rushing us out to the trenches in the middle of the rice fields we'd built up for air-raid shelters. Of course, the way the tide comes and goes there, you're in water, and you're sitting in those trenches waist deep in water.
>
> We could see Americans strafing and working over the airfield. They'd just start working toward the area we were in, and we saw them work on the underground storage tanks. They were coming along that river, and then all of a sudden they were over the top of us. They're firing at all the ships that's tied up to the docks. The only thing we hated was that one plane made a dive at a ship, and the ship's gunners must have caught it just right because that plane just almost disintegrated. We saw only one more go down.
>
> The Americans tore everything else up. They even came down that dock skip bombing into the warehouses. About noon, the Japs thought it was all over because they blew the 'all clear.' But we didn't hardly get back to camp until they were back again. They stayed the rest of the afternoon. When the sun was going down that afternoon, we saw the last two leaving way off at the side. While it was going on, we were hollering, 'Give 'em hell! I hope they don't get too close over us; we'll watch the show from here.' Most of us thought we were watching a show. We said, 'Well, at least they're getting close.'

When the war ended Slate was sent from Saigon to the Army hospital in Calcutta, and then to Halloran General Hospital on Staten Island, New

York. He was mustered out of the service at Camp Fannin in Tyler, Texas, but immediately reenlisted as a recruiting sergeant. He later served tours of duty in Europe and across the United States, but mostly at Fort Hood, Texas.

He retired with twenty years' service in 1960, and subsequently sold real estate, owned a photo finishing lab, and, primarily, worked for the United States Postal Service. He now "takes things easy and doesn't worry." He does not trust the Japanese and Koreans and, while taking the "Brits as they come," he does not "think too much of them." But of the "Aussies," he says, "They're like the Texans of frontier days!"

Chapter 4

The Death Railway

Arnold C. Brackman, in *The Other Nuremberg: The Untold Story of the Tokyo War Crimes Trials*, writes that "by all accounts the worst POW and forced-labor camps during World War II were located along a 258-mile strip of railroad track running through the almost impenetrable jungles of Thailand and Burma. The infamous Siam-Burma Death Railway was built by Allied prisoners of war and Asian slave laborers during 1942 and 1943 under conditions so vile that 27 percent of the POWs and more than half of the Asian press gangs perished." Although one might find minor fault with Brackman's statistics regarding POW mortality, with the gist of his statement there can be no disagreement. If we are to believe witnesses from the many POW camps that held American servicemen during World War II, those who survived the "death camps" of the Death Railway endured the worst. With the nearly 50,000 Australian, British, and Dutch POWs and perhaps 250,000 native forced laborers* were 668 men of the Second Battalion and the crew of the *Houston*, the only Americans to work on the line. Before their task was completed almost 20 percent, or 133 of them, had perished.

The railroad that these Americans helped build was a Japanese effort to link two existing railways: one that ran from Singapore at the tip of the Malay peninsula to Ban Pong and then to Bangkok in Thailand, and another that ran from Ye on the Andaman coast to Rangoon and was entirely within Burma. The Japanese successfully united the two by establishing a line from Ban Pong to Thanbyuzayat, a village about fifty miles north of Ye.

---

*Although it may seem difficult to believe, the native workers were treated more viciously than the POWs, in defiance of the rhetoric claiming "Asia for Asians." Rohan D. Rivett, in *Behind Bamboo: An Inside Story of the Japanese Prison Camps*, estimates that a minimum of 100,000 natives died while working on the railway.

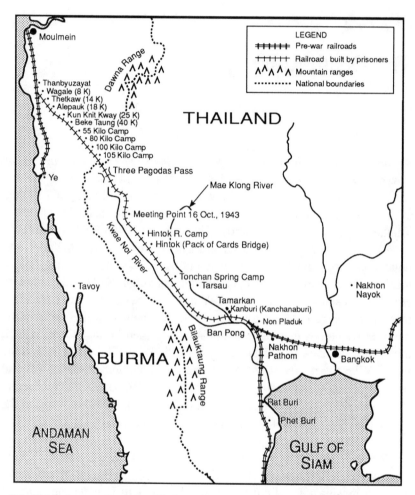

Sites of Primary Japanese Labor Camps along the Death Railway

The connecting railroad when finished followed the Mae Klong River from Ban Pong to Kanchanaburi, where it crossed the river. It then swung northwest to parallel the Kwae Noi River along its eastern bank until the headwaters were reached in the mountains of western Thailand. At the frontier of Burma the road cut through the Three Pagodas Pass* and slowly wound its way through a mountainous area of southern Burma before finally reaching Thanbyuzayat, which lay a few miles inland on the coastal plain of the Gulf of Martaban. When completed, the road was 261 miles (421 kilometers) long. It traversed rugged mountains, monsoon-flooded plains, swift-moving rivers, and inhospitable jungle. Moreover, it was located in one of the more disease-ridden areas of Southeast Asia.

A variety of factors made the railway desirable. Primarily, the Japanese needed to supply their army, which was fighting British forces in northern Burma. Japan lacked a merchant marine adequate to its imperial designs, and the railroad, by shortening the sea distance from the homeland to Rangoon, would ease the demand for ships to supply Burma, at the same time aiding the Japanese in preparations to invade India. A second purpose for the extension was to facilitate the transport of Burmese timber, oil, tungsten, and rice to metropolitan Japan.† Access to raw materials was the major reason for the creation of the Greater East Asia Co-Prosperity Sphere— Japan's imperialistic objective in Southeast Asia. The Japanese assumed that a more direct route to Rangoon would save time and money, making the co-prosperity sphere even more lucrative.

Furthermore, as the war progressed, American submarines and Allied aircraft threatened Japanese vessels once they passed through the Strait of Malacca and into the Indian Ocean. Thus, the railroad would hypothetically provide for greater security by landing cargoes at Bangkok instead of Burmese ports. Time, of course, would prove this assumption false, for no sooner was the railway completed than Allied bombers began to interrupt operations along its route.

Although the decision to use prisoners was not a primary reason for building the railroad, their use made the project more valuable to the Japanese. The Imperial Army had not expected to capture the large number of enemy troops that surrendered to them in Singapore, Sumatra, and Java.

---

*This pass, used for centuries by traders and their caravans, is located on the Burma-Thailand border and is so named because three Buddhist pagodas stand close together there. It is near the site where the northern and southern branches of the Burma-Thailand railway joined and construction crews met.

†Some writers suggest that the Japanese were developing an atomic bomb and needed the uranium deposits of Burma for fissionable material.

They did not relish feeding, housing, or otherwise attending to soldiers who, according to Japanese views, had disgraced themselves by surrendering. Nevertheless, some Japanese leaders felt bound by the conventions to which their nation had agreed regarding POWs and compelled by them to provide at least minimal sustenance to the prisoners. To the Japanese, it seemed logical that in return for food and housing the prisoners should work; what better place to set them to their chores, they thought, than in a nearly impenetrable jungle serving as a prison camp with a thousand-mile wall that could not be scaled. Although the Japanese decision seemed hypocritical to the POWs and a violation of the Geneva Convention, the men of the Rising Sun believed they were honoring the dishonorable by allowing their defeated foe the opportunity to work on a project sanctioned by the emperor.

The Japanese decided to construct the railroad at a time when their war effort was at floodtide, but they were not the first to envision this connection. During the late nineteenth century British planners had discussed it, and an English surveying party mapped the route later that was followed by Japanese engineers in 1942 and 1943. The British had given up their idea of building the railway in the prewar period, citing excessive requirements of both time and money. Japanese engineers at first estimated it would take five or six years to build the road, but when Tokyo gave permission to the Japanese Southern Army's commander, Field Marshal Count Juichi Terauchi, to use Allied POWs, the engineers reduced their estimate to eighteen months. Work was to begin in June 1942 but did not actually start until later. Nevertheless, the completion date of November 1943 remained the same. The Japanese later shortened the work period even more. In February 1943, Tokyo announced August of that year as the new target for finishing.

At first, the Americans who worked on the railroad did so in three groups. As time passed, a variety of circumstances intervened, and they slowly became separated from each other. The greatest number of them worked in A Force, commanded by the Australian Brigadier A. L. Varley, and were assigned to either Group 3 or Group 5 of the Thai POW administration.* Those in Group 3 included the 191 men commanded by Captain Fitzsimmons.† These were the first Americans to work on the line; they

---

*The Japanese ultimately had six POW groups, Groups 1 through 6, working on the railway. At times a group would be referred to as a branch.

†With the exception of the figure of 668 Americans working on the railroad, the numbers presented here are approximate. There is no way of knowing absolutely if 191, 458, and 19 are correct. Not only do the various prisoners interviewed disagree at times concerning numbers, but also do the several books written about

began work on October 30, 1942. The other body, headed by Colonel Tharp, consisted of 458 Americans, the largest number of Lost Battalion members to work as a unit anywhere. As part of Group 5, they began their labors on January 21, 1943, and were used mostly in Burma, from Thanbyuzayat to the Thai border, a distance of 70 miles (113 kilometers).*

Approximately nineteen other Americans were included in H Force, a group of aged and sick prisoners sent up in May 1943 from Singapore during the "Hurry-Hurry" or Speedo campaign. Although they labored the fewest number of days, they did some of the most grueling work. The Japanese used them on a thirteen-mile stretch between Tonchan and Hintok in the Dawna mountain range of western Thailand. They were the only Americans originally assigned to the area south of the Three Pagodas Pass. According to the Japanese organizational scheme, these men were part of the Ninth Railway Regiment, Southern Army Railway Corps, headquartered in Kanchanaburi, while their counterparts in Burma were part of the Fifth Railway Regiment, Southern Army Railway Corps, in Thanbyuzayat. Japanese commanders were in all cases the incompetents and misfits of the Imperial Army, and the guards were mostly Korean conscripts, whom one POW called the "Bully Boys of China," and another considered as "purely amoral coolie vermin . . . brutal by nature as well as by orders."

Regardless of where the Japanese located the prisoners, certain conditions existed in common. For work purposes they placed the Americans in *kumis*, units of fifty men, or in a *han*, composed of two *kumis*, headed by *kumichos* or *hanchos*. The work they did is described in the interviews, as are their labor conditions, living quarters, camp routines, the conduct of their guards, their food, and medical conditions. Their situation was primitive, brutal, and barbaric, with human kindness almost totally lacking in their Japanese and Korean captors.

The attitude of one of the Japanese commanders illustrates the situation in which the Americans found themselves during most of 1943. Major Mizdani, Japanese commander of Group 5, said that Japan would build the railroad even if it were necessary to starve the sick and let them die. He was responsible for the policy of "No Work, No Food" and reasoned that this would provide more food for the healthier prisoners, who would work harder as a result. In what seemed to be contemptuous mockery, he added,

---

the railroad. These are, however, close approximations. Fitzsimmons's men worked in Black Force, headed by an Australian, Lieutenant Colonel C. M. Black, commanding officer of the Second/Third Reserve Motor Transportation Company.
*For chronologies of the movements of Groups 3 and 5, see Appendix A.

"Any sick man who staggers to the line to lay one sleeper [railroad tie] will not have died in vain."

The most famous speech* to be given the prisoners was that of Lieutenant Colonel Yoshitida Nagatomo, commander of Group 3, who said, "We will build the railroad if we have to build it over the white man's body. It gives me great pleasure to have a fast-moving defeated nation in my power. You are merely rubble, but I will not feel bad because it is your rulers. If you want anything you will have to come through me for same and there will be many of you who will not see your homes again. Work cheerfully at my command." Among the endearing names Nagatomo called those who bothered to listen to his speech, which he delivered to all who worked in Burma and had posted at all camps there, were "a few remaining skeletons," "pitiful victims," and "merely rabble." To deter escape, he also mentioned the "ill-omened matters . . . in Singapore," where, he said, more than a thousand Chinese civilians were massacred.

Two quotations from POWs also help illuminate the scene. Ernest Gordon, in his memoir *Through the Valley of the Kwai*, writes, "During the four years they were in control, the Japanese military violated every civilized code. They murdered prisoners overtly by bayoneting, shooting, drowning, or decapitation; they murdered them covertly by working them beyond human endurance, starving them, torturing them, and denying them medical care." An officer in a Scottish regiment, Gordon became an American citizen after the war, joined the clergy of the Presbyterian Church, and served for many years as the dean of the chapel at Princeton University. Gordon's memoir reflects his tremendous piety.

Benjamin Dunn, in his reminiscence *The Bamboo Express*, has many telling passages about the cruelty of the Japanese and the suffering of Americans. None is more poignant than this simple statement: "Even though we heard *Taps* almost daily, we never got used to hearing it, for we knew that another of our friends would be left in the jungle. Even today, when I hear it, I always think of all those guys and tears come to my eyes." Allied servicemen of all nationalities died at a rate of 5.5 per mile of track; about fourteen thousand perished in one year.[†]

Of course, each interview that follows reinforces the impressions provided here. At camp after camp, which were numbered in kilos according to

---

*For the text of Lieutenant Colonel Nagatomo's speech, see Appendix B.
[†]The actual number is not known. Some writers place the number of POW dead at 16,000, or 64.5 per mile. After reading many varying accounts, the editors find 14,000 to be the most reliable estimate.

the distance from the base camp at either Thanbyuzayat, Burma, or Kanchanaburi, Thailand, the terror and agony continued. Still, as one reads the interviews there is something special about 80 Kilo Camp, the travesty called Hospital Camp, which was in fact a death camp. Prisoners dreaded the day they might be sent there, and many, although desperately sick, continued to work on the railway to delay that day. It was a place where the practice of the medical arts was truly art, for the doctors ministered without drugs or the other paraphernalia of their science.

In February 1943, because the war was turning against them, the Japanese moved the completion date for the railroad from November to August. Despite an effort that overworked the prisoners and native labor beyond human endurance—the Speedo campaign—that deadline could not be met. In late October and November, after the railroad was finished, the Japanese held memorial ceremonies and other celebrations at all the POW cemeteries and operational camps in Burma and Thailand to honor the dead and to commemorate the line's completion.

The prisoners despised the shamelessness and two-faced hypocrisy of the Japanese. At ceremonies in Burma's POW cemeteries, Nagatomo had a "letter of condolences" read to those who died building the railroad. He asked them to "please accept my deepest sympathy and regards and may you sleep peacefully and eternally." Moreover, the Japanese made the healthiest prisoners attend and used the occasion for propaganda, with movie cameras at work. Their efforts were for naught. October 25 marked the first day a train could run the length of the railroad. By that day, however, Allied bombing raids had rendered the road almost useless to Japan.

Later, in March 1944, the Japanese repeated the commemorative services in an even more bizarre affair at Camp Tamarkan, where a pyramid-shaped, twenty-five-foot cenotaph was raised. In his recollection *Prisoner of War: History of the Lost Battalion*, former Lieutenant Clyde Fillmore, Headquarters Battery, Second Battalion, 131st Field Artillery, writes that "this stone and concrete structure was the greatest travesty of all. It denied the very date it was dedicated, all the freedoms, liberties, and human dignity that men should accord one another. It was built by slave labor and thus became a symbol of the monstrous perfidy, treachery, and cruelty of a nation. I hoped it would stand forever in condemnation of what the Japanese had done to us."

At the end of 1943 and early in 1944 the Japanese began concentrating most of the POWs around Kanchanaburi, placing them in one of the following camps: Chungkai, Tamarkan, Kanburi, Nakhon Pathom, Non

Pladuk, and Tamauang (Tamuan). Groups 3 and 5 were integrated at Tamarkan, which became the new unit's headquarters. The nineteen men from H Force were now back in Singapore at the Sime Road Camp. For the Americans, the year of their most intense suffering was over, but they would remain prisoners for twenty-one more months.

Edward Fung
Battery F

Eddie Fung was born on June 20, 1922, in San Francisco. When he was sixteen he finished the tenth grade and ran away from home. He wanted to work with horses, so he went first to West Texas. He worked as a butcher and cowhand on ranches in Seminole, and in Tucumcari, New Mexico, before settling near Lubbock, Texas. He tried to join the cavalry but was too young, and his mother would not give her consent. Finally, in May 1940 he enlisted in Battery C, First Battalion, Texas National Guard. He was federalized with his unit in November and voluntarily transferred to Battery F, Second Battalion, just before it left Camp Bowie for the Orient.

As an American artilleryman of Chinese descent in the Second Battalion, Fung was unique, but, according to him, his treatment did not differ because of his ethnic background. When the battalion surrendered in Java, he felt badly, later stating, "I think we all had the feeling that we hadn't done enough, even though we didn't have anything to do it with. But you still have a feeling that you didn't do a good job. Maybe that hurt as much as anything."

Fung spent his years as a POW about as normally as could be expected for an American soldier in a Japanese prison camp during World War II. In the following pages he describes his ordeal while working as part of Black Force or Group 3, a "mobile force" that worked up and down the line on the Burma-Thailand Railroad.

"FROM MOULMEIN, we marched down to the railroad station, 191 of us in the Fitzsimmons group, and there I encountered an experience of humanity that I'll never forget. The Japanese had occupied Burma; they were the victors; they were winning all the way, and as far as anyone could see, they were going to take it all over. Here the whole population of Moulmein was along the route of our march from the prison to the railroad station tossing out cigarettes, bananas, candy, and all sorts of things.

"The Japanese tried to stop them, but it didn't do any good. There just weren't enough guards, and they weren't willing to shoot or harm the population. I guess they were trying to be on their good side. I had never seen grown men break down and cry, but we did. I mean, it was just that kind of an experience. The Burmese were out there for only one purpose, and that was to try to give us something—fruit, cigarettes, candy. So by the time we got down to the station, why, all of us had something that they'd given to us.

"After we got to the train station, we got on board trains to take us to the so-called base camp at Thanbyuzayat. We were railroaded in all the way. That was when we got our first sight of what we commonly called 'jungle camps'—of bamboo and atap roofs. The camps were a lot alike except for size. The huts would run, say, roughly 50 meters wide, about 150 meters long. There'd be an aisleway down the middle; there'd be wide platforms made of bamboo slats on each side. Total construction would be bamboo. Sometimes they would be put together with wires, but most of the time it would be jungle vine. The roof would be atap. They would cram in as many men as they could.

"If you were lucky, you would be off the ground so that during the rainy season, if the water ran through the hut, you wouldn't get completely wet. Still, the atap roof might leak, but if it didn't, the wind would still drive the rain in, because the huts were open-sided, open-ended as a rule. It was difficult to get any restful sleep, because aside from the fact that there were bedbugs in the bamboo slats, just being out in the open was enough to be uncomfortable.

"In the camp there would be a hut set aside to be called the hospital. It was just another hut except that all the people in there would be sick. One end maybe would be for a treatment room, say, for an orderly in case it was a dysentery hut where he would have to attend the people all through the night. There would be a cook shack, basically an open area where cooks would build mud fireplaces, with a roof over it. All the huts were alike; they just had different names. The camps themselves were maintained as cleanly as possible by camp personnel. By this time, the Japanese had equipped us with *wajans*, popularly known as woks nowadays. But they were large woks. The cooks had learned how to cook rice, so the rice was well prepared, although there was really not much else other than a very thin vegetable soup.

"A small camp might have 4,000 men; I guess a large camp, a working camp, might be as many as 8,000 or 10,000. Our advance group of Americans had 191 men, and even the larger group behind us couldn't have been more than, what, 600, but we never really met up with them. The Fitzsimmons group, mine, was lucky in the sense that we got there well before the end of the dry season, before the rainy season, and got used to the place. The second group that came in behind us, we heard, had been bombed and sustained casualties. They came up sort of close to the start of the rainy season. They were a larger group, but Americans were a minority in the camps.

"Thanbyuzayat was the beginning of the railroad, as far as the Japanese were concerned. When we got there, we got together on the parade ground, and we heard a formal lecture, I guess from Colonel Nagatomo, who got up on the reviewing stand and gave us a fine speech about what we were going to be doing under supervision of the Japanese. He spoke through an interpreter, I believe, although we heard rumors that he could speak English. I remember him saying, 'Be cheerful in your work' and all this sort of thing, that 'Work is good for you' and all that. At that time, why, it didn't seem that comical or cynical either. We thought, 'Okay, he's just giving us his sales pitch.'

"I think we stayed at Thanbyuzayat for about two or three days. I remember we stayed at least overnight, because the following morning we saw some Japanese doing physical punishment. Four Japanese soldiers had a small telephone pole, say about twenty feet long, held over their heads, and they were literally going around in circles at a fast jog. We thought, 'Holy smoke! They must have done something terrible to deserve that kind of physical punishment!' We found out that they had just been drunk. So we were wondering, 'What do they do when you do something bad?' Of course, by this time, we were really beginning to wonder about the Japanese. But after two or three days, they told us, 'We're moving up country,' and our first camp was going to be 40 Kilo Camp.

"As it turned out, the reason that we were going up to 40 Kilo Camp was that we were going to clear ground from 40 Kilo backwards toward Thanbyuzayat as well as working forward from 40 Kilo. Some progress and some track had been laid, I believe, as far as 25 Kilo Camp. We arrived in the jungle in October or early November 1942, because Kershner* and I set aside one can of bully beef—corned beef—for Thanksgiving. That was at 40 Kilo, so probably we got there in early November. From 40 Kilo, we went backwards to 25 Kilo once we found that there was inadequate water available.

"Forty Kilo Camp had been made up for and by natives, but it had deteriorated. We were told that we would be trucked all the way, and as it turned out, we were not. So we were walking, carrying our gear—there was

---

*Horace Kershner, of Battery D, died of stomach cancer on March 25, 1987, in Albuquerque, New Mexico.

a road alongside the right-of-way. When we got to 40 Kilo, why, we got settled in our huts. Mostly Australians were there. The first job we had to do was dig a well so we would have a supply of water. We were there for a matter of only two or three weeks, because it turned out that we did not have an adequate water supply. We did go out on some work parties starting to clear the right-of-way. That was when we found out what the work was going to be like, at least, we got a general idea. At that time, the work was relatively easy. We started out moving about three-quarters of a cubic meter of dirt. That was per man, including the officer in charge. A Japanese engineer would pace it out and stake it, and you would dig it out and carry it to the places that required the fill. It was soft dirt; it wasn't rocky, or it wasn't muddy or anything like that. It was still the dry season. The rainy season had not really gotten too heavy yet.

"I'm not a competitive person myself, but I realize that most Americans are. So the first few days, we would get out there, say, at four or five o'clock in the morning and be through by noon. The Japanese were very smart; they'd let us do it. On the way back, the Australians would tell us, 'Yanks, you're crazy! They're going to move it up!' And, sure enough, they moved it up a meter and then 1.2 meters. We were still doing it with relative ease. But the Australians were telling us, 'Take all day to do it. Don't do it in the shortest time possible, because they'll just keep adding on.' But the natural competitiveness of the American soldier, I guess, was enough to make him want to be the first one off the job.

"As I say, the work wasn't that difficult yet. We were in very good physical condition. The shovels were still pretty good; the picks were pretty good. But carrying the dirt away was when we came face-to-face with the primitiveness of the material we had to work with. Everyone was looking for wheelbarrows or something like that. What we had was a big rice sack with two poles on it: like a stretcher and two people, you know, one person on each end. It was just something you had to learn how to do. This was how we started. It was awhile before we got to the 'yo-ho pole' with the sacks on each end of the pole.*

"I don't know how the expression 'yo-ho pole' came about. It definitely was not a native expression. But the pole oscillates with the natural rhythm of the jogger. Once you get the natural rhythm of the pole, it's a very easy way to carry things. I remember at the racetrack in Java, a lady came by. She

---

*The 'yo-ho pole' had a sack hung at each end and was carried over the shoulder. Americans called it a 'yo-yo' or 'yo-ho' pole because of the sound uttered by the natives as they trotted along with their load.

had to be sixty years old or at least appeared to be. She had her merchandise on these two baskets on the end of a pole, so she set it down to trade with the soldiers. Miller* indicated that he wanted to try to lift the load. She looked at him and said, 'Go ahead.' Miller got under the stick, and he tried to lift it up. He would be off balance, and it would go one way down and one way up; he could never get the hang of it. Once he got it up on his shoulders, he could never really move with it any distance. A bunch of other fellows wanted to try, and they had no more success. When the woman got through trading, why, she just shrugged her shoulders a little bit, got the pole under her shoulders, and just jogged off laughing all the way. That was when I found out there had to be a trick to everything, just like carrying one hundred kilos. You couldn't just carry dead weight; you had to make it live.

"We had Korean guards at 25 Kilo Camp, because there we met Christian George. We hung nicknames on all of the them, and he was one of the more humorous Koreans. For instance, one time he was disciplined for having a dirty rifle, and he was told to clean it. So he took it down to the creek and got some soap and water. He just got into more trouble. They wouldn't feed him, so he would get in chow line with the prisoners and ask if it was all right if he got some rice from us because they wouldn't feed him in the Japanese kitchen. He said he was a Christian, and he seemed to be. I mean, he never bashed anyone around.

"The general run of the Korean guards was not humorous at all. Just as the Chinese are known as the Jews of the Orient, the Koreans are known as the Bullies of the Orient. There are reasons for it, probably, because they'd been overrun by the Chinese on the one hand, the Japanese on the other hand. I mean, I can understand it, but I can never feel anything but intense hate for these Koreans. He was low man on the totem pole, so he took it out on anyone who was available. But dammit, he did it with too much pleasure; that was the thing that I don't forgive him for.

"Again, you know, there's a story about Christian George when he came across two prisoners of war trading with the natives. He knew something was wrong; someone had done some wrong, and somebody had to pay for it, because those were the rules. So he gave the bullock which was pulling the cart a kick, and he decided that would square everything. He was one of the few guards that never hit a prisoner, which was very unusual, and he was greatly appreciated.

---

*Everett W. Miller was a member of Battery E, the battery that was sent to Japan. Miller now lives in Stillwater, Oklahoma.

"Formally, we were not allowed to contact the natives at all. But if you happened to come across one, you could buy things from them, and the Japanese would not bother you too much. It was at 25 Kilo when Colonel Black started the Red Cross fund. All the officers were paid according to rank, except that for some strange reason they all wound up with twenty dollars. The explanation was that the Japanese were charging them for room and board and setting aside money in banks in Japan so that after the war was over they'd have something to start with. So just by coincidence all of the officers wound up with twenty dollars.

"Colonel Black decided all officers were going to contribute half of their pay to set up a common fund to buy Red Cross supplies: soap, toothpaste, fruits and vegetables, bananas for the sick people. At the time we were being paid ten cents a day, fifteen cents a day for noncoms. So if you worked thirty days, you'd earn as much as three dollars. No, you couldn't work thirty days. The Japanese worked on a ten-day basis—ten days work and one day off. So you could earn as much as, say, two-fifty. So for the officers, who didn't really work, to have ten dollars was quite a sum.

"Also we bartered. We learned that the natives were after anything of material value, like clothing or if you had a watch. Because they were being paid in Japanese occupational money, which was just run off the printing press. So they decided they would trade that kind of paper for anything of material value. So you could sell a shirt, sweater, pants, shoes, socks, or an item of great value like wristwatches or cameras. I think some people even had guns; some of the Australians had guns and what they called mill bombs, hand grenades. There was an amazing accumulation of junk that the prisoners picked up and retained and kept as long as they could.

"Well, we worked to 25 Kilo Camp, and from there, because the railroad progressed up, our next camp was 55 Kilo. That's where I picked up malaria and dysentery. Then from 55 Kilo, I believe we moved up to about the eighty-kilometer mark, 80 Kilo to about 105 Kilo. The 105 Kilo was probably the worst period, because 105 Kilo was the farthest extent of the railroad from Thanbyuzayat to the supply line. The farther you were from supplies, why, the less you got. Of course, by this time we're speaking of the end of 1943. Your physical condition has deteriorated.

"By the time I got to 55 Kilo the work was getting harder; there were fewer people able to work, so there was more work to be done. There was also beginning to be a different kind of work. We were building small bridges. The country was changing from level to more hilly. As we got toward the 100 Kilo, it became downright mountainous, so that there were more bridges to be built, which was a different kind of work from just digging out dirt and carrying it away or putting it someplace else. I mean, here we're talking about pile driving, sawing down trees, and dragging them down to make pilings to begin with. We didn't have good tools to work with; the axes weren't sharp. Just generally speaking the work was becoming more difficult, and we were getting weaker, and there were fewer of us.

"I was intrigued by Japanese bridge building, because I was amazed at their ingenuity. Again, we go back to stereotypes, and you think of the Japanese as being what they are. Here we were in intimate contact with them; we're seeing them, sure, as conquerors and prisoners, but also as human beings. So on the first big project we had, we were wondering how in the world are they going to build a bridge that has to be one hundred yards long. We were wondering, 'How in the devil are they going to do that? This isn't just knocking something together to cross a little ditch.' By golly, we learned. They could do it and do it with what was available. It didn't require advanced technology, steel, nails, or bolts or anything else. Whatever was available in the jungle was going to do the job.

"Always in our minds we tried to figure out, 'Now what would we do if we had to build it?' It never turned out our way, because the Nips had a different approach to things. Right off the bat, we cut down trees to make the piles. Then we cut down enough different kinds of trees for scaffolding. We started to build the scaffold. Then as we got part of the scaffolding built, we'd stand up piles and lock them into position—not drive them, just stand them in position. We'd get hundreds of these piles just standing up in this scaffold framework. Then we'd set up the scaffolding for the pile driver, which was nothing more than a five hundred-kilo block with a smaller hole through it, with a stationary bar that acted as a guide on which it went up and down. The bar was driven into the top of the piling, which was sharpened on one end and had a hole drilled in the other where the guide bar was put in. We built the scaffolding so that it had pulleys on top, then ropes radiating out from the top, and twenty men on a rope pulling up the pile driver along the bar and then letting it drop.

"Of course, we started to employ tricks, not just to sabotage the works but to cut the workload. The piling would be started with a hole that was dug maybe about a meter deep. Next the Japanese would mark the pole to the depth that they wanted it driven. So what we would do is fill the hole with brush and dirt on top, and we would saw the pole off. If we had to drive it in, say, ten feet, why, we would saw off five feet of it, never realizing that somebody's going to have to ride over this bridge sometime in the future. Eventually, the piling would sink, of course, but by that time, we were long gone. We were employing every trick we could to make out as if we had fulfilled our work quota. We were taking short cuts so that we had, at least from the Japanese point of view, fulfilled our work quota. But it wasn't really an intentional act of sabotage. You might look upon it almost like a game. I guess it was. It was nothing like *Hogan's Heroes* or anything like that, but it was a game. The Japanese were at a disadvantage. There were never a great number of them, so they could never cover all of the ground.

"Well, by the time of 55 Kilo Camp most of us had lost some weight. Let's see, I'm trying to think what was the worst camp. Well, there's no such thing as the worst camp. We probably had lost 50 percent of what we were going to lose. It was just general overwork and exposure to the weather. We were on short rations, roughly a quarter-pound of rice a day. We were not skin and bones; we were mostly muscle. But the elements were beginning to get to us, the mosquitoes and the constant harassment of hot and cold, wet and dry.

"We were at the beginning of the Speedo campaign. We found out later that Nagatomo had one year to complete his job, and he could see that it was not going to be finished in that time. The word was that he would have to commit hara-kiri, or he would be beheaded if he didn't do his job. I guess he was determined that neither thing was going to happen to him. That was why the Speedo period was instituted, although later on I believe he did get a two-month extension. It took us about fourteen months to finish the road. The Japanese and Koreans started a reign of terror. They would start bashing for no apparent reason, except they thought that it would help speed up work. I think workloads got up to about 2.5 meters a day.

"Our favorite expression for our work day then was 'from can't see to can't see,' or from four o'clock in the morning to whenever you finished. There was no such thing as hoping that if you didn't finish your job they would send you home. You stayed out there until it was finished. One time there was a bombing raid; they bombed and hit a cut and it filled in, and we worked five days and nights continuously to clear it. No sleep. That was when we found out that the Japanese had no intention of not building the road. So it was the common consensus that, 'They're determined to build this road, so let's get the damn thing built!' We didn't think in terms of helping the war effort or anything else. They wanted it and the only way out was to get out the other end; it was as simple as that. It was probably the worst six or eight months of the whole fourteen-month period.

"It's bad enough to carry dirt, but to carry waterlogged dirt just adds to the load. Of course, by this time most people had no shoes, so carrying even fifty pounds on slippery ground was just almost impossible. In many cases it was impossible. You had to take roundabout ways of getting your dirt to an area which might have formerly taken fifty feet. It would now take you several hundred yards. It was so bad you'd just literally sink down. We had to go out and rescue trucks. They could not negotiate, and there wasn't enough track laid that supply trains could get up to the railhead.

"You were never dry, not even when you got into bed, because, you know, it was just incredible, the amount of rain that comes down at one time. Of course, by this time a lot of people didn't even have blankets, or they were getting pretty threadbare. The humidity just chewed everything up. That was one reason that earlier—before the Speedo period—a lot of people were beginning to sell their items. They realized that the humidity was going to wreck everything, and that they would never be able to realize any benefits out of them. So they decided that they may as well get some money out of them.

"Clothing was getting to be a problem. We were getting into the G-string era. I think it was Brimhall* that first made and put on a G-string. He felt kind of silly, because he was the first American. We still hung onto shorts and things like that. Brimhall still had shorts, but he decided that in order to stretch his clothing that he was going to have to make them into G-strings. But it wasn't long after that that we were all wearing G-strings. That was all that was available. As much as possible, people hung onto their razors as long as they could, and they would sharpen their razor blades on the beer bottles and things of that nature. Of course, a prized item would be the Britishers' Rolls type of thing that comes with a self-sharpening kit of some sort. Anyway, the Americans didn't have it, so they would make their double-edged blades last as long as possible.

"The other thing, of course, was to just grow a beard. Haircuts were by the camp barber, and ours was Paul Leatherwood.[†] I scrounged him a straight-edged razor and hair clippers from the Japanese. He had that for years, even after the war. You paid for haircuts, so I kept mine long. I didn't have facial hair, and I didn't have lice. I spent my money on soap, and I think once I even splurged and got some toothpaste. That didn't help because I didn't have a toothbrush. I frayed the end of a twig. After that, I lost most of my teeth; it didn't help. I bought this stuff at the canteen in camp run by the prisoners but supplied by the Japanese. You could buy eggs, soap, tobacco, toothpaste, things like that.

---

*Clifford O. Brimhall of Battery F now lives in Mesquite, Texas, a Dallas suburb.
†Leatherwood was in Battery F. He now lives in Kermit, Texas, forty-five miles west of Odessa, near the southeastern corner of New Mexico.

"The Japanese fed us always in the same way regardless of what the conditions were; you took food out with you. You'd leave in the morning, and you didn't come back until you were done. When you came back, you got your evening meal. The cooks were always good enough to stay up until work parties were fed. But your noon meal—whatever it was—was taken out with you. You might get a half-hour break for lunch but no more than that.

"Basically, we ate rice. The only thing that we really found in the jungle were scorpions and centipedes, gigantic centipedes! Six inches wide, two feet long! I never saw sights like that before! You'd be digging and all of a sudden something would crawl out of a hole, and you couldn't believe your eyes. But of edible things, there were no dogs or cats. We heard monkeys in the jungle but never could catch any. The only thing I remember, we did catch a python one time, and that was all. It was cooked up in a soup. Everybody got something out of it. We had to borrow a Japanese rifle to kill it. The guard was going to kill it, but after a few misses one of the prisoners suggested that he pass the rifle over, and he shot the snake. But we probably could have choked it to death, because it had just finished a meal and was very lethargic. But we decided to play it safe and shoot it.

"The only place you could scrounge anything was from the Japanese. My favorite target was the Japanese kitchen. Some of the people who worked there—Slug [Wright] was one of the American prisoners who worked for the Japanese kitchen—told me that they started mining the kitchen because there was so much pilfering from there. So I decided I had to watch to see which way the Japanese went in, because there had to be a safe way in and out. So it didn't slow us down too much, except that we had to be careful.

"The mosquitoes were the things you couldn't protect yourself against. At 55 Kilo Camp I had malaria, and the standard treatment for malaria, of course, was quinine. It was available in small quantities, and it was powder, not tablets. So it was difficult to swallow. Unfortunately, I was allergic to quinine. I found that out the first time they dosed me. Luckily, Doc Hekking, who we met up with at the 25 Kilo Camp, got me out of it. He told me, 'Eddie, you can't take quinine. It is poisonous to your system.' 'So,' he said, 'from now on when you get malaria, all you can do is cover up when you get chills. Sweat it out. I can't help you.' So it was just a matter of sweating it out. The first bout lasted about four weeks before I could shake it off. A year and a half later, I could shake it off in a matter of ten days or a couple of weeks.

"Doctor Hekking was the Dutch doctor that stayed with us most of the way and who understood the use of jungle herbs, because he learned some of that in Indonesia where he was from. On the job you'd get cuts and bruises, and they wouldn't heal; they'd become ulcerous. Once your skin was open, all sorts of infections can occur. This particular thing, I believe, is like a spirochete. It digs inward. It can be a very small wound, but it goes deep. In severe cases, it ate clear around the shinbone of the leg. In the average case, a good-sized ulcer would be about two to four inches long and about an inch or two wide in the leg area. The average-sized scar, if you were lucky and caught the ulcer in time, might be only about an inch in diameter.

"We had no way of treating them except for Doctor Hekking's famous silver spoon, where he'd scrape down through the ulcer and draw blood. Hopefully, it would scab over without pus being entrapped underneath. All you could do was keep it clean and hope it scabs over without pus underneath. If you see yellow underneath, which is pus, you had to break it open and scrape some more. It was a matter of withstanding pain. The only reason you could stand the pain was because you knew the alternative was to have your damn leg cut off. If the scraping didn't work, if it went beyond that, it became almost hopeless. Many times, doctors had to amputate.

"Some fellows put maggots in the ulcers, but I never did. They would get the wound as clean as possible and put in X number of maggots. All you had to do was walk to the latrine. It was crawling in maggots. Anyhow, they'd put in, say, ten maggots and let them eat the wound clean, and hopefully they'd get ten out. They had to make sure they got all ten out! There were two things that were highly prized, one more than the other. One was a so-called sulfanilamide pill, which you could scrape a little powder from, and that would really help. The other one was iodoform, which is kind of like an iodine-type thing. This was like gold. So your best hope was to keep the wound covered with a clean cloth—you'd just boil the hell out of it to keep it clean—and just hope.

"Now I had dysentery, and, again, the treatment was makeshift. Charcoal was the favorite way of getting something into your stomach and intestinal lining. Ground charcoal, ground or powdered charcoal, you'd eat it. But there wasn't anything that the medical people could do. They could sympathize with you. By this time, if you went to the hospital, you were really sick. If you had any sense at all, you'd try to stay out of there, because you knew that the chances were not that good that you would ever come out of there. The hospital wasn't too bad yet at 55 Kilo Camp, but it gradually got to the point that the farther up you got, the closer the hospital came to being a death house.

"I was never off the job except for malaria or dysentery. From my own personal experiences, I could have gone off the job by reporting to sick call. But I never wanted to go because of two reasons. I was afraid to admit to myself that I was sick, and I knew that they couldn't do anything for me in the hospital that I couldn't do outside. The other thing was, as long as I could report to work, there was a full ration. The camp was not given a full ration for you if you were sick, so therefore the camp suffered, since they would share everybody's rations with the sick person. Besides, I was deathly afraid of becoming sick. Except for about a week of malaria that I stayed out, why, I more or less worked all the way through.

"Well, from the time I moved from 55 Kilo, it gradually got worse and worse and worse until 105 Kilo Camp was absolutely the bottom of the pit. It was more mountainous, and it was high in the mountains and definitely cold at night. You were already in a weakened condition. You were still in the monsoon season. Supplies were short. I even had to go scrounge for rice, I mean, for our basic camp supplies, not just for my own use. So that was the worst. I guess once we got over that and were going to Thailand, well, we were in good shape. The difference between 80 Kilo and 105 Kilo Camp was minor. The work was basically still cuts and fills; you're breaking up rocks for ballast, you're cutting timber, or you're doing carpentry work. You're doing the usual things like gathering firewood for the camp cook houses. You're boiling water for your own drinking supply.

"If you're inside the camp, if you're a cook, that's a pretty good job. There was no question that they ate a little better than the average prisoner. Another good job would be the cashier officer. For instance, Captain Fitzsimmons went down to the base camp and got the cash and brought it back. You could be a hospital orderly. It was a distasteful job, but it wasn't strenuous. Many people who couldn't work or contribute would volunteer as orderlies. For instance, one Britisher volunteered for smallpox orderly because he had had smallpox. Many people volunteered for distasteful things, because they knew they had to be done. The good jobs out on the road would be any job which gave you an opportunity to scrounge something. It didn't matter what the job was as long as there was an opportunity to scrounge. Of course, it had to be from the Japanese.

"During the fourteen months of the building of the railroad the death rate went to a peak just about at the middle of our stay. [Lieutenant Roy] Stensland had made a bar graph, and it was very graphic. Starting in

October, the middle of fourteen months would be about April or May 1943. Again, we were right in the rainy season. They tried to give a man a decent burial. I remember the first one at 40 Kilo. They made a shroud, tried to make a coffin. They got contingents from each nationality to have an honor guard. But all that deteriorated to where if a man was lucky, he had a rice sack for a shroud; and depending on the weather, if we could dig a hold to cover him, we would. If it was the dry season, many times you were lucky to dig a hole a foot deep. If it was the rainy season, the hole would fill with water. You tried because it was the decent thing to do, but that was all.

"The burial site maps were made for every American. There are no Americans buried in Kanchanaburi or the Chungkai cemetery. I went over and looked through them. All Americans were brought back home, because the military had accurate information about everyone that was buried. Now, the Fitzsimmons group lost very few people—eleven or twelve out of 191.

"Some men gave up on life. I remember the classic example distinctly. I didn't believe him at the time. He was a little Dutchman, a native of Holland. He said in 1942 that if he wasn't free by a certain date in early 1943 that he wouldn't live anyway, and so he killed himself. Now, of course, he had a self-fulfilling prophecy. But other people just gave up. I don't know any classic cases. They'd just start thinking about how depressing conditions were and what it was like at home and how great it would be to be home again, not realizing that they had to get through this period of hell. Somewhere in between, they'd just not make it.

"Some stopped eating. Most of them did. In fact, that's how a lot of people in the hospital made it. If they had the will to live, they could scrounge more rations, because some people either didn't have the appetite to eat or took not eating as a way out. I know it sounds hard-hearted, but my attitude was that if a man didn't want to live, there's no way to instill the will into him. If he wanted to live, I'd help him in every way I could. But if he gave me the impression or showed me the attitude that he didn't care, I just didn't have enough energy to expend on him. We never resented the fact that men were sick and didn't draw rations from the Japanese for themselves on paper. My own personal point of view was that I hoped these guys would get better and get out of the hospital. I never resented their being there or wanting to die; no, I was always sorry when I heard that people had died. Not because of the additional workload, but just because they died so uselessly.

"When I heard about the cholera and people dying wholesale, you know, it horrified me. I was brought up by a mother who lived in the United

States for sixty years, and she never drank a drop of water that was not boiled. She said because, 'When I was a little girl, I saw some people die from cholera.' It didn't make an impression on me until I saw cholera. People literally die before your eyes. I mean, they vomit, and they excrete; they die from both ends. You can see a person melt down, literally die before your very eyes. There was this British camp between 80 and 115 Kilo Camps. You could smell it for miles. They were dying from cholera. Even the Japanese gave the camp the detour. From what we heard, before the British left that camp, they were burning up people who were really not dead yet, but they had to leave, and they couldn't take the chance.

"There was one time that I lived in total fear for my life. I ran out of water when I was out on a working party. I came across a running brook. Remembering my Boy Scout training, why, this had to be purified water, because it had been running for X number of miles. I took a drink, and from that minute on I lived in apprehension. I swore that from that day on every drop of water I drank was going to be boiled.

"During this time the thing constantly on my mind was scrounging, you know, being aware of what was scroungeable and whether I could scrounge it or not; hell, it was always food I wanted. Because even when you're scrounging you're scrounging for food. For instance, I was sort of the camp tinsmith. I made buckets for people to boil water with or made frying pans whenever we could scrounge the material. My scrounging led to a hatchet, pliers, hammers, and chisels. But all that was to get food, and tobacco.

"You not only talk about food that you've had; you talk about food that you're going to have; you talk about how you would prepare it or what you would order. You usually only talk about these things after you've had a meal, because otherwise it would literally drive you up the wall to even think about food, because your gastric juices would operate without anything else encouraging them. There were times like the emperor's birthday when they would give you a day off, and you would even get paid for it. They would give extras. They might give you a whole hog for the camp; they might give you a little sake. The cooks would put out an extra effort to make it festive. They might even organize a race day. Everyone tried to make it a festive day. But on days like that, if you've had a relatively satisfying meal, then you sit around talking about more food.

"The next thing you talked about is family. You would think a bunch of men would talk about sex, but that's so far down the line that it was almost never talked about, because there were so many more important things to talk and feel about. Food and family were definitely the main topics, and especially around Christmastide. I mean, especially with us in the camps. The feeling of Christmas was genuine. I'm not a Christian, never have been, probably never will be, not in the formal sense. I didn't pray to God for strength or anything else. But Christmas had real meaning, not just this business about exchanging gifts or anything like that.

"Let's see, it wasn't until we got to Thailand that we got mail. In terms of sending out word, I believe there were two opportunities. I remember at Singapore, we were given a postcard to fill in. You might say, 'I am well; I am not well,' so on and so forth. I believe you could write ten words, and they cautioned you to be sure it was, shall we say, noncontroversial, noncommittal. I sent a postcard home. We were given an opportunity further down the line; I can't remember exactly when. I know it was during the jungle period. I did not utilize that opportunity. I thought, 'Okay, if the first card got home, my mother would know I was alive. But now that I'm in this situation, I'm not going to encourage her anymore, because I might not make it out of here.' So I did not write.

"Well, we finally got out of the jungle, let's see, in January 1944. We went to Kanburi. We saw the other half of the railroad, and we realized that the workers on that half had a more difficult task than we did. They were building bridges in rocky conditions. They were dynamiting and blasting to get their work done. But at least we could ride; we rode on the railroad. We were a little apprehensive about how good the builders had been or how diligent they had been. But we got down to Kanburi, and by comparison, why, it was like heaven. It was a literal change from hell to heaven."

From the camp near Kanchanaburi, Tamarkan Camp, Fung went to Chungkai and then to Nakhon Nayok, northeast of Bangkok. Here, he spent the remainder of the war, building a camp "from scratch." The prisoners dug caves, cleared roads, and helped fortify the area where, apparently, the Japanese intended to make a last stand. Along the way, Fung came under American air attack several times and complained that "you've just gotten out of the jungle period, and now your own people are after you, and you know that they are much more efficient than the Japanese."

The end of the war was somewhat anticlimactic for Fung. When the Japanese announced the war had ended, he and his fellow prisoners stood in stunned silence for several minutes before reacting with some cheers. Each nationality constructed its national flag to fly in the camp. Fung followed the usual route of American POWs home, through the military hospital in Calcutta. Back in the States he had trouble getting used to eating. He also felt uneasy about his role in the war and the hero's welcome he received after it. He said, "They were treating us as if we were something extraordinary. My own personal feeling was that we hadn't really contributed anything to winning the war." After the war, Fung returned to civilian life in December 1946 and worked as a metallurgist. He has since retired but still continues to "live each day to the fullest" in his hometown of San Francisco.

Crayton R. ("Quaty") Gordon
Service Battery

Not all the Americans who helped build the Burma-Thailand railway were part of A Force, the unit that worked south out of Burma to Thailand. The Japanese attached "Quaty" Gordon and nineteen* other Americans to H Force, a company of 3,270 Dutch, Australian, and British POWs working northward. The Americans were those left behind at the Changi compound when the others shipped to Moulmein in October 1942 and January 1943. Like Gordon, the others stayed because they were ailing. In fact, most of this later levy of Changi prisoners included the aged and ill, some of whom had not yet recovered completely. Gordon, who suffered from a terrible case of malnutrition, had an infected papilloma removed by a British physician at Changi compound in late 1942. As a result, he did not leave Singapore until May 5, 1943.

Gordon was born in Itasca, a town thirty-five miles south of Fort Worth, Texas, on July 8, 1919, and after graduation from high school moved to Lubbock, where he attended Texas Technological College while working a full shift at the Good Eats Bakery. He joined Battery C, Second Battalion, 131st Field Artillery, in May 1940 for the money and because his friends belonged. He became a cook, but before the unit settled in at Camp Bowie, he transferred to Service Battery as a dispatcher. He did not cook again until he temporarily took over mess duties for the Nineteenth Bomb Group at Singosari, Java.

While being shipped from Pearl Harbor to Brisbane, Australia, seamen from the USAT *Republic* roughed up Gordon during ceremonies when the vessel crossed the equator. He had his right shoulder dislocated, received a concussion, and had "both knees all bunged up!" The shoulder would be a problem all during captivity, since it regularly slipped out of joint and medics reset it without anesthetics. The magnitude of his difficulties were not clear until he became a POW. "Being twenty-two years old," he stated, "it didn't all sink in; it really didn't. See, that's why they get young men for

---

*Another member of the group, John W. Wisecup, whose interview is in this chapter, says there were thirteen.

soldiers." After being captured he was one of the small group of Americans kept at the Chinese School in Batavia before going to Bicycle Camp. At the camp he suffered a severe bout of amebic dysentery, dropping to one hundred pounds before recovering. A Korean guard, "the Brown Bomber, a little banty-legged bastard," also dislocated the shoulder again.

Gordon's interview is unique because he spent most of his time with non-American troops, and, although his experiences were not essentially different from those of most of the other Americans, they do concern a different phase of the railroad's construction.

"WE WERE AT KANBURI SEVERAL DAYS before we started the journey up into the jungle. I could have remained behind because of my shoulder, but I chose to go because I think I was the only NCO in the group. I hoped in the back of my mind that in the jungle on the railroad or somewhere I'd meet our other people. That's what I hoped. We didn't know they were going to Burma when they left Singapore. So I thought I might run into them. We started walking by day, and we crossed this so-called Bridge on the River Kwai, you know, the one which was not over the Kwai River. I believe that it was on the Mae Klong River.* The bridge was over that river, and the railroad was built along the east bank of the Mae Klong. It was just an old trestle-type bridge. From then on, we walked by day, and how many days I don't know!

"We were on a path, and the Japanese were using the same path to move their troops up into Burma, or maybe India. The jungle off to the side of the path was real thick with bamboo; bamboo clusters were everywhere and huge teakwood trees and various other trees. The only other one I remember was the one they called an ironwood. We used a great deal of teakwood in the trestles of the bridges.

"We first went to a place called Tarsau, and then to Tamarkan. We passed through them. Of course, we would get food as we went up the route. We finally got to an area where we ran across some Australians who had been in Bicycle Camp. This was at a place called Hintok. They had two

---

*Gordon is correct. Two bridges, one of wood and the other of steel and concrete, were built across the Mae Klong near its confluence with the Kwae Noi at Kanchanaburi, Thailand. These are assumed to be at the site depicted in the movie *The Bridge on the River Kwai*. The men who built the bridges lived in the nearby Chungkai Camp, which was on the banks of the Kwae Noi. The wooden bridge was destroyed and the steel bridge heavily damaged by RAF and USAAF bombers in 1944 and 1945.

camps called Hintok, or maybe they just moved one from the first Hintok down the river and into the jungle, and it carried the same name. I don't know.

"But anyhow, they moved us, oh, to within several hundred yards of this group of Australians who were in F Force. It appeared that they had a good food supply, because they had cattle, onions, and, of course, rice. I believe it was pumpkin or sweet potatoes that they had in their stew. But they were supplied out of a Bangkok command, and we were under the Singapore command, and we had nothing; our supplies were extremely skimpy. The Australians gave us some of their food, but then their guards told them that if they had too much food, and they could afford to give it away, then they were getting too damn much, and so they became afraid of losing their own rations if they gave us anymore. Since I had some friends there, sometimes I'd go over late at night and get extra rice or maybe beef broth.

"Our quarters were tents, old British tents. Most of the other camps along the line were bamboo huts, but this one was tents. The Australians had built a reservoir, a water reservoir with a dam. Using all the bamboo that was available, man, they had the most elaborate pipe system you've ever seen—water piped everywhere. As it turned out, the water was contaminated with cholera. But it was nice for showers. You'd keep your mouth shut. We could pull a plug out of a trough going by, and here came a good stream of water down on you.

"We had to walk approximately four miles to the work site, which was a trestle; that was the project of this particular camp. We built more bridges on our part of the railroad going north, because after you crossed the Three Pagodas Pass in Burma, the river started. I assume more tributaries fed into the river also. They'd build trestles across draws or canyons instead of filling them up and building drainage underneath. My God, you'd have had to carry a helluva lot of dirt in peck-sized baskets to fill up a big fill. But they trestled across these ravines. You'd start off getting the trestle's footing ready to go. The ground was cleared, and the dirt cleaned off of the rock. Star drills and a sledgehammer were used to drill holes for dynamite. The Japs used dynamite or possibly some gelignite for blasting the rocks. Where the concrete—the cement—came from, I don't know, but they'd level off the area when they got the rock down far enough, and they'd pour a foundation.

"We benefited from the dynamite, which I'll relate later on. But this hand drilling for the dynamite was slow, and it was a helluva lot of work slinging a sledgehammer. But anyhow, we got the base poured. Then they'd use a base log to start the trestle. It was a teakwood log, oh, thirty inches, three feet in diameter, and they'd use an adz to square it. They'd use chisels to hollow out sockets in this log for uprights. The part of the trestle that I was working on was a three-tiered thing approximately ten or twelve feet high per tier. We'd cut trees right out of the jungle alongside the right-of-way and haul them down. The Japs did have one big, round power saw. It was used primarily to saw the cross-brace supports to go across the uprights. They'd just rip an ironwood log into a long slender log and use it for cross timbers, and, of course, we'd drill holes with a hand drill and bolt the logs together.

"I worked on this trestle for quite a long time, until I dislocated my shoulder again. I had dislocated it again shortly before I had gone up to Thailand from Singapore. Anyhow, I dislocated my shoulder once more on the trestle. I was lowered to the ground by a fellow who was working with me. I was tightening a bolt and slipped. I dropped my wrench, and, of course, dislocated my shoulder and was hanging on with my left hand. Some fellows—Americans—helped me get down to the ground.

"When I got to the ground, why, a Korean guard beat the hell out of me again, because he assumed that I was throwing the wrench at him, you see. There again, the beating wasn't too severe, or it didn't feel as severe as it might have had my shoulder not been hurting. But I got beat up quite extensively with a handle similar to a pick handle, and I got teeth knocked loose. The amazing thing is that I pushed them back in place, and damn if they didn't tighten up. I was very, very fortunate.

"My shoulder was out of socket this time about sixteen hours. We went back to camp, and the English doctors tried to put my shoulder back in place, and they just could not manage it. They got permission from the Japanese to let one of the men go to the camp below, Kanu II, I believe. They had Kanu I and Kanu II, and Kanu II was more the headquarters for H Force and was primarily Australian. The Japs let a man go there, and he got some chloroform and brought it back, and they gave me some chloroform to reduce the pain in my shoulder. But sitting there trying to be immobile, and muscle spasms and all, it was torture, literally torture!

"This was in July. I was hurt in July of '43. I had two full months of work there, May to July, and counting Hintok and the river, May to October of '43. Of course, by October of '43, we were down on the river, the Kwae Noi River, but I'll come to that a little bit later. The Speedo campaign was on, and it meant long hours of work. The work parties would be formed long before daylight, and we'd draw our bit of rice to eat. We got a couple of rice balls to take to work with us. We would fill our canteens with tea. Of course, we had all the tea in the world. We absolutely boiled our water. Well, we'd go out. The sand flies were terrible. Little ol' sand flies, they were very, very small. They'd just bite the hell out of you before daylight. Then we would walk in the dark to work and reach the work area at approximately daylight. Many times it would be into the night before we would get back to camp again. The work hours were anywhere from fourteen to eighteen hours a day.

"All this time we had the monsoons. One overlapped the other, Speedo and the monsoons, you know. Hell, getting to work was the worst part, because, you know, you'd be pulling through mud, and you'd be absolutely exhausted by the time you got to the work area. Working on the trestle wasn't bad in the rain, but getting to work was where it was so terrible. As I say, I got hurt on this trestle—got this severe beating, too. The Japanese in charge of the segment where we were working didn't seem like a soldier; he was more or less like a civilian, maybe an engineer, I don't know. But he spoke English very well, and he was a decent sort of fellow. After I got this beating, he said in perfect English, 'That was all uncalled for.' He wrote me out a little piece of paper in Japanese and said, 'You keep this, and this will state that you were injured on the job, and you won't have to come back to work until you get well.' Hell, I never did get well! I went back to this hospital camp, and, my God, it was terrible!

"This is where men went to die—strictly. There was no medicine, nothing. You got well or you died, but mostly you died. But I went to the hospital; I had to so as not to have to go to work. I was with the British, and we had a few Australians in this group. For example, on my row there was an Australian here, next was an Englishman, and then me. Well, this Englishman died between us, so we thought it might be a good idea not to tell anybody for a couple of days and draw his rations. So we split them. But then he got to stinking so bad, we had to tell them he was dead. So they started to haul him away, and he had a pretty good blanket. So we said, 'Hell, he won't need that blanket where he's going,' so we took turns using his blanket. God Almighty!

"We had some bad ulcer cases in the jungle. A guy named Cy Moore* bumped his leg on bamboo, and his ulcer developed finally to where he was immobile. He just couldn't walk. He got in terrible shape and had no facilities, no bandages, no medicine, no nothing. This tropical ulcer was a thing that is just almost unimaginable to someone who hasn't seen it. In

---

*Gordon is referring to Glenn E. ("Cy") Moore of Headquarters Battery, who died at the hospital camp in Kanchanaburi, Thailand, in November 1943. Gordon describes Moore's death from dysentery later in the interview.

severe cases, it would take half of a man's leg. It was a huge sore filled with pus and scabbed over. Maggots could be used to your advantage on it, if you did it right.

"Ralph Hauk, an Englishman, had an ulcer on his leg, and he was very alarmed at it, because he could see death every day from this thing. So we had heard from an Englishman about putting maggots in it. We convinced Hauk that we ought to put maggots in his leg, and we did. Of course, maggots were everywhere. They were an advantage up to a point. After they cleaned the dead flesh, they'd start eating on the proud flesh if you didn't keep them under control. When I was a kid, the way we kept maggots under control on the cattle was with chloroform. But we had no chloroform. We would put a specific number of maggots in an ulcer if it wasn't too large, you see, and take out the same number. The only other way a maggot could get in there would be from a blow fly. So we took out the same number we put in. We let them eat the rotten flesh, pus, stuff like that. If they didn't get to the good raw meat, then it was advantageous, but Cy had gone beyond that stage. He had a leg that was half covered with an ulcer.

"I had a small ulcer. I had this remedy that was used on small ulcers. There was a fly in the area that would drill through the scab of any sore and get down to that proud meat and just tear you up terribly—a bad sting. It hurt. So I got some yellow clay, and I put a thick layer of this clay on the ulcer to keep the fly off, kept it from drilling through the scab. Well, I'd come in at night and take the clay off; off would come the scab, pus, and leave it clean so that it healed up. I don't know what the yellow clay was, but I'd make it good and thick, and it would dry. It would keep the flies off, and it actually healed my leg.

"Have you ever heard the name 'Spoonsma?' Well, there was this Doctor Philip Bloemsma, a Dutch doctor. They nicknamed him Spoonsma because he used a spoon to scrape the ulcers clean; that's how he would treat them. He was a colleague of Doctor Hekking; they knew each other well. Anyhow, I heard this; I wasn't associated with him at all. Sometimes maggots would get in the ulcers, and they'd get beyond control; men would go mad from it. Possibly they would die before they went mad. If they went mad, why, maybe that was a relief before they died. Who knows? I've seen them both ways—go mad, and die from it. I've also seen them amputate legs.

"As things got progressively worse, there was only one saw, and the Japs had it in their kitchen. We had to wait until it was not being used and take it and sterilize it to amputate legs—a damn big ol' toothed saw, one where you pulled to cut rather than pushed. It was very primitive, of course, but it was the only saw available. We'd have to wait until they were through with it to sterilize it in boiling water to do the amputations, saw the bone. It was very coarse toothed, but it was all we had. Rarely did a man live after an amputation, because he could be standing on crutches, and you could see the pus drip from the stub of the leg. Gangrene soon took over, and it was impossible to recover. Amputations soon stopped, because we had no anesthetic, and a man couldn't take an amputation without anesthetic. I've seen it tried without anesthetic, but no way.

"I saw men very, very sick, not far from death, who would just give up. They would become very quiet. If they had a blanket they would wrap up in it; if they didn't, they'd be just laying there and possibly will themselves dead. Of course, they had a lot of help from disease, but it didn't take them long to go. Some stopped eating, and you damn near had to force them to eat. They wouldn't even get up for rations. At this stage of the game, it came down to the fact that maybe a man was a shirker who died. I know that's hard to believe, but a shirker put more of a load on the next guy. Hell, he'd wind up and die, you see, and then put more work on somebody else. I mean, that's a hell of an expression, but you get so callused, so very callused. In other words, sometimes you'd think it was an out for a man to die, because it wasn't no problem to die, and you'd be through with it. It worked on your mind.

"Cholera set in before I got hurt, and we'd have to burn all the cholera victims. There were a few who got put in the ground, but we tried to burn all that we could because we would destroy the germ; otherwise it comes right back out of the ground in season. It was quite a trying experience to go to work in the mornings, or maybe coming home at night, and see these piles of wood put up in advance because otherwise you couldn't keep up with the deaths. You thought when you went past the piles of wood—and we had to go by the damn area every day—you wondered, 'Who in the hell is going to be next?' Would it be me, one of my close friends, or who? I had to help build the piles, but I never actually put a body on them, nor did I ever participate in a burning. But I have seen many a one burned in various stages.

"By this time we all wore G-strings; the men worked in G-strings. Oh, I had a pair of shorts. If a man would die and if he had a pair of shorts, you'd get hold of them. There were so many men who died where I was, that there were bits of rags and clothing everywhere. There's no need to bury a man in anything, because he didn't need it. So many died that nobody kept track. There wasn't any marked grave area where I was. There was just laxity. Down in Kanburi there were good records kept, and in Tamarkan, too, but not in the jungle. Now, I understand that the Americans had a better organization, kept records. Of course, I was only in the jungle during the Speedo campaign.

"At this time our supplies came up the river. Then they were hauled on your back from the river. We also ate a few snails, just plain ol' snails. You would crack open the shell and get them out and boil them a little bit. They were tough as damn leather, but they were pretty good chewing. We ate some bamboo shoots, dried bamboo shoots, and there was always rice—always. Not a helluva lot, but some. Vegetables were very slim pickings; meat was out of the question. This group of F Force, that I mentioned earlier, they had cattle. Everytime they killed one, they couldn't give us the meat, but they would dump the entrails. Man, we were like a damn bunch of vultures in there on them. Every little particle of suet was stripped off.

"Have you ever heard of British tripe? Well, you know what it is? It's the waste bag of the animal. Well, these damn Britishers tried to make some tripe, you know. We had a few little onions, so they tried to clean the waste bag. Hell, it was impossible. But I guess the stuff that was left in it just added a little bit of seasoning, I don't know. I tried once to get the little particles of suet off the entrails, every little bit that I possibly could, but I never tried to again.

"There were baboons there, but they were more vicious than the damn prisoners. Boy, in the morning they made the damnedest commotion you ever heard at about daylight or a bit before. Along the creek where our camp was, to the southwest of us, there was a cliff, and this is where the tribe of baboons was. They raised holy hell early every morning; it was the damnedest thing! Of course, a few of our fellows thought they'd try to tackle one. You'd run across one in the jungle every now and then. Hell, he looked meaner than you did, so that was that. I tried cobra meat, I damn sure did. An Australian caught it. It was beautiful meat, really, a pinkish meat, and, of course, it became white when it was cooked. It tasted between a fish and a chicken to me. The only trouble I found with it was that I just never could get enough of it.

"We didn't have soap. My toothbrush wore out, and I chewed the end of a stick and worked it up as a toothbrush. Of course, you didn't have a hell of a lot to brush or pick out of your teeth. I had a GI mess kit knife. It had excellent steel to it, and that's what I used to shave with. I sharpened it on a piece of slate.

"Where I was we didn't have a priest or minister. There was one with H Force, a Catholic priest from Sidney, a Father L. T. Marsden, I believe. He was much of a man, much of a man. He is the one who later at Kanburi mapped all the cemeteries, had a diagram for where each man was buried, who was buried where. Up in the jungle men got religion, and even an atheist would become desperate for something. There damn sure had to be something greater than a man himself to bring him out of that place. That was what men thought, myself as well; there had to be something. I wondered many times, 'Why was I chosen to be punished so damn much?' Or, 'Why did I live and others die?' There were a lot of questions that came up that I couldn't answer. All you can do is have faith; that's all.

"I think there was unintentional sabotage on the railroad from the word go. What we built, in my opinion, damn sure wouldn't carry much traffic. We had elephants, you see, and they wouldn't walk across that damn trestle; no, indeed, they wouldn't. Yet, later, after they brought us out of the jungle, I rode on some segments of the railroad from Tarsau to Tamarkan to Kanburi. But as far as sabotage per se, there wasn't any, no, not really. You didn't have any damn thing in mind about sabotage; you were merely trying to stay alive. I constantly thought, 'When will this be over?' Not necessarily the war but this particular confinement. It had to be over someday, because, if not, there would have been far, far more buried than we buried over there. See, we wound up in the jungle with about 525 in my group. When we got back to Singapore in December '43, 116 were all that was left. You can see how they were dying.

"I also thought about the food business that I was going to go into—a restaurant. I said, 'Hell, I never want to be very far from food!' That was a thought I had many times, going into the restaurant business. Thinking about food, hell, you'd just go damn near mad, you see. But thank God for the British. I had them to vent my anger on. Pardon my language, but that was the only son-of-a-bitch you could take anything out on, you see. You didn't want to do it to your own people, and you didn't dare to do it to the Japs, who had rifles, so the poor ol' Englishman caught hell!

"We'd cuss them, you know, call him what he was. You vented your anger in his direction. Possibly some of this came up so often because you began to believe what you said about them. Their life was so different from ours—not the Japs—I'm talking about the British. It didn't seem like they had the will to live quite as much as we Americans did. I think I wanted to live a helluva lot worse than some of them did. I believe that's why so many of them died. I've seen Englishmen lay down extremely sick with maggots working both ends of them. I've seen maggots in and out of their rear end, up the rear end, in their mouth—and they're conscious! You knew they're going to die, but yet you couldn't put them out of it. You couldn't or wouldn't. You weren't built that way.

"I'll say this, however, that as bad as it got I never saw a man curry favor with the Japs at the expense of his fellow man; I didn't see any of that. Now I've seen men gain favors from the Jap guards up in the jungle to get something to eat. The Japs had them waiting on them, and after they helped cook the Japs' food, maybe they'd get some food while the Japs were eating, or when they cleared the table they'd take scraps—things like that. I don't blame them; I don't blame them a bit. Working in the Jap kitchen was the best job you could get.

"The Englishmen were damn poor cooks. Of course, they didn't have a helluva lot to cook with, but they were still damn poor cooks. After I got out of the jungle down to Kanburi, they wanted Americans in the kitchen, and the British knew that I had had a lot of experience in the kitchen, and after I got hurt I helped them set up some better kitchen facilities in the jungle. But they wanted me to run the hospital kitchen in Kanburi, but I wouldn't. I didn't want the responsibility. I did work there for a while boiling water. We boiled all the water, even rainwater that we'd catch because of the contamination of the building, the atap.

"There was this Doctor Phillips, Stewart Phillips. He's now deceased. He was an Englishman and a man if there ever was one. He would hold sick call with no equipment whatever, no medicine—strictly a psychological thing. He had a huge ulcer on his leg that he couldn't heal. Men would go into his tent and carry him out and set him on a log, and he'd hold what the British called sick parade. As I say, he had no equipment, no medicine, no nothing, just strictly encouragement, assurance, or something like that. He'd hold sick parade, and then they'd take him back into his tent.

"I really hurt my back in the jungle, very badly, and it got to where I couldn't hardly walk after I got to Singapore. Doctor Phillips, through therapy with his hands, got me back to where I could walk again, and walk well. He would make me walk to his quarters. He said, 'If you'll come to my quarters, I'll see if I can help you,' and he would do this hands-type therapy. He got me in good shape. I thought he ought to come to me; but he was making me walk that distance for a reason: to keep me in as good a condition as possible.

"Everybody had malaria in the jungle. I think they did. Cerebral malaria was the most deadly. Any of the diseases in the jungle was a contributing fact to the death of a man. You would get, say, malaria. You'd have malaria, several bouts of malaria; it would get you in a weakened condition. Then dysentery would kill you. An ulcer on your leg would sap strength out of your body, naturally. Then dysentery would kill you. One would get you in a condition where the other would kill you. This happened time and time again.

"A lot of things were psychological. Like I said before, you know, venting your anger on a dead man. It helped you out. You'd think, 'The son-of-a-bitch died to get out of this, and now I've got to bury him.' One of the worst episodes that I went through as far as relating my feelings to other men was men dying—the Britishers. See, now I feel terrible, but we had a parade before we went to work, and they asked for volunteers to bury three or four Britishers who had died during the night, and no one volunteered. Then this lieutenant, who was a friend, asked me if I would get up a party and bury them. I blew my stack. I called him a 'low-bred son-of-a-bitch,' you know. I said that if they would stoop so low that they wouldn't bury their own dead, they were beyond the realm of human beings. I really let off steam. I belittled them real, real bad. I vented that 'if one of the Americans died, I'd kill the son-of-a-bitch who buried him,' because it was our job as Americans, and they'd better not touch our dead.

"This came back later when one of our men died, and we didn't know about it until he was already buried. But, you know, you vent your anger, get it out of your system, and keep your teeth in your head. You know, otherwise the Japs would knock them out, if you vented anger on them. But back to this burying thing. I buried a lot of men in unmarked graves. They were mass graves. You would start off with, say, six or seven to bury. By the day's end, by the time you got the hole dug, why, they've already brought you some more corpses. It was a helluva job. Damn right it was! It was a helluva job—roots, mud—and you'd have to clear an area.

"When you'd start digging, because it was wet, you'd pick an area where there wasn't water in the first place. Then you'd put a mound of dirt around the grave to keep the water from coming in while you were working. Of course, you'd still have slop in the bottom, so you'd work barefooted. I buried as high as seventeen in one grave. I started off with nine dead one morning and wound up putting seventeen in the hole. It all gets very impersonal, very callous; it never bothered me one iota, not one iota. Of course, I never buried one of my own—I mean an American. There was an English captain who would always conduct the prayer at a burial. You know, he'd say, 'Dust to dust, and ashes to ashes.' There was always a prayer. We weren't that callused. But you were callused to death itself, not to an individual's death but to death in general. I say callused, it's like a continuous sore, you learn to live with it. So we became callused.

"The death of a man didn't bother you later like it did at the beginning. We carried dead men on the train and on the walk going up. Had we known the ultimate goal, that they'd wind up in a damn slop-hole grave, you'd have left them there. But you became callused later, and death didn't bother you. It did at the beginning. But it would have been far better not to have carried any men that were bad off, let him stop at the side of the road, let a Jap either put a bayonet through him or a bullet through his head, and that would have been the end of it. As it was, you carried him and let him go through all the agonies of hell in that jungle. But that was clinging to life; that's what it amounted to.

"In the latter part of October, I went into Kanburi hospital camp, the old town of Kanchanaburi. It was strictly a hospital camp right beside the railroad. I believe it was in a field or maybe a rice paddy, because it was very low. When it rained, water was everywhere. Our part of the camp wasn't too big, but just across the fence there was a native segment: Indians, Chinese, probably Thais. What this place really was, as I see it now, was a place to let those die who were going to die and the remainder, if they got well, carry them back to Singapore. That is, of our group—H Force.

"About the Indians across the fence. I had an Australian friend, a staff sergeant who was a medical student in Melbourne, and I had a scalpel with me, and I gave it to him. It had gotten rusty, but I carried it in my gear. It was a surgical scalpel. I gave it to this Aussie, and he went over to practice on some of these Indians. He worked on one in particular that had an ulcer. I watched him for a little while, but I couldn't bear to watch him anymore. The Indian had a huge ulcer around his spine; you could see the backbone in there. The sergeant was going to clean it out, and he literally tied the Indian to a bamboo fence, of course with permission. He started to work on the ulcer without any anesthetic whatsoever. Naturally, the fellow screamed. It hurt. Soon he passed out from the pain. The reason the sergeant tied him up like that was so all the pus and stuff would drain out. Anyway, the Aussie got to try out his new scalpel.

"I worked in the kitchen boiling water at this place. We lost two Americans here. We lost one coming out of the jungle and had to leave him at Tarsau. He had dysentery very bad; he couldn't walk, and we had to leave him at the camp there. Then we lost Glenn Moore, Cy, in this hospital camp. Of course, there was no work here, but rations weren't too plentiful either. They were better than in the jungle. However, water was extremely short. All the water had to be hauled in from a well across the railroad, and you had to get permission to go get it.

"We had atap huts with bamboo sleeping platforms. It was a hospital camp where I got to see some very primitive surgery performed. They had an operating theater set up. It had a mosquito netting around one end of the hut where the theater was. I saw an emergency appendectomy one night; it was amazing. One of the doctors, Doctor Kevin J. Fagan, an Australian major, I believe, and a miracle man, performed the surgery. They had a light in the equipment that he was going to use, but the batteries were gone, you know, used up. They had an oil lamp—no chimney—just a flame on a wick to do the damn appendectomy, and there was soot flying all around from the lamp. I watched it.

"I had this Indian friend, Nickel Marcell, we called him Nick, and he was an Indian in the British Army. He was a medical orderly. He gave me a powder substance that I used on another ulcer I had right back of my big toe's toenail. We became friends and talked with each other a great deal. I was visiting him, and we talked in the theater, because there were no mosquitoes there. That's when the emergency appendectomy happened. So Nick said, 'Oh, sit where you are. You're not going to be in the way.' They had a bamboo table as the operating table—a bamboo table. They had anesthetic that they administered.

"The food was some better, but I still had scabies real bad there. I guess it was a lack of various vitamins, especially vitamin C. There was this fellow, Doc Morrow,* from Wichita Falls, who cooked rice in the cook shack. We would get some water and scrub each other at night with a brush. We got hold of a brush made from a coconut husk. It had fibers sticking out. We trimmed it off and scrubbed these scabies; we were just raw as hell. We had some ointment that we put on them. It had sulfa in it, and we got in pretty good shape that way.

"We were also taking care of Cy Moore. We had pilfered a little bit of salt from the kitchen, and we'd made a saline solution to clean his ulcer. I had left Java with a sarong that I used in my bedding, and I had torn that up, and I had two bandages. We would bandage Cy's leg; we'd change the bandages daily and wash it. We'd take sand, and we'd clean the bandages of all the mucus and pus and stuff and then boil them. We got his ulcer to where he could walk again. Then he took dysentery. He had gone through hell. They had to put him in isolation with the dysentery, and that killed his will. He got up to go to the latrine one night and fell and hemorrhaged to death. He was one of our casualties.

"Billy Thomas[†] from Romeo, Michigan, also died in the hospital camp from a combination of things—dysentery and malnutrition and whatever.

---

*Adolphus C. ("Doc") Morrow, of Battery D, still lives in Wichita Falls, Texas.
†Thomas, of Battery E, died on November 27, 1943, at Kanchanaburi. He was one of the few men in Battery E who did not go to Japan, having been left in Singapore due to illness when the rest of his unit passed through.

He got in such a bad condition that he couldn't hold his head up; it just rolled on his shoulders. I think Billy was a religious man and knew he was dying. He didn't fight it; he didn't give up, by any means, but he didn't fight it a great deal. Let's see, we lost this other guy up at Tarsau—a sailor named Roszell.* I don't know where he was from. He and a boy from Woodward, Oklahoma, Norman Stevens,† were very close. Norman still lives in Woodward. They were always talking about escaping in the jungle. Where in the hell would you go if you escaped? But, anyway, we left Kanburi and Thailand after two months, in December of 1943. They sent us to Singapore— all of H Force, or all that was left. See, here's the Oriental mind again. They used the same number of boxcars to take us back as they brought us up in. So there was just one prisoner every now and then in a boxcar—plenty of room. But that's the Oriental mind.

"The trip was great. Hell, yes, it was great, just as long as you were headed south away from that jungle, you see. We went to a camp called Sime Road, and we met up with the other six Americans who had been separated from us on the way up to the jungle. They were already back there. Camp Sime was pretty good, pretty good."

To the POWs, Sime Road Camp was more than a pretty good place. Gordon began to make wine and cook whiskey while he was there. Of his sour mash, he said, "There were nineteen headaches to every damn swallow. It made you drunk as hell!" But good things never lasted in Southeast Asia during the early forties. In May 1944, "beer-belly and all," he was sent to Changi jail—not the garrison, which was disbanded by now. A British colonel soon sentenced him to fourteen days of solitary confinement for possessing a cassava root that he was not supposed to have. Gordon thinks the colonel committed suicide soon after the war ended, but wonders why he was not murdered since all the prisoners, regardless of nationality— American, English, Australian—hated him.

As the war concluded, he watched American bombers blast the docks of Johore Bahru and Singapore. "You clapped with one hand," he stated, "and you told the bombers to get the hell out with the other." Gordon still suffered physically, having dysentery again, malaria twice, and his shoulder dislocated several times. A man of 190 pounds when captured in Java, he now weighed 108, almost the same as he had in the jungle. He was liberated

---

*L. T. Roszell, of the USS *Houston*, died of dysentery on August 5, 1943, at Tarsau, Thailand.
†Norman E. ("Steve") Stevens, of the USS *Houston*, still lives in Woodward.

on September 7, 1945, when an American C-54 flew him to Calcutta for a reunion with men of the 131st Field Artillery that he had not seen since January 1943.

Back in the United States, he was in and out of hospitals for many months, fighting amebic dysentery and having his shoulder rebuilt. He met a young woman at Walter Reed Army Hospital in the District of Columbia and married. They had three children before divorcing. He attended Texas Christian University for two years, worked for a paving company in Washington, D.C., and then returned to Texas in 1951, opening a hardware and military surplus store instead of a restaurant. He retired in 1975 on the advice of his physician. Having remarried, he recently said: "I have three wonderful children and a wonderful wife who is understanding. We make the best of every day God gives us. I hope our United States will never endure another conflict like this one ever again." The Gordons live in Keller, Texas.

Charley L. Pryor, USMC
USS *Houston*

Born on February 9, 1920, at a farm in Gavin County, in the southcentral part of the state near the Arbuckle Mountains, Charley Pryor was an Oklahoma sharecropper's son. Unlike the California-bound Okies in John Steinbeck's *The Grapes of Wrath*, when Pryor was nine his kinfolk moved to Dickens County, in West Texas, about sixty miles east of Lubbock. He attended school sporadically, quitting in January 1939 to join the Marines, both to help the family financially and as "a fugitive from a cotton sack." Following boot camp in San Diego, he shipped on the USS *Henderson* from Mare Island to Shanghai, where he joined the crew of the USS *Augusta*, flagship of the Asiatic Fleet. He had volunteered for sea duty. When the *"Augie"* returned to the United States in November 1940, Pryor managed a transfer to the *Houston*.

The Japanese captured Pryor at sea when the *Houston* sank on March 1, 1942. He worked unloading and carting goods inland for the enemy's army and was later placed in the Serang jail. He next went to Bicycle Camp, then to Changi with the second group, and finally to Moulmein to work on the railroad. In his interview, along with other topics he discusses life in the Hospital Camp, 80 Kilo, where he spent considerable time.

"THEY MOVED US OUT OF MOULMEIN on up to the railroad. The first camp we went to was 18 Kilo Camp, eighteen kilometers from Thanbyuzayat, the base camp or terminus for the railroad. The Japs had a native camp there, too, and the natives had been working for some time. The camps we lived in were built by native labor, conscripted labor. The Japs would seek these natives out of the woods and jungle, and they would actually construct the camp. Sometimes a clearing might be done by prisoners of war for a camp, but the natives would construct the camp while you were working in a camp back below the one they built. So camps just leapfrogged along the construction right-of-way.

"Our first introduction to work was with picks and shovels and the yo-ho pole for moving dirt. I guess the yo-ho pole got its name from hearing the natives when they carried anything on these poles set up a chant as a kind of rhythm that sounded something like, 'yo-ho, yo-ho, yo-ho, yo-ho.' So we called it a yo-ho pole. It made a springing weight that was not a dead weight and thus easier to carry.

"So we started working. We were divided into groups, oh, a group of about forty to forty-five men that they called a *kumi*. Then you'd have your task, either to move dirt out of a cut or to move it in order to make a fill. Eighteen Kilo was a dry camp, so we were confronted with perpetual thirst. The Japanese told us that when we finished, we'd go *mandi*, Malayan for bath. Well, we got out and fought like we were putting out a grass fire. We wanted to be the first *kumi* to get through and get our bath. We were first. We were through with our first day's task shortly after midday, and the Japanese were true to their word. They let us go take a bath. The next day they gave us a larger task. The first day we had to move 1.1 cubic meters of dirt. The next day we had 1.2 cubic meters to do.

"This old business of do so much and then *yasumi** and *mandi* always worked. We always fell for it. I know that about the time the railroad work was ending, Americans were doing about 2.5 cubic meters of dirt per man and under very trying circumstances. It was the rainy season, and you moved that much mud. The Dutch were still probably doing no more than 1.5 cubic meters. The Japanese used to rate us. 'Americans,' he'd say, 'number one.' And Americans would be given more work than anybody else. 'Australians, number two.' And then, 'Englishmen, number five.' They never had a three or four, but 'Englishmen, number five.' And '*Oranda*'—that's what the Japs called the Dutch—'*Oranda*, number ten.' *Joto nai*, that's what they used to say—*Joto nai*.† I know that we always did a great deal more work than the Indonesians—the Dutch—ever did.§ Of course, the reward would be to get a bath.

"We were still pretty healthy at this time. We had not had any serious illness, injuries. They were yet to come. The work was hard, but I think most of us didn't mind hard work. We were in shape to do the work. The most undesirable part of that period was the lack of water, particularly drinking water. You can live in filth and dirt. The same dirt doesn't stay on you day after day because you get out there and the temperature creeps up to a hundred, and you're working, and the sweat just drips off of you in a constant stream. Out there almost in your nakedness, you do not acquire

---

*A Japanese word denoting a holiday or rest period.

†A Japanese word denoting that something or someone is not acceptable or okay.

§The Indonesians to whom Pryor is referring were natives of the Dutch East Indies serving in the Dutch Army. They were also referred to as the "Black Dutch."

much of a suntan because as you sweat you just bleach out. I'd be no darker than I am right now.

"The most desirable job out on this road would be using a shovel. Not many wanted to use the pick. Probably the hardest work of all was swinging the pick to break up the dirt. Then it was shoveled into either a sack or basket hung from the yo-ho pole. Then there'd be one guy to carry the pole. It was not terribly difficult work, but we didn't particularly like that yo-ho work anyhow. Using the shovel was the most desirable job, and usually you'd swap off between *yasumi*. We'd work maybe a couple of hours, and then we'd get a ten-minute *yasumi*. Then we'd swap off the various chores. Not many liked the pick, but I used it all the time. I never used anything but the pick. The only tools we had were the pick and shovel. There was not any other kind of sophisticated gear. It was interesting, I guess, to see how much can be done with such crude implements. The guards weren't bad here. They never bothered us. We worked; we worked hard. The Japs could get food to us. So there was really not much the guards had to do. They never had much pretext or justification to bash us. We came into camp and did what we had to do and stayed in our huts because we got in quite late. Then we'd be up and working again the next day. We never had many days off.

"I think we worked six weeks before we had our first day off, our first *yasumi* day. I know when that first day came, well, some of the guys that had any talent put on a concert; we gathered on a bit of high ground out there and let that be the performing stage. Those that could do anything sang a song or recited a poem or something. We had a Dutchman with us who was a professional magician. Of course, he was a good entertainer. I understand that he had worked on Dutch liners between the United States and Holland as a magician in civilian life. I know that we were all out there watching him, and a bunch of natives came across a rice paddy. Their camp was about 250 yards from our own. They came across to watch. This Dutch magician went to work doing all manner of sleight-of-hand tricks, and then he had one trick with a silk handkerchief. He made that handkerchief dance across the stage and then rise in the air suspended and then flutter through the air. Boy, when he started with that handkerchief and made it rise in the air and flutter, these natives WHSSST! I mean they took off! That was too much magic for them!

"They were hill people and probably Cochin or Nagas.* The Japanese could never keep them on the job very long. They could round them up and

---

*He is referring to inhabitants of the hill region of Assam and Burma, including Naga and Patkai Hills. The Nagas were headhunters overcome by British expeditions (1865–1880).

run them down there to work on this road, and, by thunder, some dark night
they'd look around, and there wouldn't be a one of them left. They'd all be
gone back to the hills. Later on a lot of them died. That's the thing you'll
note among Orientals. They're fatalists, and when one of them gets seriously ill, well, you can just mark him off the books because he's had it. They
lose their will to live with adversity. They just don't have the tenacious will
to hang on and beat their illness. Of course, this was particularly true of the
Indonesians that we were with. Their casualty rate was higher than ours.

"Eighteen Kilo Camp was pretty much out of the foothills. It was in a
level plain; this was plains country. There was jungle, but this was open
country more or less. When we got to our next camp—we leapfrogged from
18 Kilo to 85 Kilo Camp—there you're in the jungle. You're in real jungle.
We cleared right-of-way there in both directions. They weren't laying track
yet. The only road was a service road, truck road. They moved us up to 85
Kilo in trucks. We never had to march it as we usually had to, but they
moved us in trucks. It was in the dry season, and the dust would be inches
deep on the roads. At 85 Kilo the rainy season began.

"Soon after we got there, I got a fever, and this fever, I got it at work one
day, and the next day I saw our doctor, and he said, 'Well, you stay in.' They
were not pushing us too much then; if you were sick, you stayed in camp. I
think in the first few days of this fever, they moved us from 85 Kilo Camp to
80 Kilo Camp; we moved back down a camp to 80. In this place I almost
saw the end of me. I had fever for eighteen days. They didn't know what it
was. We had some Dutch doctors there, too, and they understood tropical
diseases. They thought that I had some form of malaria, maybe a light touch
of cerebral malaria. It hangs on for a long period of time. Usually, it's fatal.
Then they thought I had some other form of jungle fever along with cerebral
malaria.

"One evening, I had a temperature of 107.5. Well, a fever of 105 is not
uncommon with some of the jungle fevers. They're quite intense for a brief
period of time, but they don't last. Even malaria doesn't last eighteen
days—other than, as we came to know, cerebral malaria. It would last that
long, and you usually died. I only knew one man who recovered from it—a
big, strong Dutchman. I had this for eighteen days. We had no medicine, not
a bit. It was hot. One day I thought I was dying. I had the worst chill I'd ever
had, early in the morning, and then when the chill broke my fever started
going up, and shortly after midday I passed out from the fever. I came to
sometime after the middle of the afternoon. I asked our corpsman to borrow
a towel for me and go down and wet it at the creek and put it on me. I was
burning up; I was just on fire. He did, and he spread it over me and put

another one over my head. Well, that night when they took my temperature, I still had over a 105 fever. I believe that during that afternoon that if a man ever had 110 fever, I had, because I was hotter than when I had the 107.5.

"We had another guy who had 108. I can't remember his name, but I know he had 108, and he survived. I got to where I couldn't even hold water. I could swallow water, and I couldn't even keep it down. I couldn't keep food down, of course. I'd swallow it, and it would come back up. Some boys came around in the morning to see if I had died. There wasn't anybody at the end of the time that thought I weighed over 75 pounds. When I was captured, I weighed 188 pounds, and here now I was down to, they say, not more than 75 pounds.* I was just nothing but the skin stretched over my bones. On the eighteenth day my fever left me. I got the fever on the fourth of April and had it for eighteen days.

"On the day after the fever left me, the Japanese decided to move me down to Thanbyuzayat to the hospital, so I was sent down there in the back of a truck along with four or five others who were ill. At some camp down there the truck stopped, and this ol' boy went in to see some of his buddies. One of them came out and wanted to practice driving, and the fool didn't know how to drive a truck. He got in and let the clutch out, and the truck jumped and bucked. Of course, that just jarred you around. I cussed the bugger in Japanese, Malay, English, Spanish; anything that I knew I used on that clown. When he left, he parked right out in the sun. When the other one came back to the truck, that fool wouldn't park it where we could be under some shade about fifteen feet up ahead.

"Well, we went into Thanbyuzayat, and I never had any more fever. There wasn't anything wrong with me; it was just a matter of recuperating. They had a bit more food there. We had a bit more vegetables in the soup on your rice, and you had sugar and sweetened water on your rice in the morning. You could buy from the natives, and they had a canteen where if you had money you could purchase something. One of my good buddies, the one that was killed a year ago—Hugh Faulk, a Marine—had given me his shirt and told me to sell it and buy me an egg and some bananas. I was able to sell it and buy a little bit of extra food. Just before I left there, they brought our first sergeant on the *Houston* down, a Marine by the name of Harley Harold Dupler.† He died there in camp. I have just finished reading a

---

*Pryor was 6' 1" tall and weighed about 190 pounds when selected to be a member of the seagoing Marine unit, which required approximately these measurements.
†H. H. Dupler, of the *Houston*, is listed as dying of dysentery at Thanbyuzayat, Burma, on May 14, 1943.

book *Through the Valley of the Kwai,* and they mention an Australian doctor, Colonel Coates. He was a King's Surgeon. That's the highest honor you can have. Coates, who was Dupler's friend, looked after him. Dupler was from Indiana and knew Chicago well, and Coates had gone to the University of Chicago. We buried Dupler there. I was at the hospital about twenty days, and then I went back to the railroad to work.

"When I was recuperating I got a form of pellagra. The Aussies called it 'happy feet.' It's a form of vitaminosis and pellagra. Pellagra usually works on your stomach, but this worked on your shins and legs. They looked inflamed, and you had red streaks run up them and intense pains. You could hardly touch the balls of your feet to the ground. You feel like you've got to get out and walk. You couldn't rest, so you'd walk pretty much on the heel of your foot. I guess I only experienced that for about a week, and as I began to recover and get my strength back and put on more weight, well, it went away.

"Soon after I got back up to the railroad, I got a back injury that still gives me trouble. I was carrying this lumber, this timber. We had an elephant or two around to help us, but an elephant's a smart bugger. He'd test these logs before he put any effort into them, and if they seemed heavy, well, he'd back off from it. He wouldn't work with it. So when an elephant wouldn't move it, well, the Nips would yell for about eight POWs to get over there and do what the elephant wouldn't. One of the guys helping carry the log fell, and I was under the front end of the log and injured my back. It still gives me trouble at times. We worked out of this place, and then from 80 Kilo Camp we went to 100 Kilo Camp.

"Supply was getting to be a big problem now that the rainy season had set in with fierceness of purpose. From now on we had steady rain. One Hundred Kilo was one of the most unlikely campsites that we had on the road. It was built more or less in a swamp. The whole camp was nothing but a swamp. You'd wade around there in the water and in the mud, and we'd clear right-of-way, make cuts and fills, and make bridges. There was no bottom to all the mud. The Japs had three trucks that moved in the area. All three had been captured from the British, but they were American trucks— a six-wheel drive Studebaker, a four-wheel drive Chevrolet, and I think the other one was a six-wheel drive Reo. They all had front mounted winches. They were sold by the U.S. Army to the English and then captured. They were all that would move, and they just moved essential supplies. So our rations were drastically reduced.

"We were just as hungry as we had been in the first few days. We were not able to get near enough to satisfy your wants. At this time fever and dysentery became a common thing for our people, and in the midst of this rainy season we began to get tropical ulcers. Any scratch or cut would get infected and start to spread. We had nothing: no dressings, nor any sort of medicine with any kind of antiseptic power or antibiotic to combat infection. So the ulcers would grow. I know I got one just from a cut. We were making ballast for the roads, trying to improve the service roads so we could get supplies. So I was working on that, and a piece of rock cut my shin.

"We never experienced these tropical ulcers until the rainy season came along, and when we talk of the rainy season there, by gosh, it rains every day. I know in one period—I believe in July 1943—we counted that it rained fourteen days and nights. Of course, we were out in it all the time. Our camp was built in a mudhole. You're in mud and filth all the time, and in the jungle everything is decaying vegetation. So any scratch you'd get would become infected by nightfall. That was my experience. I got a scratch early in the morning, and by nightfall it was infected, and within a week the ulcer had spread to three or four inches in diameter. It had eaten to the bone in a week.

"I'm not a medical authority, but I think the ulcers were peculiar to this rainy season and condition of filth you lived in. We never experienced them in the dry season. As time went along our bodies became more wasted away, deteriorated. We suffered from malnourishment, malnutrition, as much as we ever had, but we never experienced these tropical ulcers again. I'm satisfied it was peculiar to that time and place in Burma and Thailand. I know when I got this one I had nothing to treat it with, so it began to spread and eat and grow, and it was attendant with excruciating pain. The thing ate faster than a cancer. All we had to treat it was boiling water. Every available minute I'd sit there and boil water, and I'd put a rag over the ulcer and drop boiling water on it. I couldn't keep my fingers in the water, but I could stand the water on it.

"I suppose I had this thing about a month, and then the Japs sent those of us who had the worst ulcers, suffered a good deal from dysentery and malaria, or most generally had a combination of these things back down to 80 Kilo Camp. They sent about forty-five Americans, about forty Australians, and about two hundred Dutch prisoners of war—those in the worst physical condition—from 100 Kilo Camp, where we were, back down to 80 Kilo. It was now an abandoned camp. After we built the railroad through an area, well, they'd just abandon the camp and let them fall apart. The termites would get into them, and so very soon they're eaten out and became a hull of bamboo. You certainly didn't welcome being sent back. I suppose our doctors did it, but certainly it had to be approved and cleared with the

Japanese and justified to them. Of course, the Japanese didn't believe in feeding sick people. They had an established ration there, but they couldn't support it. In this rainy season transport came to a halt, even Japanese military transport.

"From our experience, 100 Kilo Camp was the worst-situated camp. It was built altogether in a swamp, and there seemed no bottom to the mud at the place. You just lived in perpetual wetness. It was intolerable. Now, 80 Kilo Camp wasn't too poorly situated. It was well drained and adjacent to a stream, so we fared fairly well that way. But the other conditions here in these impossible times, like getting food and provisions, and they cut back the sick men's rations down to less than half of what a working person was getting—now that was intolerable.

"So when they moved us back there, I know that of the forty Australians only two of them were on their feet. Both of them had been wounded in a bombing attack at Thanbyuzayat. They had been in the hospital camp when the Allied bombers—I don't know whether they were American or English—came over and bombed the place. They bombed adjacent to the hospital, and a number of prisoners were killed and a large number injured. One of them had his eye put out and his cheekbone all crushed in. The other one lost his left arm up near the shoulder. They were on their feet and got about and helped out. I was the only American there at one time on my feet, so we went about the task of doing what we could for those who were completely bedridden.

"There were no medical facilities at 80 Kilo Camp. We thought they'd just sent us there to die. They thought most of us would not recover, and so they'd have us out of the way of those in better physical condition. They sent a doctor back with us—our senior medical officer off the *Houston*, Commander Epstein.* But he didn't have anything to work with. He was a doctor without medication. I know that of the number that went back with me originally, there's only two of us still alive today. The rest of them have died.

"I helped do all the burying at this place. As the Aussies and Americans died, well, I just felt that they had to be buried, and so I did this. As they passed away, we would go up and dig a hole on the side of a hill, a well-drained place at the edge of the jungle. We'd dig the grave, come back, wrap the body up in rice-straw sacks or a mat, put a couple of bamboo poles under the back so he could be carried easily, and we'd bury him. I think my busiest

---

*William A. Epstein died of pneumonia and cardiac arrest on November 29, 1982, in Oakland, California.

time was when I buried ten in three days. I would expect that I buried them either by myself or sometimes I had help, but I imagine that in the time that we were there—some four months—that I buried eighty people.

"Most of us had little, few possessions, but what a man did have we kept and put it to use. We knew prisoners who would need a canteen, and we would pass one on to him if we thought he had the most need for a particular item left by a man who died. So a man's belongings—what he had—still continued to be put to some use. The doctor kept death records, and he submitted a death certificate of sorts to the Japanese identifying him by name, rank, service, and nationality, and then his Japanese POW number. My number was 10131. I did make a map, a plat, of the cemetery there. Of course, the Dutch used the same facilities.

"When we had been in this camp before, one of my good buddies, Sergeant Joe Lusk,* died. I was in Thanbyuzayat in the hospital with the fever then. I was not in camp when Egghead—we used to call him Egg-head—died. His grave had already undergone settling, and so I reworked it, rocked it over. The cross at the head of his grave was four-inch teakwood; we called it 'ironwood.' It was black, and the doggoned wood wouldn't float. You'd drop it in water, and it was just like a petrified log because it just sank like a rock. You'd whack it with an ax, and the ax'd jump back up in the air. We made his cross out of that and chiseled his name out, just like you would on granite. From his grave I measured the distance and the direction to every other grave, so from this map of the cemetery that we had drawn, we could locate any person's grave that we might be looking for.

"We had two Japanese guards there with us, when we first went down there. When the first two or three people died, they came down to see it— see if he was in fact dead. But when you come down and you're in the midst of 250 people and they're covered with great ulcers sometimes from the knee to the foot, well, that doesn't last. The ulcers eat the flesh away and turn black. Then flies get to them, and soon they're just completely alive with maggots. By this time you were so far removed that your glandular system couldn't absorb the poison, and then the blood system began to absorb it. As this weakens your body, well, you'd catch anything that came along: malaria, dysentery. You just can't describe the stench and the smell that attended one of these ulcers. It was rotten flesh in the grossest way, the basest way. So the Japs would come down these first two or three times, and that was the last.

---

*J. M. Lusk died at 18 Kilo Camp, Burma, on March 22, 1943.

"They got to where they never came down, so I toyed with the idea a couple of times of escaping because the Japanese would never look for me. I thought that I'd go down, and if the doctor wouldn't fill me out one of these certificates, I'd just fill one out for myself, take it down there, report me as being dead, go up and fill in a hole on the side of the hill, and the Japanese would report that person was dead. They would never verify that I had died or was dead. They wouldn't have looked for me then. They'd never know a POW had escaped. But you can't live in the jungle long without knowing that the jungle is a formidable barrier and the harshest enemy you would have. There was nowhere to go. I suppose we were at least 1,200 to 1,400 miles from the nearest friendly troops. You would have to pass through the entire Japanese Burma Army, and unlike Europe, where you could blend in with the people, there you'd just stand out glaringly.

"I suspect the Japanese had promised the natives a reward for turning in escaping prisoners. We did have instances of prisoners escaping from other camps, not in the jungle so much because most of us knew by that time what a foolish, a really foolish, foolhardy thing it would be. We never seriously entertained any idea that escape could be successful. Even in my case when I knew that they wouldn't look for me, I knew you couldn't beat the jungle. The natives couldn't beat it; the animals that lived in it didn't beat it.

"This was an unusual time. I can describe conditions that existed there, but I don't know if anyone would understand them. You almost have to live them to be able to understand them—some of the things that you see with all the filth and stink and the unending hunger. Then, there were those for whom food had no appeal during their last days of life. That seemed to be characteristic with most who died. Their appetites would go, oh, some two weeks before the last day. Generally as they lay there, life just slowly left them—just a little bit, day by day.

"I think the first sign that death would be within the next two, three, or four days was when they'd become irrational. They'd hallucinate just like a person today, I guess, under the influence of some of your narcotic drugs. They'd seem so rational, and at the same time you knew they were completely irrational. One of our POWs—he used to be a native of Dallas—in the days before he died, his bed had fallen through the bamboo floor, and so he laid there. These white ants had hollowed out the inside of the bamboo where he had put his bed, and, well, it had broken in, and so he laid there like he was laying in a teacup or some such thing, extremely uncomfortable.

"In the last three or four days before he died, he wanted me to get him a mattress—an air mattress. He told me one day when I passed by, 'Charley, you remember when we came through 80 Kilo Camp before?' I said, 'Yes.'

He said, 'Did you ever know what was in that house across the creek that the Japanese built on stilts?' Of course, I didn't know of any house, but I said, 'No, I have no idea.' He said, 'That house is full of air mattresses. I sure wish you'd sneak over there and get me one of those.' I said, 'Okay, I'll see about it this afternoon.' When I walked away, he said, 'Hey, if there's not anybody watching, steal one of those pillows, too. Bring me one of those pillows.' Well, I knew that it would be just a matter of a few days then until he was dead, and I thought, 'Well, he'll forget all about this.' About two days later, I came by again, and he said, 'Well, what did you ever find out about those air mattresses?' I said, 'Well, there wasn't any in there.' 'Oh, my gosh,' he said, 'I was sure counting on you getting me one of those air mattresses.'

"Another sailor of ours planned to go home on leave during the two days before he died, and in his hallucinations he encountered more trouble, just more trouble, than I guess any sailor in the fleet ever had trying to get gone on leave. In the first place, they had signed his leave papers, and then they couldn't find them. Somebody misplaced them. Then he'd gone down and bought a bus ticket home—he lived in Arkansas—and so after he bought the ticket home, well, then in his mind he knew that he was going to get on the wrong bus. He was worried to death about getting on the wrong bus and not winding up at home. He died the next morning, but in the afternoon the day before he died, I came back there, and he told me, 'Charley, somebody's went and stole my uniform that I was going to wear home on leave. I had it all pressed and laying out, and now, by thunder, I go to get it and it's gone. Will you help me find it? I wish you'd go down and see the master-at-arms.' That's the ship's security people. He said, 'I wish you'd see the master-at-arms and have him conduct a search and see if he can't find my dress whites.' Well, you become callused to all of this. In such a situation where you see it, where you live it every minute of every day, and still yet when you see something like this, it's just so dad-blamed pathetic that you just wonder, 'Well, how can all this be this way?'

"I buried another ol' boy who committed suicide. There's no way that I'd mention his name, but he just in effect committed suicide. I believe he was the laziest man that I've ever met anywhere, anytime, anyplace. As we worked on that railroad, the rest of the people who worked in his *kumi* usually had to do his work because he just wouldn't put out. Then when he saw that the Japanese weren't making some of the people with ulcers work, and they'd let them stay in and have the doctor treat them, well, he began to cultivate one. We'd catch him sitting there picking at a raw sore with a sliver of bamboo, and that bamboo was just as poisonous as could be. He'd pick at that thing, and you'd find him rubbing old mud in it. I was not surprised after I'd been sent to 80 Kilo to see him come down with one of the following groups, and he had an ulcer that didn't need any cultivation then. It was tremendous, and he didn't last, I think, only about four days after they sent him down there. He died in the middle of the night. I thought I was used to any condition. I thought I'd run into all unusual conditions until I met the case of this man.

"I could pick these dead people up, and the great sores and all that pus and corruption would get on my body, on my chest—the worms from the sores and wounds—and it wouldn't affect me. I'd become accustomed to it all. But when this man died in the night, and the next morning I went around and saw that he'd died and came back after digging his grave to wrap him up and put him in it and rigor mortis had set in, I met something different. His arms were in an unusual position, and I wanted to put them across his chest because this would facilitate burying him. As I got over him . . . I had one of my good buddies helping me, Hugh Faulk, the Marine corporal that I mentioned was killed a year ago. Faulk was there for a brief time, and he was helping me bury people. Faulk was helping me put this guy's arms down, and we pushed his arms down over his chest—he had died with his lungs full of air—and in pushing his arms down we decompressed the lungs, and all this dead air came out into our face. I have come onto unusual things in the way of smells, but there has been nothing like that was. There has been nothing that was so sickening. Faulk vomited. I thought I was going to. I don't know why I didn't. Probably there was nothing in my stomach to come up.

"Then we saw another case of a man that got his ulcer in his mouth. I came along there one day and found him with a pair of pliers—I don't know where he got them—trying to pull his teeth. I took them away from him, and he tried to pull his teeth with his fingers, which was not difficult after two or three days of letting that ulcer spread. He had worms in his mouth, and, of course, it was not unusual for a man to get worms in and around his anus, you know, because they had dysentery, and the flies would get around the anus. This was not unusual. It must have been a painful thing because I know at times I'd come around some of them who were suffering from such a thing, and ofttimes in their subconscious mind they would undertake some action. You know, they'd be back there with their hands or maybe with a little stick if they could find one or come by one and try to do something. So I know that this was a thing that gave them misery.

"All of the men were suffering from a combination of fever, dysentery, ulcers, and I daresay the ulcers influenced the others more than they influenced the ulcer. I guess this was the most intolerable place as far as the treatment of people was concerned that there was along the railroad. I do not know of any other place where we had so little to do with, and the loss of life was so pronounced and so heavy. But at the end of the rainy season, they took us away from this place and sent us to 105 Kilo Camp. We were at 80 Kilo about four months, then we went to 105 Kilo, and it was quite a large camp. I'd imagine that there must have been about eight thousand Australians in the camp. We went beyond the camp where most Americans still were at 100 Kilo.

"The railroad was nearing completion. There was still some finishing work, particularly a good bit of ballasting work going on yet. At 105 Kilo, there was some railroad work, but then most of the work was directed toward cutting wood in the jungle and taking it and stacking it by the railroad so that the trains could use it. They fired the steam engines with wood. We'd stack wood by the road, and, of course, they'd just load a train with it and take it to some supply point along the track. Ofttimes a train would stop and take a load on for its own use.

"In a very short while our own people came up from 100 Kilo. I guess it must have been along toward maybe January 1944, I believe, after the first of the year. We organized again into units of Americans, Australians, Dutch, and so forth as had been our custom before. We were concerned with cutting wood and trying to keep warm at night. We were quite high up. As you look at a map, you might note that the camp was right next to Three Pagodas Pass, and that's the pass over the mountains that run the length of Malaysia and into Sumatra and Java. At night it became bitter cold, and we began to sleep as early in the evening as we could because with insufficient blankets and so forth it was impossible to sleep from along about 1:30 to 2:00 A.M. on. So we'd get up and sit next to the bamboo fires that we'd make in the hut so that we could keep halfway warm. A bamboo fire is much like sitting in front of a fireplace; you scorch on one side and on the other side you get frozen. But this was the best job that I had on the railroad, cutting wood for these trains.

"They organized us into teams of four men, and each four-man team would get a saw, an ax, a sledge, and a wedge. We'd cut this wood into half-meter lengths. A meter is about 39 inches. So we'd cut the wood in half-meter lengths, and the four-man task for the day would be to cut a rick 1.1 meters high and 4 meters in length. This Hugh Faulk again worked with my team, and Faulk was the best man on a saw that I've ever seen. The saw just ran itself when he was on the other end of it. Then one of the other sailors had worked as a lumberjack in Idaho in civilian life, so he was an accomplished woodsman. Modesty now deserts me. I only saw one man in all the prison camps that could beat me with an ax. We had an Aussie that could cut more wood with an ax than I could. But I had grown up in West Texas, and during my life as a young boy, our fuel in the wintertime was mesquite stumps, and, by thunder, you get proficient right quick with an ax when you have to work on these mesquite stumps. So this served me well.

"So Faulk and this sailor would get on the saw, and I would use the ax while they were sawing the butt cuts. I'd be working up the limbs. Our fourth man would stack it. He carried it out beside the railroad and stacked it. That's all he did. Some days, if we got a good sharp saw, we'd get out there, and we might do four days' work in one day and leave that wood stacked way out in the jungle. And so the next day, if we got poor tools or didn't want to do anything, we'd sleep all day, lay back there in the jungle and sleep, because the Japanese guards didn't go around out there in the jungle looking for you. We would sleep to midafternoon and then carry our daily quota and stack it up beside the railroad. That's why I say this was the easiest time that we had on the railroad, the time that we worked cutting wood.

"In this area we had quite a lot of balsa—like you make model airplanes out of. Occasionally, for spite, we'd cut one of the balsa trees. It wasn't as easy as you might think. It was like sawing paper. We'd go stack it up, and when the train crews passed through, they would see us stacking up the balsa, and they'd just have a fit. They'd call us everything impolite in the Japanese language that they could think of. But that didn't bother us. We didn't work for them. We worked for another bunch of Japanese, and they didn't care what we brought out there—just as long as it was wood and it was stacked up to 1.1 meters and 4 meters long. They weren't going to throw it into the firebox of a train.

"That's one thing we often noted: the complete and utter lack of cooperation between organizations of the Japanese. Ofttimes you'd see some of these Japanese military units as they passed through when we were at 100 Kilo, where we were breaking ballast. We had two Caterpillars—a DC-6 and a DC-4—with winches, and the only thing we used the winches for was to wrap around a good-sized granitelike boulder and drag it off the mountainside down to the foot of the hill so we could jump on it with sledges and make small ones out of the large one. Well, another Japanese unit would come by with some motor transport gear and get stuck out in the mud, and do you think these Japanese would go out there with their Caterpillars and drag them out? They wouldn't do it. The soldiers that were stuck would have to walk off and leave their transports right there in the mudhole because these Japs wouldn't help them out. You wonder how they ever got as far as they did with such an uncooperative nature as they displayed.

"Well, we fared fairly well by now. The rainy season was over. The bashings never did stop altogether, but they saw the futility in it about as much as we did, I think, and decided that it was just wasted effort. Not that they became any better humored, but they just said, 'Well, I'm just spinning my wheels if I go over and bash him, so there's not much use in it.' Of course, our guards were occupation troops. For the most part they were Koreans officered by Japanese, and I'd imagine that the officers were not the most brilliant nor efficient ones they had. That's why they shunted them back here in the first place. This might or might not be true of noncoms.

"Now this commander in charge of our branch of prisoners of war in Burma, by the name of Nagatomo,* he was the senior Japanese officer, and, I knew of him. I saw him a number of times. His headquarters were at Thanbyuzayat, and when I was there for that period of time, I would see him around camp. Of course, our senior POW commander was an Australian Brigadier, Varley.† I understand Varley was lost on a ship bound for Japan and sunk by our submarines. I know that in *The Bridge on the River Kwai* the Japanese characterization there is much like that that we entertained of Nagatomo, and the British officer was very much—in many ways—characteristic of Varley. Varley was much of a man. He was a holder of the Victoria Cross, and the British don't give that Victoria Cross lightly. I had a great deal of respect for him. He looked after his POWs in an unusual way, and, I'm satisfied, ofttimes at a complete disregard for his own well-being. It seems this is the general idea of how he conducted himself.

"Well, I cut wood probably from late November until March 1944. Then in March things were winding down on the railroad, and the work for the most part was devoted to cutting wood. The work of building the railroad was finished. Of course, they just didn't run up there and say, 'Well, it's finished right now.' They always had to have repair crews doing this and that. A flood in the mountains would wash out a bridge, so you had to have somebody fix it. Or a mudslide or some such thing would disrupt the line, and so you always had to have crews to go along and repair. But what remained were skeleton crews.

---

*Nagatomo was actually commander of Group 3 but the senior officer in rank.
†Brigadier A. L. Varley was POW commander of A Force. He died aboard a Japanese ship bound for Japan in September 1944.

"By March some of the prisoners had gone on, headed for Japan. A lot of them didn't make it. Well, we heard they wanted to ship some people out, and whoever they shipped out would be going to Japan. I didn't have any desire to get on a Japanese ship and go anywhere because we were bombed going to Moulmein. So they lined us up, and they asked us all, 'What was your civilian occupation?' They asked us and two or three of us got wise, and we told them that we were peach-fur pickers. This Japanese was sitting there with his brush that they write with, and we told him 'peach-fur pickers,' and their English leaves them when they got confronted this way, and so he says, '*Nani?*' *Nani* is 'what.' So we repeated again, 'Peach-fur pickers. We pick fur off peaches.' So he thought a little bit, and I guess he couldn't translate or figure out this peach-fur picking, picking fur off peaches. So he thought on it a little bit, and then he stabbed his brush over there in the ink, this lampblack-like stuff they use for ink, and he hesitated a minute, and then he put down a couple of explanatory marks, and he thought a little bit, and then he dashed off four or five more marks right quick, just like the enlightenment had sunk in all of a sudden. I've often wondered what that silly rascal actually put down.

"Anyway, when the Japanese began to divide us up and move us out in mid-March, I was selected with nine other Americans to go to somewhere, but we didn't know where. We were just ten Americans out of all this number that they picked to go somewhere. We were told on the train that we were going to Thailand, but we had no idea what we would be doing there or what we would be in for. Of course, you don't travel like riding on the Santa Fe Chief. You're bundled up in these little cooped-up boxcars, and it seemed that they might have a string of twenty empty cars, and they'd have to put forty men in one car that would accommodate maybe fifteen. There was no room for all of you to lie down at one time or even stand up at one time. I don't know why they do that, but this seemed to be one of their failings. So we went to this place in Thailand, and they took us off the train at this camp at Tamarkan. This was a big camp, the largest that we'd been in. It was a relief to know we weren't going to wind up in a port city."

Pryor never went to Japan, but a few days later he moved to Non Pladuk, where he helped build a huge foundry and machine-shop complex for the railroad. He laid water pipe to the various buildings. Later he herded cows and cut wood. He found out from Chinese technicians at the shops that the war was over on August 15, two days before the Japanese made the formal announcement. Two weeks later he was sent to Rat Buri and then Phet Buri in southern Thailand. From there he flew to Rangoon, through Calcutta, and was back home in Texas by November 1945.

Pryor's adjustment to freedom was easy; he was only a bit restless. He remained in the Marine Corps first as a recruiter and then as first sergeant of an antiaircraft artillery battalion. At the time of the Korean War he was commissioned a second lieutenant and stayed with the Marine antiaircraft artillery. He retired from the corps after twenty years of service, graduated from Baylor University in Waco, Texas, and later taught history in the state's public school system. In 1966 he began graduate study as a doctoral candidate in political science but never finished the degree. For his valor as a POW he received several military awards, including the Navy Commendation Medal in 1945.

Roy M. ("Max") Offerle
Battery D

"Just barely" sixteen when he enlisted in 1937, Roy M. ("Max") Offerle joined the Texas National Guard because his older brother, Oscar, was a member, and because he wanted the money he would earn attending regular meetings. Offerle was born on October 4, 1921, in Electra, Texas, a small town twenty-five miles northwest of Wichita Falls on Highway 287. When he was four years old the family moved to Wichita Falls. By the time the unit was federalized, he was a gunnery sergeant in charge of the third gun section of Battery D, Second Battalion, 131st Field Artillery. He was a recent graduate of Wichita Falls High School and more interested in the current popular songs than in world affairs.

With minor exceptions, Offerle's experiences were typical of those described in the preceding interviews, up to the time of the departure of the unit from Changi as POWs bound for work on the Death Railway. In the jungle camps, Offerle would "buddy up" with Keith F. ("Zeke") Naylor[*] and Edgar C. Bruner[†] once they began work on the railroad, but his closest friend in the unit was Oscar, who was also captured by the Japanese. "When we were very young," Roy said, "my father told Oscar that he was the oldest and that it was his duty and obligation to look after me. He took it literally, so he did this up until he died. He always shared everything with me." As Offerle's interview describes, Oscar died from a tropical ulcer at 80 Kilo Camp on November 18, 1943.

Offerle's opinion of the conduct of the American POWs compared to the British agrees with the Scotsman Ernest Gordon's assessment in the memoir *Through the Valley of the Kwai*. Gordon wrote of the British Army: "We lived by the rule of the jungle, 'red in tooth and claw'—the evolutionary law of the survival of the fittest. It was a case of 'I look out for myself and to hell with everyone else.' This became our norm. . . . The weak were trampled underfoot, the sick ignored or resented, the dead forgotten. When

---

[*]Naylor, who was also in Battery D, now lives in Mansfield, Texas.
[†]Bruner, of Battery D, died of a gunshot wound on March 20, 1959, at Megargel, Texas.

169

a man lay dying we had no word of mercy. When he cried for help, we averted our heads. . . . Everyone was his own keeper. It was free enterprise at its worst, with all the restraints of morality gone." Offerle's memories of the Americans are more favorable: "One thing I can say about the Americans— I'm very proud of them—they were clean, and they were neat; they stuck together. Although a lot of them stole, and they did this and that, very little, if any, was from Americans. They stole from the Japs. They were very good about helping each other in every way that they could. I'm very proud of that fact."

Aboard the *Dai Moji Maru*, Offerle contracted dysentery. As a result he stayed behind in Moulmein while the rest of his mates went forward to work on the railroad. His interview begins when he rejoined his unit at 18 Kilo Camp.

" A S I RECOLLECT, Thanbyuzayat was about fifty kilometers out of Moulmein. The first camp to my knowledge, where our people went, was 18 Kilo Camp. That's where I joined them. You see, when I left Moulmein, I was transferred to Thanbyuzayat, which was a base camp. The Japs had a hospital there, or they had barracks that they called a hospital. I was getting better. They asked anybody who was going to the latrine more than five times a day to go into one hut, and less than that, in another. I went in the wrong hut, and I could see that everybody in there was dying, so I got out as soon as I could.

"Well, I started getting better, and the first thing you know, I was well enough to be transferred out to 18 Kilo. When you're sick, you don't worry. I didn't worry too much at the time. Of course, I didn't know what the future held. We had some scares in Thanbyuzayat; they bombed an area away from the camp. Later, after I had gone up to 18 Kilo, they bombed the camp itself. I think the Japs had a railhead or something there that the Americans were coming after.

"For all practical purposes my dysentery was over when I went to 18 Kilo Camp. There are two basic types of dysentery—amebic and bacillary—and I had bacillary dysentery, which would kill you faster. It's very severe, and if you can live over a couple of weeks, well, then you can generally recover. Amebic is the one that you never get rid of. Unless they've got medication to get rid of it since then, you had it the rest of your life. But it wasn't so severe that it would kill you. This other kind would kill you very rapidly—almost like cholera. But I was over it, and I was picking up weight; and when I got to 18 Kilo, I was in fairly good shape. It wasn't but a few days, and I was well enough to go to work there.

"Basically, 18 Kilo was like one of the many camps we were to be in in the future. You're talking about, like, maybe three, four, five thousand men in these camps, a lot of men. They had long huts made out of bamboo frames tied together with atap, which are leaves wrapped over thin pieces of bamboo about three feet long. They'd leave the walls open, and they had atap leaf roofs that were overhanging. My brother was working in the cookhouse and then on the wood detail, cutting wood for the kitchen. Anybody related to the kitchen got a little better food. When I got there, he started bringing me some extra food, and it helped me get well fast. The quality wasn't too good, but the quantity was fair.

"The first job we had was a fill about three blocks long. It was forty meters across the top of the depression; there was a natural slope to it, which went about twenty feet deep.* It took four or five thousand men working a month or two to build this fill. This is when I got with ol' Ed Bruner and Zeke Naylor. Ed and I worked the first few days together. Ed was in good shape; he'd been working, and he like to killed me. The men worked hard because they knew they were off as soon as they moved a meter of dirt. After we got accustomed to pick-and-shovel work and carrying dirt, we would finish at three or four o'clock in the afternoon.

"Well, then the Japs just gave us a larger quota. So we went to a meter-and-a-tenth, a meter-and-a-quarter, a meter-and-a-half per man per day. Later on up country, they went to two meters of dirt. When they went to one-and-a-half meters of dirt, you'd get in about dark. Two meters of dirt would get you in at about ten or eleven o'clock at night. They eventually went to this, and by then, too, we got food that didn't have all of your vitamins. You weren't keeping your strength up. The men's physical strength gradually wore down, and our quotas gradually went up, which set us up for disease and sickness and a lot of the things that were to follow.

"At this time, our group, which was one of the largest groups of Americans working on the railroad, hadn't yet experienced real hardship. We were getting a little sickness, some malaria, maybe a few people hurt. From 18 Kilo, we went to 80 Kilo Camp. Now, we had larger quotas to meet. We were up in a lot more jungle. Conditions were not so good. We were farther away, so supplies were harder to get up there. We got away from canteens and extra food that you could buy.

"From 80 Kilo, which was a smaller camp, we went to 100 Kilo, which was a larger camp. Incidentally, we were at 85 Kilo Camp for a while—80,

---

*Dimensions of projects described by the POWs may not be correct. Apparently precise measurements were not taken and considerable time has intervened since the men were employed on the railroad.

85, 100. But 100 Kilo Camp seemed to be a larger camp. I believe it was in 100 Kilo Camp where we got the full brunt of the rainy season. When you talk about rainy season in Burma, you're talking about three or four months where it comes out like you're pouring it from a bucket, day in and day out. It's possibly three or four hundred inches of rain in a season.* Actually, creeks and rivers form, and you can almost watch vegetation grow. The rainy or monsoon season turned everything to soup or mud, and they couldn't get supplies up there easily. Then the speedup on work came. We went from one meter, to a meter-and-a-half, to two meters of dirt per day. Well, the men's health broke down. We started getting lots of malaria, beriberi, dysentery, and tropical ulcers, because it seemed that the germ that causes tropical ulcers was more prevalent in the rainy season. We started getting a multitude of diseases.

"The more people that got sick, the less the Japs had for working parties, so more sick people had to work. They'd set a quota of men everyday that had to go out, and they'd fill it. I worked all this time. I hadn't been sick, although I lost weight. I didn't have malaria, beriberi, or any diseases. So I worked. This *kumi* of fifty men that I was in was originally all sergeants, and it was down after the rainy season started to thirteen or fourteen men. That didn't mean they were all dead; some of them were, but most of them were just sick. They were sick enough that if they had been in the United States, they'd have been in an isolation ward with a nurse twenty-four hours a day. Yet here they were in a bamboo hut in the rainy season eating a little rice and water stew; no medication and no one to take care of them, except our own medics and doctor who had no medicine.

"This developed into a situation where we started losing men fast. The Japs would force the sick out. If they wanted a *kumi* of twenty-five to go out, and they had fourteen healthy there, that meant eleven sick had to go out. So they would come down through the sick barracks. The first time I stayed in, I had malaria and was sick as a dog. I was shaking and felt terrible and had a high fever and chills. I asked the doctor if I could stay in, and he said, 'Yes, you haven't been in, so stay in.' So here come the Japs down for extra men to go to work. Well, I got off the heavy-duty job, but they said they had to send me out on light duty. The doctor said, 'There are some men sicker than you. Can you go out on light duty?' I said, 'Well, if I have to, I will.' He said, 'Yes, you'd better go out.' These Japs raised Cain, and they started beating everybody and giving the doctors and medics a hard time. So, light duty was

---

*The highest annual average rainfall in Burma is 200 inches, but other POWs say it was 300 inches where they were in mid-1943.

busting rocks with a sledgehammer—putting rocks on the roads—because they were just a sea of mud, and they were trying to fix the roads enough to get trucks up them with supplies.

"While our doctor, Captain Lumpkin, was alive, I think they gave him a quota, and he would try to get the right men out. He'd decide who among the sick could work. Later on, I remember this one little Jap that was in charge—I think he was a Jap sergeant—and he'd come down and decide. He knew Luther Prunty* real well. Prunty had been on the wood detail, and he got to know this Jap. Prunty had a bad tropical ulcer. The Jap would shake his head, but he always let Prunty stay in. But he'd come down and ask one of the medics, 'What's wrong with this man?' The medic would say, 'dysentery' or 'malaria.' The Jap'd look him over, and, if he thought the man looked all right, the Jap'd say, 'All right, you go.' If a man was too sick, he'd argue with the Jap. But if a man looked like he could hold up, well, the Jap'd send him out.

"We had a hospital hut; actually we had more than one hospital hut. We got a lot of men with tropical ulcers, so they made one whole hut or most of it for men with tropical ulcers only. I was never in the hospital hut, because by the time I got sick where I couldn't work, they had so many sick men that they filled up the hospital hut. Of course, men got to where they didn't want to go to the hospital hut, because most of the men that went over there died. In other words, they put the real, real sick over there. They tried everything in the world to save them, but some would quit eating and just give up. They would box them and slap their ears, cuss them, threaten them—everything to try to get them to eat or to make them mad or to give them an incentive to live. But some never gave up, and some would just give up. It was pitiful, but they would do it because we'd been prisoners for so long, and the weather was so bad, and the conditions were so terrible that some of them just didn't have any will or reason to live. So they just gave up.

"This is where I got my tropical ulcer. On light duty, making little rocks out of big rocks, busting them with a sledgehammer. I hit a rock, and a chip of it cut me below the left knee, and that night it was kind of infected. I washed it out and put a rag around it. The next day I went out, and I came in and it was about as big as a silver dollar—kind of gray, rotten flesh. It kept getting larger. I guess over a period of the next few weeks, it got about three inches in diameter. I was all covered with rotten flesh with a kind of seepage oozing out of it.

---

*Prunty's interview appears in Chapter 1, "The Capture."

"The Japs started selling a little bit of drugs there. They got some American Red Cross medicine, and they were selling it to us. If you had a gold watch or ring, you could buy a little iodoform or sulfa drug. But I had already sold my watch, and I didn't have a ring, so I didn't get any drugs. All I had was hot water to flush it out a little bit. This ulcer ate part of the nerves away, so I had no pain. If you had nerves that were exposed, or if it was still very tender, it was an excruciatingly painful experience to go through if you had no drugs to deaden the pain. Incidentally, my brother got an ulcer about this time. He had a very small one, at first. It didn't go deep like mine did, but it went around his leg. It got larger and larger until it was almost from his ankle to his knee. It lacked about a half of an inch from joining at the back of his leg. So we both were with ulcers at the same time.

"It took about a year for mine to cure. We were in 100 Kilo Camp for a while, and then the Japs decided to send all of the heavy sick back to 80 Kilo Camp. I've heard it described since as the Death Camp. They sent anybody that couldn't walk back there. They only had two little Korean guards there. Both Ed and Zeke had been sick, but we had a little money saved. They paid noncoms fifteen cents a day. Ed came to me and said, 'They're sending all the heavy sick back to 80 Kilo, and Oscar will have to go, because he can't walk.' I could hobble on crutches by then, and I was getting a little better. He said, 'You'd better go with him because blood is thicker than water, and he's your brother.' So I said, 'Okay.' He said, 'I want to give you the money we got, because you'll need it worse than we will.' I said, 'No, I'm not going to take it, because you guys are sick, too.' He had about a dollar-and-a-half. He said, 'Let me help you pack.' By then I had picked up the nickname of Little Offerle, and they called Oscar Big Offerle. Ed called me Little 'Un or Junior. He said, 'Little 'Un, you had better go with Oscar.' I saw him put this money in my bag, so I didn't say anything. I took it, and it came in handy later on. But that was all the money that they had to their names. I've never forgotten that.

"We were taken in a truck, and it was a wild and rough ride. My brother's ulcer went bad on him because of the truck ride. It turned gray and black in spots. It was a camp full of heavy sick on their deathbed at 80 Kilo. There were about two or three hundred men down there. There were about six men who could walk and a few men in the kitchen. Just six men had to feed all these sick people, carry their food to them and everything, take care of them. Charley Pryor,* a Marine, and Roy Morrow† worked there. Two

---

*Pryor's interview appears in this chapter.
†Morrow, who was in Headquarters Battery, died of a heart attack on Christmas Eve, 1982, at his home in Richmond, Virginia.

Australians wounded on the ship that was bombed coming up were there. One had lost an arm, and one had lost an eye. There were two or three others: Harris,* the medic, Andy Mitchell, an Australian medic off the *Perth*. We had an old black witch doctor, a Dutch doctor. Harris and Andy were the only two medics. This is what took care of those two hundred people.

"Of course, I was getting better. I would keep flushing out the poison and flushing out rotten flesh. Oh! I stood in the river—there was a little stream there—and minnows will eat rotten flesh, but they won't eat the good flesh. So I used to go down to the river and stand, and it doesn't hurt. You'd just feel them nibbling at the place. I would stand in the water to just over this sore, and they would clean it out real good. The main thing was to get the ulcer clean and keep it clean. Then little points of proud flesh would come through the sore. It was about an inch deep. I was scared it would get in my knee and ruin my whole leg, but it never did. There was one officer— I never have told this—who had a little sulfa drugs, that they would mix with rice powder to make it go further. Sulfa was so scarce that they couldn't get much, but they would mix it with rice powder. Harris swiped a little from this officer and put it on my leg, and this is really when it started getting well. He just dosed it once or twice, because he didn't have much. But it did start getting well, and I was getting around to where I could walk.

"At 100 Kilo Camp I was next to an 'ol boy called Dan Buzzo;† he was a sergeant. We were together for a long time. He had an ulcer on his big toe. Well, I left my leg in one position for several weeks, and then when I went to straighten it, it wouldn't straighten. The tendons had drawn up. So Buzzo would massage my leg behind the muscles and underneath my knee and down my leg. He massaged it for all one day, and he got it limbered up to where I could straighten it. Then dumb me I left it straight for several days, and I couldn't bend it. So he went through the whole procedure again. You found that you got to know men real well, some of them as well as a brother, and they did help each other a lot—especially in your little groups.

"I guess one of the finest things a man ever did for me was when I had diarrhea while I suffered from this ulcer. To go to the head, I had to crawl backwards on my feet and on my hands. One day I started out and had diarrhea, so I messed my pants. I was very disgusted and disheartened, and I guess I was feeling sorry for myself. So I was sitting there crying, and ol' Zeke came in from work, and he said, 'Junior, what in the world is the

---

*Claude R. Harris, of the Medical Detachment, now lives in Boise, Idaho.

†Dan C. Buzzo, who was in Headquarters Battery, now lives in Spring, Texas.

matter with you?' I said, 'I just dirtied my pants.' He said, 'Take the blankety-blank things off, and I'll wash them for you.' I thought that was one of the finest things a man could do for me, and I'll never forget it. We really helped each other out real good. We really did.

"At 80 Kilo I was more or less looking after my brother. Where they put me, an Australian right next to me died within two days. An Australian right behind me died within two or three days. They moved all the heavy, heavy sick in one hut, which my brother went to. Oscar died there. By then his ulcer had spread all up and down his leg, between his knee and ankle, and had gone around to within a half-inch of closing on the other side. It started to get deep holes within the ulcer. In fact, it started eating around the bone of his leg, the main bone. Right before he died there was about two inches of bone showing. The ulcer had eaten around behind it, too. This waste or material that came out of the ulcer—blood, pus, mucus, or whatever it was—had dripped down on his ankle on the top of his foot, and another large ulcer was there.

"He had an old beat-up blanket that he had put underneath his leg to catch all this dripping, and it was saturated. I would take it down to the river and wash it out every day, and it would just be saturated with this stuff. It would take maybe five, ten, fifteen minutes to wash it out. There would be so much of it in it that you had to scrub it and wash it and scrub it and wash it and then take it back and put it underneath. Actually, outside of hot water, they didn't have anything to use on the ulcers.

"I didn't realize my brother was going to die, even though he was as sick as he was. With something like that, I guess your mind won't accept that he might die. Charley Pryor, who was one of the well ones there, came to me and said, 'Little 'Un, I want to talk to you about your brother.' I said, 'Okay, what about him?' He said, 'I want to tell you. I don't think you realize it, but I don't think he's going to make it. He's pretty sick, and I've seen men not as sick as he is that have died.' He said, 'I just want to let you know, because you've got to kind of adjust to the fact. I don't think you realize that.' I said, 'No, Charley, maybe we can get him out! Maybe we can save him! Maybe we can! Maybe he'll get better!' He said, 'Well, from the way it looks now, I don't think we can get out of here in time to save him.'

"I was going over to see him every day, and help feed him, and give him medication and this and that. He told me, he says, 'I'm getting blackouts. When I sit up, I get black spots before my eyes. I don't know whether I'm going to make it.' I said, 'Well, hang on. I hear they have been moving some out to another camp that's got doctors and medicine and everything. Just try to hang on and see what you can do.' I had heard rumors, but you hear anything that you want to hear.

"So I went to Kanamura, this little Korean guard in the camp who befriended us, and I told him that my brother was very sick. He said that he would go see him. The next day he came to me and said he talked to Oscar and said, 'Your brother is very sick.' I said, 'Can you help him or get medicine?' He said, 'I don't know, but I'll try.' That night he went to different camps up and down the railroad within a four- or five-kilometer area and tried to get some sulfa drugs or medicine or anything he could. He said he was just a little private, so what could he do. He said, 'I couldn't find any.' But I thought it was nice of him that he tried. But we couldn't get medication—nothing at all. I went over to the heavy sick hut a day or two later, late in the afternoon. Oscar was semiconscious, and he was hot. I put his head in my lap, and he died.

"We buried Oscar at 80 Kilo Camp. We had got hold of a bunch of teakwood, and they made crosses out of teak. Where the boys had dogtags—which Oscar had—they buried one with the body. They wrapped him up. He was buried in a woven mat—straw mat—and they wrapped him in that and tied it, buried a dogtag with him, and then they tied one to the cross or nailed one to the cross. I think they were able to identify him fairly easy later. They had one or two men working all the time making crosses.

"The Japs put out an order at one of the places—I think it was 100 Kilo Camp—that said nobody could die in the mornings because it was inconvenient or something. Of course, the people that died just ignored them; they died when they got ready. It was weird because they always played taps when an American died. You heard it all the time in 80 and 100 Kilo Camps; it just played all the time. We had so many men dying. I think we lost more Americans in those camps—80 and 100 Kilo—than any other place up and down the river. Of course, the Australians were losing a lot. They would play their taps, too. Somebody was dying all the time, all the time.

"Oscar died on November 18, 1943, and I had Christmas at 105 Kilo Camp. So sometime between November 18th and Christmas, the Japs finally pulled out the ones that hadn't died at 80 Kilo and moved us to 105 Kilo, which was an old, established camp. This was the first time we were there, however. We had Christmas there. Americans were very good about not stealing from each other, but somebody seen a Dutchman steal some dried fish from the Jap kitchen. They saw where he put them, so Charley Pryor and somebody stole the dried fish from the Dutchman. So we had dried fish for Christmas.

"Actually, the food was lousy at 105. Somebody might have a can or two of something there that they opened. But they had a lot of these long, white radishes, Chinese radishes or what-have-you. We ate radish stew for what seemed like months. It took me about twenty years to get to where I could even look at a radish. I'll tell you something I discovered. They'd bring in sacks of big, ol', dried peppers which were absolutely like chewing on a piece of paper as far as trying to eat them. But you could toast them over a fire—don't breathe the smoke, because it would knock the top off your head—and you could crumble them up and put them on rice, and they tasted just like toasted peanuts. This was a welcome change. It was very good to eat.

"I had started baking cakes. I got acquainted with the Black Dutch— they're part Dutch; they had one-fourth or one-eighth Dutch in them. We were going out in the jungle and getting weeds and stuff to eat. I thought, 'Well, we need vitamins, and these guys know all about that.' So I made friends with one of them, and within a week or two, why, I found out about twenty different items that you could eat out in the jungle—things I never dreamed of. We were getting vitamins we needed to fight beriberi. I got beriberi, but I never got it real, real bad. Your chest swells up, and you swell up all over. Your testicles swell as big as grapefruits, your legs swell; your face sticks out. It's just horrible looking. But I had it in my chest. My chest swelled up, and I was short of breath at nights.

"Well, I could hobble around, and I started making cakes with a tropical plant called lemon grass. I learned how to make these cakes from other guys. You take this rice and soak it in water, and then you pound it with a club, and it makes a coarselike consistency of cornmeal. Then you would take a bottle and roll the meal on a board and make flour out of it. Then you take some sugar and mix it with cooked rice—real thin—to make what they called pap. Then you would put this out in the sun or near a fire, and it would ferment and make a kind of yeast. Then you would mix this yeast with some of the rice and the flour. Then you take banana leaves—they used them for everything, even raincoats—and use them for grease; tender, young banana leaves, and you line your meat can with banana leaves and make your batter and put a little lemon grass water in with your cake. You put the rice batter with water and the yeast, and you had the cake made. You put a lid on the meat can and then bury it in coals, and the cake puffs up and makes a beautiful dish. You had to learn how to time it; it took about twenty minutes. Then you take it out and pull the banana leaves off of it. You make an icing from the lemon grass. You'd boil it to get the flavor of lemon. You'd get some sugar and put it in there and when it cooled off again, it turned into like an icing. With this icing you had a beautiful cake. It'd cost about a dollar to make, and I would sell them for three dollars, and I could sell all I could make.

"This is the first time I learned to look after myself. I'd make five or six cakes a day, every two or three days. The first thing you know, I ended up with twenty, thirty, forty, or fifty bucks, which was like $50,000. My two buddies, ol' Zeke and Ed, I sent them each five dollars and a cake to pay them back for the money they had given me when I went down to 80 Kilo. The cakes were very good because people were starved for anything other than rice and stew, which is basically what we had. The stew didn't have much in it. They used some kind of roots which tasted like lumps of starch. They used pumpkin and something like squash and all kind of oddball things that had very little flavor or nutrition.

"The Japs liked snake, so we very seldom got a chance to eat snake. I didn't know it, but Burma was the home of the chicken. They had wild chickens there. Some of the boys who were Boy Scouts—incidentally, the things I learned in the Boy Scouts came out and helped in a lot of ways— would make figure-four traps and trap chickens. Then we would have chicken, which was delicious. I used to catch little bitty fish about three or four inches long in the stream. I would gut them, put them on a piece of wire I had, wrap them, and cook them in the coals with the skin and head and everything—minus the guts. You'd peel off that skin, and they were delicious. I supplemented my diet a little with that. They were small. You could scoop them out with pieces of cloth like a net or block up a part of the stream and drain the water off and catch them that way.

"Well, back at 105 Kilo, we just stopped there for a short period of time. I never dug dirt again. I was on a wood-chopping detail, but that was quite a bit later. The railroad by this time had been finished as far as laying the rails. They had trains running on it. I had never wore a G-string. When the war was over, I had an old pair of Dutch shorts that had fifty patches on them, but I never got to a G-string. I ran out of shoes. I went for a year or two without shoes. But I had pride in the way I looked, and I wanted to dress well, regardless, so I wore patched shorts. I tried to grow a beard, but it itched so much. I did have a mustache all during the war. Some fellows had beards four, five, six inches long, but I never did. It worried me too much. The Japs kept our hair short. This was good. If you're baldheaded, you can cut out lice and bugs and everything. My hair was never over a half-inch long on my head.

"At the big camps they had radios, and we heard the major news: when the Allies landed in North Africa, when they landed in Italy, the islands they were fighting on in the Pacific. We knew generally that the war was going our way slowly, that we were winning. We didn't know the small details about it, though. But news is like scuttlebutt; you hear it, but you're still here, so you forget about it. I lived day-by-day. I didn't worry about yesterday or tomorrow. To me that was the best way to keep my sanity and my wits—just what's going to happen today. I handled everything better that way.

"We had some mean Korean guards and some good ones, but mostly mean ones. We nicknamed them all. We had Dillinger, Mickey Mouse, Liver Lips. He was a mean one—great, big, ugly, wore glasses, little eyes, big lips, and mean as hell. He bashed everybody he got around. All he knew was bang, bang, bash, bash—very mean. You just stayed away, and, if you couldn't, you got beat up. A few people got shot. They had one Jap officer that would stay drunk all the time, and I think he killed a man with his sword and maybe shot one or two. There were a lot of beatings—a lot of atrocities going on.

"There are a lot of bridges on that railroad besides the one over the River Kwai. There were a lot of small ones, and they were built with teak. The natives would make these big teak logs about twelve or fifteen inches square and fifteen or twenty feet long. Teak is very hard, and it doesn't rot, and it's as heavy as iron. Up in the 100 Kilo area once, we were building a bridge. We had a fifteen-man detail: five to ride the truck, ten to go in the jungle and pull these logs out, and fifteen to load it on the truck and take it down to where the bridge was and dump it. We got hold of one that we couldn't pick up, and this gray-eyed Jap—the only one that I had ever seen in my life—got a bamboo pole about six foot, and he beat us, and he beat us, but we never picked it up—it was too heavy. We finally ended up dragging it out of the jungle. We couldn't pick it up—it was too heavy—even with a beating.

"There were lots of beatings. They had found one Aussie—I believe in 80 Kilo—who had written about 'dirty little slope-headed, slant-eyed, SOBs.' They found this and read it, and they beat him day and night and made him kneel down over a bamboo behind his knees, which cuts off all of your circulation, and made him look into the sun, which blinds you. They beat on him and like to have killed him, but he lived. They kept him up there two or three days beating on him. We had this going on—torture and beating and the 'go, go, go' when they were finishing the railroad. There was lots of that. The only real hard beating that I got, when I was knocked around and slapped around a few times, was when we were pulling this log, and the Jap worked us over. I was so mad I would have given all of my back pay to get hold of this guy with my bare hands. I wouldn't want to shoot him; I wanted to strangle him to death with my bare hands and make it last so he could suffer. But I thought, 'If I kill him, they'll kill me.' I thought my life was worth more than his, so I didn't do it.

"I wanted to settle the score at the time, but after I got home, I bore no animosity whatsoever. I guess over a period of years I adjusted my mind to it, but I don't have any animosity. A lot of the men still do. They hate Japs, and they don't want anything that's made in Japan. Some of them don't even like rice. I'm a gourmet cook. I cook all kinds of Oriental dishes. I have no animosity. At the time, I did. I would liked to have paid back some scores for things. I guess my biggest regret, really, is that I lost my brother over there. But I have no animosity. I just figure that when you harbor something like that over a period of years, it hurts you as much or more than the people you have these feelings against. There's no use in it. Really, there was a war. They did wrong things; other people have done wrong things. I had no animosity, really.

"We did a lousy job on the railroad. Really, I would hate to ride over the thing today if it was still going, because we did lousy work. Every chance we got, we just messed up. Once we were working on a bridge, on a pile driver with a real tall bamboo scaffold. They wanted to move it, and everybody got kind of weak or something, because the big tower, which was three or four stories tall, started to weave. The Japs started to scream and holler and tell us to do everything. Well, what we did, we dropped it, to make a long story short, and broke it into a million pieces. Of course, they had to build another one, and that delayed work for about two or three days. The Japs were screaming and hollering, and we just sat around and laughed. But every chance we got, which weren't a lot, we did a lousy job.

"Once going up-country, we were on a train, and we passed another train, and they stopped and let us off to get relief. We unhitched the train, and then we got back up there and sat and watched to see what was going to happen. When that train pulled out going the other way, instead of twenty cars, it had about three cars. All of the Japs were running up and down screaming and hollering and wondering what was going on. They came back and saw that it was unhitched, and they looked at us and gave us dirty looks and cussed us. We acted like we didn't know what went on. So they finally backed it up and hooked on.

"We were forever stealing. I became a professional thief. We stole everything we could from them. If you got caught, the circumstances were very dire; they would beat you and stand you at attention and this or that. I was very fortunate. Considering the things I did, I was very fortunate that I never got caught. Some other men got caught, and their punishment was very severe. A lot that we stole was food. The Japs had more and better food, and we would steal it to eat.

"From 105 Kilo Camp we went out of the jungle into Thailand to Tamarkan. This is the big camp by the so-called famous Bridge on the River Kwai; it was right next to it. It was a huge camp—Australians, Dutch, a few Americans. You have to remember that the Americans were in the minority of all the prisoners there all during the war. I guess that up in the jungle there were maybe not over five hundred to six hundred of us. To our way of thinking this was a nice camp. The food was good. They had Australian doctors. They had a better hospital setup. They were well-organized. Thailand had more to offer than Burma. They were more self-sufficient; they grew rice, and they had vegetables, and they had fruit and things. We were only four or five kilometers from a little town called Kanburi or Kanchanaburi. I was what you call a hospital case when I got to Tamarkan.

"I still had the ulcer; I couldn't get rid of it. But I finally got rid of it there. This is where I ran across the scraping of ulcers. I had heard stories where they had to get four or five men to hold a man down and scrape his ulcer when the nerves showed. But the nerves had been eaten out of mine, this area. In fact, today, I still got a spot as big as the palm of your hand that is dead. The nerves had been eaten out, and when they scraped, it didn't hurt. It didn't hurt me but some of them ol' boys you could hear them yell for a country mile. They didn't have any dope to put on them, so they'd scrape them. They would sharpen a spoon or curve a knife and sharpen one end of it and scrape all the rotten flesh out, and this seemed to make them heal better.

"Mine got down to about the size of a dime, and it wouldn't close and wouldn't close, and these Australian officers said, 'We found out that they do that. To make them close completely, you get off your feet.' You can't walk anywhere. You lay down, and you stay that way for a week or two. This is what I did, and this is what it did. It closed up finally to where I got just a big scar now. The thing just closed completely. Then you would get rags and kind of tie them around there as a kind of buffer, because the skin was very thin. It was easy to bump it and get it started again, but we would wear a cushion over the area of our ulcer to kind of protect it.

"As long as the ulcer didn't kill me, I didn't worry too much about it. What I was happy about was to get good food again and to get out of that jungle. However, we did have something that was a new threat to us there, and that was the darn bridge and the Allied planes. This was the camp where the men came from that built the bridge that the movie was made about. The river splits right below where the bridge is built. The big river, which is actually the Mae Klong, is the one that the bridge is over. Down below it, it splits off to the left, there's another river which is really the Kwai. The Mae Klong was a large river, especially during the rainy season; it would get very deep and very swift. I'd say the river—counting the beds—is close to a hundred yards wide.

"The movie bridge was wood, but this one had huge concrete emplacements. Pinky King, one of the Marines, said that the Japs had brought these steel parts from Java, from a bridge there. From the pictures I've seen of the English building it, they built the concrete emplacements. Originally, they had a wooden bridge there, and they built this concrete base and then put up the steel bridge. We came out of the jungle in the latter part of '43 or early '44. In '44 the Allies decided to shoot up the railroad and start bombing the bridges, just tearing up the place. That is what they did, and, although our camp was huge, the corner nearest the bridge was just a stone's throw from it. You could take a rock and chuck it and almost hit the bridge from this corner, so we were very close. In addition, the Japs put up four ack-ack guns there from which the shrapnel fell in our camp.

"They had a raid the week before we got there, and a string of bombs had fallen in the camp, and blew up one or two huts, and killed and wounded a lot of people. So everybody was on edge when we got there. We weren't there a week when we had another big raid, so we started getting shellacked by our own people. You'd want to cheer them for tearing up the bridge, and you'd want to cuss them for trying to kill you. But it was fun to watch, and we were tickled to death to see that they were still around and doing something."

Offerle's companions, Naylor and Bruner, joined him at Tamarkan, although Bruner was sent on to Saigon while the others missed the levy because of illnesses. The two ultimately moved over to the camp at Chungkai, a few kilometers from Tamarkan, where the English soldiers who built the bridges were really imprisoned. Because he could sneak out of camp easily, Offerle began to buy clothing in the camp and then sell it to the natives on the outside.* He lived better as a result, having money to spend on food at the canteen. The Japanese next sent him to a smaller camp to cut wood and then shipped him on to Phet Buri, where he helped dig wells for troops constructing an airfield in the vicinity.

---

*Cloth of any kind was a scarce commodity at the time.

He was at Phet Buri when the war ended and followed the route of most American POWs in the area through Rangoon to Calcutta and then to New York. Within a few weeks of his liberation he was back in Texas, hospitalized first in McKinney and then in San Antonio. He mustered out of the service in 1946 and spent thirty-two years working for "a large corporation in sales" before retiring. He has written that his experiences as a POW "made me more aware of the suffering people go through, the cruelty of man against his fellow man." His opinion of Japanese is that they are cruel, Koreans are both good and bad, and the Thai people are "the best, very kind when able." He and his wife toured Thailand, Malaysia, and Singapore in May and June of 1991.

Houston Tom ("Slug") Wright
Battery F

"Slug" Wright was born on January 4, 1915, in the Wilson County jail in Floresville, Texas, where his father was county sheriff at the time. Floresville is a small town thirty miles southeast of San Antonio, but Wright lived several places in the state after his father became a captain and commanding officer of Company A, Texas Rangers. In fact, Wright thought of himself as a West Texan, and he did live in Marfa, Fort Stockton, and Salt Flats before attending the University of New Mexico. He later worked for the Standard Oil Company in Arizona.

Wright was twenty-six years old when he entered the Army on January 24, 1941. He had his name moved up on the selective service list after coming back to Texas. He wanted to serve in the Second Battalion, 131st Field Artillery, because two of his brothers served in the battalion during World War I. His receiving sergeant was a member of the Texas National Guard, who had Wright sent to Camp Bowie, near Brownwood, to become a member of Battery F of the Second Battalion.

Primarily a radioman, Wright acted also as a meteorologist and worked for the supply sergeant during the year the battalion was a fighting unit. He boarded the USAT *Republic* with the Second in San Francisco, claiming in his interview that the vessel had first been the German ship *Wilhelm der Grosse* before the British acquired her and sold her to the United States Army. While in Honolulu, he encountered someone he knew from back home:

> I never will forget that at the end of our pass I ran into some boys who wanted to go see some prostitutes, and I went with them. I didn't have any money, but I went anyway. I went up in a waiting room, and while I was in this room, a girl walked out, and it was a girl that I knew in Corpus Christi, Texas. I was shocked because she was in the same church I was in and belonged to the BYTU [Baptist Youth Training Union] and everything. She was shocked, of course, to see me and begged me never to tell that I had seen her. After she got off duty, she went with me. We talked and she bought me a flower lei. So when I got back aboard ship, all of the guys thought that she and I had had an affair, which we really didn't have. They would never believe me that I hadn't. But I never told on her either, you know.

Once the battalion reached Java, Wright became one of the few Texans to exchange rifle fire with the Japanese. He was on a scouting patrol and came upon members of an advance Japanese force. He fired at them and then fled. In his haste, he stumbled through a rice paddy, got separated from the rest of the patrol, and lost his rifle. Ultimately, he was reunited with the main body of troops and stayed with them from the racetrack near Garut until he left with the Fitzsimmons group, the first detachment to go to Changi. On the trip from Changi to Burma, Slug was badly beaten by a Japanese guard when he disobeyed an order by trying to get a drink of water from a leaky steampipe. He had his nose broken and, when the guard threw him in the hold of the ship, he had ribs broken and his chest caved in. This was his condition when the interview begins, and, as is apparent, these injuries bothered him all during his captivity.

"I FOUND OUT WHERE WE WERE, because there was a sailor, and he said, 'I know where we are.' I said, 'Where are we?' He said, 'We're in Rangoon, Burma.' His name was Donald Brain.* I said, 'How do you know?' He said, 'I used to live here.' I said, 'You lived here?' He said, 'Well, up the river. I've been here a number of times. My dad was an oilman, so when I was a boy, I was right here in Rangoon.' That's when I found out where we were.

"Okay, my cartilage in my nose was broken, my chest was caved in on one side more than the other—it will always be that way—and I had broken ribs. So I formed my nose back with my hands. I held it for, oh, well, goldang, I really can't tell you how long. But I just formed it back with my hands. The inside of the thing is still all screwed up, but I never have let them operate on it since a surgeon told me it would probably cause me more problems than it'd be worth. So I just live with it. Of course, I have trouble breathing with it.

"To top things off I slept in a leper ward the first night we moved to Moulmein. They had a sign, but I didn't see it because it was dark. When I got up the next morning and saw it was a leper ward, I wondered if I was going to get leprosy. But I didn't. Evidently lepers hadn't been there for a long time. Well, I was none too happy in Moulmein. Then, we got a train and went into Thanbyuzayat, which was called the railhead. That's where it all started. It wasn't too far from Moulmein to Thanbyuzayat, but it seemed like a long ways at the time.

---

*Brain's interview appears in the preceding chapter, "The Road to Burma."

"Well, this Nagatomo got us out there, and he gave us this famous speech that we were the rabble of the decayed democracy; that our leaders had got us into this awful fix; that he doesn't hate us, but we have to pay for it. So we got to keep smiling through this whole business. You may have read this speech, because they have copies of this famous Nagatomo speech. I don't know how they got it, but I have seen it someplace. I wasn't nearly as interested in the speech when it was given as I was later on when I read what he said, because he gave it through an interpreter. We stayed there for a little while, and then we went to the 40 Kilo Camp.

"We got out in the virgin jungle. We were the farthest group out on this side of the railroad. Of course, we didn't know it at the time, but there was another group working from the other side, and our job was to put up an embankment. Generally, when they laid rails in the United States, they lay them as they go along; but the Japs knew the monsoon season was coming, so they wanted the embankment put up and sodded with grass, so that when the monsoons came, they wouldn't wash out this roadbed. They wanted the embankment first, and the rail crew would come along later and lay rails. The 40 Kilo Camp was almost our undoing. It was an atap-type camp. You know, it was open on the side. It seemed like even though the water was boiled and everything else, there was a hell of a lot of flies out there, and, boy, people started coming down with dysentery and started getting sick almost immediately. We had open latrines and flies like you'd never seen before. We weren't the only ones there; they had English, Dutch, and Australians there.

"We slept five to a bay, they called it there. You had approximately twenty-four inches, just about, per man, and you slept right together. I came down with dysentery after I got there. I had been working on the railroad. I can't remember how long I worked, but it wasn't long. It's a wonder that I worked over a day. I could have worked longer, but I was in a sorry condition, and the work was hard. I got bacillary dysentery, and I'm going to the latrine like a son-of-a-gun and feeling bad. We had a fire there at the latrine, because those damn Limeys were crapping on the trail going to the latrine, and you would step in it. They were doggone sons-of-a-gun. You know, you're barefooted.

"Anyway, we had a fire up there. Well, I was up there relieving myself, and a damn tiger passed by that fire. I saw his big eyes looking into the fire. I guess he smelled me because that would drive him off more than a gun. But he passed me like a freight train going by, and he was long. You know something, that's the best cure in the world for dysentery. I was so damned scared, boy, and after I got back, I didn't go back outside that night.

"One of my first experiences there was funny. We were laying there one night, and I felt something going over me, and I thought somebody had thrown a leg or something over me, and I reached down and said, 'Get your doggone leg off of me!' It didn't work, because it was a python. It was a long son-of-a-gun. So I jumped up and yelled, 'Snake!!' Boy, I'll tell you, it sounded like a machine gun going off, because of those guys hitting that bamboo. So the snake climbed up in the atap on top, you know, in the cross pieces up there.

"A Dutchman heard that we had a python up there. He said, 'Don't let him get away! Don't let him get away!' Well, hell, I didn't want anything to do with the son-of-a-gun, and so he reached up there and got hold of the python's tail and pulled the son-of-a-gun down, and he had a machete, and he said, 'I'll show you how to do it! I'll show you!' He cut the snake's head off. Then he took the knife and cut a ridge all around and then at the same time he pulled this snake's skin, and it was just like taking a woman's hose off. The snake had entrails, a ribcage, and everything; and it had an animal in it. The gastric juices of those pythons are so strong that I got a little of it on my skin, and it took the pigment right out of my skin. So one of the guys had made a skillet out of a fender of a Chevrolet, and they had it greased, you know, with fat from the python, so we fried that sucker up and had it for breakfast. It was good eating. That was one experience at 40 Kilo Camp.

"This is where we got our famous Doctor Hekking. Jimmy Lattimore and Captain Fitzsimmons traded the Japs two wristwatches—Jimmy's and one that Fitzsimmons had—and we got Doctor Hekking. Before that, all we had was an Australian dietitian, and he didn't know for nothing. But we got Hekking, and he was the one that really started all kinds of things to help us out. We bribed the Japs to get Doctor Hekking. He was in a Dutch camp down the road with a lot of doctors; he and Bloemsma and a number of other Dutchmen were all in one camp. They had more doctors than they needed. I don't think we asked the Japs for a particular doctor. We told them that we needed a doctor, and Doctor Hekking volunteered to come out and help the Australians and the Americans. He was a real man. He wanted to help us. I can tell you quite a bit about him, because later on I became his medical orderly along with a guy by the name of 'Doc' Hanley.*

"Anyway, some of his remedies: say, for instance, for dysentery, he used ground-up charcoal and a type of clay to absorb some of the mucus.

---

*Robert L. ("Doc") Hanley was a corpsman from the *Houston*. He now lives in Alamo, Texas.

First, he would want to know which dysentery you had, amebic or bacillary. Then he got some lousy creosote tablets, but they weren't worth a darn; that's about all he had there. Then later, for tropical ulcers, when a man got hurt and got an ulcer, he used the scalpel method where he dug out the ulcer, and the anesthetic is where the doctor yells louder than the patient. He used a tea poultice to clean the ulcer up. He used gasoline like you would alcohol. He used leaves and the latex around the leaves to cover the ulcer—to keep flies from blowing it. So he used all kinds of methods: gasoline for alcohol; kapok for cotton; leaves for bandages; and latex to make them stick on, as an adhesive. He used all kinds of stuff.

"He was the first man that I ever heard of who treated a man as a unit. He claimed that a man had to be cured two ways: the body is only a small part of it; the mind is important as well. So he cured the mind and the body together. He was using psychosomatic medicine before I ever heard of anybody using it. Also, he was using the mold from a palmetto in lieu of what we later found out was penicillin.* Well, he was using that, and he said his grandmother used it years before that, you know, on tropical ulcers. The palmetto is like a grapefruit or a citrus fruit. The Indonesians called them 'silver dimes.' Where they got that silver dime, I don't know. I never knew that they called dimes anything over there in the Orient, but that's what they called them—silver dimes.

"Doctor Hekking decided who would work at 40 Kilo if you were sick. You went before him, and, if he said you shouldn't go out, then you could stay there. But the Japs came along, and, if they didn't have their quota of men out on the job, they took you whether you were sick or not. In fact, many times Doctor Hekking got the hell beat out of him, and other doctors did as well, because they tried to keep the sick men in, because they knew what it was doing to them.

"Well, I was just kind of wandering there at 40 Kilo. I never will forget one time when I went through sick call with Doctor Hekking. He told me something I already knew—that I stunk, I needed a bath, and that I ought to take a bath. I was very down. It was a long way from the camp to the creek. But I took his advice, and I started walking down, and I'd lay on the side of the road—a trail was what it was, no road—because the cooks had to go down there for water, and they had to yo-ho the water back on a pole in a fifty-five-gallon drum that was cut off. I don't know how many times I laid

---

*Identified in the laboratory by Sir Alexander Fleming in 1928, penicillin is derived from mold, including that of certain fruits.

down, but I finally got there, and I got in the creek. I was skin and bones, you know. It refreshed me. But hell, by the time I got back to camp, I had had to lay down on the road so much that the dust got on me, and I was as dirty when I got back as when I left. But it was clean dirt! Doctor Hekking did a number of things at 40 Kilo before he sent me back to the base camp at Thanbyuzayat. He used to get guys to argue with each other, and he said it was good for them. Guys were just laying there. In fact, I saw some guys who would just barely have enough strength to hit the other guy a little bit, and then the other guy would hit him back. Doctor Hekking used to say that it helped pep them up, kept them stimulated, in other words.

"I had tropical ulcers at 40 Kilo, but not big ones. My biggest ulcer wasn't but about as big as my thumbnail, but Doctor Hekking got hold of it. We did have some people who had them get big, like osteomyelitis. Glen Self* had osteomyelitis, a bone disease, and he had to be operated on. I saw guys go to the creek, and these little minnows would eat the diseased flesh. But Hekking was unique. With his attention, we were so much better off than the other American group that was right in the same area that we were.

"If you talk to the men as you go along, you'll never find one—at least I never found one—that said one little bad thing against Doctor Hekking. In fact, many men have said, 'Without Doctor Hekking I would have died. He saved my life.' I can say that not once, but I can say it many times that he saved me. I weighed eighty-some-odd pounds at one time. When I went into the service I was at 139 pounds, and I got down to the eighties.

"I wasn't Doctor Hekking's orderly at first, because I was a dead loss, as they said, but later on I became his orderly. I don't know how I got dysentery. I really don't know. I just started going to the latrine after everything else that I had gone through. Then Doctor Hekking sent me from 40 Kilo to Thanbyuzayat, where they had what they called the Death Ward. The reason they called it the Death Ward was because people went in there alive, and they came out dead. A few others went back there before I did, like, Kenny,† and a Marine by the name of Lloyd Willey§ who went blind in Singapore. Well, not completely blind, because you could be standing there, and he would see an outline, but he couldn't recognize you.

"They sent me down to Thanbyuzayat and put me into the Death Ward, and I got a wonderful Dutch doctor there by the name of Doctor Stein.

---

*Self served in Battery F. He now lives in Lubbock, Texas.

†Robert W. ("Bobby") Kenny, Battery D, now lives in Wichita Falls, Texas.

§Willey, of the *Houston*, now lives in Vista, California.

Believe it or not, he was a contemporary of Doctor Hekking's and a friend of his; and I told him Doctor Hekking was my doctor, and he told me what a fine man he was, and we were lucky to have him. But the only thing, I was depressed, very depressed. By nature, I am a very happy-go-lucky man; I see the bright side of everything. But I got inside this hospital hut, and it was dark as heck with very little air circulating through it, and the ward was loaded with very, very sick men, all with dysentery.

"Oh, the stink was awful! The food was what the Dutch call pap. It's like broken rice with a few little pieces of vegetables in it, but it was a gummy substance. And the worse thing was that there was nobody around who felt like talking. They were so depressed. You're weak. I got down to where I couldn't get to the latrine, and that's when I got scared! I got scared to death! I was pooping myself, and it was running down my leg. I was begging for something to clean myself with, because I couldn't live like that.

"The mental depression you go through when you have dysentery is as bad on your mind as your bowels are on your body. My anus turned wrong side out because it lost its elasticity, and I couldn't control it or tighten it to stop the flow. That is depressing, and it stinks. I was a miserable human being, and I was going to die. But I was trying to live. There was an Australian—I wish to God I could tell you his name; I wish I knew where he lives—they called him Blue. He had red hair. He came in there and talked to me, and he said, 'Yank, what you need is some tucker in your belly.' I said, 'I sure do.' He said, 'I'm going to sneak you in something to eat.'

"He was skinny as hell with scrawny red hair, and they called him Blue. I couldn't tell you his name. But, anyway, without anybody knowing it, he brought in some fried pumpkin, some tomatoes, and something else. I don't know what it was, but it was all fried up. Oh, it was a little fried rice, that's what it was. I ate that and I felt better; I got a little strength. So then when he'd come back, I said, 'Boy, that did the trick! That helped me out like you never saw before!' He said, 'If I could get you out of here, I could cure you.' That's what the little Australian said. He told me, 'I'll bring you some more.' So he did. He brought me some more. But why he'd come in that place with all that stink and everything, I still don't know. Most of the people in there were Dutch. No Americans that I can remember, just me.

"He liked Yanks, he said. Well, anyway, he got me a little more to eat and everything. Then Doctor Stein came by, and I lied to him. He asked me, 'How are you doing, Sloop?' He called me 'Sloop' instead of 'Slug.' He called me Sloop because he never could understand this Slug deal. I was named after Bob Burns's deal,* not a worm, but this Dutchman couldn't understand why a nice guy like me would be named after a worm. Anyway, I told him I was better. He said, 'You get better, and I'll transfer you out. How many bowel movements have you had?' I said, 'I'm barely going! I'm barely going!' Like hell! I was going like a son-of-a-gun, but I wanted out of there. I thought I might have a fighting chance if I could get out of that place. I felt that if I didn't get out, I was going to die in there.

"I got out of there. They discharged me. Blue said if I got out of there, he'd get me well. I got out of there, and he took me over. He got me two rice sacks strung between poles, and where the two sacks came together, he left them open. I pooped through there. They had ashes, and they would throw ashes on the poop and bury it. Old Blue was doing all the work. Hell, I couldn't get around. He had to carry me from the hospital. He got me a bath, and I got cleaned up good, but I was still going. But, by golly, I started getting better. I started getting my strength back. One beautiful thing about bacillary dysentery, you either die, or you start getting better. With amebic dysentery, it goes to your liver, and if you don't get proper care, you have it for the rest of your life. Some of the boys still suffer from it.

"Anyway, to make a long story short, I started getting a little stronger, and then an old Australian gave me a job. There were all kinds of rackets inside this prison camp. He had some coconut oil, and he had some rice bars. We would deep-fry these rice bars and then bring them up and put a sugar coating around them, and then I would sell them for twenty cents apiece. He paid me a dollar a day. Do you know what a dollar a day is? Two eggs! I ate two eggs a day while I was working for that Aussie! I started coming out of it. I never was strong, but I came from death's doorstep; boy, I was there!

"Oh, yes, another thing. I had beriberi. You get that from dysentery, you know. I had beriberi bad. I had dry beriberi and my balls—excuse the expression—got awfully big, almost the size of a grapefruit. But I started coming out of it. Colonel Fisher[†] had seen me selling these candy bars one day. They had a little money that they used to buy the sick eggs. So I had been buying my own eggs. He saw me—he knew me—and he said, 'Slug, how are you doing?' I told him, 'I'm getting there.' He knew how bad of a shape I was in. He said, 'Who's your doctor?' I said, 'Doctor Stein.' He

---

*Burns was a Will Rogers-style, folksy comedian called "The Arkansas Traveler." He was from Van Buren, Arkansas, and had his own radio show, on which he talked about life back home, where his "drinking uncle," Uncle Slug, lived.
†Major W. E. ("Ted") Fisher was an Australian physician and commander c Thanbyuzayat Hospital.

said, 'I want you to give Doctor Stein my compliments and tell him I want to put you on a three eggs a day diet.' Do you know what three eggs a day are? That's the most wonderful thing that can ever happen to a human being!

"I was in a regular ward by now. The day they brought in my three eggs, we had a bombing raid. Do you know where the bombs hit? My bunk! I lost everything I had except my glasses and mess kit, every damn thing. From then on, all I had was a gunny sack, G-string, Chevrolet hubcap, and a spoon made out of a coconut. That's all I owned in this world. Just think, I almost got three eggs a day. I would eat them hard-boiled on the rice. The only eggs I ever got—I didn't get any free ones—I got for working for this Australian selling his 'camouflaged rice,' that's what I called it. But I was in better shape. With that bombing, we had to evacuate the camp.

"Before I go on, I'll tell you about another air raid experience that I had. The Allies were bombing the railroad, and as weak as I was, I got outside my hut and dug myself a slit trench, which was about four feet deep and about two feet wide. I did a pretty good job. A lot of guys wouldn't do anything, but I did. Well, this day they really bombed the hell out of us, and I was on the other side of the camp. There was an ammunition dump there, and when the planes started coming over, I wanted to get as far away from the dump as I could, but I couldn't maneuver too fast. Still I started moving across the camp, away from that place. Okay, I got over to my slit trench, and I couldn't even get in my own trench. Some guys were in it; it was loaded! So I was up there abusing them. I said, 'You sons-of-bitches, make room for me! I dug that damn thing!' I was really scared. This story's in that book *Behind Bamboo*.* But I couldn't get in the trench.

"So I started off, and a damn bomb hit, and I hit the deck. If this would have been a concussion bomb, I mean, if it would have exploded when it hit the surface of the ground, I would be dead. I wouldn't be here. But that thing went down in the ground, and then it went off. It came up like a V. That didn't do my poor old caved-in chest any good, and with all the rest now I couldn't hear. I couldn't hear. It seems like I was always in the wrong place at the wrong time. I should have stayed at the ammunition dump, but I was so scared. It's hard to tell you how scared I was. I wasn't scared in Java, but I was sure the hell scared in these bombing raids.

"In fact, it got so bad at Thanbyuzayat that we built a big red cross. The Japs finally allowed us to take red sand and make this big red cross. You

---

*This story is not in the first edition of Rivett's book but may appear in subsequent editions. See Rohan D. Rivett, *Behind Bamboo: An Inside Story of the Japanese Prison Camps*.

know something? The Allies came over and put a bomb right in the middle of that damn thing. They didn't believe it. Later, I talked to some of the Air Force people, and they didn't know who we were. As far as they were concerned, we were natives. We had no clothes; we were brown as could be. We looked just like natives. It wasn't the Air Force's fault, but they bombed the hell out of us. In fact, one time they came over, and they dropped flares on parachutes, and then they really bombed the heck out of us.

"We had an American by the name of Bobby Kenny that I had volunteered to help any time I could. He was paralyzed. He had beriberi so bad, he couldn't speak. They dropped a bomb, and it shook him up so bad that when his bunk fell, he said, 'Goddamn son-of-a-bitch!' They were the first words he said for over a year. I ran into him at a reunion. He's a fine guy. He said, 'Slug, I want you to meet my wife and tell her all about me.' I said, 'Kenny, it's hard for me to believe you're alive!' It wasn't me that saved him, though. Charley Pryor massaged him and kept him going. But it must have been something psychological, too, as well as the beriberi. When he got that shock, he started talking and getting well after it.

"At Thanbyuzayat, we weren't too far from the coast. Of course, Lord Mountbatten was in charge of operations there, and one time he came in there and shelled the coast on a moonlit night.* It was an old saying by the British that when they get a good moonlit night and shell the coast, they were getting ready for an invasion. We were ready to go down there and meet them! It's a good thing we didn't because they shoved off after shelling the damn coast. We were going to go and take the Japs on. I mean, we could've gotten ourselves into real serious trouble.

"After that last bombing of Thanbyuzayat, we had the famous death walk of our own. You heard of the one in the Philippines, but we had one out of Thanbyuzayat that would make that Bataan one look silly because we had been prisoners of war for a long time. This was strictly a hospital camp, too; everybody there was sick. If they were not sick, they were sent back to the railroad with the exception of medical orderlies and doctors. When the Japanese told us that we were going to move, and that they didn't have the facilities to take us and that we would walk out of there, that's when I don't know how many people died. I walked out with this Rivett who wrote *Behind Bamboo*, and I carried his stuff out of that camp. He was in worse shape than I was. He tells about the death walk out of Thanbyuzayat. I think he does an excellent job at it, but it sure didn't do me any good.

---

*This event could not be verified, but it may have occurred.

"This march was pitiful. Actually, the first march we made was only about eight kilos, approximately five miles, and that isn't too far. But we were real sick. My dysentery was not as bad as my inability to walk. My trouble was beriberi. That is where my problem was. It was the biggest problem that I had facing me, and I could only take short steps. My legs were in terrible shape. Energy I didn't have, and how we made it to the 8 Kilo Camp is beyond me. But one thing that saved me was the tastiest drink that I have ever had. You probably heard of this sweetened cream. Rivett pulled out a can of sweetened cream, and he split it between me, himself, and another Australian. By the way, he's got that story in the book, too. That was probably the tastiest drink I've had, and I don't know why but that one-third of a can of sweetened cream really gave me a lift.

"But that trip—that walk—was dreadful for me more for what I saw. You know, if a man has any feelings at all, he'll have them for somebody else rather than for himself. When I saw somebody who was going to die, and it was needless for him to die, because all he needed was a helping hand, and you couldn't give it to him, well, you feel so damn helpless. Man's inhumanity to man is terrible! The Japs didn't give a damn. They didn't have to let this happen to people. It was almost like they were getting even with us for being bombed.

"I can't say the Japs went around beating people, because we weren't moving fast enough. They did that, I understand, on the famous Bataan Death March. But they kept hurrying us. They knew they would kill all of us in that eight kilo march if they did. People died by the droves anyway. They should have put us in a truck or something and moved us. They could have done it easy, but they weren't going to waste gasoline on a bunch of good-for-nothing POWs.

"There weren't too many guards along it. Some of the British and Australians seemed rejuvenated a little by getting out and walking. From somewhere they got internal strength to do it. It took all of one day. From Thanbyuzayat to 8 Kilo Camp, it was five miles. When people dropped dead, the Japs just left them there. I don't know what happened to them. Some died right away, and some were alive laying there. I hoped that some natives with carts would bring them along. Not so. I don't know what happened to them, what happened to their bodies. Later the Japs brought some healthy men down to work on the railroad, and they told me that a lot of those guys were buried down there in a cemetery in Thanbyuzayat. I made it all the way to 8 Kilo, and I stayed there for two or three days. There was no shelter or such, you know. You just laid out in the grass and so forth. I didn't have anything except a hubcap, a gunny sack, a G-string, my glasses, and that's all. In fact, the rest of the time I was in prison camp, all I owned were my glasses, G-strings, a Chevrolet hubcap, a gunny sack, and that's all I owned.

"Then I got a ride—I didn't have to walk—to either the 26 or 36 Kilo Camp. I can't remember which one, because I was in such bad shape that I can't remember all the details. But I did get a ride. I was returned to the Fitzsimmons group, but Captain Fitzsimmons couldn't use me on the road, so he sent me down to work with Doctor Hekking and Hanley. My first job was cleaning up patients and getting underneath their slats and cleaning. It wasn't a hard job. I also helped serve the men their meals. I wasn't a real medical orderly at that time. I was more of a helper. I mean, I just cleaned up men. Somebody had to do it, and I didn't mind. When Hanley got moved out, that's when I helped Doc.

"Now when I got there the rainy or monsoon season had started, and it was then that the Japs had this 'speed up' or Speedo campaign. I'll tell you, I saw water come down like you couldn't believe. Guys were under wet blankets, and they got out and squeezed the blankets and crawled back under them. See, in the dry season you could dig down forty or fifty feet and not hit water, and, if you did, it would be a handful of muddy water. Then in the monsoon season, there was just so much water, three hundred inches. It doesn't seem possible.

"You'd have raging rivers. I never will forget one detail that I did go on about this time or sometime or another. They had me carrying stuff across a river. An Australian and I were working together. I lost my footing—there was water on my glasses and all over—and I fell off of this doggone bridge into this roaring torrent. The luckiest damn thing happened. Although I don't remember what happened, all of a sudden something hit me in the stomach. I hit a sandbar downstream a ways. I was able to pull myself out of the current; otherwise I would have drowned. This Australian was yelling, 'Slug, Slug, you dirty bastard! Where are you?' I said, 'I'm coming.' He said, 'Where the bloody hell have you been?' I told him I fell off. He said, 'The Japs are raising bloody hell because you're not carrying something! Don't do that again!' I said, 'You know where I've been? I went off into that danged river and damn near drowned, and here you're up here yelling!' We had terrible experiences like that. Now I look back on them, and I think they're kind of amusing. But at the time I didn't.

"Well, of course, the Japs worked the poor sons-of-a-gun to death during this speed-up time. I wasn't on the railroad; I was doctoring them with Doctor Hekking. It was pitiful. They would come in at night, and, of course, they didn't want to go back out, so they'd come down and see Doc, and Doc would try to keep the worst ones in. The Japs would come down and raise hell and beat up Doctor Hekking. They'd come in, and then if they didn't have enough workers, they would go right through the ward and take them out of the sickbay. Many times, too, I looked so bad that Doc would have a real sick guy who looked good, and Doc would use me for him and take me in front of the guards and say, 'This poor son-of-a-gun is sick, and he can't make it.' He would put on an act, and, by golly, they would say, 'Get out of the way!' But he would save that guy that I was from going out. I was the guinea pig. They'd use me for things like that until Hanley left.

"I graduated when Hanley left. I was Doc's assistant. They used to call me a dadgummed dead loss, because I couldn't work on the railroad. But I worked for Doc, and I survived, and I thank Doc for keeping me alive. I also thank Fitzsimmons and the rest of them for letting me stay with Doc, because I think otherwise, if they would have had me out on the railroad, I wouldn't have made it. I have done many things with this man. We did autopsies, and they were strictly dishonest. The Japs made Doc put phony things down that men died of, and we would see that the man's gut was ulcerated, and he starved to death because there was no food getting into his intestines. It never was malnutrition. It was always a heart attack or some phony deal. But most of our deaths were directly or indirectly caused by malnutrition.

"Doctor Hekking lost very few men. I don't know if you know that or not. Compared to the rest, he never lost an amputee. Not one of us had a leg amputated. He never lost one from a tropical ulcer. He did lose a guy to tuberculosis, a fellow named Simpson.* Doc did lots of things. He made yeast out of pumpkins. He fermented the stuff in a big ol' bamboo deal. It was awful tasting, but, if you drank enough, you'd get drunker than a coot; it was almost like beer. Hell, I'd take a couple of slugs. At first I was scared of the jungle, but with Doc's help I learned to like it. He would pick green chilis, wild chilis, and we would pick all kinds of leaves. In fact, sometimes I felt like a cow because I ate so many doggone weeds. But rice and weeds are very good. He'd show me all the different types to eat.

"He made different kinds of salves. Say, for instance, he'd use beef tallow and a little acetylsalicylic acid for athlete's feet. Then he got some sake and some iodine crystals, and he made up iodine, and we'd paint patients with that. One time we would use iodine, and the next time we would use acetylsalicylic acid. That did some good. We'd go down to these

---

*Ward H. Simpson, of Battery F, died of tuberculosis on January 30, 1944, at Kanchanaburi, Thailand.

native *kam pongs*,* and we would have a regular line-up of native people. For lots of them, he would have to uncurl their eyes. Underneath there they would have little skin ulcers, and he used to clean those up. He had a little ointment made out of zinc oxide and tallow, and he would put that on them. Hell, they would give us presents and all kinds of things that we could take back to the sick.

"Someway Fitzsimmons got some sulfapyridine, MB-693, from a Chinese, and he paid for it. He gave it to me, not Doc. It isn't that he didn't trust Doc, but Doc saw no distinction among people. He would give anything we had to anybody. But we felt more close to Americans. Since it was American money, Fitzsimmons would give the MB-693 to me. Then when Doc needed it, I acted like I had to go get it, and then I would turn it over to Doc. But Doc used a pill of MB-693 very carefully. He would shave just a little bit, say, on an ulcer.

"Another thing that Doc did was swap medicine with the Japanese. He made a mold from an MB-693 tablet, and he cast—I don't know how many—pills that were made out of rice flour and plaster of Paris. The Japs would get venereal diseases, and they couldn't go to their own doctors. They would come to Doctor Hekking, and he would say, 'Okay, I'll fix you up, but you have to give me some medicine.' So he would give them some phony sulfapyridine, and we would get quinine and other things we needed. The poor sons-of-a-gun, it didn't help them a bit. But we had to do things like that to survive.

"Finally, Doc started sending me out on a few of the details because when a man hurt himself on a job, the Japs wouldn't let him come in. So Doc gave me a Red Cross band—that I couldn't wear on my arm because there was no way to attach it—and I put it on my G-string, and I went out on the job. But I didn't have to work. All I had to do was walk up and down among the men. One day I was out, and the Jap started yelling for a medical orderly—doctor—so I went down to see what he was yelling about. I got down there, and he told me to get into this boxcar. Well, I looked in the boxcar, and I heard somebody moaning in there, and it was a woman and she was pregnant, and she was in labor. I mean she was in labor in this filthy dadgummed coal car where they had charcoal. So I yelled at the guys, and I said, 'Hey, some of you guys bring me some grass.' So they cut some grass and threw it in the door. I got it and got the woman on it, and I could tell she needed medical help, not me.

---

*A *kam pong* is a native village or encampment.

"So I told the Jap guard to go get a doctor. He said, 'No! You!' I said, 'No! No good! I'm number ten! The number one doctor, get him!' I was frantic. I could see that this gal needed help like nobody's business. That son-of-a-gun wouldn't do anything for me, and here I was in there with this gal, and she's in labor. The poor thing looked like hell, so I yelled again for help. They brought me a Japanese bucket made out of wood, and they had some so-called tea. It was weak. I got a little piece of burlap, and I started cleaning her up because she had been laying around getting all dirtied up.

"You know something, she started having the baby. Golly, I liked to have had a fit. Here we had a damn cord and everything and no way to cut it. I yelled again. I said, 'Anybody got a knife?' They didn't. One of them said, 'Bite it in two, Slug! That's what the animals do!' So I went back, and I bit it in two. I bit that son-of-a-gun in two! That's the only way I could do it. I tied her up, by golly. I always wondered what they did with bedsheets and water in the movies. But, by golly, I cleaned that baby up with the dadgummed tea and burlap. I always thought a baby had to be pulled up by its feet and given a whack to get it crying. That thing came out like a big rat crying like nobody's business.

"I had no more than got that baby in its mother's arms and everything, and here comes a Jap down the railroad track with an old woman, and I was never so grateful in my whole life. I was wrung out. I was really glad to see them coming down. So that was my experience on the railroad. I was glad to get back to camp. I told Doc, 'I sure missed you today! I could have used you!' He said, 'Now, you see, you just remember that. That's what a woman goes through for every child that is born.'

"Well, from 36 Kilo we made a fairly big jump to 114 Kilo, which is also known as Three Pagodas Pass. This is another camp where we had a malaria problem. By then the monsoons and Speedo campaign were over. One thing I remember is that I was cold at the 114 Kilo Camp—bitterly cold. It was cold up there. We were divided at this camp. Doctor Hekking was at the top level up there, and I was at a small hospital at the lower level. This is one place where Doc got real sick. This is where I lost Swede Ecklund.* I lost him there. I will say this, too, Fitzsimmons did everything to keep ol' Swede from dying. I can't say anything but fine things about Captain Fitzsimmons, especially in the jungle. They put him on the railroad digging right along with the men. He came in very weary, you know, and he got compassion for his own men like he had never had before.

---

*R. L. Ecklund, Battery F, is listed as dying of beriberi at 103 Kilo Camp, Burma, on January 5, 1944. Perhaps what Wright calls the "lower level" was Camp 103.

"This was near the end of the line for us. Three Pagodas Pass or 114 Kilo Camp was the end of our line. I was involved inside the camp, and I wasn't on details outside. But there was a lot of loading there. The railroad was completed, and they had the driving of the 'golden spike.'* People came out of the hills with their wives and harems and so forth. Tojo was supposed to have been there, but I didn't see him.† I wasn't close to this. I saw it from a distance. They even put up a little deal above the cemetery. It was terrible. It was terrible to think that after all of those men died on that railroad, they would do a thing like that; but they did.

"I really can't say how long I was at 114 Kilo Camp before we moved to Kanburi. I had malaria very bad there. In fact, altogether during the whole time I was a prisoner of war, I had three different kinds of malaria. But mostly I took care of the sick there because there was nobody else to do it. I had a handmade 'thunder seat,' a toilet out of a five-gallon can. The guys would use it and then yell for me to 'clean up the damn place, it stinks around here!' So I would pull myself together and try. I would feed them and clean them. It was the dead loss looking after the dead losses. They had nobody else. One American looking after other Americans. I lost some men there. Thank the Lord that Doc got a little better.

"I want to tell you of an experience that happened to me between 114 Kilo and Kanburi when we moved. We stopped at a place on the side of the road, and the Japanese let us off. They put us to work on a train that had come in from Burma. It was loaded with their soldiers who had got wounded in battle, and they were really shot up. I had gotten a hand of bananas, and, boy, I couldn't wait to eat them. Then I had a bamboo with water in it; it must have had a gallon or a gallon-and-a-half. I was walking by this freight car, and I heard moaning and groaning, and I looked in. It was loaded with Japanese amputees and beat-up soldiers.

"There was a Japanese woman, a nurse, in the boxcar, and she said in perfect English, 'Do you have anything to eat or any water?' Well, I had both. Then she asked me, 'Are you English?' 'No, I'm American.' 'Oh, American!' She says, 'These men haven't had anything to eat and nothing to drink.' I almost said, 'Big deal!' But I didn't. I hadn't talked to a woman that could speak English for a long time. She wasn't pretty, just a nice-

---

*According to other POWs the spike was copper or gold plated, and one survivor suggested that a prisoner stole it later to sell.
†Hideki Tojo, Japanese general and statesman, was not present at the completion ceremonies.

looking lady. So I says, 'Oh, Slug, you son-of-a-bitch!' So I handed her the bamboo, and I gave her my damn bananas. This woman was an opera singer, and she sang—now, goddamn, if I can't remember what she sang, I'm going to cut my throat—'Columbia, the Gem of the Ocean,' and beautifully! I stood there and bawled like a baby. I didn't dare tell my fellow POWs what happened; they'd have been ashamed of me. But that was one time in my life that I am not ashamed of what I did. That was the enemy, but I couldn't do to them what they had done to me. I bawled like a baby.

"We got to Kanburi, and the first meal was like dining at the Savoy in Hollywood as far as I'm concerned. Ol' Doc Hekking invited me in. I don't know where he got the food. He had a number of sardine-type deep-fried fish, and on top of rice was an egg; oh, that was nothing like you ever ate before. So we set up a hospital there, and I was like king of the mountain. My physical being got better at Kanburi, even though we had cholera and bubonic plague there. They were isolated cases. We had a Scotsman named Jock, and he complained. He looked like he had taken a chicken net and dipped it in potash and permanganate, because he had splotches all over his body. When I called Doc, he said, 'Isolate this whole area. Isolate it.' So I did. We buried poor ol' Jock, and we stayed there, but nobody else got bubonic plague.

"That reminds me. My wife says I have a wonderful memory—and I have—but there are some things that may never again surface. I think we have a habit of burying things. Until now, I haven't thought about this story in I don't know how many years. I think I blocked it out, but sometime or other, they sent me back up toward 114 Kilo. They sent me to a camp, and I can't remember where it was, but it was a cholera camp. Doctor Hekking didn't want me to go, but he had to send me. I had to go, and I stayed there for three days, and all I did was rake dead people off on stretchers and dump them in a fire and burn them up. They were all British. There wasn't an American in the whole camp. They ended up shooting the ones who were left. A British major took the gun away from a Jap who was doing a lousy job and shot his own men.

"Well, I started getting better now. I never was as bad as I had been in the jungle. I didn't weigh much, but my step got better. It's a good thing, because I made a hell of a walk after that up north. Finally, they moved me out of this camp with some other dead losses to a place called Tamauang. It wasn't far from Kanburi, ten or twelve kilos."

At Tamauang, Wright was placed under "close arrest" by a British officer for talking back to the Englishman. He was defended by an Australian officer at the subsequent court-martial and released after the Australian convinced the court that Japanese, not British, rules applied to American POWs. Wright's urge to speak his piece had gotten him beaten up rather severely by a Japanese officer earlier. He had lectured his captor on the Geneva Convention rules of treatment of prisoners of war.

From Tamauang, Wright went to a camp near Bangkok, probably Nakhon Nayok, where he was put to work digging tunnels for ammunition and gun emplacements. Later he went north and worked on an airfield. American planes flew over and dropped leaflets stating they were going to bomb the area and drop paratroopers. Of course, many Americans knew the Japanese planned to massacre them if an invasion occurred. Wright remembers: "Well, the Japanese read that, too. They knew what the hell was going on, so they told us that they were sorry, but they were going to have to shoot us. They knew darn well if the Americans came in, then they were going to have to shoot us. But the atomic bomb was dropped and stopped that whole operation. So anybody that says the atomic bomb was a bad deal, it might have been a bad deal for Nagasaki and Hiroshima, but it certainly wasn't a bad deal for us guys—the Americans and me—who were up there at that place. It saved our lives."

Having heard the war was over two days before it actually ended, Wright, Cosby R. ("Pupsey") Sherrill, Ardie N. Mabe, and Stephen N. Feuchack* left camp only to be recaptured at Lat Buri. They were taken to *Kempei Tai* headquarters in Bangkok, where an OSS officer freed them and arranged for their passage home. Wright was back in the United States by September 11, 1945, but not separated from the service until April 1946.

His old boss, R. A. Smith of Standard Oil of California, helped him buy a service station in Oceanside, California. A Republican in party politics, he helped Richard M. Nixon in the former president's first senatorial campaign. Entering politics himself, Wright was elected to the Oceanside city council, where he served fourteen years before becoming the town's mayor. He was active in civic clubs, the American Legion, and served as a director of Oceanside's harbor district and regional hospital. A heart condition forced his retirement. Recently, in reflecting on his POW experiences, he said, "The only hero among our group was Doctor Hekking, and they never

---

*Sherrill, who was in Battery F, now lives outside of Jacksboro, Texas. Mabe, of Headquarters Battery, died of a heart attack on June 19, 1983, at his home in Hillsboro, Texas. Feuchack, from the *Houston*, died of a heart attack on March 1, 1962, in Somers Point, New Jersey.

gave him a medal." On recommendation from Captain Fitzsimmons, Wright received the Bronze Star for valor. He also holds the Purple Heart and POW's Medal.

Ilo Hard
Battery F

Ilo Hard was a bit older than most of the soldiers in the Second Battalion. He was born on December 21, 1914, near Mansfield, Texas, in Tarrant County, a few miles southeast of Fort Worth. When he was eight years old his family moved to near Shallowater, Lubbock County, where he was reared on the family farm, but after graduating from high school he bought his own garage in town. He did not pay much for the business. Although he wanted to join the military, he felt that he could not because of the low pay, eighteen dollars per month, and the need for him to help his father and mother through the Great Depression.

In 1937 he decided that he could lead a military life and still be a dutiful son. He joined the Texas National Guard and was assigned to Battery C, First Battalion, 131st Field Artillery Regiment. During the next several years he passed a series of examinations for potential National Guard officers and in January 1940 received a "war pool reserve commission." In August of that year, while on the police force in Lubbock, he was raised from staff sergeant to second lieutenant in the guard. When the Army reorganized its divisions following maneuvers in Louisiana in 1941, he shifted from the First Battalion to the Second, joining Battery F. Although he was married, he agreed to go overseas with the unit, believing that this move might provide him with a permanent position in the military. As an officer, he was involved in many of the decisions made for the Second Battalion. His guns were the ones fired in support of the Australian troops during the brief battle with the Japanese Army in Java.

After capture, he made the usual moves—from the locations near Garut, to Tanjong Priok, to Bicycle Camp, to Changi, and then on to Burma. Although officers were billeted separately from the enlisted personnel, their experiences, according to Hard, were not much different. Contrary to the opinion voiced by some rank-and-file troops, officers did not receive better food or more commodious quarters. On the railroad many were given supervisory chores, although some worked at times with pick and shovel. If Hard and other POWs are correct, officers generally received more punishment than the enlisted personnel from Japanese guards, because they tried to act as buffers for their men. They were, however, allowed orderlies, and despite misgivings accepted them so that they might shield men suffering most from the killing tasks of building the railroad.

"AFTER WE LEFT MOULMEIN, I'm not sure whether we stopped at Thanbyuzayat or not. My next clear recall is moving into 18 Kilo Camp. We moved there by truck. I do remember Colonel Nagatomo making his speech when we first got to Burma, but I don't remember where it was. I guess it was at Thanbyuzayat, the Burma base camp.

"We were Branch 5. Branch 3 was ahead of us. It was mostly Australian. I believe it amounted to about ten thousand people or something like that. The rest of our branch, who were additional prisoners to bring us partially up to strength, were caught by a submarine attack off Sumatra. My old sergeant, Miller,* was in that group. He'd been injured in a railroad yard accident in Batavia just before we left and couldn't come with us. We only had two thousand in our branch. I'm not sure whether our branch was to have been ten thousand or five thousand—that's a big difference—but, anyway, it was short by thousands of men.

"The kilo designation of camps was the distance from the one end or the other of the railroad. In our case, the Burma end, where the road branched off of the Moulmein-Tavoy Line, where it began at Thanbyuzayat, it was built out in a rice paddy on what had been a level plain. We were still in the rice paddy country—pretty flat, not true jungle. The huts generally were all bamboo structures. They all consisted of just a roof and two tiers of flooring with an open hallway down the middle. We were given a space, and that was our living space, and we put our bunk there. There was a cookhouse, central cookhouse, and some kind of water source.

"We started there during January. It was right in the latter end of past midway in the dry season, and it was very hot and dry. It was dusty. The prisoners marching back and forth, going along the right-of-way, would build up just a flour-fine dust. At night it would be cold because it was so dry there, but not as cold as it was farther up in the jungle, after we got up in the high country. The nights were cool, but the days were real, real hot.

"Well, we started living by the meter. We went out on the right-of-way, and an ol' Jap counted the number of men in each work party, and he

---

*If Hard is correct and Miller did make it to Burma, as seems to be the case, misfortune continued to dog him, because G. R. ("Brodie") Miller, of Battery F, died when his vessel was sunk en route to Japan on September 18, 1944.

measured out the surface of a cubic meter on the ground for each man and designated the area. They outlined it with stakes. We'd taken tools with us, I guess, and in very simple language he told us that it was for every man to dig out that meter and put it on the railroad grade that had been staked out. When we finished we'd go back to camp. We started at one man, one meter. We were broken into *kumis* of fifty men, although we sometimes were in smaller work parties. The battalion commander assigned us to each group. I caught Number Seven. Number One was officer personnel—doctors and so forth, the battalion commander. Well, we were all in Number One *kumi*, but seven of us were assigned as regular work party officers in charge.

"Some of us worked, and some of us didn't at first. Sometimes a Jap wouldn't let us work. We were allowed only to supervise. It all depended on the individual Jap. Sometimes he would count the officer, and sometimes he wouldn't. If I were counted as in the party, personally, I figured I had to move my share of dirt, if the Jap would let me. There were a few times when they actually put the Number One *kumi* out, made up only of officers. They'd go out and do some work. They would never get a whole lot out of them. They didn't get as much out of them as they did the enlisted men frankly because most of them were never physically able, fit, to do the work like the ones that had been going out regularly and working.

"At that time the Japanese were fairly generous in leaving us with a sanitation detail to take care of the latrine and keep the grounds cleaned up and firewood cut and keep a water supply on hand, if it had to be dipped out of a stream or hauled up out of a well or whatever. The medics didn't have to work, the ones that had a medical card. They established a sick bay. But that didn't last long.

"This was also one of the times that we had difficulty, a basic problem, with the enlisted men. At first, when we'd finish on the railroad with that one meter, the Japs would let us go in. Well, we'd go by a stream there and take a bath in the creek and go back in, and the men would play cards or goof off or rest. As we kept getting more proficient and hardened to the work, we'd get through earlier. Well, the officers thought we could see the handwriting on the wall. In fact, we got out there one morning, and the Jap said, 'One man, 1.1 meter.' I don't remember when this took place, but the Japs also played nationality off against nationality—Australians and Americans against each other, and against the Dutch. They'd play one *kumi*, one work party, against the other, trying to get more work done.

"Some of us could see the light, so we started telling the men to hold back and put in the whole day and pretend that it was the limit of our physical capability. We said we'd be better off that way. I had bitter words with some of the people in my group because even though they would kind of goof off in the early part of the day, when they could see the end in sight—and we'd be saving a little island out in the middle to piddle away the rest of the day—they'd say, 'Oh, the hell with this! Let's get through and go on in!' They'd tie into it, and it took—I won't say when it was used—physical restraint to stop them. There was some bitterness over that, but I proved to be correct. I had some people that I had pretty bitter words with who thanked me later on, because the Japs just kept adding more work.

"I remember one day very distinctly, and this was after we left 18 Kilo and moved on up to 80 Kilo, I guess. I'm not sure whether we went to 80 or 100 Kilo first, but we moved on up. I remember on May 5—that's when they got the word that the convoy had been sunk down off of Sumatra and that we weren't going to get any additional troops in Group 5. The Japs came around, and first they broke out the International Red Cross postcards. The men who were working that day were given an International Red Cross card to send home. They had the preprinted phrases: 'I am well,' 'I am working for pay,' 'I am happy,' 'I'm with friends,' or something like that. Then, that same day they came around and said, 'One man, 2 meters.' That's really more than a human can do, but, I believe, we did as much as 2.5 meters at one time.

"They had surveyed the road, and the part of Group 3 people who were ahead of us had cleared the right-of-way, and the grade was all surveyed and staked out. Our jobs were simple: we piled the dirt and built the grade that was required, or made cuts in the hills, or, when we came to a stream, we built a bridge. I believe we made cuts as deep as three meters and fills as high as four meters. Our bridges were usually a one-, two-, or three-story structure. We'd drive the pilings, build a scaffold, and put our pile driver, which was manual, out on this scaffolding, and we'd hoist the piling out there and drive it as deep as we could. Then we'd cut the top off, even. Depending on how high the grade was, how deep the gorge was, we'd make a trestlelike structure. There would be a beam with four or six upright vertical members mortised into it and then another cross beam. We'd put a beam across the top of the piling, and we'd set this trestle up on there and pack it in place with a peculiar breed of tool that the Japs used, a great, big overgrown staplelike thing. We'd make the scaffolding or bracework where they would intersect and then drive a staple in that. We'd use wire or 'string bark,' a tie material that we got off of the trees. Anyway, we'd hold that trestle in place, brace it, and then we'd set another one on top of that. Sometimes we had pilings and then three of these trestles, and each trestle was two or three meters high, stacked on top of that.

"We'd get up before daybreak, and we'd have our roll call, work call, just about daybreak, barely after daybreak. We'd finish when we completed the work that was assigned. Sometimes they'd haul dinner out on an ox cart, and sometimes we'd have to send a detail in, and they'd carry it on yo-ho poles. We'd line up by *kumi* with somebody keeping track of the roster and the mess officer or sergeant telling who got to eat first and who was first in line for the 'back-ups.' We ate supper whenever we got back in, and we always tried to keep the mess gear washed.

"At first the food was fairly good. It wasn't too bad until the rainy season started. That's when we began to hurt. Then it wasn't good. I mean, when the rainy season set in in May and the bridges were washed out, there just wasn't any rations to be had, and we started starving. What rations did come through, the Japs ate them. They latched on to them.

"We had only one real redeeming factor there, and that was that cholera broke out ahead of us in the native work camps, and their oxen got loose. This ol' Korean guard, a good one, Hirano, he was out and around all the time at the camp, and when one of those oxen would stray by, well, one of our butchers was named Jones,* and Hirano would call, 'Jones-o, Jones-o.' We had one American, one Australian, and two Dutch as butchers. The Dutch were a couple of brothers in the Dutch regular army who had been top wrestlers, and they were big geezers. They did the butchering. Well, ol' Hirano would start squalling for 'Jones-o,' and that meant 'Butcher.' They'd fall out, and he'd shoot this work oxen that had been released up ahead, and they'd butcher it right on the spot. Jones and the Australians would come in with a forequarter apiece, and the two big Dutchmen would come in with the hindquarters, and that was meat. Had it not been for that, I doubt if any of us could have gotten out of the jungle, out of our side over there. We wouldn't have made it out of there.

"We had some obnoxious guards, and we gave them names. The one I had my most serious trouble with was Makan. He was a chow hound, and that's where he got that name.† Then we had Liver Lips and Snake Eyes and Hollywood and Pock Face and Black Shirt. They were the main ones that I recall. This ol' Liver Lips, we figured that his parentage must have been a

---

*Clyde E. ("Butcher") Jones, of Battery E, now lives in Chehalis, Washington.
†Benjamin Dunn, in *The Bamboo Express*, says the guard's real name was Kanako and that the POWs called him Makan, the Malayan word for eat or food. Although never mentioned in the interviews, some of the guards had multiple nicknames, depending on their most recent activity. For example, the guard named Tiemoto was first known as the Peanut and later, after he committed a particularly brutal act, was called Dillinger.

cross between a prostitute and an African Negro—that's where he got his lips from, from his liver-lipped parents. Snake Eyes got his name simply because that's what he had: little beady snake eyes. Hollywood thought he was real good-looking—quite vain, an egotistical character. Pock Face had either the pox or eczema or something, acne.

"Well, on the fifth of May, as I mentioned, the Japs evidently learned that the additional people to fill up Group 5 weren't going to get there. See, our ship was the last ship that came into Moulmein, and evidently they had learned that we weren't going to get any more help on that end of the road, so that's when they said, 'One man, 2 meters.' That's when the monsoons started. You could've almost made a calendar by the monsoon seasons. During the two years I was there, they started about mid-May and ended about mid-November, almost exactly. I was either at 80 or 100 Kilo Camp when the first season started. Now these were rough camps. We were in both of them during the monsoon season. We were in the one where we had a major cemetery built across the railroad from the camp.*

"When the rains arrived they were in the form of a real wound-up Texas thunderstorm: lightning, wind, rain, downpour. It was kind of frightening. In the dry season all the underbrush and everything withered and died away, that which the natives didn't burn. The ground was very porous, loose, due to all the vegetation withering and the roots dying. Then comes this downpour of rain and hard winds, and some of those huge trees were blown over, and we could hear them fall. It's awesome to hear a huge tree, three or four feet in diameter, fall that way in the jungle. It just shook the ground. That happened once or twice, and then it just set in and rained. It rained for twenty-four hours sometimes and never let up.

"Working in the mud, it seemed too futile to try to move dirt under those conditions. You dig the stuff and move it, put it in the basket or on the yo-ho pole. One time we were building a grade through a swamp, a pretty high grade, and we couldn't climb the grade with the yo-ho poles, so we put the dirt in baskets and passed it up, like a fire bucket brigade, and we dumped it. By the time you got it to the top of the grade in the rain, you'd dump it up there and have only a good shovelful in the basket. I've forgotten the exact number of days now, but from the fifth of May it was something like 127 days that I remember working straight. I don't think I missed a day. Quite a few of the other people did the same thing. When we started on the

---

*He probably means 80 Kilo Camp. This was the hospital camp where, according to Dunn, forty-nine Americans were buried. However, the Lost Battalion Association roster notes forty-seven buried at 80 Kilo and fifty-two buried at 100 Kilo.

fifth of May, we had 315 men working out on the job that day. Some 120 days later, we had forty-some-odd people who could pretend to get out of the gate and do a day's work. That's what we wound up with: forty-some.

"We started getting diarrhea. A lot of times we didn't have lab facilities to tell exactly what it was, but it was a severe diarrhea, and no doubt most of it was amebic dysentery. That went with, well, oh, a fever. We had some cases of pneumonia. We had vitamin deficiencies and pellagra. I believe that's what they said it was. Our mouths would crack in the corners, and sores would form in our noses. Sometimes sores would form, or there'd be irritations on the scrotum. We had two kinds of beriberi; we called them wet and dry. Some men would swell, and others would lose weight and just wither away.

"When we started breaking ballast for the railroad, breaking the rocks by hand, the chips or sharp fragments would fly and break the skin. Any kind of an opening became infected, and a tropical ulcer would take hold. They contributed to the loss of several of our people. The whole thing was that with the fatigue, starvation, disease, either malaria, dysentery, whatever it might have been, plus the blood being poisoned by a tropical ulcer, this caused a person's whole system to just collapse. He just didn't have the resistance to fight anything off, and that would be the end. In a civilized autopsy, I don't know what would have been termed the cause of death, specifically.

"I had a small tropical ulcer, one very small one. I was very, very fortunate. I just soaked it in hot water at night. That was all I ever had—just one very small one when I had my run-in with Makan, and he tore up my leg with his hobnails, and just one spot became ulcerated. I had this run-in right at the beginning of the monsoons. There was a storm cloud coming up, approaching, and at that time they let us quit to try to get to camp and out of it. So the work parties all fell in. We had to wash our tools, and there was a water hole on the opposite side of the grade where we had water to wash the tools. One of the men in the *kumi* went over with the tools to wash them. We fell in and everybody else got ready to go, and this one man wasn't back. I thought he'd show up any minute. Ol' Makan was the guard, and I didn't want to irritate him if I could avoid it, so I reported that the *kumi* was ready to go with the rest of them. But about the time they started to move out, the toolwasher still wasn't there. He wasn't back. So I called to Makan and told him I made a mistake—one man short—because I didn't dare to go any farther with it.

"Well, Makan went into a tantrum; he accused me of helping the man escape. So he called back a buddy of his, and I made a mistake. I was carrying a meter stick—just for a walking cane. I made one and marked it off in 100 centimeters, so we could measure out the groundwork we were doing. Well, he promptly had his other guard keep me covered, and he took that stick away from me and made splinters out of it. Then he took his rifle and went to work on me with that and his hobnails. About that time the boy showed up, and he had the tools, but Makan still wasn't satisfied, and he worked me over more. We got into camp, and he did what they really liked to do. He was going to turn me over to the guards at the guardhouse.

"Well, this ol' Hirano, the good Korean I mentioned, happened to be sergeant-of-the-guard, and for some reason I'd got on his good side through no fault of my own except I always tried to have good behavior in the ranks, always tried to be lined up properly when he'd go by to count. He asked Ira Fowler* my name. He learned my name, and in the morning he'd speak to me—call me by my name. Well, he not only wouldn't let Makan turn me over to the guard, he made Makan and the other guard turn in their weapons at the guardhouse.

"But Makan still wasn't satisfied. He took me down to headquarters and got his other buddy. I've forgotten his name, but he was a Korean who didn't even have the rank of private. But he was camp commander at this time. Hirahita, I think, was his name.† He boasted that he was educated in an American mission in Korea, but he had to learn an entirely new vocabulary when he started working with prisoners. Well, the two of them gave me a thorough working over, but, thanks to Hirano, I didn't have to stay in the guardhouse. Usually, when anybody spent twelve or twenty-four hours at the guardhouse, they weren't good for anything after that.

"In May, Major Mizdani made his speech to Colonel Tharp and the senior officers. Ira was present, I believe. That's when they started trying to make us cut rations for the sick—give one ration to the working people and try to cut the ration to the sick. They'd have a regular work call in the morning, and we'd turn out everybody we thought was halfway able to work; then we'd have to have another work call, and all the sick that could walk would go out. Some of the Japs would determine who could work and who couldn't. But it was during that time that we were trying to reason with Mizdani, and he made the remark, 'A sick man is no use to Nippon; he's no use to himself. He's better off dead. In fact, I will help him die.' I believe the old Navy commander, Doctor Epstein, was present for that little speech.

---

*Fowler was an officer in Battery D. He died of a pulmonary condition on August 25, 1991, in Temple, Texas.
†Dunn refers to a guard called Hitohara, who may be the individual that Hard mentions.

"It was during this period that we lost Lumpkin and Hampton.* Hugh and Wade died very close together. Both of them were in the same cubicle with me at the time that they died. I think we were in one of those double-bay huts—Hugh, Wade, Hud Wright, Windy Rogers, and me. I believe we were in that cubicle when they died. It was rough.

"Actually, Hugh Lumpkin hadn't been that effective with our people, but he did the best he could, the best he knew. Our medical people didn't know how to deal with these tropical diseases. Hugh made the remark one time that in his opinion any experienced Dutch doctor, a doctor trained and experienced in the Dutch East Indian Army, knew more about tropical diseases than the combined knowledge of the American Medical Association. But, as I say, Hugh did the best he could. It was a blow not to have a doctor, but we had a young Dutch doctor who took over Hugh's place until later on, when Doctor Hekking, who had been with Fitz's group, came in and took over.

"I was involved in very few burials. Ira Fowler and some of the kitchen people, and Ike Parker, the ones who didn't go out on work details, attended to most of the burials. I made some, but I don't remember exactly how many. It was a matter of the deceased being wrapped in a straw mat, a hole being dug big and deep enough for adequate burial—four to six feet deep—a very brief reading, and they were buried with a marker of some kind placed on their graves. Fowler kept a detailed sketch of the sites—good enough that when the burial group went back there after the war, they were able to make recoveries. They used the trestle on the railroad and, I think, a tree or something as reference points.

"I never witnessed this one death, but there was a Marine first sergeant, Dupler, for one, who everybody felt gave up. For example, I had a sergeant, Ed Worthington,† who was terribly sick with a fever and ulcers at the same time when Sergeant Dupler was ill. Dupler was a picturesque Marine first sergeant, had everything going for him, and when he became ill, everyone was concerned. I know I split some rations that I had stashed, a can of Eagle Brand sweetened condensed milk that I'd stolen on the dock in Batavia. But other people chipped in, too, trying to get him something that he would eat. Well, he wouldn't eat; he just wouldn't do anything. One evening after I came in, I asked Doc Lumpkin the condition of Sergeant Dupler. He said if

---

*R. Wade Hampton was in Battery D. He died of dysentery at 100 Kilo Camp, Burma, on July 31, 1943.

†Charles E. ("Ed") Worthington, Battery F, lives in Midwest City, Oklahoma.

Dupler were half as sick as Sergeant Worthington, he would have already been dead. The next thing I knew, he was dead, and Sergeant Worthington survived. Not many men gave up. There was a real important point: it was between the time a man could hobble out and pretend to do a day's work and when he had to give up and go to the sick bay.

"The closest I ever came to seeing a man actually in the act of dying was the one who as a result of his death I swore out an indictment against one of the Japs. Petty Officer Trim,* a Navy petty officer, was extremely weak, but he was still going out to work, and he had to stop to relieve himself on the way in. I asked the guard for permission for him to stop, and he agreed to it. Here this one character—I don't know whether it was Makan or not; I've forgotten who it was, which Jap it was—came up on this petty officer who'd stopped to relieve himself because he had dysentery. The Jap used that as an excuse to say that Trim was trying to escape, so he beat him until he died that night. We got Trim back to camp, and I sat with him, and I was there when he died.

"We put in twenty hours one day. They had a very simple term for it: 'No finish, no come back.' It was something like two or three in the morning when we got in, and we had to get up at four or five o'clock. I think that night we got only three hours in the bunk from the time we tried to eat something until chow call the next morning. We always had some form of an evening meal when we got in. That was when we had supper. We had three meals a day, and that's when we got our last meal, when we got back to camp.

"We did what we could to keep men off of the railroad. Anything was better than working on the railroad: sanitation detail, digging drainage ditches around the huts, improving and building new latrines, cutting firewood, anything. If the Japs had a special detail, helping with their supplies, we did anything to get men off the railroad. In fact, we—I mean the officers—were authorized to have orderlies, and we took advantage of it. We'd try to pick somebody who was weaker than the others. We tried to pick somebody who was younger, weaker, smaller—just not up to working out. We would have as many orderlies as the Japs would allow us to have. I think every American officer got down to where they were only allowed one. Anyway, we had whatever the Japs allowed.

"I think we fared much better in a tropical climate than we would have if we'd have been in a temperate climate. I always said if I had to be

---

*D. P. Trim, of the *Houston*, is listed as dying of a tropical ulcer at 105 Kilo Camp, Burma, on December 11, 1943.

prisoner, I'd take it in the tropics because we didn't wear any clothes to speak of, our huts were nothing but skeletons, our beds were light, and we could scrub with whatever water we could get. We didn't have trouble with body lice and things of that sort like they do in a temperate place. Our clothes were about all gone. I know I made myself a couple of G-strings out of the ground cloth from an old mosquito net. I had one pair of shorts and a shirt left that I saved for liberation day, that I was hanging on to. Some other fellows made G-strings out of my ground cloth, the old-time GI mosquito net with a big, generous herringbone weave ground cloth. It was a good material.

"On the railroad we had very little to help supplement our food rations. I made one good trade there. In one of those camps during that rough season, a little ol' Jap was going home, and the Japs like luggage, anything in the way of luggage. So he asked Captain Fowler if anybody had a suitcase or bag, any kind of handbag, that he could trade for or buy. I had one of these, what you refer to as an 'AWOL bag,' that I had been carrying all the time, so I negotiated a trade through Ira with this Jap. I traded him this little, ol' worn-out zipper bag for a twenty-five-pound burlap peanut bag full of dried fish. There were five or six of us that it helped over the hump. Hud, Windy, several of us, we'd take that ol' dried fish—some of it was shark and would cut like a rope—and we'd take a piece of it and cut it off and stick it in the coals to clean it, you know, get it hot enough to kill the bugs that might be in it, and it was good eating. It helped, but that was about all. One time some of the enterprising Dutch got hold of some dogs, and we were getting some dog stew. The market became so competitive that we lost out on that.

"The only snake that I helped to eat was a big ol' snake about six meters long. It got into the sick bay one night—got up in the roof. There were poor characters in there who hadn't walked in a week who got out of there. When we finally got him down, they killed him, skinned him out, chopped him up in sections, and then passed him around, and people roasted him and ate him. That was the only snake; a decent snake wouldn't stay around us.

"I got pretty sick one time before we finished the railroad, but never too sick not to go out. Actually, my worst condition came after the railroad was built. I stayed over in Burma. Like an idiot, I believed the propaganda that the Allied Air Force was dropping on us—leaflets—that they were going to reinvade and reoccupy Burma. I was still in pretty good condition physically, and I wanted to get loose and get back in the war. The Japs said there'd be so many men to stay and cut firewood for the locomotives and repair the bomb damage, so I volunteered, but not for the sake of the Japs. I raised a ruckus with Colonel Tharp to have him let me stay. So I stayed behind, and malaria hit me in April of 1944 when I was still in the jungle.

"Most Americans had left by then, but there were a few of us who stayed. I don't remember now whether there were any more Americans there when I finally got hauled out. I was so sick, frankly, by June, when they hauled me out, that I don't remember a great deal about who was with me. The work wasn't grueling or long hours. Planes would come over and knock out a bridge or something, and we'd go repair it, or we'd go out and cut some firewood for the locomotives. It wasn't anything as hard as building a grade during the monsoons. Only about two hundred stayed.

"Every night I'd make a tally of whether I was ahead or whether the Japs were ahead. If I felt a little better than I did the night before, I'd mark one up for my side; but if I felt a little worse than I had the night before, I'd mark one up for the Japs' side. In April and May 1944 there was a period when I didn't know whether I was going to make it or not. I didn't want to become so weak that I was helpless and just laid down and died. If I could see the end coming, I wanted to get out in the camp and give an account of myself. It would have brought reprisals on others, but I could have taken quite a few Japs with me. That was a big question with me during the monsoon season, whether to go ahead and try to survive or go sell out at the best possible price and call it quits. That was the biggest, roughest decision that I had to make.

"I don't know what I weighed, but we had the semblance of an Australian doctor with us and a great supply of quinine. His cure for malaria was these great big pills. I don't know how many grains was in them, but we'd turn in with malaria, and he'd dish them out—nine a day for nine days and six a day for six days, which was a fifteen-day treatment. Well, at the end of that time, after I went through the routine, fifteen days, it hit me again, and I went back and went through the same thing. I did that in May and June. In June they hauled me out on a litter to Thailand, and that's when little Shorty Ingram,* and I don't remember who else, met me. They got word somehow that people were coming in, and they met me with a litter and hauled me into a hut. I was real sick then. It took me two or three months before I started picking up again.

"I was taken to Kanchanaburi, the camp over by the rice mill on the southeast of the bridge over the river.† Well, it was a Utopia there. About

---

*William M. Ingram, Jr., of the *Houston*, lives in Jacksonville, Florida.
†The POW camp is undoubtedly Tamarkan, although Hard was uncertain regarding the camps he was in at this time. Clyde Fillmore, in his memoir *Prisoner of War: History of the Lost Battalion*, correctly notes that most Americans went from

that time I think the Japs had a change of heart and decided they were going to try to take care of the ones who were left. I think they had a change of mind, and they wanted some of us to survive. I'm convinced that in the jungle they meant what they said—they didn't care whether any of us survived or not—because they were still winning the war. They never thought they'd have to answer to anybody for anything, even as late as, well, June, July, and August of 1943, the rough months in the jungle. They were still winning the war, but they saw that change."

Just before Japan surrendered, Hard was transferred to a new camp for officers a bit northeast of Bangkok, near Nakhon Nayok. After recovering from malaria, he had herded cattle, but at this new site he was helping build the camp. He knew something was amiss from the usual routine, when he passed the "worst Jap we ever had, the one we called the Undertaker,"* on a trail in camp one morning and the Undertaker stepped aside and bowed and said, "Good morning, sir." That night they received word that the war had ended. While at the hospital in Calcutta, Hard gave his deposition against the Japanese guard responsible for Petty Officer Trim's death.

Back in the United States, Ilo Hard left the Army, but before establishing himself in civilian life reenlisted at the rank of tech sergeant. He went through "retread training" at Fort Knox, Kentucky, and was assigned to the Aberdeen Proving Grounds in Maryland and then to the Pentagon. He was recommissioned and ultimately served twenty-six years in the military, including his National Guard service. He retired as a colonel in July 1963. He had since been a deputy sheriff in Austin, Travis County, Texas, and a stock farmer. Hard, who retired to Florence, Texas, just north of Austin in Williamson County, died at Fort Hood of heart disease on April 12, 1992.

---

the Burma jungle to Tamarkan, with some at Chungkai and Kanburi. Although Hard came out of the jungle later than most, it seems reasonable that he too went to one of these camps. The bridge to which he refers is no doubt the so-called Bridge on the River Kwai. One other prison camp in its vicinity was Tha Makham.

*According to Rivett, *Behind Bamboo*, the Undertaker's name was Kanaishii, and he was a Korean.

John W. Wisecup, USMC
USS *Houston*

Trouble caused John Wisecup to work on the Death Railway. As a young Marine in San Diego, he habitually got into fights, took extended, unauthorized liberties, and once "went over the hill"—was AWOL. To rid his unit of him, the topkick sent him to the Far East to serve on the Asiatic Fleet's flagship, the USS *Augusta*. Of course, once aboard he again got into trouble and was in the brig when the ship was to sail for home. Before she left, the skipper had him transferred under arrest to the new flag, the USS *Houston*. Wisecup may have been one of those rare, unfortunate characters destined for trouble. Having been born in New Orleans, Louisiana, on May 15, 1919, he left the city following his junior year in high school. He was on the West Coast serving in a Civilian Conservation Corps camp when he enlisted in the Marines in November 1939.

When not being punished for misconduct, Wisecup was an ammunition handler on one of the ship's antiaircraft guns. Following the sinking of the *Houston*, he was in the water for three days and spent three more in the jungle before being captured. He is a bit uncertain about where he was kept before joining the main body but remembers the trip to Bicycle Camp: "On the way over there, the Nips marched us down these narrow streets, and the natives were hollering at us. They were hollering 'Mac mac,' which means 'fuck you' or something, and they were throwing buckets of crap down on us from the second deck."

He was one of the few enlisted men interviewed who recognized the value of commissioned personnel. "The officers," he said, "had it harder than the enlisted guy because they were right in the middle. If something went wrong, whether it was their responsibility or not, they got the shit kicked out of them first." Wisecup got a serious case of dysentery at Bicycle Camp and still had it when the group arrived at Changi. He was cured there with emetine, made from the ipecac root, but his illness kept him from going to Burma with the main body of the Lost Battalion. Instead he was with Quaty Gordon and the other Americans who shipped out with Englishmen and Australians as part of H Force to work at the southern end of the railroad. Wisecup's story begins with a ten-day march, after the six hundred-man Allied contingent arrived in Ban Pong, Thailand.

"WE WALKED, I think, for ten days. We didn't lose as many men as they did in the Bataan Death March, but what we lost on the railroad made that death march look like a picnic. I'll tell you what was bad about our march—not with the Americans but with all the others. Most of the limeys and other guys were culls; they were sick people. We lost quite a few going up, and the Japs just left them in the jungle. We walked ninety-six miles. I've looked it up on the map and figured it out: Ban Pong to Hintok. It may have been more than that because in those days there was no railroad. I'm following the old route; it's highway now from Ban Pong to Kanchanaburi and then on up to Hintok. On the map it shows ninety-six miles. What made it hard was that you had to carry a lot of gear. We carried tents, which we shouldn't have brought, because the bastards leaked like sieves. We were carrying them and all the cooking gear and all kinds of shit. Plus, some of the guys carried a whole gang of gear that they discarded on the way.

"What we did was march at night because it was so hot. We'd march all night until daybreak. We'd take breaks about every hour, I think, for maybe five minutes. The guards kept you going. The guys in the rear were kicked and punched and beat. If someone couldn't make it, if he had to fall out, that was that. You just left him there. I don't know how many we left. I couldn't give you an accurate number, but we must have lost quite a few. But we didn't lose any Americans, although some of them got sick en route. The hell of it was that when we got to the goddamned place, Hintok, we didn't even get a day's rest to put up a camp. We went right to work, and it started raining the day we got there!

"The monsoons had just started. It rained a little bit every day; it was just the beginning. Well, we did get our tents up, and we got the place ready. Then after we did that, oh, Jesus, the rain started coming down. It rained constantly. You were wet all the time. Your tent was wet; your bunk was wet; your clothes were wet; your feet were wet. You'd fall down; you'd get muddy; you were dirty. You got body lice that you can't get rid of, and you've got bamboo lice. My strongest memory is of guys sitting around a smoking fire, because it's raining, and they're trying to keep that fire going at night because they can't sleep. They're scratching and fighting bugs. Everybody had them. Nobody could sleep, and we were in the mud constantly.

"After that, cholera hit, and guys started getting dysentery, and nobody could make it to the latrine. They'd just walk outside of the tent, if they could make it, and they'd crap there. The camp area looked like a pigpen in the morning. It looked like where ducks had been. One guy's job was to cover it up. All day long, he'd bring ashes around, covering up the droppings. It was filthy. The Nips, when they came down to call out a working party, would never come into the camp. They stood outside and hollered down because it was that filthy down there.

"The Americans stayed together pretty good. We didn't have to—and sometimes, you know, you'd get separated—but we stayed together pretty good. When the Speedo period started, the Japs were, well, belligerent. You know, they'd get the hell kicked out of them if they didn't produce. They had a deadline, and so they'd work you over real bad to make you produce. Plenty of guys almost got beat to death up there. 'Quaty' Gordon, when his shoulder went out of place, instead of helping him, they beat the hell out of him. Guys were falling off the damn uprights for the bridge when we first put them up, and they got hurt. Quite a few guys fell off; the bridge was pretty high.

"The Korean guards were like slaves to the Japs, and the ones you had up there were the bottom of the barrel. Christ, they were on the muscle all the time. Hell, they were much harder, much tougher, and a whole lot crueler than the Japs. Let me give you one example. We used to have working parties that would go from Hintok to the river to pick up supplies. We'd have an officer in charge. One time we had a British officer whom I will never forget. There was another camp down from us where they had quite a few British. We only had one guard with us. Nobody was going to escape in the jungle. He'd lag along behind, or he'd go way ahead. So the British officer is with us—about six of us. Halfway there he told me, 'Look, I'm going to piss off, mate, and go down there and see some of my friends at this other camp. When you come back, I'll meet you at such-and-such a time halfway here.' There was a cutting in the jungle, and this would be about the halfway mark. It was about four miles into the jungle to the river where we were going to get the supplies. I said, 'Okay.'

"We went to the river and loaded up to come back, and the Korean started to ask us where the officer was. I said, 'Oh, *benjo!*' In other words, I said he had stopped to take a crap. The Korean asked if he was sick, and I said that he was. So that satisfied him. So we keep going and get up to the cut, and we're walking slow to give the Englishman a chance to get up there, and he wasn't back. So the Korean started raising hell and wants to know where he is. I said, 'Well, he stopped here somewhere.' Directly, here he comes. So this Korean starts asking where he was. Well, this stupid bastard, instead of using a little couth and saying he was out in the jungle sick, you know, and had to take a crap and all, he told him where he went. Man, that Korean beat him to pieces. This was a big Korean; he weighed about 165 or 170 pounds, and we were all in poor shape.

"We had no use for the limeys, anyhow. There were three Americans in this party. We didn't particularly like this officer. This shows how callous you get when you're a prisoner. The Korean beat that guy and kicked him, and we just stood back there and looked at him. As I can recall, there was no emotion whatsoever. It just shows you how you get when you're a prisoner. The guy asked for it in the first damn place. He was snotty. I often thought of that, you know, how you get under those conditions. But that's the worst beating I've ever seen. Oh, man, he beat him up.

"When we first got there, we had to lay the groundwork for the bridge. This is the one at Hell Fire Pass, the Hintok Bridge. We had to do the drilling. We'd drill out holes and blast so they could put the pilings down. That's the first job I had—Gordon, [Norman] Stevens, and I. The Japs did the blasting, but we did the drilling. We'd drill out holes to bedrock so they could put the original piling down and your cement and what-have-you. When we got that done, crews in the jungle cut down the green teak and hauled it down there. They'd just hook up almost like in a harness and pull the teak out of the jungle. Then it was cut to size, which we did with hand tools—no mechanical stuff. Our winches were all hand-operated pulleys. All this was hoisted up by hand-operated pulleys.

"I'll tell you one funny thing. We had this winch, an old hand winch. You've got one guy on this side and one guy on the other; you've got your cables, and you've got your log. Your timber would have been about twenty feet long. They'd hoist it up to the second stage of the bridge. Me and another guy worked all day on this. And they had a Nip up on the top—a Korean—and everytime we would hoist one up—every second or third time—he didn't like the way we'd hoist it. So he'd come all the way down the ladder, walk over, take a couple of punches at us, and then go back up there. I used to tell the other guy, 'Here he comes, mate.' He'd say, 'He'll be out of gas by the time he gets here. Don't worry.' He would, too. He'd be all out of breath. He'd yell, and then he'd go back up there. Well, we built this bridge at Hell Fire Pass. You've got mountains all around there full of green timber, which we cut and hauled down. You'd call this bridge at Hintok a trestle back home. It spanned a gully. It was a quarter-of-a-mile long and sixty to seventy feet high. We got up there in May and were finished in

October or November—somewhere around there—and then we went back to Kanchanaburi. I worked a little on the Kwai River Bridge* after we got back to Kanchanaburi.

"Now I didn't work the whole time. I got ulcers on my feet and legs, and then I got beriberi and couldn't really walk from the camp to the Hintok Bridge. It was about seven miles, I think. They put the camp so far away because they had running water in that area. That was the nearest spot. There was none by the bridge. See, they had to have water for the camp facilities. That's the closest fresh water they had running. They used it for bathing, cooking, and everything else. It was a creek running down the mountain.

"They put me on light duty burying guys who were dying of cholera. We were burying fifteen, sixteen, seventeen a day. We dug one big hole and put them all in there. It was me and another guy. His hand was almost rotted off with an ulcer. I never will forget that. About three weeks before they slacked off on the bridge, they came and got me again, and I went out there because there were only about thirty guys able to work by now. When I got out there at first, because I couldn't walk, they had me cutting wood and making tea. Everybody drank tea all day long.

"These guys didn't know how to use an ax. By this time, they were putting braces on the side of the bridge, and the Nips wanted them to be squared off. They wanted them hewed square. Now these limeys, most of them, ain't never seen an ax except some headman in a movie cutting off somebody's head. So they're trying to square these things off, and they don't put a notch in the log. They come down on it straight, and the ax glances off and hits them in the shins and damn near cuts them off. That happened to three or four of them.

"One of the Nips came up, and I'm making the tea. He kicked me in the leg, grunts, and gives me the ax. He figures he's going to have some fun with me, I guess. So he tells me he wants this log squared away. I've done this before. I notched it, and he's watching. I notched it, and then I squared it on one side. I notched the other side and hewed it. I did that to two, and he said, 'Yasumi! Yasumi!' He goes and gets me a cup of tea and gives me a cigarette, because I was the only one who knew how to do this. The rest of them were killing themselves. Finally, he brings the Jap sergeant to show him me doing this. That's the easiest job I had the last three weeks on that bridge.

---

*He is referring to the Mae Klong River bridge.

"Now, my shoes gave out about the second week after we got to Hintok. So I'm working barefooted, which I'm used to. Anyhow, I'm working down there and swinging the maul; you got your drill bits, and you twist them around. The way I got my first tropical ulcer was from rocks and chips flying around there. The Nips never did say nothing about when they'd fire the hole like they do on a construction site. They'd just shoot. So some of it flew over and hit me in the leg. It knocked the hide off of my leg. That started one. I thought it was going to heal up, but in the jungle nothing heals that fast. Even now, it wouldn't—if you were to go there now. It's so hot and festering. Well, that one started on my leg.

"Then I told you about working on the winch. I'm working out there one day, and I got beriberi by now. My legs are swelled up with water. So I got a blister on the top of my foot because you got a lot of water in your leg and in your feet. A blister popped up on my foot. Well, I popped the blister, and I took some grease off of the winch to put on top of it. That was the beginning of the son-of-a-bitch. Later on, I put mud on it and covered it. Then at the end of the day, I'd pull the mud off and clean it.

"Well, them bastards, once they get started, within a week's time, Christ, they can cover six or eight inches on your shin and expose the bone. But I was lucky. You could smell the damn thing. It rots. Then maggots get in them. You've got to watch the flies, you know. They lay eggs on there, and the maggots hatch, and they will go in and get behind the bone, if you don't watch. I've seen guys die with that. Geez, boy, that would stink; Jesus Christ, it smelled terrible. And they're painful. And that's where the Nips'd kick you—right in them goddamned ulcers. But I was lucky. I had them, but they never got big. My leg puffed up, but I was lucky. I got scars on my legs, small ones, and I got them all over my feet. They went clear to the bone. But I was lucky. I got out of the jungle and got down to Kanchanaburi. It took a year for them bastards to heal up. Actually, I was back in Changi before they healed. But I was lucky.

"At Hintok the only thing I could do is cover them with mud during the day, and at night I could sometimes make a solution of hot water and salt and pour it on them. You never had any bandages or nothing to put on the sons-of-bitches, so you'd have to doctor them the best you could. We had no medical treatment up there. Beriberi was what made my ulcers so they wouldn't heal. Nothing heals when you got beriberi. You couldn't get rid of it while you were up there, because you ain't getting the right food. You were getting rice, but you weren't getting enough vegetables and greens to go with it.

"I can still smell the huts at Kanchanaburi where they kept ulcer people. When you first went in, it was overpowering. Maybe a hundred guys had ulcers rotting away. But after you were there a day or two, you became callused to it, and you didn't pay any attention. You'd sit down and eat your chow, and it didn't even bother you. You'd know who died, and you'd get his chow and eat it. That's how you got after a while. Now, if I smelled something like that today, it would make me deathly sick. But I was lucky with the ulcers, I'm going to tell you. I was lucky.

"You know, you didn't dwell on things like that then. You were busy trying to get something to eat and thinking about a cigarette and a rest. You were worn out all the time. You couldn't sleep at night when you got back to camp because the damn rain was coming in. And you were scratching the lice. You never had time to worry. Now some guys did, and they didn't last too long. I saw guys die when they had nothing wrong with them. I swear. They flat-ass had no interest in anything anymore. They'd say, 'I'm finished. I'm gone.' Well, you didn't worry about him. That was his business.

"Up there, on the bridge, you had to be lucky. Don't get me wrong. I don't care how strong you were or what you did, you had to have luck. Because cholera can hit anybody, and you're dead in about two days. You dehydrate. Well, about three weeks after we got up there, to Hintok, we had the first cholera case. I helped carry him off. He was working on Hell Fire Pass. Around two o'clock in the afternoon, someone came down and said, 'Does anyone want to help carry a sick Aussie back?' I said, 'I'll do it.' So I got over there. I think there were six of us. Two would spell the other four. We went right up over the mountain, and this guy was groaning and puking and shitting—just water. He's the one that started it. Then it hit the camp, and we started losing about sixteen, seventeen guys a day or something like that. I mean, boy, they were all over. We'd find them laying out there outside the tents. So me and this other guy had to pick them up. They got me first. After my legs got bad and I couldn't get out on the bridge, they put me on that. At first we made individual graves, and then there were so many of them that we just couldn't keep up with it.

"There was this little Irishman from Dublin—very religious—I will never forget that. 'Hey, Paddy,' I said, 'we can't make individual graves.' He said, 'What are you going to do, lad?' I said, 'Just dig one big hole. It'll take us all morning to dig a hole about ten feet square, and we'll throw them in there.' Now, he was religious, and he says, 'Oh, mate, that's sacrilegious.' I said, 'Yeah, but we ain't going to be able to do it individually!' So he finally agreed that we'd do that, and then we'd throw them in there.

"I never will forget one rainy morning. They got these bamboo shoots that grow up overnight. And here we are. I'm barefooted, and Paddy had some shoes. The path out into the jungle was about six, seven, eight inches deep with mud, and I'm walking along, you know, out in front, Paddy in the back. We don't have this stiff head first; we got him with his feet toward me. I ain't got no ass left in my britches, and I'm walking along, and I'm miserable, and the lice are eating me, and the dead guy's feet keep hitting me. I never will forget. Jesus Christ, I start cussing. I never will forget this, never to the end of my days. I stopped and turned around, grabbed hold of the stretcher, and threw the whole bunch into the jungle. I said, 'Leave that son-of-a-bitch over there!' So Paddy says, 'John!' I said, 'What?' He says, 'We can't do that, lad. No good will come of it.' He says, 'You can't blaspheme the dead.' I says, 'Goddamnit, he's out of it, the son-of-a-bitch! Leave the bastard laying over there!' In a few minutes, I cooled down and went and got him. I can remember that just so clear: them cold feet kicking me in the ass. I was thinking, 'Look at him! He's out of it! He ain't got to put up with this shit anymore!' Now this is how you get. We used to take what clothing they had on them worth using, if they weren't stripped by the time we got there. We never had any graveside service. We had no time for that.

"I was real strong again. I was hurt, but I was still strong. I didn't have dysentery anymore, and luckily all the time I was there I never got malaria. I didn't get malaria until I got back to Singapore. I could eat like a horse, whenever I got anything. When we'd go on these working parties down to the river, we used to get some dried fish. It looked like shark. This was for the Nips. It was about three feet long and had a thick skin, just gray skin like a shark. The meat was oily, but it was beautiful! Well, en route through the jungle, we would stash some of it under logs. Then the next day we'd sneak back, or at night, and get it. By this time the maggots had gotten to it. Then we'd get back to camp, build a big fire, and beat the damned fish, and maggots would fly like salt and snow. Then we'd boil it up and eat it. It was oily, but, Jesus, that was good. I could eat anything.

"If someone died, we didn't report it right away because you could get their chow. We'd do it all the time. Sometimes we wouldn't let the Japs know for a couple of days because you couldn't smell them in the sick hut because of all the rotten flesh from ulcers and stench from dysentery. You never noticed the dead guys. This was at Kanchanaburi where we did that— me and Paddy Grubb; not the Irish guy—Grubb was a British Columbian, and he'd been in the Argyll Regiment. He's living in New Zealand now.

"You know, you've got to eat. You look back now, and you think about what a foul place that was. Holy Christ! When I worked in that ward, there were only two of us taking care of about seventy or eighty ulcer cases in Kanchanaburi. What you did, you had your urine bottles that we made out of sections of bamboo. Also, you had your shit pan made out of cut bamboo. We had to help them go—hold them up. Like one guy who had ulcers on his buttocks, and we helped him so that the maggots wouldn't get into it. Well, they got in and all the way around it. They had to operate on him, and they cut off half of the poor bastard's butt. You could see all the ligaments and everything. Well, he had to lay on his belly and it got gangrenous. We used to hold that bastard up to take a crap, you know. Man, he died horribly. That poor son-of-a-bitch! I never will forget that. Boy, let me tell you, that's a hard way to go, with them ulcers. There ain't no worse. Just before you die, two or three days before, that gangrene affects your mind and everything else.

"The Japs at Hintok wouldn't come down into the camp unless they absolutely had to, and, if they couldn't make up the work quota, they'd start beating up on people. They'd beat up on a sergeant and what-have-you who was in charge, and he'd come down there and drag somebody out of there, sick or not. They had to have them. But only under those conditions would they come into that camp.

"People who were sick didn't get any rations. That was understood. If you didn't work, you didn't eat. If somebody didn't bring the sick guy food, if you didn't have somebody to bring you food, you were in trouble. And there's very little that they got. I'm going to tell you right now. They had to go round scrounging. If the guy was so sick that he couldn't get out of his hut, he was in bad shape. But we Americans all stuck together. I wouldn't say we were real tight. That group that we had go up there to Hintok had no officer, no senior NCO. We had nothing. We stuck together. Nobody beat up on an American or anything like that.

"As I look back now, I'd say, 'Well, some guys are loners and down.' You always got that. Me, you know, I really believe there are some things you're born with. I don't know. But I was always an optimist to some extent. I always looked at it like, 'Well, things are going to get better.' They never have, but . . . ! We had guys on the ship before we sunk that you didn't want to talk to. I got away from them! They'd say, 'Man, we can't make it out of this.' I'd walk away from these kinds of people; I didn't even want to hear this. Oh, I knew it was true, probably, but, still, I didn't want to hear it.

"But as far as despising anybody out in the jungle, I don't think it came to that. You were so goddamned preoccupied with getting something to eat and surviving that you didn't think about these things. As far as sticking together, we must have stuck pretty good up there because we were the only

Americans. Christ, there were six hundred originally of all these different nationalities, mostly English. You can't say we were buddy-buddy or anything like that, but we helped each other out pretty good. Three of our thirteen died. That's all. The last one died at Kanchanaburi, I think. One died in Hintok, and the other one died at Tarsau on the way back down. We tried like a son-of-a-bitch to keep them going. I can't remember their names now. Gordon would know them. He knows all that stuff.

"You know, Hintok was the pits. There just wasn't any way to make it up there. You just wanted to get it over with and get the hell out of there. We went up there in May and left in October or something like that. We went down to Tarsau. First, we went someplace down the river, and we were there about two weeks. Then they brought us to some little place where the railroad ran next to the river. They put us on the train, and we went to Tarsau. We stayed overnight in Tarsau, and the next day they put us on flatcars—regular flatcars, and it took a day-and-a-half or something like that to get to Kanchanaburi—in the rain. This time we had plenty of room. All we had to do was keep from falling off the flatcar.

"Kanchanaburi* looked like a big city. Geez, I don't know how many men were there. There were not a hell of a lot of Americans, I know. It was just us at that time. I've heard the number estimated all the way from seven thousand to ten thousand prisoners. I've seen pictures of the damn place. It had regular atap huts, and each was about a hundred yards long. They were right next to the railroad. They had a Tamil camp next to it. You had your two Kwai River bridges not far from there. They asked for people to work on the bridges. They came in and got the fittest. I worked down there a few days. I guess I got about three weeks on that Kwae River bridge. We got in on the last part where they were putting up the braces and side stays. They were bringing in ties—they called them 'sleepers'—and stuff. But they were in a hurry to finish it. Boy, they were really tough on us. You had to be careful. You'd get the hell kicked out of you quick over there. We got in on the end of the Kwai bridge. They were winding down. When we left Hintok, they already had trains going over that bridge. I never will forget the first train that went across it. I thought, 'That bastard's going to fall down.'

"A lot of guys weren't working at Kanchanaburi because you had mostly the sick, who were waiting transportation back down south, see. Most everybody was whipped when we got back there. But, like, me and Paddy Grubb and Gordon and them guys, we were the walking wounded,

---

*Although this is the town's name, and there was a camp with this name near it, he is in fact discussing Tamarkan Camp.

and they could still get a little work out of us. And they got it. They'd come around there and want a certain amount of guys to go out and work. They did have quite a bit of what we would call rest there. They used to have lectures. Some of the guys would give lectures. We had a guy who had climbed Mount Everest with Sir So-and-So. What's his name? The first guy—Hillary?*

"Well, we had a guy who had been with him, one of the officers. Another guy had spent many years in Afghanistan, and he'd also been fighting on the North-West Frontier. There were some real interesting lectures, when I was in the hospital ward especially, and I got to listen. I wish I'd had a tape recorder. One of the officers had been one of your top polo players—one of the top three in the world. You know, some of these guys had really been around. It's something you can remember, something worth listening to.

"Also, the food was a hell of a lot better than at Hintok. We could get around and hustle up something to eat because they had a black market going in there. See, the Thais were coming in and out. We went out on working parties. You could always hustle up some duck eggs. You'd trade: some of the officers had jewelry, watches; somebody had a fountain pen. Ronson lighters were good trading material. One trading item was flints for cigarette lighters. We used to cut barbed wire with a wire cutter—the same size as a flint—and sell them. They didn't have a lighter with them to try it on, so we'd trade that. All kinds of deals. If you had a newspaper, it was barter material. All kinds of things that ain't worth a goddamn now was worth plenty then. You'd wonder how guys could hang on to stuff in that goddamned place, but they did. Some guys came out with complete diaries. Look at Ben Dunn.† He kept all his notes.

"On the black market there were many things you could hustle, but rings, watches, and fountain pens were valuable. The Parker fountain pens had gold in them, I think. You would go out on working parties, and you'd get stuff off somebody and go out and try to get a bigger price than you paid. The first thing you'd do when a guy had something, you'd say, 'Well, what's on it?' In other words, 'How much do you want for it?' He says, 'Well, I want fifteen dollars.' You'd try to 'Jew' him, so you'd say, 'Look, man, I ain't gonna be able to get no more than ten dollars for this.' Well,

---

*Sir Edmund Percival Hillary began his climbs in the Himalayas after World War II and reached the summit of Mount Everest in 1953.
†Benjamin Dunn wrote *The Bamboo Express*.

outside you might sell it for thirty, see. We did that sort of thing. Then we bought mostly tobacco or sugar, fruit, and things like that which were available in that neck of the woods. For example, we had all kind of wog tobacco, but the best was from Java. It was red. It had all kinds of names. 'Wogweed,' they called it, or 'Turk's Beard.' 'Granny's Armpit' is what the Aussies used to call it. Listen, that stuff would kill your appetite and probably kill you. You know what was a premium? Japanese paper. I think it was the *Japan Times*. It was made out of rice paper, and occasionally you could get ahold of a sheet of it. If you could get hold of that, you had money. You'd cut that up and sell it for cigarette papers. Any kind of paper was used for cigarette papers, but you were going first class when you had the *Japan Times*! No kidding, man.

"I don't know why I got the job in the sick hut. First, when I got there, the Japs had me working on the bridge. Then I had a day off, I think, and I was trying to get some extra rations around there. Paddy Grubb, the British Columbian, came over, and he had been working in the sick hut. He liked Americans. He'd been on the international police force in Shanghai. So he says, 'Do you want to work in here? You get a little extra chow now and then.' He didn't tell me how I'd get that extra chow, but I found out later. You know, when somebody died, you got their chow. So I says, 'Yeah.' So I went in there, and that's how I got it.

"Oh, man, it was terrible! It was all these guys down with leg ulcers. Some of them had their shin bones exposed; some of them had ulcers on their arms. Some of them were fly blown and full of maggots. We used to come and pick the maggots out every day and couldn't get them all because they get back of the bone. Every day or so they'd amputate somebody's leg or cut off an arm. We used to carry the people outside. The operating table was between the huts, in the open. It was just a stretcher on some boxes, and they'd chloroform the guy. We'd stand and hold him until he went under. Then they'd scrape these leg ulcers or cut off the leg or whatever they had to do, and then we'd haul him back in.

"We used to take care of them, you know, bring their chow, try to clean them up. We never gave anybody a bath because there wasn't any water. The only way you got a bath in there was when it rained. Everybody went outside and got in the rain. Some of the amputees survived, believe it or not, but it wasn't too good. I think the doctors used scalpels and that stuff. But as far as sawing the bone, they didn't have that regular surgical stuff. They used a regular hacksaw blade in most cases. Sometimes the chloroform didn't do the job right. Guys would still be half-awake. We'd have to hold them down when they'd come out of it. That's painful.

"I was improving. The beriberi went down while I was there. The ulcers weren't healing, but they weren't getting any bigger. They stayed. It took over a year for them mostly to heal. I was still without shoes. They got some Red Cross supplies—American Red Cross supplies—but they didn't give them out to the Yanks. They gave them out to the British. Well, in November 1943, or it might have been early December, we went to Sime Road a few days before Christmas, sometime before Christmas. We went back by train, the same way we came up. Only from Kanchanaburi to Ban Pong, we rode the flatcars. Then when we got down there, they stuck us back in the tin cans again, but they weren't crowded like before. It was a picnic going back down compared to coming up. We went to the Sime Road Camp, which is five miles from Changi."

In early 1944 all the Americans at Sime Road were sent to the Changi jail, where Wisecup cut wood for the boilers. Later, they were transferred to an atap hut behind the jail, which Wisecup says was the hut in James Clavell's novel, *King Rat*. In fact, Wisecup maintains that Corporal King, the novel's main character, was in fact a composite of three Americans living in the hut:

> Actually, the guy who is Corporal King is a composite of three people. He calls them Corporal King, but he wrote about three people. The book is mostly based on a guy named Eddie MacArthur. Eddie was a merchant seaman. He came into Changi before we went up-country. He had been on a merchant ship sunk in the south Atlantic by a German raider. German raiders sank about seven or eight down there, and they had a whole gang of prisoners, and they had to unload them somewhere. They couldn't get back to Germany past the British. So they brought them to Singapore.
>
> Eddie MacArthur came in there, and I never will forget. When he came in all he had was a pair of dungarees, and that's all. He bummed some cigarettes off of me, and then I went up-country. When I came back down, he's running the camp. He used to go through the wire.
>
> . . . Actually, the story is mainly about him, but King is a composite. It was three guys: Bob Martin, who was a boatswain off the *Houston*, Eddie MacArthur, and a guy named Carpenter.* It's built around these three. You can see it in there. If you had been there, you'd see it. He had this locker—footlocker—and in it he had cooking utensils, eggs, and all this. I got to watch it for him a couple of times, and he'd give me a cigarette. He was in the hut. All three of them were in the hut. But these guys never left Changi; they just stayed there.

---

*Robert L. Martin died of heart disease on October 18, 1986, in Houston, Texas. Albert L. ("Buttercup") Carpenter, of Battery F, now lives in Santa Fe, New Mexico.

For his part, Wisecup did not fare as well as the fabled King Rat. He, a British cook, and two others were caught stealing rice. Although not court-martialed by the British, he was put on the top floor of the Changi jail in isolation for two weeks as punishment. In August 1945 he was one of forty Americans liberated at Singapore and flown to Calcutta. Within a few weeks he was back at Marine Corps headquarters in Washington, D.C. He received a ninety-day leave and convinced his superiors to assign him to the Marine Ammunition Depot at Belle Chasse, Louisiana, near New Orleans. When the chance came in January 1946 he left the Corps.

His experience as a POW affected Wisecup more than many. He never settled down, and his longest employment was as a merchant seaman in the Orient. He served on cargo ships during both the Korean and Vietnam wars, for which he holds Merchant Marine campaign ribbons. He was a "swamper," waiter, and bartender at The Cage, a bar and restaurant located a few blocks from the Continental Hotel in Saigon, a position that gave him an opportunity to observe newsmen covering the Vietnam War. His criticism of them is devastating: "It was my privilege to witness the news media of various publications *bravely* writing up their daily battle reports. One cannot praise the courageous efforts of these fine and dedicated scriveners enough. The media did more to defeat (hogtie is more appropriate) our military forces than Charley ever did."

Chapter 5

Liberation

As America's Lost Battalion began to relocate in camps around Kanchanaburi, Thailand, the men quickly recognized that fundamental changes were occurring. Apparently, the Japanese had become apprehensive about the dreadful treatment and heavy casualties they had inflicted on the workers building the Death Railway.* Although housing remained essentially the same—bamboo and atap huts—the prisoners' food improved. The amount was slightly greater and the contents immeasurably better. Meals now included more rice, more vegetables, and sometimes even meat in a thicker stew. Death continued to be the companion of a few, primarily those who had come from the jungle suffering the most from their exposure. But harsh treatment by the guards abated somewhat. Bashings were less frequent, and activities that had not previously been allowed or provided for suddenly became possible. The POWs began to refer sarcastically to this period as a time of "rest and recuperation."

Allied troops were located in six camps around Kanchanaburi, but Americans appear at first to have inhabited only four. The men of H Force had been taken to Chungkai before returning to Sime Road in Singapore. Groups 3 and 5 of A Force, which included most of the Americans, were placed either at Tamarkan or the camp called Kanchanaburi (or Kanburi). Only a few were located at Nakhon Pathom, where an 8,000-man hospital camp was created. In early 1944 several members of the Lost Battalion were sent to the Hashimoto Works at Non Pladuk. This industrial center included the marshaling yards and railroad shops of the Burma-Thailand Railway.

---

*E. Bartlett Kerr, in *Surrender and Survival*, notes that the American government publicly protested to the Japanese government about the treatment of American POWs in March 1944 and threatened reprisals against Japan later. He says that the vice war minister instructed camp commanders to "improve the health conditions of POWs," but adds that conditions did not improve.

The only camp that the Americans seemingly did not enter at this time was the one at Tamauang.

This period of light duty did not last. After a few months those near Kanchanaburi began to be relocated. The Japanese planned to send 10,000 of the fittest POWs to Japan. From April through August 1944, these men began to move in groups of 150 to either Saigon, Indochina, or the River Valley Camp in Singapore. Most of the Americans who went to Saigon stayed in that area until the war ended. Allied submarines in nearby waters made shipping them to the Japanese homeland impossible. The only Americans in these groups to reach Japan left Saigon for Singapore in mid-1944. They stayed several months at the River Valley Camp and late in the year sailed for the Japanese home islands. They reached Moji in January 1945 after picking their way along the Asiatic coastline to avoid American submarines, which were very active in the area. These POWs worked in coal mines on the island of Kyushu not far from Nagasaki. They were near that ill-fated city when the atomic bomb was dropped on August 9, 1945.

Earlier, in June 1944, fifteen members of the Second Battalion had died when American submarines sunk the Japanese vessel transporting them through the southwest Pacific to Japan. These were not men who had worked on the railroad, having been kept behind in Java when the main groups left in October 1942. Three additional members of the Second Battalion died on September 18, 1944, when submarines sank the *Kachidoki Maru* and *Rokyu Maru*. The majority of men killed were Australians who had been part of A Force. Brigadier A. L. Varley, commander of A Force during the building of the railroad, was one of the men who perished in the sinking. Some of the Lost Battalion survivors believe the Americans who died on September 18 were not among those who worked on the railroad, but circumstances surrounding this shipment of POWs suggest that they were. Moreover, some members of the battalion agree that these men had survived Burma only to die in the Pacific Ocean. Allegedly, the first verifiable information Americans had about what had occurred in Burma and Thailand came from survivors of the September sinking.*

Some of the Americans remained in Burma and Thailand and were put to work as part of repair crews or woodcutters on the railroad. They underwent increasingly severe attacks by Allied bombers, and, although terribly frightened by the raids and not always allowed to build shelters from them, only a few were injured. The only American known to have died

---

*Information about American POWs in Burma was sent into China in mid-1943 but was not as conclusive as it would be were the former POWs at hand.

in a bomber attack was killed during the period when the men were at work on the railroad. E. P. Wilson, of Battery D, died in a raid at the hospital in Thanbyuzayat, Burma, on June 13, 1943.

Some few Americans were put to work building Japanese air bases or improving existing ones. The majority of these men was shifted into southern Thailand near Rat Buri and Phet Buri. It was from this group that James W. ("Red") Huffman, whose interview appears in the following chapter, and another American escaped, joining an Office of Strategic Services (OSS) unit operating in the adjacent mountains. The pair confirmed the story of Japanese mistreatment of the Lost Battalion survivors for the outside world. By 1945 the Americans were widely scattered with most either near Saigon or Rat Buri and Phet Buri, or in Nakhon Pathom, Non Pladuk, Singapore, or Sendryu in Japan. Several may still have been in Burma.

As the last year of the war opened, the POWs' officers began to be removed to special camps at Kanchanaburi and Nakhon Nayok, northeast of Bangkok. Reasons for the relocations are unclear. The Japanese may have decided to live up to the Geneva Convention's requirements concerning the separation of officers and enlisted personnel. A more plausible explanation seems to be that they decided to keep enlisted men from contact with their leaders to preclude any organized resistance as the war wound down. At any rate, in January the resettlement at Kanchanaburi began, and in June the shift to Nakhon Nayok took place.

The Japanese had grisly plans for the war's end. They began to improve security where POWs were kept. Moats with high embankments were dug around camps, barbed-wire or bamboo fences were erected, and sentry posts were built and manned. Movement in and out of compounds was restricted, and food and treatment grew worse. Men were put to work digging fortifications, including innumerable caves and mazelike tunnel systems, in an obvious attempt by the Imperial Army to repel an expected attack by the Allies. At the headquarters of Field Marshal Count Terauchi, commander of the Southern Army in Saigon, plans were developed to massacre all prisoners if an invasion took place. Through various sources— natives and Korean guards—the prisoners learned of Japanese intentions.

Not only were the Americans worried about their countrymen's air raids, but also they now had divided opinions regarding a land assault. They still confronted their predicament with humor: A leaflet dropped from Allied planes said, "Take heart, we are coming," to which one POW responded, "Take cover, they are here." Two events in August saved American, Australian, British, and Dutch prisoners from being massacred.

Early in the month, the United States dropped atomic bombs on Hiroshima and Nagasaki; Russia then entered the Far Eastern war. The Japanese ambassador to the Soviet Union was informed on August 8 that to hasten peace Russia would enter the war on the next day. On August 9, Soviet troops crossed into Manchukuo [Manchuria]. After several days of discussion at an Imperial Conference, Japan surrendered on the fourteenth. Intervention by a member of the royal family, the emperor's brother Prince Chichibu, kept Terauchi from carrying out his gruesome project. Japanese authorities informed the prisoners on August 16, 1945, that the war was over.

After liberation, those POWs in Southeast Asia generally came home through Calcutta, where they received immediate medical care at the 142d General Hospital. Those in Japan came by hospital ship through the Philippines. They greeted freedom after three-and-one-half years of captivity in a variety of ways, but a quote from Benjamin Dunn's *Bamboo Express* captures the essence of their feelings when they first heard the war was over: "There was a brief moment of extreme silence and then unimaginable bedlam broke loose. There was much shouting and back-slapping which lasted for some time—then immediately following that spontaneous celebration of the long-awaited victory, the British, Australians, and Dutch produced flags from hiding and soon had them flying. The British were singing 'God Save the King' and the Dutch were singing their national anthem, but strange as it may seem the Americans sang 'God Bless America.' It seemed to express our feelings of victory and freedom and gratitude to our great country."

Granville T. Summerlin
Headquarters Battery

Born on April 24, 1919, in Hughes Springs, Texas, a small town twenty-five miles north of the Longview-Marshall area in East Texas, Granville Summerlin was one of about forty draftees the Army assigned to the Second Battalion, 131st Field Artillery in early 1941. When drafted he was working as a machinist's apprentice for the Texas and Pacific Railway. After joining the battalion he served as clerk typist in Headquarters Battery. His experiences as a prisoner of war were not substantially different from those of the majority of Americans who worked in the Burmese jungle. He was part of Group 5 and suffered the usual illnesses—malaria, dysentery—and tropical ulcers, which were treated by Doctor Philip Bloemsma.

Summerlin chummed mostly with draftees when he first joined the Second Battalion at Camp Bowie, but in prison camps his clique was composed of other members of Headquarters Battery, including J. H. ("Cheedus") Bailey, E. L. ("Kirk") Kuykendall, and the Summers boys, Jay and Mark.* They worked primarily at cuts, fills, and bridges—the usual assignments. His interview begins after the railway was completed in October 1943.

"WHEN WE LEFT THE JUNGLE, they pulled the train in, and the best I can remember, we loaded on the train. We were kind of crowded, and we rode on the railroad that we had just built. I can't remember just now what camp we were at, but it was the one that had all the monkeys. It was above the 100 Kilo Camp; it could have been 105 or something like that. We weren't there all that long.

"I think they put us in boxcar-type containers on the train. I don't remember what time of day or what particular day it was. I remember that it wasn't a very smooth ride. The rails weren't exactly straight. They were kind of wishy-washy to ride on. The train didn't go fast. I really didn't know

---

*Bailey died of chronic bronchitis on December 15, 1977, in Abilene, Texas. The others live today in Texas: Kuykendall in Diana, J. L. ("Jay") Summers in Pleasanton, and Mark Summers in Fort Worth.

whether we were going to make it or not, the way that it was built. Things looked pretty shabby, but evidently it worked. I remember the ashes from the train coming back and flying into our faces. It was an old-time train, I'll put it that way—from way back in the old days.

"I remember it was one of the days when we had a scare from airplanes strafing. We had to get off the train and run for the brush. The Japanese sounded the alarm, I think. Like I said, the best I can remember, we were in boxcars, not open cars. It seemed like the train was still moving when we jumped off of it, and they strafed it. The planes made a run, the best I can remember, but they didn't do any damage to amount to anything.

"Our destination was Kanchanaburi—across the bridge, across the river—to the large camp there: Tamarkan. Well, after being in the monsoon season, it looked good after it got dried out a little. The barracks were similar to all the others, but it seemed like they were longer. They were huge barracks made out of the same stuff—bamboo. This is the place where the Japs gave us a day off each week, and that is when the guys started putting on stage shows. I got assigned to the cattle party. I herded cattle. I don't remember why I was picked. They just called me out. I might have been a little fragile, I guess, a little too thin for anything else. But that's when I started dealing with the natives.

"They had cattle for the camp, and they had these old buffaloes or the type of cattle that they had over there. We would go out and take them to graze. At that particular time, the Jap guard would get in the shade of a tree, and we would deal with the natives and do what we wanted to do. In fact, one of the boys went out and did a little fooling around while he was there. But we would, like I say, swap gold for different things. We stayed there for quite a while, and when a guy would have a birthday in camp, we would fill up canteens with that native whiskey over there and bring it back in. But the Japs got on to that, and they caught a guy bringing it into camp, and that is when they punished him there at the gate, in front of us.

"They made him kneel down and put a round piece of bamboo behind his legs and then made him squat down on it, and that would cut the circulation off of his legs. Of course, how long that they made him squat at a time, I don't exactly know, but they would let him up for so long and start circulation again, and then they'd make him sit back down again. Well, that kind of broke up the bringing in of whiskey for birthdays. Some Jap guards were real lenient with us about letting us do things. If we got hold of whiskey, we would give some to them. I heard that one or two of them got into trouble over that. In fact, we heard them over there hollering out. They were getting beaten just like the prisoners did.

"I imagine a half dozen of us were herding cattle. Of course, we traded most to get bananas, mangoes, any kind of fruit, duck eggs, and stuff like that. I would get my trade stuff from boys in the camp and take it out and swap it. Then I would bring back what I got, and they would give me a small percentage of it. You had to survive, and that was one way; since they couldn't get out, and I could, I did. They set up a canteen, and it had a limited amount, a few things in it that you could buy with Japanese money.

"I can't remember just exactly how many air raids we had in Tamarkan, but the first time the planes came over, this antiaircraft gun that was at the river bridge fired on them. Well, that went on for three or four days, maybe a week, and we knew that eventually the Allies were going to try to eliminate that gun. I believe they were doing most of their bombing at Bangkok, but they did bomb out this bridge near our camp, oh, three or four times. The bridge was a modern metal-constructed bridge with concrete tiers under it. It looked like it was probably a quarter-of-a-mile or less long. It was part of the railroad. They bombed it several times in the day, and we would work on it at night. They kept bombing it, and eventually the Japs built some little ol' docks along the river down there, and they used barges then. They ran a spur off the line and then used the barges. I think the Allies bombed the spur a few times, too.

"During the raids they decided that they were going to take out the antiaircraft gun, too, and they sprayed shells and bombs all the way from the gun over into the camp. I think that there were about forty-some Australians killed. I don't think that they were bombing the camp. They just overshot their target at the bridge or the gun. Of course, the raids bothered us, but we knew that the Allies were getting closer. We knew something was going on, where otherwise we didn't know. We seemed to perk up at this time of the game. It was looking much better. The raids seemed to anger the Japs more, but, as far as I could tell, they still didn't seem to take it out on the prisoners, not in the camp, anyway. The planes were B-29s, four-engines, and the Japs thought that they were something because they were so large—back in those days.

"They began to give us a day off. On that day off, if you needed a haircut, you'd try to get one or a shave, or you'd just generally rest up because you wouldn't have a lot to do or take care of. They played cards, and they shot dice. In fact, I played a little blackjack, myself, and I never had played it before. Then, they let us build a stage in the middle of the compound there, and they would put on shows that day we had off. The British seemed to enjoy doing it. In fact, the Japs came to them, and they would laugh. They were what some of the jokes were about. The actors made a lot of jokes out of the Japs. I can't recall any, but they made jokes out of them.

"We also got to send out one postcard—I did. Of course, it was marked with a very few words, and you could just put an X on what you wanted to say. You didn't do any writing on it. They had 'I am well,' 'I am working,' or something like that, and you could just cross one of them. That is all that I recall of the mail that I sent the whole time. I am pretty sure that about that time everyone was allowed to send one. I don't recall the date, but I know the one my family received from me was sent from Kanburi or Tamarkan or whatever you call it. I get kind of mixed up on that. But I've got the original thing, the yellow card or yellow paper.

"They started sending people from there to Japan, and I didn't want to go because I was afraid that I would have been sunk before I got there. The war was still going on over there. I didn't want to get in it, I'll guarantee you that. I don't remember how many were shipped to Japan, but there were still a lot left in our camp. Finally, we went to Bangkok. When we got there, they put us on a dock, in a warehouse, full of mosquitoes. We were there until the next day. Then we were taken to a camp up in Thailand where we worked on gun emplacements, underground tunnels, and all that kind of stuff.*

"The officers were separated from the men here, and the officers were building their own camp over there. Of course, our camp was similar to all the camps, but the work was different—building gun emplacements and tunnels to different places. The Japs were digging in. That's what we were taken there for, to dig them in. It was a fairly pleasant, warm place, just ol' summertime temperatures. Of course, some of the places, as far as I remember, were pretty cool at night, but in the daytime it warmed up—just tropical climate.

"We weren't there long until one morning we were going out, and we got about two or three hundred yards from the gate, maybe a little farther, and they stopped us and turned us around and took us back. We didn't know what for, but the natives were standing alongside of the road saying that the war was over; and when we got back to camp, there weren't any guards there. Well, we were so happy that the war was over with, but we didn't know what to do, really. Finally, the officers got us together and told us what was happening. Sure enough, when our officers got in touch with the Thai government, the war was over. They got us some food to eat, also. When we got it, we ate all that we could eat, and it made us sick. We couldn't stand meat or anything that rich, and we had more diarrhea.

---

*The camp was near Nakhon Nayok.

"I don't think that it was much over three days or four at the most, after we heard the war was over, that the Japs came in there in trucks. Instead of putting sixty or seventy-five in a truck, they put twenty-five or thirty so that we could stand up or whatever, and they took us to the nearest airport. As far as I could tell, there were planes already waiting to take some of us back to India then. It was a happy day when I got on that plane. We stopped at one place, a Red Cross camp, on our way to Calcutta, and we got our first American sandwich. It was the first bread I had. I don't remember what we had to drink with it, but I do remember that we had a sandwich, probably a ham sandwich.

"Then we flew to Calcutta, and it seemed like we stayed in the hospital there, I don't know, a week or two. They screened each one of us—the doctors did—to find out what we really needed in a hurry and whatnot. Then we were placed in the hospital. The main thing that I remember is that they had a list of stuff that we could order to eat—whatever we wanted—and I remember ordering a bunch of stuff, and it made me sick again. I ordered meat, some type of meat, and I ordered sweet stuff. It was more than I could eat. I don't remember exactly what I weighed, but it was roughly between eighty and ninety pounds. I had weighed roughly 150 pounds.

"Well, they did some psychological tests or something on us. I guess they wanted to see if we were 'all there.' I think they wanted to find out if it had affected us mentally, that's what they were after. What do you call it? Anxiety or whatever the technical word for it is? How bad had it affected you? When we first got to the hospital, they wanted to take a group of us back to pick out certain Japs that we thought had committed crimes and so forth, so I volunteered, and [Isaac] Alvin Morgan volunteered. But before it was over with, they decided it would be best for us not to go back in there because there really weren't any Allied troops close by, and it could have caused a lot of trouble. I felt like going back because of the treatment that we went through on the durned railroad, starving us to death all those years. I didn't get beat bad, just small incidents. The sort of thing that everybody received. You might say everyday occurrences.

"After a while we were given a priority card for transportation, and we were more or less on our own after we got out of the hospital at Calcutta. They gave us this card and told us what planes we were supposed to catch, and if we missed one, then we were to just catch the next one. Of course, they were military planes. We stopped in New York at the hospital there, and I don't recall its name. We checked in, and from there they sent us to different places. They sent me to North Carolina to a hospital. There were several guys there who were in my outfit. I think that they sent me there for tropical disease, that tropical ulcer that I still had. I don't know how long I stayed there, but then I got a leave of absence to go home. Of course, that was my happy day!"

After his leave ended, Summerlin spent about a year at Army hospitals in Texas, including William Beaumont at Fort Bliss, El Paso, and Brooke Army Hospital at Fort Sam Houston, San Antonio. He had some trouble curing his leg ulcer, but his main problem was the stomach parasites from which he has never fully recovered. He was discharged in November 1946 and returned to work for the Texas and Pacific. After a few years he left the T and P to start his own paint contracting business, which he continued until retirement. Summerlin now resides in Marshall, Texas.

James W. ("Red") Huffman
USS *Houston*

In the fifty-man *kumi* to which Red Huffman and Matthew ("Matt the Greek") Marinos* were assigned, they were the only two to survive the ordeal of building the Death Railway. Part of Group 5, they were also survivors of the sinking of the cruiser *Houston*. In fact, after that ship was sunk, Huffman and several other seamen, by furtively moving around Java and a small nearby island, managed to stay free of the Japanese for six days. This accomplishment was a mixed blessing for Huffman; he was "bare naked" from the time he swam ashore until a Japanese officer bought him a sarong four days after his capture.

Huffman was born on September 29, 1916, in Los Angeles, California. He quit school after the tenth grade and joined the Navy to get away from the family ranch, enlisting on October 16, 1934. Huffman had several duty stations before being assigned in 1938 to the *Houston*, where he became the leading seaman on the deck crew. When the *Houston* was sinking, Huffman was at his battle station as pointer on a Number Two mount, an 8-inch gun, forward, under the bridge. He followed the usual route of the ship's survivors from the Serang theater to the Burma jungles, and he had the standard ailments: wet beriberi, malaria, dysentery, and tropical ulcers. His experiences after the prisoners finished work on the railroad, however, were anything but ordinary.

"WHEN I FINALLY STARTED OUT of the jungle, I believe I was at 115 Kilo Camp. We went down to a place where there were a couple of sidings, and they loaded us on a bunch of cattle cars, the kind that you can look through. After maybe several hours, a couple of engines were hooked onto us, and away we went. I got off the train at the bridge over the River Kwai, at a place called Tamarkan—a camp. That's where I went— me, ol' Pinky King,[†] and the whole bunch. The ride was a son-of-a-bitch! The railroad was the most awful thing I ever rode on. One of the guys, I

---

*Marinos now lives in Seattle, Washington.
[†]King and his antics apparently were morale builders among the Americans.

remember, said, 'Boy, we made this thing smooth! What in the hell happened to it?' Well, the Japs didn't let the dirt settle enough, and then it got wet and soggy, and it got just like the sea. Some of the guys even got seasick! They did!

"When we got to Tamarkan, we were pretty bad off. I wasn't in too good of shape—lots of malaria and malnutrition. But this Chinaman came over one night to our barracks, a guy called Marco Su.* He was cooking for the Japanese officers. He used to be a cook on our ship where he was the captain's cook. He came over to me, and he said, 'You want a good job?' He had been drinking sake. I could smell it. I said, 'Where'd you get that sake?' He said, 'You want a good job? I get you some, too.' I said, 'What do I have to do?' He said, 'You want a job? You don't want a job?' He was talking Pidgin English. 'I want a job.' He said, 'Okay, get your stuff.' He took me straight out the front gate, past the guardhouse, and over to the Jap kitchen.

"Guess who's over there? Pinky King, the Marine, and a couple of other guys, and we were the cooks. I learned to be a Jap cook pretty damned quick, and I ate good. I got well. I got well, gained weight, and so did King. He weighed 190 pounds at one time. When I was on the ship, I weighed 187 pounds, and when I weighed at a rice depot in Burma, I weighed about 118 or 119 pounds. I lost a lot of weight.

"But, oh, boy! Oh, yes, I gained weight and started feeling pretty good at Tamarkan. We ate the same food as the Japs. The cook said, 'You eat the same as us.' I ate pork, chicken, all the rice I wanted, and green stuff. You got fresh pork. They'd bring in a whole hog. We'd kill it. I got all kinds of green onions and something like spinach, and fresh fish and salted fish. There were lots of duck eggs and some chicken eggs, but I never got any chicken eggs. The Japs wouldn't give you any of them. Those were for the Japs. That's about the size of it. We had lots of fried rice with eggs and vegetables and pork in it. Boy, that was good stuff.

"I started taking on weight, and I had a mosquito net by then. I almost got rid of the malaria, but like a damned fool, when I escaped from the prison camp, when I ran away, I didn't have my mosquito bar, and in a couple of nights I had malaria again. But for a while I was lucky enough that I was in the Jap kitchen then. Hot damn! I was probably there about four months. Then one day they came in and wanted two volunteers to cook for the Japs: one officer's cook and one enlisted men's cook to go to Chungkai. Marco Su said, 'Let's go!' I said, 'Man, we got a good deal here.' He said,

---

*Su, who is carried on the *Lost Battalion Association* roster, died in 1971, but the cause of death and his whereabouts at the time are unknown.

'Maybe better deal over there.' I said, 'I go.' And away we went. We went down and got in a boat and went up to Chungkai, and I got with a whole bunch of Americans up there. I was in the Jap kitchen. But it wasn't long that they closed it, and we moved out, and I never worked in a Jap kitchen again.

"When we left Chungkai, we went down to the railroad by Tamarkan and got on a train and headed for southern Thailand. We went to a place called, oh, I can't say it, but it was on the Burma-Siam border in the mountains.* They were building airfields right along the edge of the mountains, and we started working there. I forget all the men who were with me then. I remember Luther Prunty. He was one of them. There were several Army and Navy boys. There must have been at least thirty of us there working on those airfields along with the Australians.

"We were taking those big ant hills and leveling them. I got the job of running a steamroller, back and forth, back and forth. Then the native girls carried earth on their heads from way off and dumped it in the holes where we pulled out big trees. The Japs eased off on us some. It was not like on the railroad. We went to work after it got daylight, and we were usually in by the time it was dark. None of this 'can't see to can't see' business. The food was better than on the railroad, too. It was a farming belt in there—Chinese farmers. I wouldn't write home about it, but it was better.

"When I was running this steamroller, Harris,[†] this friend of mine, was overhauling trucks, and he and I would get notes from the natives. We worked by ourselves, and we didn't have guards. We'd get notes, and we'd hide them, and we'd come in and compare them. They were from these guys with little parasols, like, a lama or Buddhist priest has. They were written like a fourth grader would write—printed, not written. They were telling us what they would do if we would go with them. There was one letter that they gave to Harris, that if anytime that we were ready to go, what to do. We were to crawl under the fence and start running, and they would have two men at any time of the day or night to take us to our friends. Harris believed it, and he got me to believing it. So we did exactly that, and what they said would happen, exactly happened.

"At noontime the guard's prostitute would bring him his food, and he would eat and have his sex. Then he would lay down, and she would keep the flies off of him. This went on day in and day out. We'd watch it. We

---

*He was in the Rat Buri and Phet Buri area of Thailand.

[†]Lanson Harris, who was also on the crew of the *Houston*, now lives in Tustin, California.

picked when he went to sleep to run off. He was the only one there. He wasn't really a guard; he was the boss. There was a split bamboo fence about eight feet high. So we threw all our gear over the fence and crawled under the hole and started running. The natives were there, and they took us by the hand. We ran and ran and ran until I couldn't run any longer. We hid in a banyan tree for the rest of the day, and the next night we took off again. We kept going and going and going—always going up higher in the mountains. They told us later at the OSS camp that the two natives were gangsters. They were turned loose by the Siamese when the Japs took over. They were pretty much renegades. They wanted weapons. They figured if they did what the lamas said, that is, take two prisoners and give them to the Allies, they would get some weapons. Then they could kill and rob Japanese. That's what they wanted to do, they said. But I don't know if the major gave them any weapons or not.

"I had been thinking about escaping as long as I was a prisoner, but I never had a chance. Anyway, the first day, when we were in the banyan tree, we saw airplanes and Japs all over the place looking for us. I know they were because we had never seen this before, these little planes. We stayed right up in the banyan tree. They're huge, cover three or four acres, a solid mass of roots. It got dark, and we came out, and away we went.

"We went with them holding our hands. Isn't that something? They demanded that; it meant something to them to be hand-in-hand. They were about thirty. Dope fiends. They 'snorted' every couple of hours. They had a little can and a little bent tube, and they'd stick it in their mouth and take some and spit, and, boy, they were ready to go again. They'd want us to take one, but no way! Remember, they were ex-prisoners, crooks; they got out of civilian prisons. They were going to take us, like the lama said, to behind our lines—Burma-India lines. That's what they thought. But that wasn't where they took us. They took us to an OSS camp that they knew was up in the mountains. They thought it was behind the lines. They weren't too smart.

"Well, pretty soon we got captured by the OSS troops or the OSS bunch. They weren't Americans; they were trained by Americans. We were going along this river this day, and there was a big tree that had fallen over—teak probably—and it made a footbridge. We went across this footbridge because we had to get on the other side of this river. We started up a little place where people had a trail going up the side of the bank, and we got about halfway up, and they jumped out on us. There must have been twenty of them—all with crazy stuff on their faces, colors. I saw my first wartime .45 submachine gun. He stuck it right in my face, and I told Harris,

'That's a .45.' Harris said, 'No, it ain't. It ain't got no disk on it,' you know, the round drum thing. I said, 'I don't give a damn what it's not got on it! That's a .45!'* We could talk just a little bit, but we didn't move. We sat there and sat there and sat there, and nobody said anything or made a move because we were scared.

"Pretty soon we heard somebody hollering, and when they heard it, they all started smiling. When the guy doing the hollering got closer, he was a Siamese Army officer, and he was hollering in American: 'My friends! My friends!' I still didn't know what was going on. Finally, when he got there, he gave us each a Hershey bar. I told Harris, 'At last, we're among friends.' He said, 'We got to be.' So we stayed all night in their camp, and they had a monkey party.† The next day we walked twelve hours to the American major's camp—the OSS major.

"The major had been in France and in the OSS. He spoke French and Canadian and American. He came straight from France and dropped into Thailand. He built this camp with all the guerrillas. That's what they were: ex-Siamese Army people. He made the whole shebang there. He had a little airfield made; he had a big ammunition dump. He had everything there to kill and screw up the Japs, which he was doing. He knew we were coming about twelve hours before we got there. By radio he found out who we were and everything. He just walked in, and he said, 'You boys in the Navy?' I guess he could tell by my tattoos. I said, 'Yep!' He said, 'Welcome aboard.' That's all there was to it, and there we stayed.

"He tried to get us out. He had orders for us to get out, but they wouldn't let us go because we couldn't get a British airplane in there. The British wouldn't give it to them because they were fighting still. The American Army and British never got along. There wasn't anyone who would give you a thing. So we didn't get out. We would have been back to the United States months before the war was over, because we stayed four months out there with that major.

"I learned to be a guerrilla trainer. I learned all this new explosive stuff, and you trained kids that did the job. The major was getting ready to send me out, not Harris, because he and the major fought all the time. But I was going to go to see what the hell they did. The major said, 'It'll be good for you. Go out and see what they do.' All of a sudden, the radio guy one night, when it came time to go on the air, dropped everything and hollered for the

---

*This Thompson submachine gun apparently had a box magazine instead of the more familiar drum magazine.
†They were eating monkeys.

major to come. He said, 'The war's over!' The major drank a fifth and had a little dance and took us down and put me on a plane, and I headed for the Bureau of Naval Personnel. The plane came out of Kandy.* That was the name of an airfield.

"I knew I was going home then because the major told me exactly what he was going to do with me. I only had to do one thing for him—call his wife when I got in the States. And I did. I used my Red Cross call to call her. Then I went to the Bureau of Naval Personnel. They told me, after I got there, that nobody in the United States knew where the *Houston* was sunk. I was working in an office with a yeoman. There were a bunch of Waves typing records and stuff. They called me to a commodore's office. He had a big room with bulkheads that were two stories high. It had world maps and atlases. He said, 'You know where the *Houston* sunk?' I said, 'Yes, sir, exactly where it sunk.' He said, 'I want you to crawl up on one of those ladders and put a pin right where it sunk.' He gave me a little pin with a ribbon in it. So I put it where it sunk. Up till then, they never knew where the *Houston* sunk. I never saw that guy again.

"Well, I had been in the Navy from 1934 to 1945, and they made me a chief. I could have been an officer, if I'd have pushed it. Everybody else did, but not me. I got what I wanted. With that much time in the Navy, I found it awful hard to quit. So I didn't. The world I came back to was completely different. Like the Jew said, 'Even the Gentiles are squawking.' The good times were gone. People had made more money than they had ever made in their lives. The only way I could get a room in D.C. was to sign my coffee and butter and sugar chits over to this woman because there was no place to live. They sent you out to civilian homes to live. You had to give all that stuff so she could buy stuff, but you never got any of it because you never ate there. You just slept there. Boy, they were getting everything from everybody that they could. It made me sick. People weren't that bad in the POW camps. At home they'd lie to you, cheat you, roll you—anything. The country went to hell during the war. I had never heard of such a thing before then.

"I wouldn't get married. I didn't get married until I had twenty years in the Navy. I'd rather be around older military guys. You went ashore with them; you drank with them; you got in trouble with them; you did every-thing together. Who likes a goddamned civilian anyway, even though I am one now? We used to say, 'Goddamned civilians got the world by the ass

---

*Kandy, on the island of Sri Lanka (Ceylon), served as the headquarters of Admiral Lord Louis Mountbatten, Supreme Allied Commander, Southeast Asia.

and want everything else!' I've had a helluva time becoming a civilian. I stayed in the Navy twenty years. I got to be a senior chief petty officer."

Huffman also served in Korean waters during the Korean War. After leaving the Navy, he operated a chicken ranch, a cattle ranch, and tried his hand at raising hogs. All of these businesses failed, and he became a welder. He said, "There isn't anything to welding. A jack rabbit can weld." He worked as a welder for fourteen years, and then, at his wife's urging, retired. He now lives in Garden Valley, California.

Marvin E. Tilghman
Battery F

Marvin Tilghman could have flown out of Java with the Nineteenth Bomb Group in late February 1942 if he had wished. The group's commanding officer asked him if he wanted to go. Tilghman said no. "I stayed," he added, "and they flew the planes out." His reason for not leaving was noble: he thought the battery and battalion needed him.

Tilghman was born on September 5, 1917, in Parker County, Texas, a bit north of Weatherford, about twenty-five miles from downtown Fort Worth. Before he reached his first birthday, his family moved to another farm west of Jacksboro in Jack County. He graduated from high school in 1936, worked for the Texaco Oil Company, and joined the Second Battalion, 131st Field Artillery, that same year. He belonged to his original unit, Battery F, when the Dutch surrendered Java to the Japanese.

Although he was one of the few Americans who avoided having dysentery while a prisoner, he did have malaria, tropical ulcers, and an extremely painful and difficult-to-treat carbuncle on his tail bone. Worst still, just before work ended on the railway he was badly beaten by a guard. He said: "I didn't do anything, but I guess I may have stopped working for a minute or two. This guard walked up, and he hit me right in the back, below the belt, with a rifle butt a couple of times, and then he slapped me around. My back bothers me yet." Tilghman's interview concerns the Americans sent to Saigon in 1944.

"I THINK WE LEFT THE JUNGLE from 100 Kilo Camp and went on in to Thailand in the latter part of October 1943. We were sure glad to go, even though we were riding a train out of there. I mean that the railroad wasn't too good; it wasn't safe. It wasn't straight like our railroads; the rails were crooked, and you didn't know if the trains were going to stay on the tracks or not. I still haven't figured out why they built it, because I don't think they ever got much use out of it.

"We went to Kanchanaburi, that was the name of the camp. It was close to the river. It was a larger camp than what we had been in. I imagine it had fifteen to twenty large buildings in it, or maybe more. They were all similar

248

to what we'd been used to, but there were more of them, and they were bigger. This time became a recuperation period. We didn't do much work. About the only labor we had to do was to have some people take supplies up to the Japs on antiaircraft guns on a tall hill right close to the camp. Then, we'd get to go down to the river and bathe nearly every day. They'd let us do that. As far as actual work, we didn't do much around the camp. They'd gotten just about all the work we had left on that railroad.

"Some of our men were still back on the railroad, doing minor work: odd jobs, repair stuff. Most of us were still pretty well intact as a group, except for the men who had died. Food was a little better here. The rice had a few more vegetables with it, and sometimes they'd allow us to have a little meat, but not much. We still had our count or roll call, but the guards were a little better, maybe. They didn't seem to harass us quite as much as they had in the past. Since the railroad was supposed to be finished, I guess the Japs'd eased up on them, so they eased up on us. They were the same Korean guards, maybe not entirely the same ones, but, if you had a bad one and he left, you seemed to get another bad one in his place. We'd talk about revenge, but I don't know whether I would have done anything. I really don't know.

"We didn't stay at Kanchanaburi very long. They came up with the idea of getting the ones who were well or in the best physical shape, and they were going to send them on to Japan. I was in that group. So one day we left Kanchanaburi on the train. I don't know the exact route we followed, but we went down through part of Thailand and into Cambodia. We wound up in Phnom Penh, on the river, where we boarded a little river boat, maybe fifty or sixty feet long. I don't think all of us got on that boat, surely not. There were about 100 to 150 of us, and the boat wasn't that large.

"Anyway, we wound down that river and around that coast into Saigon, French Indochina. When we got there, they put us in a camp. The dock area had big warehouses built by the French. Then, right behind those, there was a street, and just across the street was our camp. It may have been an army camp for the French, earlier. It wasn't a good camp; it wasn't a bad camp. It had brick and mortar buildings with tile roofs. Of course, anything in that area didn't have windows. They just had openings and shutters. The sanitation facilities weren't bad, but they weren't good either. We had a little outhouse with a place to squat. They kept a big bucket underneath that, and someone would empty it every once in a while. We had a big cement trough with water running in it all the time and a cement area around it where we could bathe. The camp had plenty of water, and the food was a little better at the camp when we first got to Saigon.

"French people were there. We'd see a lot of white people, French, which we hadn't seen in a long time. The French were friendly. They would wave at us and talk to us, if they had a chance. Most of our group were Americans, English, and some Australians, but mostly Americans. This was one of the times when they didn't send any officers with us. One officer went at first, and then they sent him away. That left only NCOs. I was in charge of working parties a lot of the time. We would store gasoline in drums. I got to be a buddy of the Jap sergeant, if you could call it that. Of course, by that time we could speak Jap pretty good.

"Being close to the dock area, we'd unload supply ships that came in. Some of us worked at a big oil refinery out of town a little ways. I worked out at a big air base the Japs built near Saigon, which later on Americans used in the Vietnam War.* We patched runways. This was quite a bit better than working on the damn railway. I worked out there about six or eight months. Being friendly with the Jap helped. I could see he really didn't care what we did, as long as we didn't get him in trouble. He let us buy from the natives. We worked, and as long as we didn't try to get him fouled up, we were all right. Some of the boys did put dirt in the gasoline barrels. It might not have hurt their airplanes, but I don't think it helped them, either.

"We knew the Japs were getting kicked a little bit in other places. This old Jap sergeant and I'd talk a lot. Finally, he got to telling me along about May or June 1945 that the war wasn't going to be going on much longer. He told me they were getting pushed around pretty good. He even told me that MacArthur had landed in the Philippines. So we knew pretty well that things were going our way, and we'd begun to see some of our planes fly over pretty regularly.

"When they first started coming over, the Americans would send some high-level bombers—B-24s, I guess. This base where we were was a fighter plane base at the time. Everytime an air-raid alarm would go off, these fighters would take off. The bombers would go over, and they would go up and shoot at them. I guess our people got tired of that, because one day while we were out working, an air-raid alarm went off, and all the Jap fighters took off. About the time they got to where the bombers were, American P-38s, about fifteen, showed up, and they shot down every one of the Japs or the Japs went back to another base to land, because none of them came back to our base. I know the Americans shot a bunch of them down, because we saw it. We had a ringside seat. It was interesting.

---

*He is undoubtedly referring to Tan Son Nhut air base, northeast of downtown Saigon on Highway 1.

"They didn't bomb our base. They were bombing over the river. The Japs had an ammunition depot over there, but we never did see it. They also bombed the oil refinery where we had worked. These raids helped our morale a whole lot. After that one time then the Jap fighters wouldn't go up much anymore. Finally, some of them came back to our bases, but, when the air-raid alarm went off, they'd get the planes out in the brush. The Japs didn't want to go up and fight anymore. Some of the Japs didn't like what was happening and got pretty horsey. They would be mad, and they'd try to get even with Americans or Australians or something.

"Along about this time, or soon after, maybe in May or June, the Navy bombed the harbor with dive-bombers. They came in early one morning—about the time we were having roll call. They hit the air base with fighters a bit earlier. They shot it up real good and didn't let any Jap planes get off the ground. When the fighters got through, here came the dive-bombers. They stayed there all day. At the back of our camp the Japs had let us build some shelters. We went to these shelters. We sat there and watched the air show all day. I think they sunk every ship in the harbor. They left about dark or a bit before. I don't know how many dive-bombers they had, but it was quite a show to see.

"We saw two of our planes get shot down that day, and another one get hit. I read an article in the *Literary Digest* after I got home, and this ol' boy who got hit was talked back to his carrier by the wing man. He couldn't see; he was blinded. A shell hit the canopy, and his wing man talked him back to the carrier. I know he was the one we saw get hit. He was over Saigon. Boy, that raid was something good to see.

"One day we got our orders to load on this ship to Japan the next morning. The next morning came, and they told us it had been postponed, that we wouldn't be going. Then we heard through the grapevine that submarines had sunk a bunch of ships at the mouth of the river, so we never did get any more orders to load up for Japan. Thank goodness! I didn't want to go anyway, period. I had made it that far and had gone through so much that I didn't want to go on a ship. My health was good, and everybody else who was there with us was in pretty good shape. I felt that unless something unusual happened, I might make it through the war. We might have it made by then.

"We were getting more vegetables, rice, and a little meat—water buffalo. The food was better. While we were here, we got a partial Red Cross package, the first ever. We had seen the Japs smoking American cigarettes, and we knew they were coming from Red Cross packages. One day they brought us enough so that each person got maybe half a package, which was pretty good. It had milk, candy, some canned stuff, and ciga-rettes. It was real good. That's the only time we ever got anything from the Red Cross. I gave my cigarettes to my buddies since I didn't smoke anymore.

"Along about now we were seeing our planes come over a lot. They'd come over on patrol and just check. Every once in a while a B-24 would come over and strafe a little bit. They wouldn't bomb, just machine-gun things. By this time we knew the war was pretty much in our favor, or the Air Force couldn't be able to do that. We began to worry about the Japs killing us if they lost the war. They made us build pillboxes around the camp. Instead of having the opening for the gun turrets pointed out away from the camp, they had them pointing in toward the camp. That made us think that if they ever had a landing around there, the Japs just might machine-gun the whole camp. We didn't know.

"One night we heard a bunch of shooting in town, and we didn't know whether somebody had landed somewhere or what. The shooting was close to where we were. We found out that it was a bunch of French. They had some Foreign Legionnaires there, and some of them got crosswise or had some kind of trouble. Of course, there was no landing, so we never got shot. But we were very much aware that those gun turrets were pointed toward us instead of away from camp. They weren't there to defend us, that's for sure.

"We had an Air Force lieutenant in there with us. He was there when we arrived, but I don't know where he came from. He was in the camp, and he went under the fence one night and got out. He got through all right, but the Japs sure did 'throw a shoe' when that happened, because they made it hard on us for a week or two. Then they finally said that they got him—captured him—and shot him. Later, after the war was over, we found out that he made it out up through China. The French underground helped him, I think, or somebody did. I heard rumors about guerrilla groups in the area, but I never did see anything like that. I don't know if it's true, but to my knowledge, I never did know of anything like that.

"One day the Japs told us that Roosevelt was dead. We didn't know what effect this might have on the war. We didn't really figure it would cause much difference. You hate to lose a president all right, but we didn't think it would change the outcome of the war. Anyway, while we were in Saigon, we went up the coast and worked for a while. We went to Nha Trang. At the end of the Vietnam War it was a big Ranger base. We went up there and then went up to a mountain resort, Da Lat, and stayed there for a couple of months, I think. We didn't have any problems going up on a train. I guess it was a cog railroad, because the grade was steep. We worked digging tunnels in the mountain. In later years, I found out that those people tunneled underground like moles or rats. I thought about all that digging we had done for them. The mountains are just honeycombed where we dug.

"This resort had a real cool climate, nice homes, and you could tell this was where the rich people used to go, when they went on vacation or something. I would imagine there were close to a hundred of us. We worked there a while, and then we worked over on the railroad part-time, transferring stuff from one side of a bridge that had been blown up to the other. We worked pretty steady, and it was hard work there, but they didn't 'rush-rush' like they did in Burma when we were finishing that railroad. The food was good, and we stayed in an old school of some sort. They had a moat around the building, but it didn't have water in it. I guess that was supposed to keep us in.

"When we were going back to Saigon, we had some close calls with some of the ol' boys who would fly down the railroad and strafe. We were riding in open cars, like what I would call gravel cars that used to haul gravel here. You could see right out. We'd stop every once in a while and get off the train. I don't know if they had some kind of warning system that told them that a plane was coming or not, but we'd get off the train and get out in the brush or out in the timber away from the railroad. Directly, here'd come a Navy bomber down the line, and it'd strafe everything as it went through. They'd just fly right down on the deck. They did that two or three times during the trip back. We knew for sure then that the war was going to be over soon—nearly all the Jap soldiers kept telling us that.

"When we got back to Saigon, they put us in another camp this time—a big French Foreign Legion camp, kind of over in town and back of the residential area. They had big, three-story barracks, nice buildings with water and sanitation and all that. It had a good place to bathe. It was a whole lot better than anything we had had. Of course, we still didn't have beds to sleep on, but we didn't mind that too much. The food was still good here, too.

"We didn't stay in this camp long. One day the planes came over and started dropping leaflets about the war being over. We knew it was really over, because some of the Japs had told us that we had dropped the big bomb on one of their towns and that town was finished. The next day, I believe, the planes came in and landed out at the air base. One of our captains, who had gone to Saigon with us and was put in another camp earlier, came in with the OSS people to make arrangements to get us out.

"We started having fun then. Of course, the Japs didn't know what to do, and most of our Korean guards had vanished. As I said, this captain came in to make arrangements to get us out, and he let us go to town if we wanted to. We still came back at night to the camp. We went in to town to visit, buy food, eat, visit with people. Some French people invited us to their homes, and we ate dinner with them. That's when the Vietnamese war started. The natives had an uprising one day in town and started shooting and ransacking the town and killing people. They didn't like anybody that was white. I had my GI khakis on, and that saved me. If they knew you were an American they didn't bother you, but you had to prove it before they'd let you go.

"We were there that day it started. About dark, I thought we might ought to get back to the camp or try to. The people that came in with the captain had set up headquarters in a hotel downtown. This was about five or six blocks from the house where the French people who had us to dinner lived. I took off walking down to the hotel, and it was about dark. You'd meet natives riding around in trucks with guns. I had my GI clothes on, and they never bothered me, but I never did know what they might do. I got to the hotel, and I caught one of the trucks going back to the camp and went back to the camp that night. I didn't go out anymore until we got ready to leave to come home.

"They took all the sick out first. I'd been driving a supply truck to town to get supplies part of the time, so I drove the truck with the sick people out to the planes that morning. When we got there and got them loaded, the ol' colonel, who came down with them, told me that there was room for me if I wanted to go. I didn't say no this time. I left that truck sitting there, and crawled in, and came out with them. I left all my stuff, but R. N. Gregg* from Decatur brought it out the next day. I wasn't going to take any chances this time. When I had the chance to go, I came on out. It was my birthday, September 5, 1945. I won't ever forget that. That's when I got out; I left Saigon for Calcutta. Every birthday I look back and think what happened on that day in 1945. It was the best birthday present I've ever had."

Tilghman became part of what the Army called Project J, an effort to get the POWs processed rapidly and back to the United States. He stayed at the 142d General Hospital in Calcutta about one and one-half weeks and then flew across the Near East, North Africa, the Azores, and to Washington, D.C. He arrived in the district in early September and was in Jacksboro by

---

*Robert N. Gregg, of Battery F, still lives in Decatur, Texas.

November 1. He was mustered out of the Army in February 1946. In civilian life he opened an upholstery shop, which he ran until 1959. For the next twenty years he was county clerk of Jack County, leaving the office for retirement on January 1, 1979. He still lives in Jacksboro.

Melford L. ("Gus") Forsman
USS *Houston*

Gus Forsman had two military careers: he served as a sailor from 1939 until 1946 and as a soldier from 1949 to 1964 and 1969 to 1972. Altogether he spent twenty-five years in the service before final retirement. Born in Alpena, South Dakota, on March 22, 1921, Forsman was raised in Minnesota and Iowa, where his father worked on the railroad. Because he wanted a military career and wished to see the world, he quit high school to join the Navy in April 1939. After boot camp at the Great Lakes Naval Training Station near Chicago, he was sent to Bremerton, Washington, to join the crew of the *Houston.*

Gus was at his battle station on a 5-inch antiaircraft gun when the *Houston* began to sink in the Sunda Strait. He successfully evaded Japanese gunfire while in the water and eventually reached the shore. Covered with oil and soon suffering from badly blistered feet, he helped pull his captors' supply carts inland before being interned in the Serang theater and jail. After time spent at Bicycle Camp, he shipped to Singapore and on to Burma with the Fitzsimmons group. He was part of Branch 3, A Force, suffering their discomforts and threats to life. He had a bad case of dysentery and a tropical ulcer that ate through to his shin bone.

After leaving the jungle, he was placed in solitary confinement in Singapore. His interview deals primarily with that phase of his captivity.

"IT SEEMS LIKE it was around December that I got out of the jungle— sometime in December. When I got out I went to Kanchanaburi. We rode the railroad part of the way, and we walked part of the way. Mostly, we did a lot of walking, I know that. Of course, I thought about the train running off the rails, too. It being a narrow-gauged railroad made it a lot different than our railroads in America. It was more or less like a Toonerville trolley. The boxcars swayed an awful lot, and you wondered—especially when you went across a bridge or something like that—whether it would hold, or whether you were going to go crashing in.

"The Kanchanaburi camp was very large, a very large camp. There were all nationalities there: Dutch, English, Australian, American, and quite a few Indians, Sikhs and Gurkhas, which we didn't have with us before. I believe they came in from Singapore, but I'm not sure. The Sikhs did all of their own cooking. I believe it was one of their religious beliefs. They were a very interesting people. They were large, soldierly-type individuals, very ramrod, and very clean.

"When I first got there, I just worked on details. Sometimes it was, oh, going out in the jungle and picking leaves. You'd put them next to the slit trenches for people who had dysentery and stuff like that. Once in a while, you'd pick a few nettles to throw in there with them, you know, give the boys a buzz. There were also wood-carrying details for the fires. In this camp we ran across quite a few people with different things to barter: watches, rings, clothing. So we would sneak out of camp at night, late at night. We'd sneak out and into the jungle, and there was a little village near there with an individual that I knew by the name of Tin Hook. How he got the name, I don't know, but they called him Tin Hook. He was head of this tribe or sect or whatever it was in them villages. Anyway, we would barter with him.

"When we'd go out, I had my friend McFadden,* who was a lookout for me, down by the goat pen because that's where I went out. I'd whistle, he'd whistle, and I'd whistle again, and if it was all clear—if no guards were in sight—he'd whistle back, and I'd sneak back in. On several occasions there, I know that we'd crouch down along a path in the jungle, and the Jap patrol would walk right past us. We could've reached out and touched them, it was so black. You think about those things afterwards—what would happen to you if you'd ever get caught.

"I was at Kanchanaburi until January or February, probably the latter part of February 1945. During that time, I got the job of herding goats. I'd have to go out every day with the goats. I had one other person helping me. I had an Australian who had one arm, and his last name was Harvey. He had one arm off, which was off between his shoulder and his elbow. He was the other goat herder. It was a very good detail because it gave you the opportunity to barter with the natives, since they only sent one guard out. I think we started with ten goats, and toward the end I think we had about forty-some. You could barter because the Jap guard couldn't stay with both of the herders at the same time. You'd be at one place, and the other guy would be at another place, so the guard generally picked a spot in between somewhere.

---

*Elmer L. McFadden, a sailor from the *Houston*, died from a heart attack on May 15, 1979, in Iowa City, Iowa.

"Every night I milked the goats and then took the milk to the Japanese cookhouse—after taking some off and taking it to our hospital and adding a little water to the goat milk, which we did all the time. The hospital derived benefits, also, from the beef and stuff, too. The Japs killed beef, and we got the skin, the entrails, the hoofs, the head, and stuff like that. We used it. They made tripe and stuff like that, which they used in the hospital. I used to ask the Japanese guards for iodine to fix a sore on a goat or something like that, and then I'd give it to the hospital. And we used to get sulfur from them, and I'd give it to the hospital. Different things like that was another way of getting stuff for yourself from the Japanese.

"While I was a goat herder, I made contact out in the jungle with a man in the French Indochina underground—a Portuguese doctor. I don't remember his name now, but, anyway, he wanted information from me as to what was in camp, how many prisoners were there, how many guards there were—just anything about the camp. So I went back in, and, of course, we had an Army officer as our commanding officer for the naval personnel. Well, at this time, it was Captain [William ("Ike")] Parker, who we called Skipper. I went back in and told him, and he says, 'Well, why don't you see if you can get us some news about what's happening and everything like that?' I'm pretty sure he in turn talked to Major [Winthrop H. ("Windy")] Rogers. So they asked me to go back out the next day and to ask him just exactly what he wanted.

"So I did and that's when he told me that he was with the French Indochina underground. Then he told me that we wouldn't be prisoners very much longer and all that. He spoke fairly good English. Anyway, I told him that we wanted news. So the following day, well, I went back in, and they gave me information as to how many sick we had and the general things about the camp and everything. I carried it out in a hollow bamboo pole which I used for guiding the goats. He gave me what was called the *Bangkok Chronicle*, which was a newspaper. I really don't know why I should have had to smuggle it because, really, everything, I believe, was censored by the Japanese. Anyway, I smuggled the newspaper back into camp and then gave it to Captain Parker, and they would glean what news they could out of it—whatever was of interest as far as the war effort. Then they would disseminate this news to the troops.

"Anyway, this went on for a while, and, also, I got a little bit of sulfathiazole one time from that man and brought it into camp. I got a little Atabrine, and I believe some quinine tablets, which were the first quinine tablets we'd seen in a long, long time. We'd normally been using quinine bark and boiling it for malaria before. Anyway, I went out there one day, and this man wasn't there. But there was another native there—or I thought he was a native—and he had all silver teeth. He didn't have a white tooth in his head. They were all silver—not a gold one, either—just all silver. He wanted to buy something, and I don't know why, but my suspicions were aroused for some reason. I told him to go away, that I didn't have anything. So that was the last I saw of him at that time. Then one day while I was out there with the goats, two Japanese soldiers came up and got me and put handcuffs on me.

"They put handcuffs on me and led me off and left this other boy there. They got another boy who was with the cattle—this Charley. They got him for some reason; I don't know what. They hauled us into town, to what they called the *Kempei Tai* headquarters there, which is, I guess, probably about equivalent to the gestapo or something. They took me in there and put me in a cell along with this big Texan by the name of Charles or Charley.* That evening they came and got me, and they took me into this conference room. It had a large table about four-by-twelve feet with huge legs—big, hand-carved legs. They made me kneel at the end there, and they handcuffed my hands around the legs, and they started interrogating me.

"Then this man with all the silver teeth came in, too, and he spoke English. Then I knew he was Japanese, that he wasn't a native. He started interrogating me. They were trying to get me to admit that I had stolen medicine and was selling it to the natives and so forth. I wouldn't admit that, and he grabbed a bamboo cane and started beating me on the back with that. I was kneeling with my hands around the leg of the table. He beat me on the back with that bamboo, and after the first couple of blows, I didn't really feel anything. I could feel the jar when they hit me, but I didn't feel any pain or anything. They broke the bamboo cane, and then took a piece of what was probably electric wire and started using that. Of course, again, that wasn't painful at the time. It wasn't painful because I was numb, and I could feel the jars when he hit me.

"I think that's one of the very few times that I really feared losing my life. I was afraid that they were either going to beat me to death, or they were going to shoot me or something, that they were definitely going to get me one way or another. They were yelling and screaming in English, so you knew what they were talking about. The guy with the silver teeth asked me if I wanted a drink or something, and I told him, 'Yeah, I sure could use

---

*Charley L. Thomas was a sailor on the *Houston*. He was killed in an airplane crash near Lake Tahoe, California, on April 22, 1979.

one.' Well, what he was talking about at the time was that he was going to take me down to the river and drown me.

"Before all this happened, Captain Parker and Major Rogers and I had a pact that if anything ever did come up, we would be the scapegoats and not involve any other people. There were other people involved in this news disseminating. In fact, the colonel of the 131st was involved in it. But they said, 'Don't involve anybody else. If you have to, go ahead and identify one or the other of us.' So, anyway, when they brought Captain Parker out, I knew, well, hell, they got him. At about the same time, Parker said, 'Yes, he's the other man.' And I said, 'Yes, he's the other man,' about the same time. We just went ahead and admitted that we were the ones giving out the news. Captain Parker saw my back, and he was really mad. It shook him up; I mean, he actually started crying. And he told them that he didn't want to see any more beatings or brutality or anything like that. They took me back to the cell.

"They had beaten him, also. So they took me back to the cell. This big boy, Charles, from Texas was in there, and he seen my back, and I thought he was going to go berserk. Oh, he really got mad, and he asked me what he could do for me, and I told him, 'Well, I'd like to have a drink of water.' So he told the guard to get me a drink of water, and the guard ignored him. Of course, he said it in Japanese. And, boy, he just thrust his arms through the cell like he was trying to get at that Jap and hollered, '*Mizu!*' which means 'water.' And then the Jap went and got some water and gave it to me. I don't know what happened to Charles. They never interrogated him at all. They just took him back to camp because I met him at one of the reunions. He was killed just not too many years ago in a plane crash. But he said he didn't know why they ever brought him in there.

"Well, then they took Captain Parker and me and Major Rogers into Bangkok for a court-martial. They didn't beat us anymore. They did take us down and let us bathe in the river. So they took us into Bangkok, and they had us on a porch at this one place. It really wasn't a military establishment; it just seemed like a huge house. Of course, they had us handcuffed and sitting on this porch. Then they called us in, and they led us in front of this big, long table. The Japanese officers filed in, and we stood at attention in front of the table. Then they read the sentence to us: six years' solitary confinement in a Japanese military prison. That's when Windy Rogers told them, 'Six years, hell! We'll be lucky if we serve six months!' Of course, immediately, the Japs knocked him to the floor.

"I couldn't believe it—six years' solitary confinement. Of course, at that time, a lot of things are racing through your mind. You're thinking,

'Am I going to make it? Will it be worse than what I've already had? How could it be worse than that?' Then when Major Rogers said that, well, that kind of perked me up a little bit. That helped my morale. I figured, 'By gosh, he knows something that I don't.' Shortly after that, they moved us to a civil jail in Bangkok. It was a regular Siamese jail, and they had civilians there. While in there, I noticed that they had this Portuguese doctor in jail. While we were there, he received numerous, severe beatings. I doubt very much if he survived it, I really do. This is in the latter part of February 1945.

"They had a Dutchman in there—I can't think of his name now—and Captain Parker, Major Rogers, and me, and there were two Englishmen, also. There were six of us. We were all in one cell. Now you either had to stand or sit at attention. You could not talk; you had to face the wall; you could not turn your head. If you had to go to the toilet, you had to call the guard and then give him your number and ask permission to go, and he'd let you go. Then immediately afterwards, you had to return to your spot again to either sit or stand at attention. This went on all day long. If they caught you talking, they might come in and bash you around a little. They made us lay down at nine o'clock in the evening, and at five o'clock in the morning they made us get up or stand up and be at attention.

"We were in this place about a week or a week-and-a-half. They came and got us one day and put us on a train to Singapore. Their Japanese prison was located at Outram Road in Singapore.* Anyway, they took us down to the train station and put us in a car similar to our cattle car—only it was a whole lot smaller—and we started our trip to Singapore. A lot of times, we were traveling by night and laying in a freight yard during the day, camouflaged with big palm leaves and branches and stuff because the Americans were very active in their bombings all through there. We saw a lot of steam engines and stuff that had been bombed. A lot of railroad yards, sheds, depots, and stuff like that were torn up. That was another harrowing experience.

"But we got to Singapore, and they loaded us on a truck and hauled us up to the Japanese military prison. They took us into a huge courtyard with a well in the center that had wooden buckets. They made us strip completely, and we drew one wooden bucket of water. We hadn't had a bath since we left Bangkok. We washed off. Then we were marched to our cells—no clothing, just bare naked like the day you were born. You were put in a cell, one person to a cell. The walls were so thick you couldn't communicate. There was a solid oak door and a little sliding panel in the

---

*The Australian official history of the events calls it the Outram Road gaol.

door, a six-by-six-inch panel where the guard could look at you, and down below another one that they used to put food in.

"I would estimate the cell to be about ten feet long, four feet wide, and fifteen feet high. Way up at the top, there was a metal grate where you could see sky now and then. I'd say it was maybe ten by four inches. They had one electric light bulb right in the center of the room at the top, which was probably a twenty-watt bulb. And an old 'honey bucket'* was in the corner. You had two pieces of board, probably one-by-eights, about sixteen inches wide, fastened on each end by a two-by-four block that held them together. Your pillow was about a four-by-four block of wood approximately twelve inches long, and you had one real thick cotton blanket. That was all you had in your cell.

"There wasn't much sitting at attention as before. Your routine there was that you couldn't sleep during daylight hours. You had to prop your bed up against the wall, and you couldn't sit on the blanket or anything. If you sat, you just sat with your bare bottom on the concrete, which got awful uncomfortable, or you'd stand. The guard checked not more than once an hour, sometimes not even that much—very seldom at night. They'd tell you generally at nine o'clock at night that you could put your bed down. Then it was the same routine in the morning. About five o'clock they'd holler at you, and you'd have to put your bed up. The only time you'd see outside your cell was when a Jap prisoner was brought around to pick up your honey bucket. Other than that, they'd never open the door. They didn't allow you out for bathing or anything else.

"We were fed twice a day, and we got about a cup of rice the size of a demitasse cup, not a regular coffee cup, twice a day, with an equal amount of tea. No water, just tea. That's the way it went for six months. I knew that I was losing weight, and I knew that I couldn't last forever in there because my weight was dropping fast. They fed at five-thirty A.M. and then at six o'clock P.M. I'd be waiting by the door, hoping that it had something different in it—everytime—hoping it'd be different, hoping it had a couple of kernels of corn, which, once in a while it did. When I got the food I took it easy. Especially the corn, I'd put it aside, and then I'd have it for dessert. I'd really savor it. I'd chew it and suck it and get everything out of it before I'd swallow it. And if there were any tea leaves, I ate them. There wasn't anything that went back.

"For several years I had never eaten with a real fork or spoon or knife. Now, in here, I used my fingers to eat with, and they were filthy. At times,

---

*A container for the disposal of human waste.

they would almost nauseate you, knowing they were so filthy. I'd have given a thousand dollars for a Dixie cup of water or something to wash my hands. I felt like an alligator probably feels with scales, because I could actually peel off the dirt. I actually peeled off the dirt. I didn't know that a human being could get so filthy, but, then, there wasn't anything I could do about it. I had a low opinion of myself, knowing how dirty and filthy I was, but at the same time, I realized that, hell, there wasn't anything I could do about it.

"Another thing was not being able to wash your teeth. I used to get the tea and swirl it around in my mouth and maybe take my finger, even though it was filthy, and rub off a little bit from my teeth. I'd kept my hair cut short before, but it was growing out and sticking out like an Afro about then. I had a little goatee. I used to sit there and twist it. I still didn't have enough hair to shave even if I could have.

"I talked to myself all day long. Asked myself questions, counted the bricks and counted the cracks in the bricks, got a fly and pulled his wings off so he couldn't fly away, and talked to him and played with him. I had an odd cell. It had 437 bricks on one wall and 435 on the opposite wall. I could never understand that, but I counted them and counted them. I lost track of days. You had no way of keeping track, so you didn't know what day it was. The light burned night and day. You had no way of knowing what was happening.

"Sometimes I'd try to remember things. I tried to remember a book I read, all the sequences of the book. I tried to remember when I was a kid and studied catechism and was confirmed. I tried to remember mechanics—the parts of a carburetor, what made it work. I just tried to occupy my mind. If I had been an intelligent person, I'd probably gone off my rocker in there, but not being that intelligent, I didn't have enough sense to go crazy. I'd just talk away sometimes, and sometimes I'd sing. The Jap never said anything to me. I don't believe I'd have cared what he said. It didn't make any difference.

"Once in a great while you'd hear a commotion. I'd holler out; I'd say, 'What in the hell's going on down there?' Then the guy next to me might say they were working over one of their own men, and they did. Every once in a while they'd haul out one of their own people, and they'd just beat him unmercifully. After I had been there three months they took this Englishman and me outside. I was shocked, and he was probably shocked by what he saw: we were filthy and losing weight and everything. The Japanese had a garden, and they took us over there to water it. I grabbed two handfuls of spinach. I never did like spinach, and I don't today, but I grabbed it and jammed it in my mouth and ate it. That was the only time that I ever got out of there. I don't know why they took us out that time to water that little garden, but they did. You hated to go back in again after breathing fresh air out there.

"You imagine all kinds of things when you're in there. You imagine them coming in and dragging you out, lining you up and shooting you. You get back in the food thing again—you imagine food, so hard that you taste it. You taste a Hershey candy bar or whatever. On several occasions I thought they forgot me, that they were just going to leave me there, and this was where I was going to end up. You know, you've seen all these movies of some guy hanging in chains and nothing but skin and bones and all. Well, there I was, only I wasn't hanging in chains. But it was about the same thing, just similar to a dungeon.

"I never went nuts like on television. On several occasions I walked and cursed a lot, just being mad, just to let off steam, but it was just another case of talking to myself. I never pounded the walls or anything like that. A lot of times I'd holler at the top of my voice. I'd call them names, whatever name I could think of, and I probably used them all. Being a sailor, I knew quite a few. I think that getting a fly or a bug or something like that was, oh, maybe unusual, but I'd derive two or three hours of entertainment out of a fly, you know. I'd pull at least one wing off so I was sure he couldn't fly away. He'd have to crawl away then.

"I walked back and forth. I didn't do any push-ups or things like that, but I did a lot of walking, a lot of pacing, back and forth, back and forth. Sometimes I'd turn. I'd make so many turns to the right and then so many turns to the left. Sometimes I'd turn to square it, you know, down this way and then square it across and back. Sometimes I'd walk backwards instead of walking forwards. I never ran. A couple of times I stood on my head in a corner. I don't know why, but I'd just stand there until my head hurt. I guess it was just most anything to do.

"I caught a cold one time, but other than that I didn't have any health problems, other than losing weight. Now I was bare naked, and at night it'd get downright chilly. I had one small blanket which I covered up with at night, which did get cool, especially being in all that concrete. In the daytime it was plenty warm, but it wasn't insufferable; I mean it wasn't a suffering heat or anything like that. Of course, not having any clothes on helped you in the daytime.

"It was rough. I tell you, it was rough. I look back on it today, and I wonder how in the hell did I ever survive it. When you think about all the different things that we went through, you know the Good Lord had to be on your side, that's all there is to it. I'm not a highly religious person, but I've always believed in the Lord. I was brought up that way. I've always thought that if you were in dire need, the Lord will take care of you. I used to say my prayers at night. I used to say the Lord's Prayer now and then, and also I'd ask Him to bless my family. As far as asking Him for anything, I don't believe I asked Him for myself. I thanked Him for letting me live another day. Well, I believe I did ask Him to help me return home.

"As bad as the jungle was, I'd have to say this was worse. I think the six months in solitary was as hard as the other three years. It was always a welcome thing at night to be able to put my bed down and lay down instead of having to stand up or sit up. Maybe if, just if, the routine would have been broken here and there, that would have made a lot of difference, but it never was—it was the same, day in, day out. What griped me most was that the information I passed on was easily available; I mean, it was Japanese-censored stuff and everything. It really didn't seem to make much difference. I don't know why I did it. I guess I thought it helped morale, but honestly I don't know why. I think what was of use was contact with the guy more than the news—the contact with the Portuguese doctor. In case something happened, if it came down to the Japanese saying, 'Hey, we gotta get out of here, but let's get rid of these prisoners of war first,' maybe that might have happened, and this doctor might have known of it beforehand and warned us. Also, he helped us get medical supplies like the Atabrine, which was beneficial, and the quinine tablets.

"Now somewhere after August 20—I don't know exactly when it was, but it was after they dropped the atomic bomb—they came along and opened my cell door, and he just motioned me to come out. The guard motioned me to come out, and I came out. I didn't know what was going to happen. Then when I stepped out, they were taking the others out, too: Captain Parker, Major Rogers, the Englishmen, and that Dutchman. They looked real terrible, in real sorry shape—skinny, they'd lost weight. They had more beard than I had, but they looked terrible, filthy, downright filthy. They smelled, too. That was one thing I noticed about them—they smelled.

"Then when the Japs took us out where this big well was, they had these stacks of clothing, which consisted of a pair of 'go-aheads'* and a G-string. They let us draw a bucket of water and bathe. Then they had us put our clothes on, and they marched us over by the gate and opened it, and he says,

---

*Go-aheads are similar to what Americans call "thongs" and were so called because one could only walk forward in them. Walking backwards would cause them to slip off. The soles of go-aheads were usually wooden or made from a piece of rubber tire.

'Go!' We just stood there, and they kept pushing us, and saying, 'Go!' I think it was Major Rogers who said, 'Well, they're going to shoot us in the back.' He says, 'They're going to say we were escaping.' So he says, 'By God, let's give them a run for their money! Run in a zigzag course!' Well, I was so weak that I couldn't run in anything else but a zigzag course. Anyway, we took off down the hill. The Japs were laughing behind us, and we figured, well, they're about to open fire. But they didn't. We got down the hill, and there we were, just standing there. We didn't know what to do, and a Chinaman came by on a bicycle, and Major Rogers said something to him. Well, he stopped and fortunately spoke some English. He told us that the war was over. Of course we didn't believe him. He said, 'No, no, they boom, boom one time! Japan finished!' We still didn't believe him, but he did get across to us that the best thing for us to do was to go to Changi, so we did. That's where we went.

"I don't know how far it was, but it seemed like ten miles to me. We walked every bit of the way. Some Chinese gave us apples and oranges, all kinds of fruit, and we ate it as fast as we could with both hands. We got to Changi, and there was a Jap guard with a wooden rifle, not a regular Japanese rifle. We started up this road, and here came a bunch of POWs from Changi, the regular Changi jail. They came running down, and there was ol' Crayton. Crayton Gordon was one of them. I remember they threw their arms around us and wanted to know where we came from. They thought when we left Thailand we were for sure dead. Anyway, they took us over to the jail and told us the war was over. They took us inside the jail, and we got introduced all over. My God, it felt like a hero's welcome."

After the usual celebrations and bouts of eating, Forsman was flown to the 142d General Hospital in Calcutta, which he remembers was on Outram Road.* He thought it strange that the "evac" hospital should be on a road with the same name as his Singapore prison, the Outram jail. After time in Washington, D.C., he went home to Iowa, but had difficulty adjusting to all the attention he received. "I still had a certain amount of guilt feeling about being a POW," he said. But the human spirit is resilient, and Forsman adjusted.

Forsman left the Navy in early 1946, and worked on construction and as a supply clerk with the Veterans Administration. He joined the Army in 1949, retired in 1964, but was called back for another three-year hitch in 1969. He was an aviation mechanic, maintenance supervisor, and flight

---

*This could not be verified.

instructor. During the Vietnam War, he was back in Southeast Asia as a crewman on an assault helicopter in Cu Chi, Vietnam. Among many decorations given him are two Bronze Star awards and a Purple Heart. During the 1970s and 1980s he was owner of Arrow Company, a construction and landscaping firm. Now retired, he lives in Morgan, Texas.

James Gee, USMC
USS *Houston*

Jimmy Gee was a freshman at the University of Texas in Austin when he decided to join the Marines in June 1940. He wanted to see the world, and the Marine Corps seemed to offer his best opportunity. He had been born and reared in Howe, Texas, about fifty miles north of Dallas on Highway 75. After boot camp at San Diego, California, he attended sea school and was assigned to the USS *Houston*.

As the *Houston* was sinking in the Sunda Strait, Gee was at his battle station in the powder magazine of a 5-inch gun. Like many of the seamen, he spent the night dodging Japanese bullets and was picked up in the morning by Japanese merchant mariners. They took him to a cargo vessel, where he helped unload supplies for the next week. He was later sent to the Serang theater and to Bicycle Camp, and then became part of the first group of Americans shipped to Singapore and on to Burma in October 1942. While working on the railway, he suffered dysentery, pellagra, malnutrition, beriberi, and tropical ulcers. He was slapped around by hand, fist, forearm, bamboo stick, and rifle butt. He was kicked and cursed; bedbugs, body lice, mosquitoes, and other insects and vermin bothered him.

For one-and-one-half years, in 1943 and 1944, he endured malaria attacks at ten- to fifteen-day intervals. At one point he lost nearly fifty pounds in a week. Gee said, "Doctor Hekking saved my life along with every life for each American in his camp before the next eighteen months were over. We all owe him a debt of gratitude. We owe him so much that we can never repay him because he not only helped us physically, he helped us mentally."

In his interview, Gee discusses his experience from the completion of the railway until liberation while in Japan.

"IT TURNED OUT that even though there wasn't anything heavenly about Kanburi, it was so much better than what we had had the last eighteen months that we thought that we were in heaven. We had a long train ride down to the camp. It was an interesting ride because we were looking at the work that other people had done, and we were comparing their fills and their bridges and their work with what we had done. And I think we all came to the conclusion that they had probably had the rougher part of it.

"I stayed in Kanburi until August 1944, when I went to Singapore. A couple of times while I was still in Thailand, I was quite sick. Believe it or not, we were at Kanburi for rest and recuperation. After I got over being sick, I regained a lot of weight. I was about 110 pounds at one time, and I gained back to 140. I was normally about 200 pounds. By the time I finished this whole thing in Japan, I weighed about 160. Our life became more routine. Even though we didn't have that much more to eat, we weren't working those deadly hours, and it was a little better.

"But this good life was pretty short lived. In August they took a small group of Americans and Aussies and put us on a train to go back to Singapore. It was very close to my birthday, August 27, 1944. On my twenty-fourth birthday we were on a train going down the Malay Peninsula. We were in a cattle car, and we could see the countryside. It was almost as beautiful as that first train ride from Moulmein to Thanbyuzayat when we arrived in Burma. Now we were weaker and not as wide-eyed, but I remember the fact that I never wanted to go to sleep because I was afraid I would miss seeing something. We stopped at little villages along the way, and people came out to look at us. The Japanese guards would really harass us at these places. They'd knock us in the head through the slats. They'd push a rifle butt in and hit you every now and then. We were packed in like cattle. We couldn't lay down. We just sat.

"I've forgotten how long it took us to get down the peninsula, but it was two or three days, and, of course, we were going night and day. It's quite a ways from Bangkok to Singapore, and these were small tracks, narrow gauge. But we were sorry that the trip ever ended, really, because we were sent back to Changi. We were put in a different set of barracks, and, boy, had they deteriorated! They were in terrible shape. They were dirtier. We were put to work right away in a detail digging a hole for a dry dock out by the beach in the harbor. It was all done by hand labor—men, wheelbarrows, picks, and shovels. We worked on that for about three months, from the first part of September until mid-December. It was a bad situation.

"By then all the Englishmen who were around, oh, had they degenerated! Some of them had been there during the war and were still working. They were a thieving bunch. They would steal the pennies off of their dead grandmother's eyes. It was just a bad situation, and we really hated to get back there. We dug this dry dock, and somebody else was to come in and do all the steel work on it. We did our part, and pretty soon our job was completed. So one day they got us together and took us down to the docks and loaded us on ships. Again, we had our hopes up. We thought maybe that they might be going to trade us for some Japanese prisoners. Every once in a while this rumor got strong. We thought that maybe the Japanese were changing their tune and would exchange us for some of their prisoners. They took us out on the dock, and, sure enough, they loaded us on this ship, and then we found out that we were really going to Japan.

"Fortunately for us, at that point, about thirty-five of us didn't get on the ship. They got it loaded, and some of us had to stay in Singapore. Well, that was the luckiest day of my life because that was the ship with 1,800 prisoners on it that was sunk off the coast of the Philippines, and only a few people were picked up by American submarines.* There have been stories written about it, but most of the POWs drowned. Most went down with the ship. Of course, a few were blown off the ship, and maybe if I had been on the ship, just maybe, I'd have been one of the lucky ones. I'd been lucky so far. It would have been a pretty slim chance. On the *Houston*, one out of three got off. On that prisoner ship, one out of ten got off. The odds don't always work for you, you know.

"Well, it wasn't a week or two until another ship came into the harbor, and they got another convoy together.† By then we knew we were going to Japan. We loaded and started to Japan. We knew that our people were retaking the Philippines about this time. We knew that they were bombing and sinking almost every Japanese ship that went through. We'd had some pretty direct stories from natives and others. So we figured our chances of getting to Japan were pretty darn small. We sat out in the harbor at Singapore a week before we left.

"Like always you didn't have room to really lay down. You just had room to sit up against somebody, and it was going to be this way for the next three weeks. The latrines were on top, and you could only go in small groups of two and three, and then they'd fuss at you all the time. You'd get on deck, and, boy, they'd be standing there with that rifle really watching you. They were pretty mean by now because they were getting beaten, but fortunately the merchant marine sailors were never as cruel as the army, and that's the only thing that saved us on this trip. We ate better, probably

---

*Gee's time sequence is a bit confused. This group sailed in September, and there were 2,300 POWs on two Japanese transports, *Kachidoki Maru* and *Rokyu Maru*, including Brigadier Varley, who was among the missing. Other Americans had died in a sinking in June 1944.

†Gee and the others loaded on December 16, 1944, and sailed ten days later aboard the *Awa Maru*, reaching Moji on January 15, 1945.

because we ate more of what the Japanese ate. I guess they didn't have the stuff they needed to make that horrible stew. As I recall, we only ate two meals a day on the ship, but they were a better grade of stuff than what we had been used to.

"We hugged the coastline all the way up. We were so close on a couple of occasions that we scraped the bottom of the ship, and we thought that a torpedo had hit her. But fortunately, we didn't damage her. We had several air-raid alarms, but they always turned out to be false. The reason we got through was that it rained from the time we left Singapore until we got to Japan, except for the time we were in the area of Hong Kong, and, sure enough, in that area where we had to get the farthest out from land it was sunny for a few days. You talk about being as nervous as cats on a hot tin roof, boy, we could just feel those subs and airplanes bearing down on us. We were sitting ducks because we had a big Japanese warship as one of our escorts. We went about eleven knots an hour, so our movement was slow, and it took weeks to get up there to Japan—well, two weeks, anyway. I believe that we got to Japan on January 16, 1945.

"We had all been through the baptism of fire, and we were a pretty determined group. We still had some high hopes, and every day we felt better. Even if we'd have been hit, we would have known that it was because the Japanese were getting beaten in the war, and, I guess, we would have been glad at that. Moreover, we didn't lose any of our men because if a person wasn't healthy enough to work, the Japanese didn't take him. You had to be healthy enough to work to be sent. They had picked what they considered to be the men who were in the best shape.

"The day we arrived in Japan it was as gray as it had been all along the way. When we got off the ship, it was snowing, and we still had that little green Dutch uniform that they'd issued us a long time back. We'd also been issued some kind of shoe, I guess they were Dutch shoes. I figure the Japanese issued them because they didn't want the people at home to think that they were being inhuman to us. So we had a fairly decent pair of shoes. Having lived in the tropics for nearly the past four years, and wearing a green summer uniform of the Dutch, all of a sudden we're thrown out in Japan. It's snowing, freezing at about 16 degrees, and we unload, and they take us out to a parade ground, an open place off the docks.

"I think Moji on Kyushu was the port where we landed. There were so many of those names, I always forget. Anyway, we stood out in this parade ground until about ten o'clock that night. It was a bitter, cold, humiliating experience. They could have taken us in a big building there any time, which they finally did. They served us dinner at about ten o'clock. It was rice in a wooden box, and it had a few pickles, pickled cucumberlike deals laying on top of it, and some seaweed. We were cold, the rice was cold, and the building was cold. For the first time in my life, as hungry as I was all the time, I could hardly eat. It was half-frozen, half-cooked; it was horrible. Somehow or another, things weren't put together right that day, and we experienced a most unpleasant introduction to Japan. It wasn't long after eating that they took us to a railway station.

"There weren't any civilians around, just army, down on this dock; maybe that's the reason they kept us there until dark. And maybe that's the reason they moved us at night into a village called Sendryu up in the mountains from Nagasaki. It was a little coal mining village then, but I heard it is part of a larger city now. They put us in a camp right in the middle of town, near the coal mine entrance, and for the remainder of the war we lived in that camp. We had older civilians as guards. We had an interpreter, and we had a camp commander who was a fairly decent fellow. When I say fairly decent, he didn't create too many problems for us. The worst thing that he did was when our people would bomb somewhere close by, as they were doing now, he would make us pack our bags, roll up our bedding with any personal belongings we had, and we'd throw these across our back, and we would have to run down through the town and practice getting out of the area where they might bomb by running to a cave in the side of the mountain. This was undignified, below our dignity, but with those bayonets behind you, you just ran right along.

"Strange as it might seem, the townspeople didn't do anything. They didn't mistreat us. Early in the war, when the Japanese brought people up, they did. But by this time they were already, I think, beginning to change their minds about how strong they were. They were short of food and clothing. They were getting short of oil and gasoline. Their Zeros were being knocked out of the sky by the dozens, and their ships were being sunk, and they knew it. They didn't like us any better, but at the same time they were afraid to treat us any worse than what they were treating us.

"In January we started planting a garden, and this is where I was introduced to the 'honey carts.' I was one of the men who worked on the honey carts. The Japanese take all human waste, and they put it in long concrete vats, and they put some chemicals with it and then let that set and ripen. After a few weeks you take it out and pour it on the grounds, and you plant your garden, and your cabbage grows and grows in that cold environment and gets to be real big. It's just fantastic. It's got to be the best fertilizer in the world. We did that. Each hut had a garden spot where we grew our own food when we weren't working in the mines.

"Their coal mining is about as ancient as their religion. To go down into the mine, which is about a mile back underground, you had a tunnel about ten feet high. It was on about a 45-degree angle and had a little railroad running down it. Off of the main tunnel, which meandered back under the earth's surface, were side tunnels. Down below, the main tunnel was eight feet high and about six to eight feet wide, just enough room for the train track and car, a little coal car. The side tunnels were a little smaller. You could walk standing up in the main tunnel, but on the side tunnels you had to sort of stoop to go along. Then off from the side tunnels, they have beehive-like things, just honeycombed with tunnels off to the side. They were the ones that you'd crawl into and dig coal. You'd go about fifty to one hundred feet in these little subtunnels. A whole line of men would get in there and about every three feet there would be a man, and you'd all be facing the seam of coal. Behind you, you'd put up supporting beams, props, little pine logs about three or four inches in diameter. You'd put those right behind you to hold up the ceiling, and all of this area back in there would be dug out.

"You'd dig three or four feet at a time and then put up these props. After you moved again, you'd knock out the first props, and let the roof gradually fall in behind you. What happens in a cave-in in a mine is that the supporting beams are under some kind of a fault line, and it caves in up to the seam of the coal, to its face. Fortunately for us, we were careful, and the Japanese did teach us a little before we went down and started digging. We had to practice topside: how to handle a shovel sitting on your haunches, how to pick on one side, and how to shovel into a trough behind you on the other side to send the coal out. It was a very precise operation; we learned the telltale marks of a cave-in right quick and, boy, when you saw one coming, you passed the word to get out. Japanese guards or no Japanese guards, we moved over them if they didn't go with us, and so we didn't lose a man. The Koreans working in the tunnel right across the way from us would lose a man almost every week. But they had the Koreans working as coal miners in there, not as guards.

"We were supposed to send out so many cars a day depending on conditions. Sometimes we worked a seam that wasn't but three feet high. We'd work eight hours, but we'd take a break for lunch and eat down the mine. We ate the same thing that we had been eating all the time, but, here again, it was a better grade of food. The Japanese guards were coal miners. The people that looked after us were coal miners, and they were more tolerant. They were compassionate. They'd know when we were sick, and they'd share their food. So, consequently, we had a different feeling entirely for the guards in this camp compared to the guards down south. I guess that accounts for the fact that when the war was over we gave our guards a chance to get out, go away. We didn't beat up on them. We didn't hurt any.

"Depending on what hours you worked in the mines, during remaining daylight hours you'd go up and work on your garden, up on the side of the mountain. From there you could see the water. You could see the town. You could see the islands of Japan, its beauty and the beauty of its carpenters. Their homes were just uniquely done. Everything was handmade, and often by quality workmanship. And the miners, gosh, they operated just like little machines. We had some Japanese miners working right along with us. They ran the machinery. They showed us how to move the equipment as we dug on up ahead. We had to move this little trough that carried the coal out. We moved it by sections, uncoupling and coupling it. We had Japanese miners helping us do it. They made sure we did things right.

"The Japanese gave us additional clothing here, and our housing situation was much better than in the jungle. For the first time we had a fairly decent cabin to live in, and about fifteen men lived in a cabin. There wasn't any heat in the bunkhouse area, but we would go out during the day when we were off and build a little fire outside. Somehow or other we kept warm, and it must have been better because we didn't seem to complain as much. Also, we were so tired from working in the mines that we would sleep when we weren't down there. We weren't out in the weather much. Where we ate, the cookhouse, it was warm. So everything worked out pretty well in Japan.

"They'd let us take baths at a community bathhouse. It was nothing to go in and have other coal miners, their families, their wives, and whoever come in. They'd get in a bathtub on one side of the room, and we'd be in one on the other side. At first, I thought, 'Hmm, am I really in the right place?' I wasn't used to having some woman walk in where I was bathing. Well, it sort of shook you up, you know. But we had a good, hot, steamy bath almost daily. We also had better medical attention. They pulled teeth, but not much better than we did in the jungle. They didn't have much stuff to deaden it. I had a friend who had a tooth pulled, and it almost killed him. They practically cut it out. But with better medical attention, a little better food, and guards who weren't so military-minded, life was a lot better here than down south.

"It was a small camp of about 150 men in all. But other than the humiliation of racing through the streets when we bombed, it wasn't bad. Some guys would steal things, and the Japanese would get upset. When that'd happen, well, naturally, they'd march us out and give us a working over, but nothing compared to what we had had. Consequently, we felt like that if we didn't get hit with bombs, we could stick it out here. We should be able to hang on until this war ended. And, sure enough, we did. I put on a little weight, and I had renewed faith that 'Boy, we're going to make it now!' And knowing Americans were bombing nearby because of that racing activity, I decided that, by golly, this thing really can't last much longer. It had to end pretty soon. Our only fear was what the Japanese would do if we invaded Japan. I felt certain that we would be shot.

"I didn't receive any letters while I was a prisoner, but by sheer chance I got a penny postcard that was mailed from my brother-in-law in Dallas. He decided to pick up a card and send it. My mother and dad paid as high as twenty-five dollars apiece for telegrams that they said they sent through the Red Cross, and I did not get a one. But this penny postcard, I received that, and it was just a short note. It said, 'I certainly hope all is going well, and we miss you and things are fine.' That's the only thing I ever got. Now Mother and Dad received about four or five letters or cards from me.

"When spring began to come, the Japanese began to talk about the United States and Japan being equals. We could tell from the way they were talking that things were beginning to form in our favor, and we were more afraid of the invasion of Japan now because of the bits and pieces we were hearing. Along about summer some of our own planes flew over, and the Japanese really began to change their tune. They didn't work us as hard. They ran us in that race a little more. We had to practice running to the caves to protect ourselves. So when we finally heard that the Americans had dropped this small bomb—and that's the way they told it to us—that's when they really did work us out about going to the caves. They said, 'Your people dropped one small bomb and killed hundreds of people.' We knew then that this might be such a thing as an atom bomb or rather that there was such a force as an atom and that it could create power beyond man's imagination. Of course, we knew nothing about the atom being harnessed or what-have-you. We felt that it was in this area of atomic power that something had been developed. And, when it hit Nagasaki a couple of days later, we could tell from the Japs' attitude that they were frightened to death.

"We were about forty-five miles from Nagasaki. Actually straight across we were more like thirty miles from Nagasaki. But by train it was about forty-five miles. We probably felt the bomb and heard the darn thing, but we didn't know it because we heard a lot of explosions that we didn't know what in the world they were. But we knew one thing: there weren't hardly any Japanese airplanes in the sky. We knew occasionally that American planes were in the area from the air raid sounds. We knew things were shaping up in our favor.

"After Hiroshima, they called us on the parade ground, and this is when we had our biggest run down through the city. This is when people were jeering at us because of the number of people that had been killed. But, anyway, Nagasaki was hit next, and we were called onto the parade ground, and the Japanese in a formal ceremony told us what had happened and said that America and Japan were now friends and that they were our friends and that they wanted to treat us the very best that they could and that they were sorry for all the hardships that we'd suffered and all that. And in just fifteen minutes' time, they switched from our major enemy to our best friend, and to seal this, to let us know that they meant it, they turned over their rifles and ammunition to us, which we accepted without hesitation. We had a man who made an American flag and had carried it with him for quite a while, and we took the Stars and Stripes and replaced that rising sun with Old Glory. That was the end of our POW days.

"Their orders were to surrender to the nearest Allies, and whatever their commanders said, that's what they did. We happened to be in this town. They also surrendered to us because they had treated us better since the men guarding us were old men. They weren't real soldiers. They may have been something else, but we considered them coal miners. We gave them, the guards, twenty-four hours to get out of town. We said, 'If you're caught in town after twenty-four hours, then we will deal with you.' I don't know what we'd have done with one of them who came back. We tried to catch him, but we didn't.

"Of course, we were pretty stunned. It was just a matter of hours until the war was over, and we were in command. That first day, we took our rifles, and we walked out across the countryside looking for food. We traded the Japanese clothes, shoes, personal things for eggs, greens, vegetables, anything to eat. We didn't take a thing off of those people by force, and we gave them something in return, always. It wasn't a matter of days, oh, maybe three or four days that we were sitting in camp one day and heard a mighty roar coming up the valley. We looked up and three planes came up the valley. They were flying so low you could see the whites of the eyes of the man sitting in the bomb bay doors. But instead of bombs they dropped parachutes. They literally filled the sky around this valley with parachutes.

"These parachutes had everything conceivable that a man could need in a tube attached to them: clothing, medicine, food, including candy bars and powdered milk. It had Spam, which everybody in the Army before then felt was the worst thing on earth. To me I can still open a can of Spam and think that it's food for a king because it was the best meat I'd had in what seemed a hundred years. One of the drops happened on my birthday, and I guess you couldn't wish for a better birthday present. I'd never seen a parachute drop before. But this was just the end of what had been a horrible nightmare for three-and-a-half years. You couldn't have asked for a more perfect ending, and Hollywood couldn't have written a better one than what we had for the windup of this whole thing."

Gee left Japan along the same route followed by other Americans at Sendryu. He departed from Nagasaki, through Okinawa, Guam, and to Oak Knoll Naval Hospital in San Francisco. He mustered out of the service in June 1946 and worked many years for the Frito-Lay Company and Dixico, Inc. He retired from Dixico as vice president and regional sales manager in 1986.

In 1956, while an officer in the Lost Battalion Association, he and others had Doctor Henri Hekking come to the United States, where they honored him in a variety of ways at their annual reunion. Gee currently lives in Dallas. His feeling toward the Japanese is mixed. He admires their hard work and economic success, but dislikes the current feeling among their younger generation of Japanese superiority. He has written, "They say if they had to go to war against one of the great powers they would choose the United States because we are on the way out." He also rues the fact that Japanese schools teach "next to nothing" about the atrocities their armed forces committed in World War II. As one who survived in the jungle because he "believed you could will yourself to live," Gee's motto today is the Golden Rule: "Do unto others as you would have them do unto you." He is active in church and social service work.

Epilogue

A half century has passed since the men of the Lost Battalion first felt the slap of their captor's hand, the jab of his rifle, or the kick of his boot, but for many it might as well have happened yesterday. Time has not erased a memory of humiliation, starvation, and death. Fortunately, only a few Americans in our national history have felt the whip of a conqueror, only a few have been prisoners of war. That few, however, belong to a fraternity that transcends time and space. Representative Sam Johnson (R, Texas), a Vietnam War POW for seven years, writing in the *Dallas Morning News* of March 13, 1991, summed up the eternal feelings of the captive. He said of Americans returning from the recent Desert Storm engagement: "Some people might say these POWs spent only a short time in captivity. That misses the point of how horrible POW camps really are—the filth, the degradation, the constant torment, the mental anguish, and, worst of all, the separation from family, friends, home, country."

The men of the USS *Houston* and the Second Battalion, 131st Field Artillery Regiment, Texas National Guard, would understand. E. Bartlett Kerr, in *Surrender and Survival*, writes that he believes that the prisoners of Japan received treatment much harsher and more humiliating than Americans captured in other areas of the war. Of course, each reader will have to decide whether Kerr's observation is correct, but many members of the Lost Battalion would agree with it. For a few, their experiences fifty years ago mightily influence how they feel today toward Japan and the Japanese. Red Huffman recently wrote that "the Japanese are a race of people who boast 4,000 years of civilization, and now claim to be richer and smarter than any other nation, but they still use human manure to grow their food. That is as low as you can be! Kill every one of the bastards!"

Others express feelings more restrained but not much more favorable. Otto Schwarz has a "deep-seated hatred of them," and Ilo Hard "dislikes and distrusts Japs." Marvin Tilghman does "not think well of them." The

POWs' attitudes toward Japanese also color their views of Asiatics in general. Gus Forsman has said, "I have no use for any Asian and avoid any contact with them." He then echoes an oft-stated opinion: "I refrain from buying any item or material not made in the United States." Few, indeed, drive Japanese automobiles. About the only neutral comment was from Luther Prunty, who stated, "I'll leave them alone, if they'll leave me alone!"

Still, time has mellowed others. Charley Pryor "admires the Japanese for their initiative and perseverance." Seldon Reese's wife writes, "He liked all Asians except for the Koreans. He believed the Japanese soldiers were just following orders." Quaty Gordon elaborated on this view. He said, "The hard treatment, lack of food and medical care, as well as the hard work we had to perform were caused by their religious beliefs, their standard of living, and their discipline."

Of those replying to the question, "What is your opinion of Koreans?" only one POW, Pryor, had anything favorable to say, although his comment did not apply to his Korean guards. "I sympathize with the Koreans," he wrote. "Theirs was a lot, such as ours as Japanese POWs, during the Korean Conflict." The attitude of Edward Fung was more typical. He opined, "I will dislike Koreans to the day I die!" Prunty thought they were "ignorant, sadistic, cruel." Jack Burge said, "Bastards all!"

The American attitude toward the Javanese was not much better than that toward the Japanese or Koreans. The prisoners disliked what they saw as a two-faced, hypocritical attitude. Apparently, before the Japanese invasion the people of Java had treated Americans fairly, but afterward they became an angry egg-and-vegetable-throwing mob. Despite a few POWs who disliked Asians in general, most were complimentary of the Burmese, who treated them kindly, and of the Thais, who sided with the Allied cause by the time Americans arrived there in any number. They universally respected the Chinese, who tried to help and feed them whenever they could.

The opinion American POWs held of the British is mentioned often in the interviews and is not a favorable one. Not only did the Yanks dislike the military formalities the British officers demanded, but they also felt the English overworked them and kept supplies from them. This complaint was commonplace among those interviewed when describing their time at Changi. Whether the Americans would have accepted British sanitation and bathing practices more graciously if they had received the Red Cross aid, which they felt the English kept from them, is moot, but they probably would have.

The American POWs were less critical of the Dutch than were the British or Australians, but they did complain about them, especially the so-called Black Dutch or Indonesian soldiers. Dutch women were another matter. The Lost Battalion men universally praised the women's courage and kindness, contrasting them often with their male countrymen, whom they considered generally less than heroic—with the exceptions of Doctors Bloemsma and Hekking. The people they praised the most were the "Aussies." One can only speculate whether their instant attraction to the Australians is related to the fact that the overwhelming majority of the Americans were from Texas and found in them men who were simpatico. This is possible, even probable. Several of the Americans remarked how similar the Australians were to their Lone Star brethren, and some decided there was no difference at all. They also appreciated the Scots, who piped them out of Changi. This was a compliment rarely bestowed on anyone by the Highlanders.

On the related question of whether the Americans sought retribution against individual Japanese or Koreans at the war's end, most felt they would like to have, and some said they did, but the great majority were more interested in getting out of Asia and back to the United States once freedom was achieved. Their need for American food and shelter after three-and-one-half years was great, and their desire for companionship with the folks back home caused them to put revenge out of their mind.

They paid some attention to the war crimes trials in Tokyo, and a few knew of the tribunals in Singapore that tried Japanese offenders. But none of them seemed to have accurate knowledge of what happened to their tormentors. Their responses most often were that they had heard from another POW that the Korean guards or Japanese camp commanders were being punished. The British did hold trials for two railway-camp commandants after the war and hanged them at Changi, and they also tried and imprisoned other Japanese and Koreans. The longest term any received was thirteen years.

Some Americans held grudges against specific fellow prisoners whom they felt were too cozy with the Japanese, but most did not mind such activities if in so doing the POW improved his lot and did not jeopardize another prisoner's welfare. They were all disdainful of men who gave up and allowed themselves to die. They were contemptuous of anyone who shirked his duties. Many enlisted men believed officers were treated better than they, especially in the matter of food, the most important element in the POW's life. Officers were treated differently, but those interviewed do not appear to have been treated any better than their noncommissioned comrades.

Members of the Lost Battalion Association appreciated their uniqueness. Feeling that they were forgotten or their whereabouts unknown, they referred to themselves as "lost," and the description stuck. The artillerymen prided themselves as the first Americans to fight on foreign soil in World War II. They believed it important that they were Texans. To them this circumstance contributed to their survival. Perhaps it did: some historians feel that soldiers who came from the same locale and were kept together did have a better chance of enduring the rigors of POW camps than those who were from widely scattered areas. The death rate of the artillerymen, who were from several small towns and country areas in West Texas, was less than that of the *Houston* survivors. The men of the Lost Battalion felt that camaraderie resulting from their place of residence contributed to their higher rate of survival. Actually, the American mortality rate was not any better or even as good as that of the Dutch or Australians who worked on the Burma part of the railroad. Of course, when the building of the entire railroad is considered, their 19 percent mortality rate was low.* Although statistics concerning native laborers on the Burma-Thailand line are uncertain, most scholars reckon that 250,000 southeast Asians worked on it and approximately 91,000 of them died there.

Probably no single individual can accurately explain why he survived the ordeal of the Death Railway and others died. Nevertheless, this question was posed to every former POW interviewed. Faith was the most frequent reason given for survival, but it was not just a simple faith in God. Gus Forsman put it this way: "I had faith—faith in everything, faith in myself, faith in the Lord, and faith in my fellow man. I mean, just faith in my comrades, knowing that if things really got rough, you could always depend on them for help in one way or another."

Among the many explanations were Granville Summerlin's view that "luck" and "determination" brought him through the ordeal. Charley Pryor designated the attitude as "perseverance," saying, "I do oftimes think that we had a perseverance that only a few other people really have." A few thought their "good physical conditioning" before they became prisoners was a reason, and Quaty Gordon attributed his survival to his "upbringing as a farm boy." Jimmy Gee said, "I learned a great deal of what to me is common sense in a small town in Texas. I don't mean from a moralistic

---

*These observations are based on information in Lionel Wigmore, *The Japanese Thrust*.

standpoint, but it's just common sense that you help your fellow man." Despite what they said, most would agree with Eddie Fung, who replied, "I can't give you an answer to why I survived. I know there are a lot of men who wanted to live who didn't make it. I mean the survivors were not all good, they were not all bad. I don't think that had anything to do with it. A lot of men had more to live for than I had, and they didn't make it. I don't know what it was. I know half a dozen men who wanted desperately to live, but they still died, and it wasn't because they didn't try. I just can't give you a reason why I survived."

Some writers and more than a few of those interviewed pointed out that the small cliques they formed, the groups of two or three men, created an informal support system that saw them through. Of course, the buddy system was always a part of American military life. It may explain the success of some who survived. The maintenance of the command system early in their captivity is pointed out by most of the officers as being a contributing factor. Whether the enlisted personnel agreed was not explored. Certainly, the use of company money by the supply officer at Bicycle Camp was important in supplementing the prisoners' diets early in their captivity.

The physical and psychological effects of their captivity have been enduring. When asked "What impact has the fact that you were a POW had on your life since then?" many listed illnesses resulting from neglect, malnourishment, and mistreatment at the hands of the Japanese. A great many have since died from heart attacks and liver and kidney diseases or failures. One ailment rarely spoken of but evident in reasons given for Lost Battalion members' deaths since 1945 is gunshot wounds. Every individual interviewed agreed that immediate adjustment to freedom and civilian life was difficult, even if it involved only diet. In the words of one of them, they went "hog-wild." Long-term damages done to personality and adjustment to normal living have been multiple. Some examples are simultaneously pathetic and humorous. Luther Prunty wrote: "I'm inclined to stock large amounts of canned food." Others are tragically poignant. Mrs. Seldon Reese, answering the questionnaire for her deceased husband, wrote: "He was a very mixed-up person. He didn't trust anybody. He was antisocial and saw the black side of everything. His children grew up afraid of him. As his wife, I can say his life was miserable."

Some members of the Lost Battalion have returned to Java, Singapore, Burma, and Thailand in recent times. Curiosity, nostalgia, and the interest of friends and relatives caused them to go. Here they lost three-and-one-half years of their life. Short of being maimed they suffered the worst fate a soldier can live to regret. But here they also earned the gratitude of succeeding generations. At times it may not seem so to them. Kerr points out that in 1948 and 1950 the United States government provided each with an added compensation of two dollars per day for every day they were deprived of adequate food rations, suffered forced labor, and received inhumane treatment. As he says, this was small reward for what they endured.

Recognizing that adequate recompense is an impossibility where these men are concerned, the thoughtful element of the nation would agree that they have earned a full measure of our appreciation. But for them, ever pragmatic, they would no doubt find Lester Rasbury's assessment more to the point. Rasbury has stated: "I probably didn't do as much in building the railroad as the ones who worked on it. But I heard them say, 'Well, we did it. They didn't think we could, but we did.' The English had surveyed that thing out, and they lost too many lives in there, and they abandoned it. We went in there and did something that other people couldn't do. Of course, it was a real big expense. The old colonel [Nagatomo] told us we were going to build it if it took a body for every crosstie, and he didn't miss it by much."

Appendix A

Otto Schwarz, whose interview is included in Chapter 1, has spent a great deal of time establishing a chronology for Groups 3 and 5. Although men were separated for various reasons from their groups, his chronology provides some idea of the whereabouts of the majority of the American POWs during their time on the railroad. The Schwarz chronologies for each group follow.

The reader should note that the individual interviews do not always agree with Schwarz's chronology.

Group 3

1942

October 29 Thanbyuzayat Base Camp
October 30 En route by foot from Thanbyuzayat to 40 Kilo Camp
October 30–November 29 40 Kilo Camp (Beke Taung)

1942–1943

November 29–March 10 25 Kilo Camp (Kun Knit Kway)

1943

March 10–20 35 Kilo Camp (Tanyin)
March 20–April 5 14 Kilo Camp (Thetkaw)
April 5–26 25 Kilo Camp (Kun Knit Kway)
April 26–May 2 45 Kilo Camp
May 2–14 18 Kilo Camp (Alepauk)
May 14–July 14 30 Kilo Camp (Retpu)

July 14–September 11 62 Kilo Camp
September 11–November 3 85 Kilo Camp

1943–1944

November 3–January 12 114 Kilo Camp
January 12, 1944 To Kanchanaburi area

Group 5

1943

January 21 Arrive by train at Thanbyuzayat Base Camp
    and leave by foot for 18 Kilo Camp
January 21–March 15 18 Kilo Camp (Alepauk)
March 15–April 1 85 Kilo Camp
April 1–May 29 80 Kilo Camp

1943–1944

May 29–January 2 100 Kilo Camp (Anganan)
January 2, 1944 To Kanchanaburi area

Appendix B

Speech Delivered by Lieutenant Colonel Y. Nagatomo to Allied Prisoners of War at Thanbyuzayat, Burma, on October 28, 1942

It is a great pleasure to me to see you at this place as I am appointed Chief of the war prisoner camp obedient to the Imperial Command issued by His Majesty the Emperor. The great East Asiatic war has broken out due to the rising of the East Asiatic Nations whose hearts were burnt with the desire to live and preserve their nations on account of the intrusion of the British and Americans for the past many years.

There is, therefore, no other reason for Japan to drive out the Anti-Asiatic powers of the arrogant and insolent British and Americans from East Asia in cooperation with our neighbors of China and other East Asiatic Nations and establish the Greater East Asia Co-Prosperity Sphere for the benefit of all human beings and establish lasting great peace in the world. During the past few centuries, Nippon has made great sacrifices and extreme endeavors to become the leader of the East Asiatic Nations, who were mercilessly and pitifully treated by the outside forces of the British and Americans, and the Nippon Army, without disgracing anybody, has been doing her best until now for fostering Nippon's real power.

You are only a few remaining skeletons after the invasion of East Asia for the past few centuries, and are pitiful victims. It is not your fault, but until your governments do not wake up from their dreams and discontinue their resistance, all of you will not be released. However, I shall not treat you badly for the sake of humanity as you have no fighting power left at all.

His Majesty the Emperor has been deeply anxious about all prisoners of war, and has ordered us to enable the operating of war prisoner camps at almost all the places in the SW countries.

The Imperial Thoughts are unestimable and the Imperial Favors are infinite and, as such, you should weep with gratitude at the greatness of them. I shall correct or mend the misleading and improper Anti-Japanese ideas. I shall meet with you hereafter and at the beginning I shall require of you the four following points:

(1) I heard that you complain about the insufficiency of various items. Although there may be lack of materials it is difficult to meet your requirements. Just turn your eyes to the present conditions of the world. It is entirely different from the prewar times. In all lands and countries materials are considerably short and it is not easy to obtain even a small piece of cigarette, and the present position is such that it is not possible even for needy women and children to get sufficient food. Needless to say, therefore, at such inconvenient places even our respectable Imperial Army is also not able to get mosquito nets, foodstuffs, medicines, and cigarettes. As conditions are such, how can you expect me to treat you better than the Imperial Army? I do not prosecute according to my own wishes and it is not due to the expense but due to the shortage of materials at such difficult places. In spite of our wishes to meet their requirements, I cannot do so with money. I shall supply you, however, if I can do so with my best efforts and I hope you will rely upon me and render your wishes before me. We will build the railroad if we have to build it over the white man's body. It gives me great pleasure to have a fast-moving defeated nation in my power. You are merely rubble, but I will not feel bad because it is your rulers. If you want anything you will have to come through me for same and there will be many of you who will not see your homes again. Work cheerfully at my command.

(2) I shall strictly manage all of your going out, coming back, meeting with friends, communications. Possessions of money shall be limited, living manners, deportment, salutation, and attitude shall be strictly according to the rules of the Nippon Army, because it is only possible to manage you all, who are merely rabble, by the order of military regulations. By this time I shall issue separate pamphlets of house rules of war prisoners and you are required to act strictly in accordance with these rules and you shall not infringe on them by any means.

(3) My biggest requirement from you is escape. The rules of escape shall naturally be severe. This rule may be quite useless and only binding to some of the war prisoners, but it is most important for all of you in the management of the camp. You should, therefore, be contented accordingly. If there is a man here who has at least 1 percent of a chance of escape, we shall make him face the extreme penalty. If there is one foolish man who is trying to escape, he shall see big jungles toward the East which are impossible for communication. Towards the West he shall see boundless ocean and, above all, in the main points of the North, South, our Nippon Armies

are guarding. You will easily understand the difficulty of complete escape. A few such cases of ill-omened matters which happened in Singapore (execution of over a thousand Chinese civilians) shall prove the above and you should not repeat such foolish things although it is a lost chance after great embarrassment.

(4) Hereafter, I shall require all of you to work as nobody is permitted to do nothing and eat at the present. In addition, the Imperial Japanese have great work to promote at the places newly occupied by them, and this is an essential and important matter. At the time of such shortness of materials your lives are preserved by the military, and all of you must award them with your labor. By the hand of the Nippon Army Railway Construction Corps to connect Thailand and Burma, the work has started to the great interest of the world. There are deep jungles where no man ever came to clear them by cutting the trees. There are also countless difficulties and suffering, but you shall have the honor to join in this great work which was never done before, and you shall also do your best effort. I shall investigate and check carefully about your coming back, attendance so that all of you except those who are unable to work shall be taken out for labor. At the same time I shall expect all of you to work earnestly and confidently henceforth you shall be guided by this motto.

Y. Nagatomo
Lieutenant Colonel
Nippon Expeditionary Force

Chief No. 3 Branch
Thailand POW Administration

Appendix C

Locations and Dates of Interviews

Donald Brain	Denton, Texas	March 11, 1981
Jack Burge	Azle, Texas	May 16, 1978
Melford Forsman	Denton, Texas	July 28, 1980
Edward Fung	Denton, Texas	December 21, 1977
James Gee	Dallas, Texas	March 6, 13, 1972
Crayton Gordon	Denton, Texas	January 31, 1977
Ilo Hard	Denton, Texas	March 26, 1980
James Huffman	Denton, Texas	April 11, 1990
Roy Offerle	Decatur, Texas	August 14, 1978
Paul Papish	Denton, Texas	January 30, 1989
C. L. Pryor	Dallas, Texas	November 4, 1972; January 22, February 20, 1973
Luther Prunty	Denton, Texas	October 20, 27, 1986
Lester Rasbury	Ft. Worth, Texas	June 10, 15, 1978
Raymond Reed	Granbury, Texas	March 13, 1979
Seldon Reese	Denton, Texas	June 21, 1978
Otto Schwarz	Granbury, Texas	August 7, 1979
Garth Slate	Denton, Texas	August 13, 1980
Granville Summerlin	Denton, Texas	June 9, 1981
Clark Taylor	Denton, Texas	September 14, 1979
Marvin Tilghman	Denton, Texas	September 6, 1978
John Wisecup	Weatherford, Texas	July 28, 1987
Houston Wright	Dallas, Texas	August 15, 1978

Sources

In preparing this volume several books have been indispensable in providing background information. Without them major errors would not have been detected, although without doubt some mistakes remain. In discussing the USS *Houston*'s fate, Duane Schultz's *The Last Battle Station: The Story of the USS Houston* (New York: St. Martin's, 1985) was used extensively. Schultz traces the cruiser's history from the laying of its keel in 1928 until Japanese gunners sank it in the Sunda Strait in 1942. He concludes with an overview of the crew's ordeal as part of the group that worked on the Burma-Thailand railway. The majority of the study deals with the period prior to the ship's sinking. Schultz used oral histories at the University of North Texas, as well as materials from the History and Museums Division, U.S. Marine Corps, and the Operational Archives Branch of the Naval Historical Center. In addition to its accuracy, the book is well written.

Another expertly written, extremely valuable study is E. Bartlett Kerr, *Surrender and Survival: The Experience of American POWs in the Pacific, 1941–1945* (New York: Morrow, 1985). As far as could be ascertained, this is the only attempt thus far at a survey history of American servicemen held captive by Japan during World War II. It is a broadly researched volume. In addition to monographs, the author used published and unpublished diaries, memoirs, and interviews and consulted documents at the Office of the Adjutant General, St. Louis, Missouri, and the Washington National Records Center in Suitland, Maryland, the library of the University of California, Berkeley, and elsewhere. Kerr's information on American POWs in Asia and the southwest Pacific provides an excellent opportunity for comparisons with the Americans in Burma and Thailand. He also supplied the data regarding Japan's official position toward military prisoners.

In trying to fathom the Japanese military mind and to understand the harshness of the actions toward captives, John W. Dower, *War without Mercy: Race and Power in the Pacific War* (New York: Pantheon Books,

1986), was valuable. An unpublished source of considerable use was Waller F. Jones, "Japanese Attitudes Toward Prisoners of War: Feudal Resurgence in *Kokutai No Hongi*" (master's thesis, University of North Texas, Denton, 1990). Jones is a Vietnam veteran and deputy sheriff in Denton County, Texas.

Lionel Wigmore, *The Japanese Thrust* (Canberra: Australian War Memorial, 1957), is part of the monumental Australian series entitled *Australia in the War of 1939-1945*. Chapters 22 through 25 deal with Australian prisoners of Japan who were captured in Singapore and Java and other areas of the Malay Peninsula and Archipelago. Chapter 24 deals with the railroad, and although the purpose is to discuss Australian military men's experiences, Americans are sometimes mentioned and the conditions discussed are similar to the stories related in the Lost Battalion interviews. Like the other two volumes, *Japanese Thrust* is generally accurate.

Another accurate and highly readable volume is Clifford Kinvig, *Death Railway* (New York: Ballantine Books, 1973). At the time Ballantine published this volume, Kinvig was a major in the British Army and a lecturer at the Royal Military Academy, Sandhurst. Part of *Ballantine's Illustrated History of the Violent Century*, it surveys the British experience, although it includes some information relative to American POWs. Of the several histories that deal exclusively with the building of the railway, this is seemingly the best.

Four memoirs by Lost Battalion members have been published. In some instances the authors have tried to provide more information about the American experience on the railway than merely what intersected the memorist's life. The one that most closely reflects this intention is Benjamin Dunn, *The Bamboo Express* (Chicago: Adams, 1979). Dunn was one of the seventeen men that the 26th Brigade transferred to Headquarters Battery, Second Battalion, 131st Field Artillery, in February 1942. He was part of the larger American group that worked on the railway, Group 5 of A Force. Most important of all, he kept notes during his captivity and used them later to write the book.

Another brief, but excellent, recollection is Clyde Fillmore, *Prisoner of War: History of the Lost Battalion* (Wichita Falls, TX: Quanah, 1973). Fillmore, an attorney-at-law who served as district attorney in his home-town of Wichita Falls after leaving the military, was a lieutenant in Battery D when the unit surrendered in March 1942. His presentation is a bit more personal than Dunn's but also deals with aspects of the captivity beyond his immediate ken.

H. Richard Charles's *Last Man Out* (Austin: Eakin, 1988) was described by its *Dallas Morning News* reviewer as a "story of courage, endurance and spirit, capturing the quintessence of heroism at both the philosophical and gut level with equal facility." Charles was a Marine antiaircraft gunner aboard the *Houston* when it sank, and has since graduated from the Medill School of Journalism at Northwestern University in Evanston, Illinois. Once a free-lance writer, Charles presents a deeply personal vision and provides a great deal of information about Doctor Hekking, who saved Charles's life.

The fourth memoir is Horace Teel, *Our Days Were Years: History of the "Lost Battalion," 2nd Battalion, 36th Division* (Quanah, TX: Nortex Press, 1978). Teel, who spent twenty-nine years as a teacher and preacher in the North Texas area, was a member of Battery F and part of the Fitzsimmons Group, Group 3 of A Force. His religious interests heavily flavor his recollections. Unfortunately, he does not often identify the men whose activities he relates. The appendix to his work gives the name and rank of members of the Second Battalion.

In addition to reminiscences by these Americans, an extensive number of personal accounts by Australian, British, and Dutch POWs has been published. Having access to the interviews of many Americans, only a few of these were used. Those consulted include Tim Bowden, *Changi Photographer: George Aspinall's Record of Captivity* (Sydney: Australian Broadcasting Corporation and Collins, 1984); Hugh V. Clarke, *A Life for Every Sleeper: A Pictorial Record of the Burma-Thailand Railway* (Sydney: Allen and Unwin, 1986); Jeffery English, *One for Every Sleeper: The Japanese Death Railway through Thailand* (London: Hale, 1989); Ernest Gordon, *Through the Valley of the Kwai* (New York: Harper, 1962); Chaim Nussbaum, *Chaplain on the River Kwai: Story of a Prisoner of War* (New York: Shapolsky, 1988); Richard Pool, *Course for Disaster: From Scapa Flow to the River Kwai* (London: Cooper, 1987); John Stewart, *To the River Kwai: Two Journeys—1943, 1979* (London: Bloomsbury, 1988); and *The Burma-Siam Railway: The Secret Diary of Dr. Robert Hardie, 1942–45* (London: Imperial War Museum, 1983).

Another memoir of sorts by an Australian reporter, who was captured by the Japanese in Singapore and interned with Australian troops who helped build the River Kwai railroad, is Rohan D. Rivett, *Behind Bamboo: An Inside Story of the Japanese Prison Camps* (Sydney and London: Angus and Robertson, 1946). Its first edition was used frequently. The volume has since been revised and issued in several editions. Rivett had a newsman's eye for detail and a commentator's view of general import. This is an excellent book, easy to read.

The appropriate parts of three books were consulted concerning war crimes trials after liberation: Arnold C. Brackman, *The Other Nuremberg: The Untold Story of the Tokyo War Crimes Trials* (New York: Morrow, 1987); Richard H. Minear, *Victors' Justice: The Tokyo War Crimes Trial* (Princeton: Princeton University Press, 1971); and Philip R. Piccigallo, *The Japanese on Trial: Allied War Crimes Operations in the East, 1945–1951* (Austin: University of Texas Press, 1979). One other volume used is Joan Blair and Clay Blair, Jr., *Return from the River Kwai* (New York: Simon and Schuster, 1979). The authors discuss the sinking of the *Kachidoki Maru* and *Rokyu Maru*, two Japanese transports carrying Allied POWs, in September 1944. The Blairs underestimate the number of American POWs involved but give a detailed account of the sinkings and rescues. Pierre Boulle, *Bridge over the River Kwai*, trans. Xan Fielding (New York: Vanguard, 1954), was read several times.

The *Lost Battalion Association Roster* (1985) was used extensively in its updated version. It is kept current by Shirley Dunnett of the Oral History Program at UNT, from information provided by members of the association. Both Otto Schwarz and Crayton Gordon, whose interviews are included in this volume, provided considerable information about other men of the 131st Field Artillery and the USS *Houston*.

One other item, produced by Lost Battalion Association member John W. Wisecup, is his "After the Battle: Hintok!" An undated typescript, this work includes a six-page poem, "Saga of Bamboo Jack," written in the style and meter of Samuel Taylor Coleridge's "The Rime of the Ancient Mariner," and a series of twenty-five cartoons depicting life among the prisoners at Camp Hintok.

Two master's theses need to be cited: Elmer R. Milner, "The Lost Battalion: Second Battalion, 131st Field Artillery, 1940–1945" (University of North Texas, 1975); and Frances G. Peadon, "Survival in Japanese Prison Camps" (Texas Christian University, 1967).

Index